D1590922

Paul Mason learned the practice of Transcendental Meditation when he visited Maharishi Mahesh Yogi's *ashram* at Rishikesh after hitchhiking to India in 1970. He has maintained an abiding interest in India and has produced a fair few books relating to the teaching of meditation, and about the lifestory and teachings of Swami Brahmananda Saraswati - Guru Dev.

After a chance meeting with musician Donovan, a student of Maharishi Mahesh Yogi, Paul Mason felt inspired to document The Beatles' involvement with Maharishi. After a long period of intensive research, during which he contacted many of those who had attended the meditation course in Rishikesh in 1968, he compiled a massive biography, profusely illustrated with monochrome and colour pictures, which was published in 2017 as *'The Beatles, Drugs, Mysticism & India'*.

Paul Mason is best known for having been commissioned by Element Books to compile the biography of Maharishi Mahesh Yogi, first published in 1994. Since then he kept himself appraised of Maharishi's activities and teachings, and, after being repeatedly asked to update the biography, he has chosen instead to completely re-write it, work in new material, add a vast amount of new illustrations and to offer up a concluding chapter to this work; Maharishi's extraordinary story.

Titles by Paul Mason:

The Beatles, Drugs, Mysticism & India:
Maharishi Mahesh Yogi - Transcendental Meditation - Jai Guru Deva OM

Roots of TM: The Transcendental Meditation of Guru Dev
& Maharishi Mahesh Yogi
^
Den Transcendentala Meditationens Ursprung - Turning Pages
Swedish edition 2017

108 Discourses of Guru Dev:
The Life and Teachings of Swami Brahmananda Saraswati,
Shankaracharya of Jyotirmath (1941-53) - Volume I
~
The Biography of Guru Dev:
The Life and Teachings of Swami Brahmananda Saraswati,
Shankaracharya of Jyotirmath (1941-53) - Volume II
~
Guru Dev as Presented by Maharishi Mahesh Yogi:
The Life and Teachings of Swami Brahmananda Saraswati,
Shankaracharya of Jyotirmath (1941-53) - Volume III

The Knack of Meditation:
The No-Nonsense Guide to Successful Meditation

Dandi Swami: The Story of the Guru's Will, Maharishi Mahesh Yogi, the
Shankaracharyas of Jyotir Math & Meetings with Dandi Swami Narayananand Saraswati

Via Rishikesh: A Hitch-Hiker's Tale

Mala: A String of Unexpected Meetings

Kathy's Story

The Maharishi: The Biography of the Man Who Gave
Transcendental Meditation to the World
Element Books - First English edition 1994
Evolution Books - Revised English edition 2005
Maharishi Mahesh Yogi - Aquamarin - German edition 1995
O Maharishi - Nova Era - Portuguese edition 1997

Established in Yoga, Perform Action:
Gita Bhavateet; The 'Song Transcendental' of Acharya Satyadas

MAHARISHI
MAHESH YOGI

The Biography of the Man
Who Gave Transcendental Meditation
to the World

Paul Mason

PREMANAND
www.paulmason.info
premanandpaul@yahoo.co.uk

This edition, revised, enlarged and updated
Published by Premanand 2020

© Paul Mason 1994, 2005, 2020
First published by Element Books Limited, 1994
ISBN 1-85230-571-1
Revised Paperback edition published by Evolution Publishing, 2005
ISBN 0-9550361-0-0

Cover picture by Charlie Lutes, Premanand
Cover design by Premanand

ISBN 978-0-9562228-5-5

To my parents

Acknowledgements

I would like to extend my grateful thanks to Kathy and all the many people who were, either directly or indirectly, of assistance to this work, and expressly to: Maharishi Mahesh Yogi, Yolanda Baldi, Raj Varma, Andreas Müller, Bevan Morris, Brahmachari Satyanand, Steve Jeffery, Jerry Stovin, Walt Gibbons, Vesey Crichton, Vincent Snell, Peter Russell, Prem C. Pasricha, Joan Benesh, Mary Lou Jennings, Sarah Rose, Marcus and Phillipa Saint, John Windsor, Jet Fairly, Henderson Davison, Derek Dearden, Bob Rankin, Dinah Demuth, Roger Preece, Dario Ciriello, Sally Bowen, Sarah Buret, Surjeet Husain, S. Guruvareddi, the staff of Element Books and Dhyan Vidhya Peeth, the monks of Jyotir Math, D. N. Upadhyay, and Swami Ashibananda and the other swamis of Gyaan Mandir Uttar Kashi. Also to the 'Anonymous Devotee of His Holiness Maharishiji Mahesh Yogi', Bob Hopeless, Tom Anderson, Jerry Jarvis, Carole Hamby, Vincent Daczynski, the inspiration and stimulation of Rani Anjali Mahaldar, and all the thought provoking questions from those on internet newsgroups. And such special gratitude for all those invaluable suggestions and willing assistance of Suradeva Anthony Evenson. A huge thanks goes to my loving family who have provided me with very necessary tea, sympathy, feedback and valued support; and always there to assist; Richard Mason, so much gratitude for being a sounding board, and much more, in matters computer related. Pranams to Dandi Swami Narayananandji Saraswati for his blissful blessings.

Acknowledgement and credit should also be given to the authors and publishers whose works I have quoted within the terms of 'fair usage' and to anyone else who has been of material use or support, and whom I have unintentionally omitted to mention.

Preface

Maharishi's initiative in bringing out this simple effective practice of Transcendental Meditation for all to enjoy, was both courageous and magnanimous, a gesture that won the hearts and minds of countless meditators around the world.

I recall the idea for a book came to me whilst on a walk during my lunch break; my mind suddenly lit up with a burst of strip lights! I envisioned the project being a celebration of Maharishi's original style of thinking, his fresh perspectives on age-old themes, and his optimism for the well-being, progress and happiness of all. Within a very short while Element Books commissioned me.

The compilation of Maharishi's biography was shaped by the need to offer a comprehensive understanding of his teaching in the context of his own lifestory. The work was originally undertaken under certain constraints regarding content and style. Now, in this totally revised and expanded volume, effort has been taken to improve the overall presentation and to include any important material that was previously unavailable, also to include many more illustrations, and to add an extra chapter covering Maharishi's latter years.

It is thought that this completely refreshed and re-invigorated account of Maharishi's life will be of great interest to all readers, meditators and non-meditators alike.

6 - v - 2020

जय गुरुदेव
JAI GURU DEV

Contents

PART III: *The Enlightenment Business*

PART I

—★—

The Spirit and the Flesh

'I will fill the world with love'

1

—★—

MAHESH AND HIS MASTER

I mean look how it all started. I believe he just landed in Hawaii in his nightshirt, all on his own, nobody with him … – John Lennon[1]

For San Francisco Bay Airport, Thursday, 29th January 1959 was just another working day – more flights, more passengers, just like any other day. From Honolulu, Hawaii, came yet another scheduled flight, stimulating another flurry of activity for the uniformed customs men. Baggage handlers attended to their normal duties, unloading luggage from the hold of the plane and delivering it for collection. In the arrivals lounge were the normal complement of eager, expectant faces looking out for loved ones, business colleagues and the like. There was to be nothing out of the ordinary about the passengers today, no famous actors or politicians were due in.

As the new arrivals began to emerge, attention fell on one lone individual, a visitor from somewhere far beyond Hawaii. There, walking self-assuredly upon quaint Hessian-banded wooden sandals came a figure of slight stature draped simply in a pure white robe with long, wayward, wavy black hair tumbling about his shoulders. His was a sunny, amiable countenance, with large glistening chestnut-brown eyes, broad flattened nose and cheeks both generous and shining, partially obscured by a flourishing growth of beard. On espying the carpet roll he clutched, any child might have fancied him to be an Arabian *fakir* come drifting in upon a magic spell. Much more likely was that he was a potentate from some small but wealthy kingdom, maybe a sultan or maharajah from the East who wished to travel incognito. The two Hawaiian nationals that escorted him out of the terminal could perhaps have explained something of the identity and mission of this mystery man.

The United States of America had but scant exposure to representatives of that rich cultural heritage which is India. Some sixty-five years before, the great World Parliament of Religions of 1893 had paid host to the turbaned, corpulent personage of Swami Vivekananda and listened to his monkish philosophy. More recently, in 1920, the city of Boston had hosted an International Congress of Religious Liberals which received, from a ship newly arrived after a two-month voyage from Calcutta, India, a delegate that many Americans later took to their hearts, the ochre-robed and deceptively youthful-looking Swami Paramahansa Yogananda.

With no plans to attend either parliament or congress, but nevertheless exuding unbridled confidence and virtually unbounded zeal, came India's latest emissary, known to his followers as His Holiness Maharishi Mahesh Yogi.

At his first press conference in the USA on Wednesday, 29th April 1959, he revealed his intention to spiritually regenerate the entire world, adding:

> My life truly began 19 years ago at the feet of my Master when I learned the secret of swift and deep meditation, a secret I now impart to the world.[2]

Prior to his arrival on Western shores, the man we now know as Maharishi Mahesh Yogi had spent almost his entire life in India. It was at the age of twenty-three, in his home town of Jabalpur, Madhya Pradesh, that he first met Swami Brahmananda Saraswati, a wandering holy man of some renown. He recalls:

> One day I was led by those who knew I was fond of meeting saints, to a house somewhere in the forest, and then I was led up some stairs to a terrace. It so happened that this was a very dark night and I could barely see a chair with a few people sitting around it, all quiet.[3]

> We were a few men who had gone to visit Guru Dev. We sat outside his door a long time until we were finally admitted. We sat down by the door which had been left open. Guru Dev sat in darkness. We could only sense his presence – he didn't talk to us. Suddenly a car drove by on the road and the headlights momentarily shone through the open door. For the first time I was able to see Guru Dev's face. Oh, it was a wonderful sight! I have never seen anything so wonderful. Immediately I experienced a deep reverence and devotion to him and I decided to do everything in my power to be in his surroundings.[34]

The spontaneous commitment Mahesh felt for the hermit had the young man's parents deeply concerned. Voicing their disapproval in no uncertain terms, they did their utmost to dissuade him from taking to a life of renunciation. This was not the life they wanted for their son, not at all.

If Swami Brahmananda had overheard these concerned, conscientious parents, it would probably have brought a smile of recollection to the old hermit's countenance. As a young child of barely nine years old, he had witnessed a very similar reaction to his own deeply felt convictions.

Let us take a closer look at the life of this old *swami*, for it will be seen that he plays a key role in the story of Maharishi, namely that of *guru* or master.

The city of Ayodhya, in northern India, is famous as the birthplace of Lord Rama, hero of the ancient epic poem *Ramayana*. Lord Rama is worshipped as an *avataar* (incarnation of God), and his name is held sacred by millions.

On Thursday, 21st December 1871 [*Vikram Samvat* 1928, *Marg Shirsh Shukla Dasmi*][5] in the village of Gana close to Ayodhya, Rajaram Mishra was born. His family were Brahmins (the caste which provided both teachers and priests) and were relatively affluent, being *zamindar* or landlords. They were thus able to offer Rajaram a secure, comfortable childhood.

Perhaps this young boy would never have entered the annals of history but for two incidents which awakened him to the world beyond his playthings. When he was barely seven years old he suffered the loss of his most cherished companion, his grandfather, whose lifeless body was borne away to the chant of:

"राम नाम सत्य है"

"Raam naam satya hai"
'Rama's name is truth'.[46]

Rajaram took this *mantra* as guidance in his hour of need. Already of a retiring nature, the young lad became increasingly withdrawn, dwelling as he did upon the transitory nature of existence and its temporal happiness.

A year later Rajaram was enrolled at the Sanskrit Institute, an establishment of some standing in the holy city of Benares (a very ancient city known also as Varanasi and Kashi). The very atmosphere of this pilgrim centre no doubt deepened the youngster's leanings and yearning towards a commitment to a spiritual life. As it happened he had not been studying there long before his next major upheaval. As was the custom in that era, a child marriage had been arranged for him. We can but imagine the boy's feelings, at barely nine years of age, being informed of his own impending wedding. He was not inclined to become a victim of his parents' schemes, and being a boy of unusual pluck and determination, he made ready to break free, to do a disappearing trick.

For several days Rajaram journeyed along the banks of *Ganga Ma*, the sacred 'mother' Ganges River, with faith his only companion. From Benares he made his way to Allahabad (Prayag) and onward upriver as far as Hardwar, intending then to travel via Rishikesh to the Garhwal Himalayas, an area steeped in ancient folklore. But he could be evade discovery for only so long, and some way before Rishikesh a police inspector apprehended the young runaway and returned him safely to his parents.

His family was of one voice in their condemnation of his strange behaviour and unaccountable unworldliness. According to tradition, a young man's future lay in settling down to his duties and in being a credit to his community. Undeterred by such argument he reasoned with his parents and with the local wise man, until at long last they acknowledged defeat and capitulated to his demand for freedom to seek his own path in life. His mother, in giving her permission for him to 'go and sing in praise of the Lord', exacted a promise from him.

> 'But don't become a *bhikhamangaa sadhu* (begging *sadhu*) and when you get the desire sometime, for being a *grishasthi* (householder) then come home at once.'[7]

The quest for liberation from disharmony has led many to shun the fleeting and transitory experiences of material existence in favour of a more enduring spiritual serenity. Talking to the wise, mixing with the holy, the young truth-seeker drifted where inspiration led him. For food and lodgings the *ashrams* and *dharmashalas* (religious rest houses) would have all been open to him since, then as now, India was always accommodating to sincere seekers of the truth. Notwithstanding this custom of offering alms to travellers in search of holiness, life could not always have been easy for the young boy alone. Excursions into the byways of the Himalayan hinterland threatened many dangers, for wild beasts lurked there, including boars, bears and tigers. However, Rajaram's steadfast faith in his God held good, and he ventured freely and remained unscathed. Whilst on this solitary quest for self-realization, he recognized the need for guidance and thus entertained the hope of meeting someone who might offer him spiritual tutelage.

In his search he encountered many learned and sincere devotees, but met none whom he felt comfortable enough to entrust himself. On one occasion though, after having tracked down a *mahatma* (great soul), he waited patiently for the *swami* to emerge from meditation. After offering his respects and greetings, Rajaram requested that he provide him with fire, but the *yogi*, who after his exercises had appeared so serene and blissful, on hearing the boy's request exploded in a rage, for it is well known that in the tradition of *dandi* (staff) carrying *swamis*, the use of fire is generally avoided. Rajaram patiently endured the heated outpourings before calmly asking the *swami* from where this anger sprang, if not from fire. The *swami*, thoroughly abashed, hugged the lad and apologized profusely, and over the next few days gave time to the precocious aspirant, familiarizing the young seeker in the fundamentals of *yoga* discipline.

The search for living examples of the spiritual perfection which Rajaram sought for himself continued, and, at length, at the hermitage town of Uttar Kashi, in the Himalayas, he met Shri Swami Krishnanand Saraswati. In this teacher alone the boy found the qualities he sought, those of renunciation, celibacy and mastery of philosophy. Believing him to be a man of deep realization, Rajaram offered himself as disciple to this austere teacher, took initiation and received a new name, that of Brahma Chaitanya Brahmachari.

In surrendering to the rigours and demands of monkhood, Brahma Chaitanya, along with his fellow *brahmacharin*, derived great support and love from his *guru*. In time, his dedication to the service of the master resulted in a special dispensation being accorded to him, for Shri Krishnanand 'banished' the young lad from his *ashram* and ordered him to enter a *gupha* (cave) a few miles away, on the understanding that he attend weekly visits to his teacher on the day of *Guruvar* (Thursday). However, his fellow pupils were completely unaware of the real purpose behind his 'banishment' from their community and believed him to have upset their teacher in some way. So, at length Shri Krishnanand resolved to address this situation and to that end sent a senior *brahmachari* to seek out the novice and enquire of him whether there might be some empty cave that the master could come to stay in. The reply came back that there was none.

On the next Thursday, when Brahma Chaitanya returned as usual to the *ashram* in order to receive his teacher's blessings, he found himself very unpopular with his fellow *brahmacharin*, for it was common knowledge that there were many empty caves thereabouts. His response that there were no empty caves in which the *guru* might stay, had been interpreted by them as untrue and therefore gravely insulting. So, when they were all gathered before Swami Krishnanand, Brahma Chaitanya's fellow pupils awaited the boy's punishment for his insolent behaviour. But Shri Krishnanand just sat there silently surveying the assembly, as if unaware of the ill-feeling that had arisen amongst his disciples. So someone spoke up:

> 'Maharaj [Lord], what penance is escaped by the one who disrespects the will of the *guru*? Disrespect of the will then is a kind of contempt of the *guru*. From this then is a proven insubordination of the *guru*. Then, in this way with insubordination of the *guru*, what should be the treatment?'[8]

The *guru* asked him to provide an example and the questioner hesitatingly revealed his motives for raising the issue. And when he had finished, all eyes fell on Brahma Chaitanya so it became clear to him that he was required to speak therefore he explained himself claiming that what he had said was the truth. He elaborated:

'As far as we understand Guru Charanon's abode is not in rooms of stone and clay. There should be a room in the heart of devotees for him to dwell. Since a long time all the rooms of my *panchkoshon* (five *kosha*, the receptacles within the body according to the *Vedanta* system) were adjusted to be the abode of Shri Charanon. From the day we seized the water that washed Shri Charanon (the blessed feet) of the holy soul, really at that time the emptiness of the rooms of my own heart were filled, there you became seated. Now we do not have any empty room. Guru Dev then became an occupant of the finest hairs on the body. If we had known before that day that in future you would request a place sometime, then within the *panchkoshon* I would have set some, one or two empty places, but I was ignorant of this wish and had previously filled all the rooms.

And speaking of these rooms of earth and stone, then Maharaj Ji understands that all are empty. Had he desired to dwell at that place he would really have graced it by going there. It really is not necessary to inquire from me. Therefore, I gave the answer about which rooms Maharaj Ji was asking of.'[9]

After his explanation, a prolonged silence fell upon the assembly as Brahma Chaitanya's fellow *brahmacharin* now understood something of the depth of both question and answer. With the master's permission the shamefaced and deflated pupils removed to their quarters, leaving *guru* and *chela* alone.

It is written that by the age of twenty-five the *brahmachari* had become fully established in the truth of his inner self and completed his study of the scriptures. With his *guru* he set off from Uttar Kashi to stay at a village close to Rishikesh where Shri Krishnanand is said to have assisted life to return to a dead youth's body after it had already been prepared for cremation!

Brahma Chaitanya continued to travel, in the mountains and amidst deep, dense forests pursuing the lifestyle of the religious renunciate that he was. By habit he did not fraternize with others, least of all with women. Stories abound bearing witness to his life of contemplation, his habitual prayer and his crystal-clear thinking. There are even rumours, rich in content, concerning miracle-working.

We catch up with the God-loving monk just after the turn of the century, in 1906 at the famous religious festival of Kumbh Mela in the city of Allahabad, where his *guru* decided to ordain him formally into the order of *sannyasin*. Here at Prayag, the confluence of the sacred rivers Ganga and Saraswati, Brahmachari Brahma Chaitanya was given the title of Shri

Swami Brahmananda Saraswati Maharaj and received the traditional symbols of *swami* hood, namely *kamaldalu* (a wooden pot) and *kaupeen* (loincloth). Henceforth, dressed in the flame-coloured robe of his calling, he would attract much attention as a venerated holy man, even though he was no more than thirty-six years of age. Audience with him, though sought by many, was granted only to the few who correctly interpreted his put-offs as tests of earnestness and sincerity. Those in search of his *darshan* or 'holy look' would find themselves confronted by a hand-painted message in Hindi reading *"Aaj naheen milenge"* – 'Today we will not meet.'[10] If visitors waited long enough, their patience would usually be rewarded. It seems that on such occasions he would initiate enquirers into secret *yoga* meditation techniques.

His fame spread, to such an extent that villagers desirous of his blessings would even attempt to gather dust that his feet had touched. For Swami Brahmananda, (Brahmanand or Brahmananda means 'Absolute bliss') the lure of the jungle, with its offer of protection and sustenance proved irresistible. A favourite haunt of his seems to have been a cave under a waterfall where, living a frugal existence, he practised his austerities. One of his fellow *swamis,* Swami Rama, attempted to seek him out:

> He used to live only on germinated gram seeds mixed with a little bit of salt. He lived on a hillock in a small natural cave near a mountain pool. I was led there by the villagers to that place, but I did not find anyone there and became disappointed. The next day I went again and found a few footprints on the edge of the pool made by his wooden sandals. I tried but I could not track the footprints. Finally on the fifth day of effort, early in the morning before sunrise, I went back to the pool and found him taking a bath. I greeted him saying, *'Namo Narayan'*, which is a commonly used salutation among swamis meaning, 'I bow to the divinity in you.' He was observing silence so he motioned for me to follow him to his small cave and I did so gladly. This was the eighth day of his silence, and after staying the night with him, he broke his silence and I gently spoke to him about the purpose of my visit. I wanted to know how he was living and the ways and methods of his spiritual practices.[11]

Such was Swami Brahmananda's spiritual magnetism that some of his followers nurtured the hope that he would one day grace the prestigious post of Shankaracharya of Jyotir Math, northern India (one of the four key positions in the Hindu faith), but apparently when offered he outrightly refused it. Again and again attempts were made to persuade him to accept the *gaddi* (throne) of Jyotir Math that had not been filled in well over a century. The prerequisites for this office are highly exclusive - candidates must be Brahmin by birth and life-long celibates, they must have a profound knowledge of the religious scriptures and be of Indian birth, and they must live in a state of enlightenment.

Apparently, the passing years produced no change in Swami Brahmananda's refusal of the position of Shankaracharya. In spite of this he acquired many devotees and inspired many to follow a spiritual life. His relationship with his master, Shri Krishnanand, had long since outgrown the formalities of *guru* and *chela* and instead had become transformed into one of mutual regard, each insisting that the other be accorded the greater respect. This did not prevent the silver-haired Shri Krishnanand from urging his fellow *mahatma* (great soul) to become less reclusive and to share his spiritual knowledge with the masses.

So Swami Brahmananda, whilst following his inner stream of inspiration, would occasionally surface in the midst of some town or other, and accepting a devotee's accommodation he would immerse himself in prayer and meditation. Chances to glimpse him, let alone talk to him, were rare and highly sought after. In Jabalpur in central India, there lived one Raj Varma, a photographer and artist, who like others, was repeatedly rebuffed before gaining audience with the *swami*. And in the ensuing months Raj's nephew, Mahesh, also expressed a desire to visit the wandering hermit. He was more fortunate, for when the occasion arose, access was readily provided and, fixed his eyes on the robust-looking *swami*, he became convinced that here he had found his *guru*.

Mahesh Prasad Srivastava (aka Mahesh Prasad Varma) was born on Saturday, 12th January 1918, the third of four children; with one older brother, Jageshwar Prasad Srivastava, 'J.P.', born 17th May 1911, and two sisters, Indira and Godawari. As an infant, Mahesh would have submitted to the customary shaving of the head and the writing (with honey upon a golden pen-nib) of the syllable ॐ *OM* upon his tongue. It is likely that his father's name was also Prasad for according to custom a newborn male child bears his father's name in addition to his own. Likely also is that he is of the *Kayastha* a caste of scribes, with his father believed to have been a minor official in the Department of Forestry. According to his passport he was born on 12th January 1918 in a village by the name of Pounalulla. However, many believe the year of his birth to be 1917, with his place of his birth being either Panduka village in Chhattisgarh, about 660 kilometres southeast of Bhopal in Madhya Pradesh, or at Chichli, near Gadawara, roughly 150 kilometres east of Bhopal.

As a boy Mahesh would have felt the love of his family as his father, Shri Ram Prasad Shrivastava, and mother, uncles and aunts took turns to place him upon their knee, generously sharing their sweets and affection. There were stories for little Mahesh to hear, tales of gods and demons, saints and *gurus*, and of ordinary people rich and poor. Of these stories, those concerning the mischievous god-child Krishna and the virtuous deeds of god-prince Rama would both have been firm favourites. From these tales the cultural values that were the boy's birthright became transferred, absorbed and reinforced. Mahesh was later to reflect on the process whereby personal values become cultivated:

> The children in India are told when you get up you bow down to your mother, you bow down to your father, you bow down to your elders. You go to the temple, you bow down to the Deity. You go to school, you bow down to your teacher.
>
> It provides a great shield of security and assistance from all quarters for the child to grow on right lines with great energy, with great intelligence, with great accomplishment, very great. And these feelings of love for mother and love for father supported by this ritual of bowing down, this later on develops in devotion to Almighty Great Father.[12]

In this regime of worshipful obedience, what chance of forgiveness could a child hope for should his behaviour become less than impeccable? Some reassurance could be derived from the much-loved stories of Krishna, the mischief-making boy who so easily won the hearts of everyone. When Krishna stole his mother's butter she tied him to a tree. Someone offered to free him, but he refused, preferring to wait for his mother. Perhaps that is how it was for Mahesh:

> It is the love of a mother for her child that makes her look kindly upon his mistakes. In fact, a mother enjoys the mistakes of the child because, when he commits a mistake, she is able to give him more of her love. In that love, the child grows to be better able to overcome the weakness of committing mistakes.[13]

It is said that Mahesh was possessed of a naturally cheerful disposition, but he was later to recall:

> This has been the one question in my mind ever since I was young: God is omnipresent and God is almighty and God is merciful and in the heart of everyone, why should a man suffer having God within himself? And what is the value of oneself if he keeps suffering?[14]

The growing tide of modernity sweeping the world had brought with it incitement to disobedience, but the cultivation of 'free thinking', a concept greatly valued by Westerners, was of dubious value to the highly organized structure of traditional Indian society. The suspicion was that political awareness could lead to weakening of religious values, and possibly, given time, its eventual destruction. The dilemma facing the educated classes was how the material advantages of 'progress' could be gained without losing their highly valued spiritual culture. Mahesh's parents faced the situation boldly and made sure that he received an above-average education. In a country where English quite literally ruled, they saw to it that he mastered not only the native language but that of the Raj too. And evidently he showed a certain promise in the scientific disciplines too, although, as with many other students, the ancient language of Sanskrit posed difficulties for him. Allegedly he undertook degree courses in both physics and mathematics at K.P. Intermediate College (K.P. standing for Kayastha Pathshala) Allahabad. It is difficult to verify this claim, and has even been suggested that he was registered under another name, that of M.C. Srivastava (who was listed amongst the alumni of Allahabad University), though quite why this would have occurred is difficult to understand. But, maybe the rumour is correct, that Mahesh left his family home early in life establishing close links with the family of his Uncle Raj R P Varma, and it is speculated that Mahesh spent much of his childhood with them, and perhaps temporarily assumed their family name.

According to Mahesh, referring to his time at college; the acquisition of so much information only accentuated his hunger for deeper fulfilment:

> I was completely dissatisfied with what I studied in college. Because I knew – this can't be the whole knowledge. I was searching for something complete whereby I could understand everything.[15]

Perhaps it is true, as some say that at this time he took to working as a clerical assistant, at the local Gun Carriage Factory, in Jabalpur for a brief period. But what is clear is that he had also become enamoured with the subject of *yoga*, which was not unusual, for even amongst the most worldly and irreligious of Indian people there is a desire to hear stories of saints and miracle workers. In the busy life of material advancement that Mahesh was witness to, time could always be found to contemplate ideas concerning God and religion, and to hear stories about miracle-working holy men, as Mahesh's brother, J.P. Srivastava, recalls:

> 'Visiting innumerable Sadhoos and Sanyasis during his school and college life the Maharishi at last came in contact with Gurudeo in 1939.'[16]

> One day someone in the street whispered to me, 'There has come a great saint, but he does not want to be known by the people. If you wish, then we shall go quietly one night.' I said, 'There could be nothing better than that. Taken precaution that nobody sees us, one night we went. We reached the house about 11 o'clock in the night. A small house and two to three people were there on the ground floor sitting quietly and meditating. We were a surprise to them. First thing they did was to put their fingers on their lips, and we did the same,

assuring them that we would not speak. I whispered to one of them who looked a little more sympathetic than the others. "Can I have *darshan* with Swamiji, just *darshan*, no talking; we will not disturb him. He asked, "Who told you to come here"? I quietly whispered, "There is no time for all that, don't ask me that, just *darshan*". He went upstairs and came back quietly without any information. He said, "Does not seem possible, better go and come some other day". We stood there without answering him. After about 10 minutes he motioned us to sit down. That gave some hope and we sat down. It was dark all around with only a dim lantern in the corner. After about an hour, two or three people seemed to be coming down the staircase. The man went up again and quickly came down hastily to call us up. He asked us not to talk, no sound to be made. "Go, stand, prostrate and come out", he said. We started going up the stairs, and every step brought us into more intense darkness. There was no light. Slowly we managed to come on the terrace. It was not so dark in the open but it was difficult to see clearly. It was just the time. It so happened a car took a turn a furlong away, and that was the light provided us to have Guru Dev's *darshan*. But I think that was enough to intrigue the soul. We came back and somehow managed to find out one of those 4 or 5 people who used to go there every evening.[17]

I somehow was able to speak with him. He asked me about everything I was doing, and when he heard I was student he said; 'First finish your studies'. There was nothing to argue or discuss.[18]

Allegedly, on listening to the *swami's 'upadesh'* (discourse), Mahesh was moved to say:

'This is the Divine light I have been searching for'; and he requested Gurudeo for initiation, but was told to wait for some time, "There is no hurry about it" he said[19]

This [going to visit every evening] lasted a few days, then Guru Dev was gone back to the lonely forests. It was hard to locate from where he had come and where he had gone, because those who knew him were strictly prohibited to tell others his whereabouts. There was no way to keep in contact with him.[20]

According to his brother, J.P. Srivastava, Mahesh composed the following lines of verse in January 1941:

> *'Om Lead Me To Light*
> *Om Dawn In My Sight*
> *Om Take Me To Thine*
> *Om Make Me To Shine.* '[21]

Marketplaces in India throng with vitality, the scents of fresh vegetables, fruits and freshly gathered spices, blend with the fragrance of burning *dhoop* (incense) and wood smoke from restaurants and *chaay* (tea) stalls to produce an exotic aroma. The sounds of the barking voices of traders calling attention to their wares, the tinkling cycle bells, the vain hooting of a car demanding the right of way, mixes with the creaking of horse *tangas* (taxis) and groaning grinding heavily laden ox-carts. One particular market place, on one particular day was busier than usual; it thronged with expectant, eager local citizens and was swelled by people from out of town. The city was Jabalpur (Jubbalpore) in the Central Provinces of India (modern day Madhya Pradesh - M.P.), and the year was 1942. The air crackled with electricity, for not only was this the monsoon season, when at any moment a torrent of rain might fall, but something even rarer, an event of a lifetime, was drawing ever closer.

The occasion that the growing mass of people awaited was the chance to take *darshan* of the Shankaracharya of northern India, the recently appointed head of the Hindu faith. Their religious life had for a century, perhaps longer, been without its major representative. Amongst the crowd, craning his neck for a glimpse of the parade, could be seen the expectant features of a youthful Mahesh. It had been some months since he had first met Swami Brahmananda and received his blessings and guidance.

> Shankaracharya is the head of Hindu religion. In Shankaracharya dissolve all the differences and the tensions of different sects and creeds of Hindu religion. Somehow the seat of Shankaracharya remained vacant; there were no occupants of that great throne of Shankaracharya. All the conscientious leaders of public life and good saints were concerned with this seat of Shankaracharya remaining vacant. They held national conferences to select some Shankaracharya, and on the highest circle of the saints Guru Dev was known, so they decided to approach him wherever he was. The story goes that it took him twenty years of persuasion to accept the seat of Shankaracharya. [22]

> By the time I had finished my studies, he had become Shankaracharya in Jyotir Math. I was told that many people were going to that place and I went there and found Guru Dev. [23]

Now Shankaracharya means a great institution in himself, hundreds of people surround him and all.. Great, great commotion. His life had been a complete silence. Whatever it was.. that was the time when he came to.. when Shankaracharyas used to come, they'd take him out in great processions, with great, all big paraphernalia. In one of the processions I happened to see him, and when I saw him, first time, I said 'Now, fine, this is it.' That was a flash to me.[24]

On seeing the *guru* again, draped in a saffron-coloured silk robe bearing a *danda* (staff) the sceptre of his office, amidst the sounds of jubilant chants of bystanders raining flowers down on his vehicle, Mahesh set his heart on again meeting with the *guru* and immersing himself in the man's presence. Later, the procession over, Mahesh atttended an openair gathering at Bai Ka Bageecha, Baldev Bag, Jabalpur, where, clutching a sheet of paper, he approached the organiser, Jugal Kishor Srivastava, asking:

'जगद्गुरु भगवान के शुभागमन पर मैनें एक छोटी सी कविता लिखी है

क्या मैं महराज के समक्ष इसका पाठ कर सकता हूं ?'[25]

'Jagadguru Bhagwan ke shubhagaman par mainen ek chhoti si kavita likhi hai kya main maharaj ke samaksha iska path kar sakta huun?'

'On the auspicious arrival of *Jagadguru Bhagwan* I have written a short poem. Can I recite it to *Maharaj*?'

After Swami Brahmananda arrived, a *puja* and a ritual ceremony were celebrated with some 11 *pandits* reciting Vedic *mantras*. Mahesh then read aloud the verses of his poem in the presence of the Shankaracharya.

Soon after the assembly Mahesh announced his resolve to join the *swami's ashram.* This monumental decision to become a monk and to renounce his kith and kin apparently threw his family into great confusion.

> Meditation gives us an extra means of culturing the heart. More extra, quickly, expands the heart and expands the mind and then allows the greater waves of love to come up. It's a very, very, fortunate situation in whatever set-up we have placed ourselves. Whether a *brahmachari* or a married man, and that's it.
>
> In-between is a waste of life. No good.
>
> This decision cannot come from anyone else. It has to come from within one's own mind. 'I want to lead a *brahmachari's* life', or 'I want to lead a married life'. Nobody else can decide. Marriage counsels are, they're good to help thinking here and there, but no other than man himself will be able to decide whether he wants to be a *brahmachari* or a householder. Always.
>
> When people knew my intention that I want to be a *brahmachari*, and want to go to the Himalayas and be a *yogi* and all that. Lots of persuasion; that everything you can do at home and all that, all that, all that. And people used to take me to some saints, with saints. Much in advance they would go and tell him that we are bringing a boy and you persuade him to marry and all that. And, and because I was fond of saints, they'd say, 'Oh that saint has come here and we'll go' and I'd say; 'Yes, we'll go,' and then they'd start something talking about God and later on this topic would come up and then the saint would talk to me quietly and would try then to persuade me to marry and all that.
>
> And then, it was difficult thing. I never expected a saint to talk to me like this. One saint was a very powerful saint. I loved him very much, and it was in the night and he started to persuade me like that. Then I felt very bold with him, and I said, "Do you think anyone else can make a decision for anybody else? What kind of life this would mean? Don't you think the decision should come from one's own?" And he was **shocked**. Very elderly saint, and good, I loved him, and he was a very learned saint, and nice, when he got a shock, he stopped for some time, two or three minutes, and then he said, "You have a very, right, deciding mind. No one else can decide for you, you have to decide." And I said, "Yes, this is what I was thinking." Because it's such an intimate thing, no one else can know the whole thing about anybody else's feelings, or thinking, the whole structure of life, the whole bent of life, so one will decide and when the decisions are taken on a very natural, innocent impulse of life, they'll last with man.[26]

What better choice of *guru* could he make than this revered holy man who shunned all personal glory and had no interest in matters of power or material wealth? When later asked if his parents had not wanted another career for him, he replied:

> I think this is common in the parents. It all depends ... that their son should live happily, and happiness is – he should have the comfort of a home and good family and he should live all the joys, and he should not go to the Himalayas where there is nothing and where will he sleep and do what he has to do and all that ... because monks' life is a very hard life. No home, nothing, nothing – you

sleep under the trees and meditate in the caves or wherever, whatever. So there is nothing definite in the life of a monk, particularly in India. Here in the west the monks are more organized and the church is there and they take care of it, but in India when one leaves home – he doesn't take care of himself, because he has no means to take care. He is out of society; no one asks him to do some work and pays him wages or anything – nothing. So now he is all in the faith of God – now that he is left with just his faith. So the life of a monk is a very very hard life. Therefore the parents don't generally like the children to take such hardships now – out of love.[27]

Mahesh's brother, J.P. Srivastava, tells that it was two years after Mahesh's first request for initiation, that he was actually initiated, and within a few months, started life in the *ashram.*

2

—★—

HIMALAYAN HERMITAGE

It might be wondered why Mahesh's master, Swami Brahmananda, had finally been persuaded to take the mantle of Shankaracharya when for twenty years he had steadfastly refused to succumb.

Long, long ago, some say as long ago as 2,500 years, came one who was to be known as Adi Shankara ('The First Shankara'), and the mass spiritual reawakening of the people of India at that time is attributed to him. He died at the age of thirty-three, but before departing his earthly body, he arranged for the future management of religious guidance by setting up a *math* (monastery) at each point of the compass. The first of these was headed by his disciple Trotakacharya (sometimes referred to as Totakacharya) and located at Jyotir Math (modern-day Joshimath) in the Garhwal Himalayas. Traditionally, it is held that Shankara was an incarnation of the god Shiva (also known as Shankar), the only incarnation in human form; Lord Shiva is perceived as Lord of the *Yogis* and worshipped as such by their votaries. Shiva has many names or epithets, and amongst them is that of Mahesh (Sanskrit for 'Great Lord' or 'God'). The naming of children in India is taken very seriously and a *pandit* is generally consulted for the purpose. Contemplation of one's own name is thought to encourage specific desirable qualities and tendencies if it has been correctly chosen. It is of note that Swami Brahmananda's name at birth was Rajaram (King Rama) and he later took to the chant of 'Ram *naam satya hai'*. 'Rama's name is truth'.

Adi Shankara, in setting up the *maths* had produced reference points towards which the wandering *sadhus* and *swamis* might congregate. It has been suggested that the favoured motion of such people should be in a circular flow, forever passing through the lives of everyday folks or *grihasthas* (householders). It is clear that there had been a lapse in the lineage of Jyotir Math, coinciding with British rule, so the plans of Shankara had been upset. Though Swami Brahmananda possessed the necessary credentials for office, he preferred to remain in the quietude and

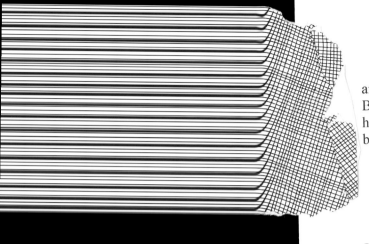

anonymity of forests and jungles. Nevertheless the requests had continued. By 1941 the situation was set to come to a head and through the efforts of his disciple Swami Karpatri, and another *swami*, Gyanandji, pressure was brought to bear on him.

> When Karpatri opened his mouth before his Guru, latter's words were "You want to put a lion to chains who moves about in the jungle freely. But if you so like, I honour your words and am ready to shoulder the responsibilities of the Peeth management. By shouldering this responsibility, I would be serving the cause for which Adi Shankaracharya stood. I fully dedicate myself for the mission".[28]

It surprised all concerned when he actually appeared to yield, so accordingly arrangements were made to bring about his installation. But only two days before the great event, he did his second significant disappearing trick (the first having been on the eve of his marriage). In truth, taking the seat of Shankara could make incalculable demands on him, so perhaps this was why he so unceremoniously slipped the net. Though there was much consternation at his conduct, rather than look elsewhere for a substitute, it was decided that the celebrations were merely postponed.

When Swami Brahmananda re-emerged in Benares some three weeks later, news of his return brought representatives running to him, begging for his co-operation. On this occasion he neither accepted nor rejected their offers - no agreements were made; he remained silent. However, since he did not disagree, the plans for his investiture were re-instituted and out of expediency commenced without delay. The traditional rites were brief but duly completed and as of Tuesday, 1st April 1941 the nation had as head of Jyotir Math, Badrikashram, Himalayas, the highly respected Jagadguru Shrimad Swami Brahmananda Saraswati Maharaj Ji. Seated crossed legged within an ornamented palanquin atop a mature elephant he allowed himself to be paraded before the people and, it is said, at a conference held in his honour that he was given an outstanding reception. The Maharajah of Darbhanga delivered a speech extolling the *swami's* greatness and amidst the celebrations, with the chanting of Vedic hymns in full swing, a feeling of great optimism settled and enveloped those gathered there. For those present it seemed as though a new era were dawning in the history of the Indian people.

During the first months of his ministry, Swami Brahmananda (or 'Shri Charanom' – 'The Blessed Feet' – as many of his disciples addressed him) made a tour of southern India and on his return attended the religious ceremony of Maharudra *yagya*, convened in Madhya Pradesh. Shortly thereafter his *ashram* took in a new member, young Mahesh Srivastava.

> Right from the beginning the whole purpose was just to breathe in his breath. This was my ideal. The whole purpose was just to attune myself with Guru Dev,

and that was all I wanted to do.[29]

"Right in the beginning, I joined the *ashram*, I came, and then I was amongst thirty or forty *brahmacharis,* and *pandits* and all that, all that. And they were very wise people, *pandits* of all the six systems of philosophy, and *pandits* of all the *smrittis, shrutis,* and all that. The whole learning round about Shankaracharya was vast retinue of learned people and I was absolutely insignificant. I had some knowledge of Hindi, and some of English, and a little bit of Sanskrit, but in that big huge learned assembly, this was absolutely insignificant, and English, of course, it was not necessary at all.

And then it was about a week and as everyone in the morning would go and do the prostrations and come out and then there was nothing to do. And one week passed and then I thought. "It's ridiculous to waste all this time." Was just once in the morning and once in the evening, go and prostrate and come out. So I made friends with a man who was cleaning his room, something like that, like that. Adjusting his table, this, this, this.

I said, "Oh, could you not take rest? You must be feeling very tired," and something, something.

And I said. "I could..."

But he said, "You can't. You can't come in this room," and this and this.

But I said, "Maybe when Guru Dev is not here, when he is taking his bath, and I could clean or something."

And he said, "Yes, that time you can come but get out quickly, and don't disturb things." Like that. So I started on that, some cleaning of the floor, something, something, adjusting something.'

During a temporary absence of a *pandit* who dealt with the clerical work of the *ashram*, Mahesh saw an opportunity for himself, and assumed the role of clerk to the *guru*, checking through the incoming mail and offering to read out loud certain of the letters addressed to Swami Brahmananda.

'One letter was there. It came for his blessing from some state in India asking that they are going to perform a big *yagya* and they want the blessings of Shankaracharya. And that letter was there and that date was approaching, about a week was left. And that I thought was a letter very responsible for the organisation to answer.

And I asked Guru Dev, "Oh, oh, the answer of this letter?"

And he would just not mind it, because in his eyes just one organisation doesn't mean anything, or something.

But, I thought it's a very great responsibility of the organisation, it's if someone wants Shankaracharya's blessing then it's for the organisation to reply, and reply his blessings and create goodwill and inspire that organisation.'

Over the following days Mahesh repeatedly attempted to solicit a response from the *guru* but without result, so then he even went so far as to suggest writing something himself. He recalls:

'One day I said, "It's only about four, five days left. Shall I make a draft and read to Guru Dev, or anything?"

And He said, "What you will write?" And that was the end he said.

Mahesh returned to his own room to gather his thoughts:

'I said, "Now come on, I have to write an answer to this. What? What? How to write? What to do? Now supposing if I was a Shankaracharya? What I'll say in that letter?" And I just imposed Shankaracharyaship on myself. And I said. "Yes, all the religious organisations look to Shankaracharya, head of the religion. The main thing is, that they should get inspiration from the blessing of Shankaracharya. As an organisation doing this great *yagya*, inspiring the people in the locality for religious life, so they should have the approval of Shankaracharya for this good act of religious value." I somehow wrote. And in the evening - it was just a very short thing, because nothing very long has to go from Shankaracharya, who is a **great** authority on religion, so very short inspiration. I made some few lines.

In the evening when I opened the door and entered and I read out that thing, in one simple breath quickly. And it sounded **so** apt, **so** appropriate.

And then he said, "Will these people get it if you write? Then send it."

I said; "Yes, they can get it, it's yet four days."

That's all he said.

Then I quickly wrote and put on a seal of Shankaracharya and did the whole paraphernalia, and sent it. From that day probably I gave an impression that I could write something useful. That was the first thing. And from there, the letters came to me for replying and I was replying and sometimes reading to him.'[30]

Wishing to get ever closer to the *guru* he attempted to attune himself closely to the master's thinking.

'And it took about two and a half years, and I thought two and a half years were wasted, but it came out to be quite early to adjust myself to his feelings. And the method that I adopted was just to sense what he wants at what time - what he wants. I picked up activity as a means to adjust to his thought, to his feelings.'

'Just about two and a half years for my thoughts to be mainly flowing in tune with his - how much perfectly, there was no way to measure, but I knew I was making very, very rare mistakes, no mistakes almost.'

'And from there on for me the whole thing was very light and beautiful, no obstacles, clear, everything. Then I was living around him without even feeling that I was living. It's a very genuine feeling of complete oneness with Guru Dev, just like that. People who have seen me moving with Guru Dev know that I was not as if in this isolated, single body or something. '[31]

'Even ignorant people like me were blessed, and this was his great, extreme value of adaptability, He could adopt [sic] himself to even such sheer ignorance, and raise the value. This adaptability is what I found most useful for me, as far as Guru Dev is concerned. Very great fortune to have found him..'

Mahesh's Uncle Raj offered this insight into his nephew's enthusiasm:

He came to the ashram as a youth bubbling over with mirth, full of energy and joy of living. He became so devoted to his master in everything …
    At night he lay down outside Guru Dev's door.[32]

Mahesh later recalled:

Out of my own experience at the *ashram* of Guru Dev - there were hundreds of pupils - no human is perfect. One comes imperfect to the *guru*, to learn how to overcome these inperfections. I had my faults also, but I did not know where. But one thing I was famous for, that I never spoke ill of anyone - always cherishing hope, that he might rise etc.[33]

At the direction of Shri 108 Dandi Swami Adwaitanand Saraswati, one of Swami Brahmananda's senior disciples, Mahesh set about preparing a book containing the lifestory and teachings of Swami Brahmananda; entitled 'Shri Shankaracharya Vaksudha' ('Nectar Speech of Shri Shankaracharya'), published in 1947, with Mahesh listed as 'Shri Mahesh Prasad Ji'.

Contained in this publication are may of Swami Brahmananda's teachings, which are firmly based on traditional wisdom, shined and polished by his own experience. We see an example of this in his reference to Patanjali's Yoga *sutras* in which the central doctrine of *yoga* is presented - '*yogash-chitta-vritti-nirodhah*' - '*yoga* is the stopping of the fluctuations of consciousness' (*YogaDarshanam* 1:2).

Shankaracharya Swami Brahmananda Saraswati clarifies:

'We are told the*"yoga"* of stopping the fluctuations of consciousness

The ultimate aim is this, that by the practice of having stopped the fluctuations of the inner self, to experience the Supreme form of the Self.

Calm without a wave in any part of the pool of water, that manner a person can see his own face.

That really is the method, stopping the fluctuations of the consciousness is really giving a clear reflection of the imperishable Self in the instrument of inner vision.

This indeed is *"darshan"* (sight) of *"atma"* (self or soul).[34]

And the old *swami* was eager to warn the unwary of being lured by those offering *siddhis* (spiritual powers).

'Nowadays most people seek the *siddhis* [paranormal powers], desiring to meet with any kind of *siddhi*. Few people have a *siddhi*, but by their greediness for *siddhi* a good many people become cheated. Our wish then is [for them] to be wary. We are like the village guard who calls *"Jagtay raho!"* ('Be awake!'), in this way we people are remaining attentive. Be cautious folks, beware of cheats. The watchman raises his voice; his *"deputy"* work is done. Later, how could he be blamed if anyone is senseless asleep! It is the one who is sleeping that gets looted. Our wish is to perform the everyday affairs of the watchman. We are awake and awakening others.[35]

A pressing task for the new Shankaracharya was that of reconstructing the monastery in the mountain town of Joshimath, which had been destroyed by an earthquake almost a century earlier, in 1851-2. But before dealing with the rebuilding programme, he had first to gain repossession of the

Jyotishpeeth land. In this matter Sir Joseph Clay, the former Deputy-Commissioner of Garhwal Himalayas and adviser to the Secretary of State, assisted the new Shankaracharya. On a hill situated between snow-clad Himalayan peaks lay the ruins of the former monastery, and in the grounds, grows the ancient mulberry tree (surviving to this day) which Adi Shankara is supposed to have planted with his own hands. Beneath the roots of this now vast tree lies the cave, or *gupha,* which served as his hermitage. Adjacent to this and a little way down the hill, lies the cave of his disciple Trotakacharya, whom Adi Shankara nominated as the first Shankaracharya. On the site of the original monastery an attractive, a simple thirty-room structure came to be built., and at the behest of the Maharajah of Darbhanga, a temple was constructed in the grounds.

> As Shankaracharya of Jyotirmath, Swami Brahmanand maintained a high Royal status. His Chhatra (Umbrella), Chanwar (Flapper), Sinhasan (Throne), Palaki (Palanquin) and Peekdan (Spittoon) were all made of pure gold. His high standard of royal life led to a new adjective in his ascetic name, 'Anant Shri Bibhushit' (Ornamented with boundless glory). [36]

The location of Jyotir Math is such as to deter all but the most ardent pilgrims from journeying there to take *darshan* of the ancient temples of their forefathers. Joshimath, at a height of 6,500ft, is a halting point for pilgrims undertaking the strenuous circuit of *Uttarakhand Yatra,* a tour of holy places in that region of the Himalayas. Whilst en route to Badrinath, a principal Hindu shrine to the god Vishnu, or to Kedarnath, the principal shrine of the god Shiva, many pilgrims also wish to pay homage to the Shankaracharya *Gaddi* 'Seat of Shankara'. After the arduous climb towards the monastery, and observing the venerated caves on the way, visitors could make their way on past the small shrine dedicated to the goddess Purnagiri Devi. After making the breathtaking ascent they would arrive at the *math,* climb the stairs at the front of the low, long, two-storey building and be welcomed into a small hall. Here was sited a highly polished wooden throne, low and wide, beautifully carved with flowers and Sanskritic texts, and strewn about with cushions.

Though Swami Brahmananda seldom visited the mountain monastery he could usually be found at his *ashram* at Varanasi. On the walls of the hall large mirrors had been carefully placed, reflecting not only the many adjacent vases of flowers but also the images of visitors as they presented themselves. Gone were the days when the best that could be hoped for was a glimpse of him or the rare opportunity to attend the half-hour prayer evenings he conducted. Now all who took the trouble to find him could partake of his *darshan* and attend his lectures.

The old *swami* wanted nothing from others and warned against trying to offer donations at *puja* (worship). Wherever he went, an information notice was displayed in front of his *shivira* (camp), stating that:

इस शिविर में कोई भेंट पूजा - द्रव्य आदि नहीं चढ़ेगा ।

"isa shivira men koee bhenta, puujaa - dravya aadi naheen chadhegaa"

NO MATERIAL OFFERING, OBJECT etc. IS TO BE OFFERED IN *PUJA* AT THIS *SHIVIRA*.

On this subject of materiality, Swami Rama, confirms that Swami Brahmanand was 'unaffected by worldly temptations and distractions'.[37] On one occasion when the Shankaracharya visited the city of Kanpur and addressed those wishing to make material offerings, he exhorted them to offer something more precious instead.

In Kanpur it is a custom to make gifts of *thaili* (small bags). But we are not someone who is contented with a *thaili* (small bag) of stones and jewels, *rupees* and *paisa* (*paisa* are small coins). You should give to me bags of the *durguna* (flaws) of mankind.'[38]

After a few years, Swami Brahmananda granted Mahesh permission to become a *brahmachari* (student) and guided him to retire to a cave in order to practice his *sadhana* (spiritual discipline) in seclusion.

In undertaking to serve as a *chela*, disciple, together with the usual vows of service and celibacy he took a new name, that of Bal Brahmachari Mahesh. The relationship of *guru* and *chela*, an ancient time-honoured Indian tradition, is not entered lightly, for the *guru*, in accepting a pupil, assumes full responsibility for his welfare. In addition to offering material security he is also expected to render such guidance and assistance as might bring about the latter's spiritual advancement. In return for this total support, the *chela* commits himself completely, dedicating his every thought, word and action to God and *guru*. Demanding and serious though this relationship most certainly is, it is not an act of total renunciation for the disciple. According to tradition those wishing to renounce material existence (and its attachments) fully are initiated into the order of *sannyasin*. Only after taking the vow of *sannyas* is the title of *swami* conferred.

As a master Swami Brahmananda was no less uncompromising as the following account indicates. Mahesh was given a specific errand to run for the *guru* urged him to run to a location high up and far away in order that he might deliver a message to a saint who dwelt there. On arriving, the breathless and exhausted young man waited for the reply. But the *sadhu*, after reading the message, merely bid him return quickly to his *guru*. Many times did the *brahmachari* find himself on such a mission and on one such occasion, as a result of his undue haste, he tripped and fell. After dusting himself down, he stooped to recover his *guru's* precious message, only to find it had become unsealed. Curiosity gained the better of him and he read the message which simply said: 'Please instruct this *brahmachari* to return immediately.' One can but imagine the novice s amazement as he read this. But how did the *brahmachari* interpret this seemingly purposeless service to his teacher?

> The disciple adjusts his likes and dislikes to the likes and dislikes of The Master, thereby elevating his mind to the status of the master's mind. In this nothing matters except obedience.[39]

In the role of Shankaracharya, Swami Brahmananda performed the function of a religious teacher, bringing out the essence of the traditional Hindu teachings for his flock. It has been said that when the *swami* met sincere seekers he would sometimes initiate them into the mysteries of *yoga* meditation. These teachings were necessarily passed on in a climate of faith and worship; so reconciling the devotional nature of Hinduism with its myriad forms of God, its multiple and varied forms of worship with the rigors of objective science must have forced Brahmachari Mahesh to more than once ponder that 'man cannot serve two masters'. However, it would be unwise to infer that the techniques the *swami* taught could only survive in a framework of religiosity. It would be equally incautious to assume the opposite. In point of fact a 'science' of the worlds of both matter and spirit has long been studied in India, although quite how closely this discipline accords with modern science is a subject for debate. But before dismissing it, we should at least be aware of our debt to Indian thinkers in the field of mathematics, for the so-called 'Arab' numerals which we use every day in point of fact originated in India.

The word *Veda* means knowledge, as does the word science. According to many, the *Rig Veda* is said to be the oldest record of human thought, and though its Aryan authors were once believed to be of European extraction,

Indians have steadfastly held the *Vedas* as their own. Descriptions of the geophysical environment in which this civilization dwelt offer much support for this latter contention. A key area of Vedic science is in its classification of energy and matter in terms of *gunas* or qualities: *sattvic* (pure), *rajasic* (energetic) and *tamasic* (impure). It is still common practice in India to refer to foods according to this code, hence *tamasic* food would be that which is over-cooked or over-processed, while *rajasic* would be most appetising and tasty, highly seasoned and spiced, but low in nutrients. A *sattvic* diet would naturally include fresh fruit and vegetables, pulse foods, cereals and dairy produce.

In spite of having become Shankararcharya of Jyotir Math, Swami Brahmananda's *ashram* in Varanasi remained his base, and in time, after renovating the mansion at Allahabad, that too became a working *ashram*. In fact he seldom visited Jyotir Math, except occasionally, during the monsoon season. So the running of the *math* fell to the *swamis* who remained there. In winter months milk was virtually unobtainable, for the cattle were taken to the lower mountain reaches. Fruit and vegetables were scarce too, so that the *swamis*, living their *sattvic* lives out on the mountainside without the conveniences of delicatessens or supermarkets, had to make do on very little. From Herbert Tichy, the European explorer and mountaineer, we gain this insight:

> In Yoshimath the Sherpa Nima and I fought a cheerful but obstinately contested battle with the aged priest Govindanand. For several weeks we had shared the Spartan life of the hermits, eating neither vegetables nor fruit, and we craved vitamins. The bazaar at Yoshimath could supply only onions and garlic, but with these we were content. When the appetising savor of the rice with onions which Nima had prepared spread through the building, however, Govindanand burst into our cell in a rage. Did we not know, he asked, that onions were an 'apple of voluptuousness,' strictly forbidden in the monastery?
>
> No, we did not know it, and we had no voluptuous desires whatever. Hostilities ensued, ending with our eating the onions, which we really did not want to forgo, raw and at a safe distance from the monastery, although this did not diminish the sinful smell that emanated from us. Nevertheless, we departed in peace and with the priest's blessing.[40]

Perhaps we should ask ourselves what had provoked the young Mahesh to give up the relative comfort and ease of his former life in exchange for austerities. In later years he many times recollected the 'flash' of his 'Guru Dev's' presence. But was this personal magnetism the sole reason for Mahesh submitting himself to a life of physical and mental endurance (it is recorded that for five years he had to abstain from the use of salt)? We find an answer in the statement made many years later, when he claimed his life only truly began nineteen years before, when he learned the secret of 'swift and deep meditation'.

Apparently, the old *swami* was not at all keen to have female followers, but despite this, there exist stories of women who were determined to take his *darshans*. In 1948, a newly widowed 20-year-old called Sitadevi Saraf (also known as 'Mataji'), was desperate for the *swami* to be her *guru* and she stopped eating, and when she appeared be be becoming ill from so much fasting, her parents beseeched Swami Brahmanand to speak with her. He met with her and she was initiated the following day.

Shankaracharya Swami Brahmananda Saraswati
at Amausi Airport, Lucknow, Saturday, 24th March 1951,
enroute from Patna to Kanpur

Swami Brahmananda Saraswati seated on mobile dais, in Mussoorie
Shankaracharya Day, Tuesday, 23rd September 1952
Man in Nehru-hat seems to be reaching out across steering wheel
to Brahmachari Mahesh

Swami Brahmananda's description of the spiritual search for oneness is captured on a 'wire' recording, of which the following is a translation:

> And that thought.... "What is mind?" Mind went in search of *"Paramatma"* (the Supersoul, Transcendental Being) and it finished going there, and was caught - and certainly it will be caught. Like an effigy made of salt, having made an image of salt, and drop it into the ocean, it will go. "Go, measure how deep this ocean is, how deep is the ocean?"

> Then the effigy will proceed, then the salt figure gets wet. There is no difficulty to go but there is difficulty to come back. There is difficulty returning, in returning from wherever it has gone. Wherever it entered the ocean, it is drowned. Who then can speak of "How deep is the ocean?" Therefore, desiring *mumukshu* (salvation), when *Paramatma* is experienced, who then will come back when the seeker experiences what *Paramatma* is, or what *atma* (individual soul) is? The *"gudha taru"* ('the tree that is concealed' – i.e. the root). He will become absorbed in That. For this reason, to speak and to listen takes us only so far; to talk and to explain, only so far whilst one has not seen *Paramatma*.[41]

It is evident from photographs and film footage that Shankaracharya Swami Brahmananda was frequently caught in solemn mood, but he could also display a radiant smile and project a lively sense of fun and jollity – an enigmatic combination, perhaps indicating two facets of the same reality, on the one side projecting his inner serenity, and on the other his joy of outer existence. Certainly he made sure that life was not all duty and tests for his *brahmacharin*; time was also given over to the study of the scriptures, prayer, contemplation and meditation.

In 16mm film footage taken during a visit to Lucknow by the Shankaracharya in April 1952, an occasion when the *guru* spoke at length, as did others, and all the speeches were recorded on wire. Brahmachari Mahesh can be seen seated waiting, and then standing speaking at a microphone addressing the congregation; where he appears very animated, intermittently gesticulating with his arms.

Shri Shankaracharya Upadesha - the *ashram* weekly newsletter

The staff of Swami Brahmananda's *ashram* produced a regular newsletter, the *Shri Shankaracharya Upadesha*, containing pictures and lectures of Swami Brahmananda, news and inspirational quotations. In addition, quotations from Swami Brahmananda Saraswati's talks were also being collected for a book to be published by the *ashram* under the title *Amrita-Kana* (Ambrosia Drop), the compilation accredited to 'Balbrahmachari Shri Maheshji'. Here is a small selection of the many Hindi quotes included in *Amrita-Kana,* translated into English:

भगवान् का भक्त होकर कोई कभी दुखी नहीं रह सक्ता । यह हमारा अनुभव है ।

Being Bhagwan's [the Lord's] devotee nobody can be unhappy, this is our experience.

ईश्वर प्राप्ति की वासना जब तक दृढ़ न होगी तब तक अनेकों वासनाओं के चक्कर में पतंग की भाँति न जाने कहाँ हाँ उड़ते फिरोगे ।

Whilst the longing to gain Ishwar (God) is not resolutely strong, and for so long as you are in the spin of many habitual tendencies, then in the manner of a kite you will fly - turned about, twisted around not knowing indeed where.

अनेक वासना–सूत्रों को इकट्ठा करके भगवद्–वासनारूपी मोटी रस्सी तैयार करो और उसी के सहारे भवकूप से बाहर निकल जाओ ।

Many threads of desire are gathered. Possessed of desire for Bhagavad (God), make ready a thick rope and enable escape beyond the *bhavakupa* (birth-well).

शक्तिशाली बनना चाहते हो तो सर्वशक्तिमान भगवान की शरण में आओ ।

You who desire to be made become strong come into the shelter of Omnipotent Bhagwan.

कुसंग से सदा बचते रहो ।

Always refrain from bad company.

यदि शान्ति चाहते हो तो व्यवहार में मन को अधिक मत फँसाओ ।

If you desire peace, do not get the mind excessively involved in your daily business.

भवसागर से पार होने के लिये मनुष्य शरीर रूपी सुन्दर नौका मिल गई है ।

सतर्क रहो कहीं ऐसा न हो कि वासना की भँवर में पड़कर नौका डूब जाय ।

The human being has got the beautiful form of body as a boat to get across to the other shore of the *bhava sagar* (ocean of birth). Be careful not to sink anywhere or to drop into a whirlpool of desire.

धन-संग्रह से अधिक प्रयत्न बुद्धि शुद्ध करने के लिए करो ।

Whilst working for a living utmost care should be taken to work with a clear mind.

फूटे घड़े से जैसे बुंद बुंद गिर कर जल कम होता जाता है वैसे ही क्षण-क्षण करके आयु समाप्त हो रही है । अभी से सावधान हो जाओ ।

Like the little drops of water that drip from a cracked earthenware pitcher, the moments of the life are passing. From right now become careful.

तुम तो स्वयं सच्चिदानन्दमय परमेश्वर के आंश हो परन्तु अपने को भूल कर अज्ञान के कारण इधर उधर लावारिस कुत्तों की तरह पूंछ हिलाते । विषयों में धक्का खाते फिरते हो ।

You are yourself a part of the Sat Chit Anand – the Absolute Bliss Consciousness - of the Almighty, but out of ignorance don't make the mistake of going here and there in the manner of stray dogs wagging the tails, as taking pleasure in worldliness pushes a return experience.[42]

On 21st April 1952 Swami Brahmanand travelled by train on the *Dehra Express* from Lucknow to Dehradun,, in a compartment adorned with garlands of flowers. After staying a few days in Dehradun, amidst the gardens of Kashmanda House, he left for Rishikesh, staying a couple of days at Atma Vigyan Bhavan, Ramnagar, in "Shri Shankaracharya Nivas" ('Dwelling place of Shri Shankaracharya'), before moving on to Mussoorie.

It is conjectured that in 1952 that Swami Brahmananda embarked on a two and a half month long *yatra* (pilgrimage) of the *Char Dham* (the four principal places of pilgrimage in the Himalayas; Badrinath, Kedarnath, Gangotri, and Yamunotri); he is also thought to have presided over a week-long *yagya* at Shri Chakreshwari Temple on Hari Parbhat hill, in Kashmir.

Whilst staying in Mussoorie, a parade was organised celebrating Shri Shankaracharya Day, and on 23rd September 1952 Shankaracharya Swami Brahmananda could be seen on an improvised float or 'Popemobile' (the comparison is a reasonable one), on which the enthroned *swami* could travel amidst a rich array of foliage and flowers, a mobile dais atop of a simple vehicle chassis with just enough space for a handful of disciples, including Brahmachari Mahesh and a very careful driver.

Such occasions gave one and all the chance to partake of the Shankaracharya's *darshan*, and thousands came to see him seated in his silk ochre robe, with his austere gaze, his bleach white beard, his long dark hair intermingled with the garlands of fresh flowers draped around his neck. He would always sit on the Dharma Sinhasana (the Lion Throne of Dharma) with gilded and carved with images of lions on the arms of the seat. To ward off the glare of the sun, an umbrella shade was placed over him, fashioned from red velvet with intricate patterns, religious symbols and text, executed in golden stitching. His forehead was daubed with sandalwood paste, a measure intended to lessen the effects of the heat, and when the vehicle halted, his disciples brought out yak whisks to cool him. Many of the general populace also took the opportunity to obtain the blessing of *tilak* (a mixture of sandalwood paste, rice and red dye) anointed upon the forehead. On his mission of spiritual revival, he travelled far and wide, presiding over many ceremonies, conferences and the like.

On Wednesday, 15th October 1952 a press conference was arranged in anticipation of the arrival of the Shankaracharya of Jyotirmath:

> ### The Great Saint of the Himalayas is Coming to Shower His Blessings on the Metropolis.
>
> The Statement issued by: BAL BRAHMACHARI SHRI MAHESH JI.
>
> Press conference convened by Shri Shankaracharya Reception Committee, Delhi on the 15th Oct., 1952 at 5 p.m. in the Young Man's Tennis Club Queen's Gardens, in connection with the visit of HIS HOLINESS SHRI JAGATGURU SHANKARACHARYA MAHARAJ OF JYOTIRMATH.
>
> ******
>
> My own self in different forms.
>
> It gives me a great pleasure to welcome you all and have your company here this afternoon. It gives me enough encouragement and support to acquaint you with the

details of the mission for whose fulfilment His Holiness Shri Jagatguru Shankaracharya Swami BRAHMANAND SARASWATI MAHARAJ will be visiting your city about the 12th of November 1952 and stay here for about a month for Dharmopdesh.

Swami Brahmanand Saraswati Maharaj, the present Shankaracharya of Jyotirmath Badarikashram (in the Himalayas) is a magnetic personality with a sweet amalgam of High Wisdom and Love of humanity. He combines in himself the Knowledge of the self with the mysterious powers -- the siddhis arising out of yogic perfection and hard penances, which he has undergone throughout his life. He is a great living yogi and scholar and is revered by millions of Hindus as their Supreme Religious head.

This great Saint of the modern age was born in U.P. in a well to do and renowned Brahman family in 1871 and was enthroned to the seat of His Holiness Jagatguru Shankaracharya in 1941 at Benares, during the ninth session of the All India Sanatan Dharma Maha Sammelan convened by the Bharat Dharma Mahamandal in conjunction with a countrywide support of almost all the ruling princes and different socio-religious institutions all over the country. It may be recalled that it was a long persuasion of about twenty years which could convince Param Virakt Swami Brahmanand Saraswati to accept the great responsibility of the Shankaracharya at the age of seventy.

From the tender age of nine when he came out of his home in Search of God, till this time, his life was mostly spent in the lonely hidden regions of the Himalayas, Vindhya Giris and the Amarkantakas which are rarely frequented by men and are chiefly inhabited by wild animals. For years together he has lived in hidden caves and thick forests where even the midday sun frets and fumes in vain to dispel the darkness that may be said to have made a permanent abode there in those solitary and distant regions.

But today he is easily accessible as he is now the presiding head of Shri Jyotirmath which is the greatest religious institution of the Hindus of Northern India, covering all different creeds and sampradayas and branches lying under the fold of Hindu Religions.

One unique principle of the great Sage that distinguishes him completely from other living saints of today is that he does not accept money as gift from his visitors or disciples.

This brief description attempts to mirror a few hurried and short glimpses of the life journey of this great living sage who has actually transformed into a living fact the inner latent potentiality of the soul. He has known the great universal Truth, whose realisation is the aim of the entire scheme of life. For him the mists of ignorance have completely disappeared and having known the Divine Reality he has verily become an embodiment of the great Divinity.

His aim of life, if the life of a realised soul can be said to possess any such aim, is to broadcast the message of the Great Divine light that he has himself realised, the Light that is the Soul of all human beings. Having himself attained the pinnacle of Self development, he aims at transforming the worldly minded people into the Godly minded, and through his inner Divine touch to change the materialistic hearts of iron into spiritual hearts of gold.

His entire personality emanates the sweet perfume of spirituality. His face radiates that rare light which comprises love, authority, serenity and self assuredness that comes only by righteous living and Divine Realisation -- one feels as if some ancient Maharishi mentioned in the pages of the Upanishads has assumed human form and feels that it is worth while leading a pious life and to strive for the realisation of the Divine.

His Spiritual teachings are simple and clear and go straight home to heart. He strictly adheres to the course of inner development laid down by the Systems of Indian Philosophy and ethics and he raises his voice never in opposition but always in firm support of the Truths and principles contained in the Hindu Scriptures.

According to the tradition from the worldly point of view, the dignity of the Shankaracharya's throne has got to be maintained by the rich paraphernalia around his Holiness, but those who have come in his contact know the fact that the private life of the Sage is quite simple and renunciation.

I believe that he is a living embodiment of titanic spiritual force. If I were asked on the basis of my personal experience, about the living saints of today, as to who is the greatest amongst them, I would unhesitatingly name Shri Jagatguru Shankaracharya Swami

Brahmanand Saraswati Maharaj of Jyotirmath the Beacon Light of the holy sanctuaries of the Himalayas.

Shri Shankaracharya Maharaj has clear insight into the mind and the thoughts of the modern age. His teaching and commandments are based on sound reasonings which are quite agreeable to any reasonable thinker. He is a great critic of prejudices and narrowmindedness arising out of irrational love of caste, creed, nationality or any "ism". His life is a living proof of the Truth of the Vedas and Shastras. He has opened a new era of renaissance of True Religion. He extends his recognition to anything that is good in any religion. He is accessible to all. Everyone can enjoy and derive benefit from his holy Darshan and elevating discourses.

He is coming shortly to shower his blessings on the busy and restless souls of the metropolis. I beseech you, my friends, to extend your hearty co-operation for the great cause in the interest of each individual of our society, in the interest of our nation and in the interest of the world at large. The great Saint of the Himalayas is coming in your midst and in the fitness of the great occasion, I appeal to your good sense to extend your valuable support so that his elevating discourses may reach the masses in every nook and corner of our country and abroad.

Thanking you for giving me a pertinent hearing, I would like to say something, in short, about the shrine of Jyotirmath, the prime spiritual centre of Northern India and the headquarter of Shri Shankaracharya Maharaj. Jyotirmath is one of four seats established by Adi Shankaracharya in this continent -- two thousand and five hundred years ago. It is situated in the heart of the Himalayas 173 miles up from Hardwar and only 18 miles south of Shri Badrinath and may be said to be the queen of the Himalayas for natural beauty and spiritual values. Jyotirmath it was that the first Shankaracharya selected for his stay in Himalayas where he taught the highest philosophy of existence -- the Vedanta - to his disciples, wrote his immortal commentaries on the eleven principle Upanishads, the Bhagavad Gita and Brahma Sutras and established a seat of Spiritual light to function as sansorium (sic), a supreme centre of the Eternal Religion of India to keep the Light of Pure civilisation and culture burning for all the millennium to come. It is an ancient culture centre of yoga, the Light House which has preserved and disseminated the Light of the Sanatan Dharma all the way down the ages.

The Shankaracharya attracted eminent visitors. Indeed, Dr S. Radhakrishnan, the famous Indian philosopher, sought guidance at his feet, as did the first President of India, Dr Rajendra Prasad, who addressed him as 'Vedanta Incarnate' or 'The embodiment of the scriptures'.

When speaking with Dr Rajendra Prasad, the Shankaracharya told him:

> 'Before, the kings would have discussions with *tapasviyon* (ascetics) and *maharshiyon* (great saints) for their advice on the tasks of government. Because of *yoga* and *tapasya* (austerity) their minds had become clear. There existed neither greed nor worldly desires, and they did not fear the king becoming displeased with what they said. Those who were given advice, that advice was beneficial for both *raja* (king) and *praja* (subject). But now things have gone to hell on account of *rajas* neglecting to keep the company of *maharishis*.'[43]

President Rajendra Prasad with Swami Brahmananda Saraswati, Shankaracharya of Jyotirmath

A photograph taken in December 1952 show the President with Swami Brahmananda, and another portrays Rajendra Babu, the President, standing beside a barefoot Brahmachari Mahesh, who was later to describe his master thus:

> His entire personality exhaled always the serene perfume of spirituality.

> His face radiated that rare light which comprises love, authority, serenity and

self-assuredness; the state that comes only by righteous living and Divine realization.

His spiritual teachings are simple and clear and go straight home to the heart. He strictly adhered to the courses of inner development laid down by the systems of Indian Philosophy and ethic...[44]

President Rajendra Prasad with Brahmachari Mahesh

Photographs taken at this time show the Shankaracharya to have aged considerably, his health having for some months given cause for much concern. Though homeopathic and allopathic (Western) medicines were administered to him they were of no avail, and he declined rapidly. He returned to Varanasi for a while before making a surprise visit to Calcutta, where an eminent doctor, thought to have been Shri Vidhan Chandra Roy (formerly Mahatma Gandhi's physician), attended to him.

But, in spite of their best efforts, the disease proved fatal. Swamiji was suffering from dropsy (Jalodar). [hydropsy or oedema - water retention, causing heart failure][45]

At about one o'clock on 20th May 1953, the doctor saw him and said, ' *"Sab thik hai"* (All is well)! The state of the heart is *"thik"* (fit). The pulse is moving, *bahut achchi* (very good).'

After the doctor went, Maharaj Shri relaxed and about ten minutes later he suddenly opened his eyes and said, ' *"Uthao"* - 'You must lift (me)!'

Having arisen, he quickly drew both his feet to sit in the posture of *sukhasana* ('easy seat' - cross-legged) and closed the eyes. In this way he was sitting.

At one-fifteen, having abandoned his own body of the five-elements he became absorbed in his own Self. The Self arose from the form of the gross body, from the surface of the world.[46]

At 1.15 pm on Wednesday, 20th May 1953, after a period of five minutes absorbed in silent meditation, Shankaracharya Swami Brahmananda Saraswati breathed his last.

Allegedly, both Brahmachari Mahesh, and Mataji Sitadevi were there in Calcutta, in the service of the *swami,* so it fell to Brahmachari Mahesh to telephone the other disciples to apprise them of the death.

On the topic of mortality, the *guru* had once given this advice:

Every day be ready, bedding packed. Nobody knows what time the "warrant" comes. Death "warrant" is the arrest "warrant" - for you there is no scope for "appeal", all at once it occurs you are to leave. Wherever one is, at that very place you will be falling down. If you are ready in the first place, then there will be no suffering at the time of death.

He who remains ready to go, from him there will never be sin. Really it is by overlooking the other world that one becomes wicked and lives sinfully. If all this is remembered every day that one day one is going to let go, then henceforth a man will never lie or behave badly.

Consider this; that when father, grandfather, great grandfather is not living then it cannot be that we will remain. When it is settled that we will go, then really if we are ready beforehand, then the travelling will be a pleasure; but if one is not ready then afterwards you will be suffering. Be careful of doing any work that you regret afterwards, at the time of going.

If you are not careful then you cannot escape falling down. The stream of worldly existence takes a downward direction. The inclination of the senses is opposed to a man and in opposition one again falls into the wheel of desires, not considering the suitability. Therefore it is always necessary to be careful.

At the time of death that which was good and bad in a man's own lifetime all come to be remembered. That sin that has been done remains, the fearful effects are remembered at the time of death - much repenting and much sadness occurs. Therefore you should be careful that no sin occurs to be regretted at the time of death.[47]

Swami Brahmananda's devotees received news of the *guru's* passing.

'When in 1953 Guru Dev left this mortal frame and attained nirvana I was at Benares, another place of pilgrimage for Hindus, and at that moment I was staying in the *ashram* of Guru Dev. Everybody knew that I am very attached to Guru Dev and devoted to Guru Dev, and then news came to Benares that Guru Dev has attained *nirvana*. I was sitting somewhere with a group of my friends and the news was relayed there. When my friends heard that Guru Dev was no more they were very anxious about me and when they conveyed that news, they were rather alert to appraise whatever reaction is and what happened, I simply, when I heard that news I became very sad, very sorry and I just kept my head on the table before me. And all of them were very anxious what will become of me. But soon after, while I was very morose, sorrow, sad, entire world was empty for me and I did not understand what to do without Guru Dev, just a half a minute or two seconds after, a flash came and it appeared to me that Guru Dev was scolding me;

"What a fool you are! You have been with me for all these many months and years, and you heard my discourses too. Is it a moment of feeling sorry? Why should you be sorry today? And you think that I am gone, where am I gone? Till now whenever you wanted to meet me, you had, you had to come to the place where I was, and today when I have attained nirvana, I am everywhere, I am omnipresent. Where have I gone? Very foolish for you to mourn on this occasion. I am with you, here, there, everywhere. Why should you be sorry?"

And the moment this flash came, my face became very brilliant, I became very cheerful. And when I raised my head, my friends who were standing there, very anxious and held in suspense, they were upset to see my brilliant and cheerful face. And then they said, "What has happened to you?" I said, "No you can't understand, nothing has happened to me, I am alright, now let me go back to the *ashram* and make the necessary arrangements".[48]

The lifeless body of Swami Brahmananda, still seated in the lotus position, was taken to Calcutta railway station and transported to Benares, where, at his *ashram* the ritual bathing of the body was conducted before being placed, with *danda* stick, in a stone (concrete) casket. Then transported to Kedareshwar Mahadev and the casket was lowered into the Ganges where the waters could enter in through several perforations.

Having arrived in the middle of the river the boat stopped and the box was lowered into Ganga Ji. Then Brahmachari Mahesh Ji jumped into the Ganga, for the box. On the arrival of the box on the riverbed he came outside for doing the final *pranaam*. The time of the *jala pravaha* having arrived, the gathering could not stop their own abundant mourning; their eyes becoming filled with tears, throats becoming obstructed and no words were coming from the mouths, and disunited they fell to crying.[49]

After Swami Brahmananda's death, people were left wondering who would be appointed in his stead. Apparently, even before his passing, the Shankaracharya had been mindful of the need to name a successor, but noted that the choice was not his alone.

Swamiji reciprocated to the loyalty and devotion of Mahesh and reposed full faith in him. Swamiji attached top value to the suggestions and advices given by Mahesh. By 1952, Mahesh came to be the most powerful man in the Ashram dynamics. He became an indispensable commodity in the matter of Math management. Sociometrically speaking, Mahesh became a near-star in the Ashram premises. Devotees touched his feet and held him in high esteem. All this, kindled in him an ambition to become the Shankaracharya of Jyotirmath after Swamiji. Sensing his ambition, one day Swamiji said to him "Mahesh, even if I myself install you as the Shankaracharya of Jyotirmath, people would not let you continue. So, exterminate this ambition from your mind."[50]

According to Shankara tradition only a *brahmana (brahmin)* can become a *sannyasi (swami)*, and only a *sannyasi* can be a *guru* and take disciples. In a scarce Hindi book of quotations of Swami Brahmananda entitled *'Shri Shankaracharya UpadeshAmrita'*, Shankaracharya Swami Brahmananda Saraswati is quoted upholding this view:

परन्तु गुरु सब नहीं बन सकते । गुरुत्व केवल ब्राह्मण ही को है ।"

parantu guru sab naheen bana sakate. gurutva keval brahmana hi ko hai."

'.. But not everyone can be a *guru*. Actually, only *brahmanas* are in the position to be a *guru*.'

So, since one of the preconditions of entitlement to the post of Shankaracharya is to be born a Brahmin. Brahmachari Mahesh, being of the Kayastha caste, was not eligible to hold this venerated office, even if he had fulfilled all of the other criteria. So, on account of being of the *varna* (caste) of *kayastha*, Brahmachari Mahesh could not have hoped to succeed his master nor could he ever become a *guru* himself, even though he had been very close to Swami Brahmananda.

Some days after the *guru's* death, a *vasiyat*, or Will, surfaced, the contents of which seemed to be a surprise to some, since it had been assumed that Swami Karpatri would succeed him. It should be understood that Karpatri was Swami Brahmananda's principal devotee, having been accepted as a *chela* in 1926, being given the name Swami Hariharananda and made a *sannyasi* by Brahmananda at Varanasi in 1932. Possibly because Karpatri had become deeply involved in politics, a new Will had been drawn up and registered on 18th December 1952. Karpatri was not listed amongst the potential candidates, namely; Swami Shantanand Saraswati, Pandit Dwarika Prasad Tripati, ('if he comes to accept *danda* [i.e. if he becomes a *sannyasi*']), Swami Vishnudevanand Saraswati, and Swami Paramanand Saraswati MA.

'Swamiji (Swami Shantanand) was at that time on the banks of the Ganges. Staying in Karnavasa he was undertaking severe penance again. In between an evening bhajan session on the banks of the Ganges he happened to hear a news telecast of one of the radio stations. Later, some devotees arrived at the hermitage of Swamiji to inform of the departure of Maharaj Shri. Swamiji left for Varanasi as soon as possible to participate in the funeral

'A meeting of all the devotees, disciples, religious leaders, saints, sages, scholars and prominent people was arranged in the leadership of Karpatri ji Maharaj. An interim committee was formulated which had the ability to take care of the entire peeth until the official formalities could be completed with the help of the Allahabad Registrar. As the name of the successor was not declared, the interim committee had the power to take all kinds of decisions including the wealth. The interim committee was supposed to hand over all the documents and power to the successor once the name was declared.'

'The interim committee was presided over by Swami Swaroopananda Saraswati with the secretary as Pt Balakrishna Mishra who was also the secretary of Bharat Dharma Mahamandal. Other members were Pt Balakrishna Mishra, Kashipathi Tripathy of Varanasi, Yugul Kishore Tandan of Etawa, Jagadish Prasad Mishra of Jabalpur, Ganga Prasad Pandey of Prayag, Pt Dwarika Prasad Tripathy, Brahmachari Mahesh ji, Brahmachari Ramprasad ji and Shankaralal ji.

On Friday, 12th June 1953 the scene was set for the induction of Swami Shantanand Saraswati as the 'Abhinava' Shankaracharya, the 'new' Shankaracharya of Jyotir Math.

'In charge of the ceremony was Swami Govindanand ji Maharaj who had left the place without informing anybody. He was in possession of the essential things for the ceremony. But the general secretary, Pt Balakrishna Mishra, with the help of other members such as Pandit Kashipathi Tripathy, Lohiya Pandey, Brahmachari Mahesh, Shankar Brahmachari, and Brahmachari Ramprasad tried hard to make all arrangements and invited all the dignitaries from across the nation. Representatives of all the religious centres, sannyasis, scholars, and spiritual leaders arrived at the pre-determined time and the ceremony began. With the blessings of saints and sages of the entire world, the ceremony was successfully completed.'[51]

But on 23rd June 1953 Karpatri challenged the Will and installed his choice, Swami Krishnabodhashram, so, now there were now two claimants to the title of Shankaracharya of Jyotir Math with Swami Shantanand running the *ashram* at Allahabad. Brahmachari Mahesh then took leave of his *gurubhaiees* (fellow devotees of Swami Brahmananda) and travelled to Uttar Kashi (northern place of Shiva) a town some way north of Rishikesh. Frequented by pilgrims on their way to Gangotri, with a temple complex close the source of the River Ganges; Uttar Kashi contains numerous temples, of which the largest and most impressive is Vishwanath Mandir.

There is an old-fashioned market place, with shops and artisans with the local inhabitants living across the river and in the hills to each side of the valley. Up until recent years the local populace lived a traditional life, preparing their food seated on the broad verandas of their simple wooden-beamed homes and storing foodstuffs for their few animals in hayricks in the upper branches of trees. Overhead fly the crows and large birds of prey: kestrels and even eagles. In former times wild animals roamed, making it unsafe for anyone to venture out after dark.

It was in this remote and ancient place that Swami Brahmananda had found his *guru* and taken initiation into the mysteries of *yoga*. The town is renowned for its community of scholars, *sadhus*, *swamis* and *mahatmas*, most of whom live in an area known as Gyan Suu. Here, where the sight of holy men and saints is considered commonplace, Brahmachari Mahesh, with his loose long black hair and covered in a simple white robe would not have attracted much attention. He stayed on the outskirts of town at an *ashram* by the name of Sri Shankaracharya Gyan Mandir, located a comfortable distance from the main Rishikesh-Gangotri road. Bordering the gurgling Bhagirathi River (an alternative name for the sacred River Ganges), the *ashram* was situated within spacious grounds whose perimeters are lined with trees (some of them fruit trees, yielding bananas and oranges) which provided a screen from the neighbouring lands. The sandy banks of the crystal-clear waters of the Ganges, provided an ideal spot for local people to wash themselves and their clothes, but over the years successive monsoons have swollen its waters, resulting in significant loss of land to the *ashram.*

The focus of the buildings of Gyan Mandir 'Knowledge Temple' was an impressive shrine, a *Shivalinga* (ancient symbol of the forces of creativity). Surrounding the temple were the buildings containing simple whitewashed cells which provided accommodation for inmates and occasional visitors. A few also contained a *gupha* or cave below floor level.

Having arrived at Gyan Mandir, Mahesh committed himself to prolonged spells of deep silence.

> Where I stay in a small Ashram in Uttar Kashi, the cave is like a very small basement under a room. The entrance is through an opening only big enough for one person to enter. Down there is quiet. No sound. Cool in summer. Warm in winter.[52]

Amongst the hermits thereabouts the prevailing attitude was abstention from everyday mundane cares. Since seeking direct contact with God or Brahman is seen as of paramount importance for a spiritual adept, then any deviation is perceived as wasted energy. Brahmachari Mahesh was to spend many months in solitude in his sandy cave. If he wanted to sleep he had only to take to the bed in the room that lay directly above the cave. He would come out only to take exercise, to deal with the normal bodily functions and take the occasional meal which a man from the town would bring and leave outside his door.

For most of the time at Uttar Kashi the *brahmachari* kept his own company, but on those occasions when he took companionship, it was usually with a fellow truth-seeker, and even then, more often than not the time would spend the time in silence. 'We hardly ever spoke ... After all, there was really nothing to talk about.'[53] After years of devoted service to his master, he had now to acclimatize himself to life without the *swami's* living presence. So he pursued his *sadhana* but in spite of the isolation (or perhaps because of it), he began to entertain the notion of travel.

> When he (Guru Dev) left his body I could not survive in the affinity of the world. I just retired to the depth of the Himalayas, the place where Guru Deva found His Guru Deva - Uttar Kashi - I was just living there. The whole consciousness was as if sunk into no activity.
>
> A thought came that I should go to Rameshwaram, south of Madras - the temple of Lord Shiva - and I could not attribute any reason to it - just a thought that I should go to Rameshwaram. Six months more went by. Sometimes I used to mention my thoughts to a few saints in Uttar Kashi. They were very wise saints, between 70 and 90 years of age. One, whom I liked very much was 90 years old and his hair fell about four feet on the ground when he stood up. One day I found him coming from the backside of the Ganges, completely shaved. I could recognise him only from his walk. When he came nearer, and only then, it was confirmed that, it was confirmed that, yes, he was he. When I asked about what he had done to his hair, he replied: "One more means of memory of the past has gone". I used to mention to him that I wanted to go to Rameshwaram somehow (and Uttar Kashi is the place of saints - the heart of the world, down below the Himalayas). Just the thought of going from that place was just, for me, stepping into mud. That is the type of air of Uttar Kashi, completely out of activity, and from there the field of activity looks like the field of mud.
>
> I had mentioned to him about my thought about Rameshwaram two or three times during a period of nine months. One day he said "Better to get this thought out of your mind"[54]

Brahmachari Mahesh was of course used to taking instructions (both implicit and explicit) and must therefore have been unfamiliar with taking full responsibility for his own actions. But the great wide world, spurned during study and *sadhana* (spiritual discipline), now awaited his return. He might have chosen any destination, but his thought had been to visit Rameshwaram, a place of religious pilgrimage in southern India. With the required permission, Mahesh readied himself to commence his journey.

3

MAHARISHI EMERGES

SO after about a year and a half spent in relative seclusion, Brahmachari Mahesh departed from Gyan Mandir in order to follow his inspiration to visit southern India.

Swami Srikanta Bharathi of Sree Matha, Hariharapura, recalls:

> Among the ardent devotees of Poojya Gurudev Brahmananda Saraswati, there was one elderly lady in Kolkatta, West Bengal, belonging to a well-known family of zamindars. Mahesh affectionately called her "Mathaji" ['Mother']. She too was most impressed by Mahesh's devotion to the great Guru, and she was fondly calling him "Beta" ['Son']. This lady was deeply hurt and felt desolate after Gurudev passed away, and became very sad and depressed. Her health failed. For necessary treatment she was advised to go to Madanapalli, in Andhra Pradesh (South India). She called "Beta" Mahesh to accompany her. Taking it as an opportunity to serve Mother as well as Gurudev, Mahesh accompanied her to Madanapalli.

> Mathaji [Mataji] was admitted into the sanatorium and Mahesh had to find a place to stay in the small town of Madanapalli.

One Krishna Iyer and his brother Narayana Iyer were running a small coffee hotel in Madanapalli Town. But there was no provision for travellers to stay overnight in that hotel. After having his meal in that hotel, Mahesh asked the Iyers for a place to stay. Since there was no provision for lodging, they suggested that he may sleep on the steps, in the nearby temple. In the rain and cold of that place it was not possible to stay outdoors. So the problem was serious. Mahesh saw a very small room next to the kitchen of the hotel and asked for permission to stay there. But it was stacked with firewood and was quite uninhabitable. Somehow Mahesh prevailed upon the owners, [then he] neatly stacked the fuel in one corner and made enough space to stretch himself. He was quite pleased with the arrangement, and the others sympathized with him too. During the day he would be spending time at the hospital to look after Mathaji and later, in the evening, he would come back to his corner at the Town

Hotel.

In Madanapalli, there is a branch of The State Bank Of Mysore, and one Mr. T. Rama Rao was its manager then. He was a well-educated person with deep interest in philosophy and was living a virtuous life. It was his routine, at the end of the day's work in the Bank, to have coffee in the local hotel of Rama Iyer and spend the evening on the steps of the temple near by, with a few of his office colleagues, talking about various matters of general interest and also covering religious and philosophical topics. During that time, one evening, they saw Mahesh sitting all alone, with a gentle smile of deep contentment. His bright eyes, the charming smile on his lips and total composure attracted Rama Rao and his friends. They enquired about Mahesh's identity. They were most impressed by his smiling response, pleasing voice, gentle laughter as well as easy handling of subjects of religious and philosophical import. Clad in unstitched pure white silk, having long black curly hair and beard, innocent, ever twinkling eyes, soft but very clear voice, easy rendering of religious and philosophical subjects, at once impressed the group. Day after day, they engaged themselves in covering topics of righteous living based on religion and Indian philosophy. They were eagerly looking forward to the meeting every evening. The hotel owner brothers too joined the group. Finally they concluded that this person was a consummate Yogi. They began to address him as "Maharishi".

Suddenly the old message - "Go South" flashed across his mind. He enquired of Sri Rama Rao where and what was there in the "South" and how far. He learnt that 200-300 miles down south of India from Madanapalli on the east coast, there was the town by name Rameshwaram, where there was a very large and ancient temple dedicated to Lord Shiva established by Lord Sri Rama himself. It has become famous over these centuries. Mahesh was thrilled to hear this and remarked - " Surely that is my destination. I must go there! I now see how and why I have been brought here by Mataji. Thank God." [55]

It has even been suggested that whilst in Madanapalle, Mahesh drew a certain amount of attention to himself by putting up a sign saying 'WHO WANTS INSTANT ENLIGHTENMENT', allegedly conferred by a blow on the forehead!

His destination, Rameshwaram, is very close to Sri Lanka, and is renowned for its religious atmosphere, drawing pilgrims from all over the subcontinent. After touring around the temples and holy shrines of Rameshvaram, the lone hermit moved down to the southernmost peninsula of Cape Comorin to spend time at Kanyakumari.

I went there [Kanyakumari] and stayed for three weeks. Just after two weeks again a thought came for going to Kanyakumari. At last I went to Kanyakumari. There one day I was sitting in silence and only silence. A revelation came to me about what Kanyakumari is. All this divine radiance - That Lila Shakti - Brahmini Shakti - that place is completely wrapped in Transcendental Reality. It took about five days for fathoming the whole depth of that place.

Just after seventeen or eighteen days stay over there, I felt like going back to Uttar Kashi. With that a very faint thought - side by side - came that, when I am going back, why not give them blessing of the Himalayas. What the blessing will be - what it will be - I know nothing about this definitely, just a thought - faint thought. After three days I decided just to go out of that place. So from there I started for Trivandrum, capital of Kerala. I reached that place at about eight o'clock at night.[56]

Whilst walking the next day to the Guruvayur Krishna Mandir temple there, he sensed that someone was following close behind him. At length he was overtaken and a stranger introduced himself and began to question the *brahmachari* as to whether or not he ever spoke in public.

I was followed by a man and he asked me to speak about the Himalayas - he arranged a 7 day lecture program and he supplied the topics.

At this stage I had never initiated anyone. [57]

Brahmachari Mahesh explained that he was unaccustomed to giving lectures but told the man where he might be contacted. The stranger returned and during the following week a series of lectures was held in the locality. Such was the interest generated by these talks that the local press was alerted and further lectures were arranged. Even after a further six months in Kerala, the *brahmachari* still had no immediate plans to return to his cave at Uttar Kashi. When he was not busy lecturing he would spend much time in the company of the prominent lawyer, Shri A. N. Menon, responsible for arranging his schedule of talks.

...the first such thing happened somewhere in Kerala, where I went from Uttar Kashi to Kerala, *dakshina* [Hindi for 'south'].. South India, and people wanted to learn this practice of meditation.

I thought: "What to do, what to do, what to do?" then I thought, "I should teach them all in the name of Guru Dev. I should design a system, a system of *puja* to Guru Dev." [58]

During his time in the south, the *brahmachari* spent several months in Kerala moving from town to town, advocating a method of meditation. The technique he was teaching necessitated repetition of a *mantra*, and he claimed that the practice was easy and very effective at bestowing happiness. Responding to an advertisement in a local paper, Mrs Thankamma N Menon and her husband attended a three and a half-hour talk at Ernakulam and afterwards met with the speaker.

'Maharshi asked us about our Ishta-Devata [favoured deity] and advised us to go to him the next morning for Pada Pooja of Guru Deva, Maha Yogi Raj Ananta

Sri Vibhushith Sree Sankaracharya Brahmananda Saraswathi Maharaj of Jyothir Math who was going to be our Guru.' [59]

Many other people were interested in learning this easy method of meditation, amongst them Sri C R Vaidyanathan.

'Somebody said that Swamiji was giving initiations and if one followed his directions he would get Bliss quickly. I was really sceptic about this "Ananda"[Bliss] business.'

'I presented myself with the necessary puja materials on Thursday. Swamiji made me offer puja to Guru Deva and under closed doors gave me Mantra of the Ishta Devata I chose and asked me to repeat the same and also gave the necessary instructions in the new method for meditation.' [60]

Someone else who attended the session was Professor P S Atchuthan Pillai, who observed:

'His talk, behaviour and everything about him are as though he is in constant contact with his Gurudev. That is a feature which has surprised many of us closely moving with him. Maharshi Bala Brahmachari always acts as the messiah between his "Gurudev" and his own disciples. He modestly claims to be only the conduit pipe conveying the Gurudeva's blessing on to his devotees in Kerala, or to use his own expression, he is only the "bulb through which the spiritual electrical current from Gurudev shines in radiating light on all".' [61]

Teaching in the name of his *guru,* Brahmachari Mahesh began promoting a seemingly novel philosophy, offering assurance that the quest for spiritual fulfilment does not require one to forgo any material comforts (the theory being that only a *sannyasi* can benefit from **abandoning** desires whereas the householder only finds happiness in the **fulfilment** of desires). He explained:

'Obviously enough there are two ways of life, the way of the Sanyasi and the way of life of a householder. One is quite opposed to the other. A Sanyasi renounces everything of the world, whereas a householder needs and accumulates everything.'

'The one realises, through renunciation and detachment, while the other goes through all attachments and accumulation of all that is needed for physical life. We have two different sets of Mantras to suit the two ways of life. Mantras for the Sanyasis have the effect of increasing the sense of detachment and renunciation and also have the power of destroying the objects of worldly affections, if there should survive any such objects for him. Quite contrary to this are the Mantras suitable for the householder which have the efficacy of harmonising and enriching the material aspect of life also.'[62]

A group was formed in the city of Alleppey to found and dedicate the Adhyatmic Vikas Mandal (the Society for Spiritual Development) and at nearby Cochin arrangements were made for *yagyas* (religious rituals) to be performed from 23rd to 26th October 1955. Led by Vedic *pandits* daily ceremonies were performed and there followed conferences which took personal development as their topic. These events were accompanied by a grand parade along local thoroughfares in which Brahmachari Mahesh appears to have been the centre of attraction, being the only person present pictured wearing a garland of flowers.

Inside the hall, to the centre of the low wide stage was placed an ornate throne upon which was set a garlanded framed picture of the late Shankaracharya Swami Brahmananda. The framed portrait of the revered teacher was illuminated from above by a standard lamp, its shade shiny and lined with tassels, resembling the parasol formerly associated with the departed *swami*. In festive spirit, coloured paper decorations were suspended from the ceiling and hung about the walls. The congregation, comprising young boys sitting at the front, their elders behind them and women in a group to one side, sat in rapt attention upon cotton matting strewn about the floor. The assembly was estimated at over 10,000, although it is doubtful whether the hall itself contained more than a few hundred. Messages of goodwill were read to the assembly, messages from the current Shankaracharyas of Jyotir and Shringeri Maths.

Various speakers took to the microphone, including the Maharajah of Cochin, and the barrister Shri A.N. Menon, who noted:

> The world has known saints performing miracles of various nature, but here is a saint whose miracle works in the inner man to glorify it.[63]

The star of the occasion was 'Maharshi' (Great Sage) Bala Brahmachari Mahesh Yogi Maharaj of Uttar Kasi, Himalayas, who commenced his lecture by saying:

> It gives me great pleasure this afternoon to be in the company of you all here assembled in the close vicinity of the Maha Yagna Mandapam. From the early morning the atmosphere here is being surcharged with the Divine Vibrations of Rig Veda and Yajur Veda Parayanam and the chantings of the Maha Yagna *Mantras*.[64]

As he moved through the formalities of first paying homage to the previous speaker (the Maharajah of Cochin) and to those well-wishers who had written messages to the assembly, then he indicated that the occasion was 'graciously sanctified by the presence of the great Lord Shiva and his retinue'. The *brahmachari's* own message of hope centered on the promise that *sat-chit-anandam* (unlimited bliss) is accessible to all:

> Then why waste time in helplessness and suffer any agony in life? Why suffer when you can enjoy? Why be miserable when you can be happy? Now, let the

days of misery and peacelessness be over and let their operation become tales of the past. Allow not the past history of agony to be continued in the present. Be happy and gay.[65]

After introducing his philosophy in a general way, he then boldly claimed to hold answers which could solve the dilemma of suffering mankind. The next day of the 'Maha Sammelan' ('Great Conference'), he gave the second of his lectures during which he held forth on the physical location of the *sat-chit-anandam* he had referred to, stating:

> Electrons and protons of the modern science, seen through the Indian system of analysis of the universe, are manifestations of Agni-Tatwa and Vayu-Tatwa combined. The energy of the electrons and protons is due to the Agni-Tatwa and motion in them is due to Vayu-Tatwa. Thus we find, the present day science has reached up to Vayu-Tatwa in the field of analysis of the universe.[66]

Naming the successively finer strata of creation as *Agni, Vayu, Akash, Aham, Mahat* and *Prakriti*, he concluded:

> And finer than the Prakriti-Tatwa and the very cause of it is the Brahma-Tatwa which is the Ultimate Reality, the subtlest 'Anoraniyan', Sat-Chit-Anandam.[67]

For this audience of exclusively Indian composition, so recently released from the grip of Western rule and knowing the scorn that had been heaped upon their traditional beliefs, this elucidation must have been as pure nectar. Although his explanation might have been confusing to them, they here was a man who appeared able reconcile the most modern beliefs with those of their forefathers.

This 'miracle' that 'works in the inner man' is undoubtedly an allusion to the system of meditation that was being taught by Mahesh. Although it is difficult to identify the precise technique, it appears to have centered on the use of a personal *mantra* or special sound to be intoned by the practitioner. Mention of the efficacy of certain recommended *mantras* was made, although warning to 'householders' was given against use of the magic syllable '*om*'. This advice strongly echoes the counsel of the Mahesh's own *guru* who specifically advised women to avoid the use of '*om*' and in its stead to use the syllable '*shri*', holding that the repetition of '*om*' could create a potentially disastrous mentality of unworldliness. The Mahesh addressed the same topic:

> 'Om' is the *Mantra* for the Sanyasi. The Sanyasi repeats 'Om Om Om'. It is given to him at the time of 'Sanyas-Diksha', at the time when he has completely renounced attachment to the world. Renunciation and detachment increase with the repetition of 'Om'. 'Om' is chanted aloud by a Sanyasi to put an end to his desires. Desires are destroyed by loudly chanting the *mantra* 'Om'. And if there is any desire deeply rooted in the mind of a Sanyasi, the chanting of 'Om' will

result in the destruction of the object of such desire in order to make the Sanyasi, wholly desireless.[68]

The audience, hanging on every syllable of his words, gazed attentively as 'Maharshi' Mahesh continued:

> If unfortunately, the householder begins to repeat the pranava *Mantra* viz. 'Om', 'Om', 'Om' he experiences destructive effects in his material life. The effect starts with monetary loss and then goes on to destroy objects of affection, one by one. Such a man, when he finds loss of money and separation from the dear ones, he is reduced to utter peacelessness and frustration.[69]

He remained all the while seated upon a deerskin in the cross-legged lotus posture, his large dark eyes flashing to the flow of his speech. Simply attired in a white *dhoti*, garlands of fresh marigolds around his flourishing full beard and long black hair, he possessed many outward symbols of his vocation, which emphasized the authority of his words. After the stern warning with regard to dabbling in mystical practices he then reinforced this view with great clarity:

> It is not at all necessary for the householder to go for direct practice of 'Tyaga' or 'Vairagya' [Renunciation] for realisation. That practice is unnatural for him, antagonistic to his nature and opposed to his way of life.[70]

The philosophy of detachment had permeated Indian thinking for centuries, but at a stroke Brahmachari Mahesh was attempting that such beliefs be set at nought! Just strip away the Sanskritic terms and his message stands revealed: 'You don't have to become a monk or adopt a monkish mode of life to experience the highest of spiritual goals.' This was a message that many wished to hear as few if any present would have found the hermit life alluring. But on the other hand, how can real peace of mind be experienced whilst one is caught up in the thick of everyday life, with its disappointments and unavoidable miseries?

Mahesh went on to expound his philosophy yet further by pointing out that attachment to material life lies solely in the area of thought and that since even the greatest material treasures are seldom located upon one's person, it is really only the thought of wealth that confers the sense of ownership. He explained that for a householder to experience a state of 'non-attachment', what is needed is simply the ability to go beyond thoughts related to the outer world.

In less than a year Brahmachari Mahesh had so far distanced himself from his life of abstinence and seclusion as to be lecturing the people of southern India that they were missing nothing that could not be had in the comfort of their own homes. Understandably, in their search for *sat-chit-ananda*, many took him at his word and asked for instruction into meditation.

The end of the three-day conference was marked by a rousing cheer of 'Jai Shri Guru Deva' (Glory to the Blessed Guru Divine) in praise of the guru of Mahesh. To commemorate the conference, a souvenir booklet was published under the name Beacon Light of the Himalayas, subtitled 'The Dawn of a Happy New Era in the Field of Spiritual Practices Mind Control, Peace & Atmananda – Through simple & easy methods of Spiritual Sadhana propounded by Maharshi Bala Brahmachari Mahesh Yogi Maharaj of Uttar Kasi, Himalayas'. This publication (now lamentably difficult to acquire) contains a full transcript of speeches from Brahmachari Mahesh, the Maharajah of Cochin and others including the barrister A.N. Menon. It provides a wealth of interesting perspectives into the early ministrations of the man who would henceforward be referred to as the 'Maharishi'.

'In South India this word is more prevalent for good saints, and when I travelled South India the newspapers wrote, and then it came from one newspaper to the other, like that, just, a spontaneous thing, and this is not a title conferred as a degree in a college or somewhere. It's the, I think, just like a 'sage', or a 'seer', or a 'saint', they're not the degrees, it's the symptom of a man, a symptom, a feature, and then people start calling him, but there is no confirmation of the title or anything. That is it.'

'Rishi' and 'Maharishi' - 'rishi' is a Sanskrit word and that means 'the seer of the mantras', 'the seer of truth' - the mantras and are the Vedic hymns.'

'So "rishi" is equivalent to "a seer", a seer sees the truth, "maha rishi" means "great seer", "maha" is "great".'

'Generally, people don't remember the name. A North Indian name [viz. Brahmachari Mahesh] is not so easily remembered by the South Indians, like that, like that.'

'I didn't object to it. (audience laughter) Otherwise I have to explain why they should **not** call me "Maharishi", but just call me something else.'[71]

Shri Ratan Lal Chamaria, a 'leading businessman of Calcutta' wrote:

It has really given us great joy and satisfaction that Kerala has recognised the inner divine radiance of our revered Bala Brahmachariji and that he is generously flashing out the Divine Light blazed by Shri Guru Deva in his noble and serene heart.

It gives us great satisfaction and encouragement to note from your pamphlets that the Great 'Brahma-Leen' Spirit of Shri Guru Deva has started to work out His Divine Programme of spiritual development of the nation through His beloved disciple who is worthy of it.[72]

BEACON LIGHT OF THE HIMALAYAS

ADHYATMIC VIKAS MANDAL

FLAG HOISTING

THE DAWN OF A HAPPY NEW ERA

IN THE FIELD OF SPIRITUAL PRACTICES

MIND CONTROL, PEACE

&

ATMANANDA

Through simple & easy methods of Spiritual Sadhana

propounded

by

Maharshi Bala Brahmachari Mahesh Yogi Maharaj

OF

UTTAR KASI, HIMALAYAS.

SOUVENIR OF THE GREAT SPIRITUAL DEVELOPMENT CONFERENCE OF KERALA., OCTOBER, 1955.

Oh ye of the peaceless and suffering humanity! My happiness desires to root out your suffering. Will you extend your arm and allow me to lift you up from the mire of misery and peacelessness?

Come on, here is the call of peace and joy for you. Here is an invitation, a cordial invitation for you all to come and enjoy the Blissful Grace and All Powerful Blessings of my Lord the Great Swami Brahmanand Saraswati, the Great among the greats of the Himalayas. I have found a treasure in the Dust of His Lotus Feet and now I invite you to share it with me and make yourself happy.

Come on; I invite you to get into the Blissful Realm of His Universal Benevolence. See, the path is straight and entry is free. Come on with faith and you will find that the very cause of your peacelessness and misery will be eradicated and you will be adorned with lasting peace and real happiness in your day to day life.

Feel not disappointment in life and shirk not from your responsibilities in despair. Whatever are your circumstances, rich or poor, if you are not in peace and if you want peace and happiness, come on with faith and you will have it. Here is the message of hope for you. Here is the Divine call of rescue for you. Peace and joy of living await you. Do not reject it. Come on and have it.

The sun of Guru Deva's Blessings is now up on the horizon. Wake up from the deep slumber of apathy and agony and enjoy all glories of life material and divine.

Bal Brahmachari Mahesh.

29.11.55

The *Beacon Light of the Himalayas* booklet opens with a short handwritten message penned and signed by Bal Brhmachari Mahsh (sic):

Maharshi's Message to the Peaceless and Suffering

Oh ye of the peaceless and suffering humanity!

My happiness desires to root out your suffering. Will you extend your arm and allow me to lift you up from the mire of misery and peacelessness?

Come on, here is the call of peace and joy for you. Here is an invitation, a cordial invitation for you all to come and enjoy the Blissful Grace and All Powerful Blessings of my Lord the Great Swami Brahmanand Saraswati, the Great among the greats of the Himalayas. I have found a treasure in the Dust of His Lotus Feet and now I invite you to share it with me and make yourself happy.

Come on; I invite you to get into the Blissful Realm of His Universal Benevolence. See, the path is straight and entry is free. Come on with faith and you will find that the very cause of your peacelessness and misery will be eradicated and you will be adorned with lasting peace and real happiness in your day to day life.[73]

Brahmachari Mahesh signed his name as 'Bal Brhmachari Mahsh'; and it is interesting to observe that 'Mahsh' is phonetically very close to what he was now being called, i.e. 'Maharshi' (also written Maharishi).

Chamaria House, Calcutta

After his successful trip to southern India, Brahmachari Mahesh then went to stay in Calcutta, at the house of businessman Ratan Lal Chamaria, who had been supportive of the conference in Kerala. From there the *brahmachari* - Maharishi - took to propagating his message in the various other provinces of India, and by April 1956 he was in Hardwar to attend Ardh Kumbh Mela, a major Hindu festival with a huge influx of sadhus attending.

> By the time I arrived at Haridwar, it happened to be the time of Kumbha Mela - the whole philosophy was clear. The only one point of emphasis was that it is simple for the mind to turn within.

> When the Mela ended, some people were coming to Kashmir, it was the month of April, it was hot and they asked me "Why don't you come to Kashmir?" I said "Alright". At Pahalgam, a peace camp was arranged. I met some persons from Ahmedabad there and they took me to Ahmedabad. I was continuously emphasizing the same thing, that for the mind it is easy to traverse within. People who heard me readily accepted this message. And every time I initiated someone, next day I was more convinced that it works efficiently.[74]

After holding a meditation camp in Ahmedabad, he visited the cities of Bombay (Mumbai), Madras (Chennai) and Calcutta (Kolkata), and at numerous other venues.

How different was his daily life was from that of his teacher, who at his age was secluded in a dense jungle, in prayer and contemplation.

On 30th November 1957, Maharishi attended the 15th session of the World Vegetarian Congress at Madras, and addressed the audience there.

> How are we going to change the 'killing world' of today into a non-killing world of tomorrow? How are we going to change the spirit of killing, the spirit of aggression, the spirit of violence into the spirit of *kindness and love* - overflowing love for the whole creation? How are we going to change hardness and cruelty of heart to softness and overflowing love for everybody?

He pointed out to his audience that all the major religions condemn killing, and then he declared:

> The killer knows that he is killing and in return he will be killed. The sinner knows that he is committing a sin and that he will be punished for it. Not that he does not know. He knows it. But, with this information, the cruel is not afraid - his cruelty is hardened still. The killer declares his action is the role of a saviour, he kills in the name of life, he kills in the name of saving life, he kills in the name of maintaining life. He kills and murders ruthlessly in the name of protections and peace. In the name of world peace and protection have been

waged the deadliest of wars. In the name of peace and protection are preparations being made for the murder of man and creation. Shame to the greatness of the human intelligence which fails to recognise the Judge Supreme!![75]

An impassioned speech albeit that he was preaching to the converted, but what hope could he offer that things might change?

> Our task of the day is to find a cure for this major ill of humanity. The heart of man is be changed. The inner man has to be transformed. If we want to establish real and good vegetarianism in the world we have to rise with a practical formula to transform the inner man.

> My experience says the inner man *is instantaneously transformed by a flash of Divine Experience*. A direct experience of the Blissful nature of Soul, the inner man is completely transformed. The mind experiencing the Great Bliss feels satisfaction and this satisfaction of the mind results in right understanding and virtuous action, kindness, love and compassion for all.

Although hundreds, sometimes thousands, turned out to hear Maharishi's lectures about meditation (it is even said that mass initiations were not uncommon), his desire to spread his message to ever greater numbers of people steered him to ever greater success. After many months of touring he returned to southern India once more, and this time using the city of Madras as his base, he hatched plans for a rather remarkable event. Invitations were dispatched widely with a view to drawing together disciples of the late Swami Brahmananda for a great celebration of his memory. The Seminar of Spiritual Luminaries was to be held in Mylapore, and 'eminent saints and philosophers of all countries' were exhorted to attend. The stated reason for calling together these people was 'to contribute their experience in finding out a practical formula of spiritual regeneration of the world'.

To some extent this seminar was, in reality, perhaps a gesture of goodwill, for Maharishi could not hope to pursue his endeavours without first gaining the support of the late Shankaracharya's other disciples. Be that as it may, the wording of the invitation seems to imply that Maharishi's techniques of 'mind control' were still open to improvement. It is possible that even now he entertained doubts about his methods and hoped that this event might prove an opportunity to garner important feedback, most especially from his peer group. It is likely that he also looked forward to hearing testimonies in support of his seemingly extravagant claims, endorsing and confirming as a *maharishi* the erstwhile *brahmachari*, he who had told his audience in Kerala:

> Here is no empty promise of Heaven after death. Here is the positive experience of 'Heavenly Bliss' during lifetime. Come on who desires for it…[76]

It is said that the Seminar of Luminaries was attended by over 10,000 people and that as it drew to a close Maharishi felt inclined to ask those assembled there: 'Why can't we spiritually regenerate the world through this technique?' Apparently his question drew tumultuous applause, prompting him to arrange a day's extension to the festivities. The Seminar's invitation to find 'a practical formula of spiritual regeneration of the world' proved to be somewhat self-fulfilling for on Wednesday, 1st January 1958 Maharishi announced:

> The one aim of the Spiritual Regeneration Movement is to provide a simple and easy method of meditation and infuse this system of meditation in the daily life of everybody everywhere on earth. To meet this end, this Movement had been started to work for the construction of meditation centres everywhere in every part of human habitation.[77]

Maharishi later explained:

> It was the concern of Guru Deva, His Divinity Swami Brahmananda Saraswati, to enlighten all men everywhere that resulted in the foundation of the world-wide Spiritual Regeneration Movement in 1958, five years after his departure from us.[78]

In the following months, in addition to the holding of several more spiritual development camps, some twenty-five meditation centres were opened across India. It was at Bangalore in the spring of 1958 that Maharishi appears to have been inspired to make his next move.

> One fine morning I thoughtfully reviewed the work done and calculated how much time it will take for the whole world with this rate and I found out that it will take 200 years (laughter).
>   Then I said 'No, I must change my ways of work'; then I thought what to do. Then I thought: I must go to the most advanced country because I thought – the country is most advanced because the people of that country would try something new very readily.[79]

> It so happened that one businessman from Rangoon who attended the meetings during the three day Seminar at Madras, came to me and said: "Whenever you decide to go abroad, your first country to visit should be Burma. I will organise and because I have heard your message - it is beautiful - I must do whatever I can in my country." So that morning when I realised that it will take 200 years and to speed up I must go to a country which is most highly developed because my appeal is very simple and natural, but I must speak to those who are in habit of adopting new things - countries which are not developed means; the individuals knowing that the thing is good, they don't adopt it, so nation does not advance. I asked that man to write three letters: one to Calcutta, one to Madras and one to Bombay - that now, I want to go to the United States and how soon can they arrange it. I did not know myself what arrangement would be needed.

Within a week a reply came from Calcutta that send Maharishi here and that he would stay with us for about two months, because it takes about that much time for getting the passport, etc. Then I came to know that there is one more item - passport. I had absolutely no sense of this type of civilization. I went to Calcutta and things were arranged. [80]

Some people in Calcutta, when I was staying there, my preparations were going on, some businessmen said: "You give us three months and we will give you good contacts." I said: "No. Your contacts would be business contacts and through business contacts I will not be able to benefit the people with no money wherever I go. Therefore, business contacts will not help me. I will just walk on the streets and I will have my contacts.

There was only one confidence in me that I have some knowledge that other people are in need of and they don't know. I know it. Everywhere is my home and everywhere are my people. [81]

With the trip to America delayed, a short tour of Kerala was arranged.

On Sunday, 27th April 1958 Maharishi made for Calcutta Airport, not to catch a flight to the United States of America, but to make the relatively short hop across the Bay of Bengal to the capital of neighbouring Burma. His arrival in Rangoon contrasted greatly with his massive send-off from India; for there was only one individual waiting to meet him there. Before long however, the wandering *brahmachari* had attracted considerable attention and several lecture dates were organized. As a result of these talks, many wished to learn how to practice his style of meditation. And, curiously, an unexpected boost came about after the prediction of an aged Buddhist monk became known; allegedly, a year before he had foretold that a great Indian *yogi* would visit Rangoon on *Bodhipurnima* Day. This prophecy brought forth visits from monks, high-ranking officials and a large complement of local men, women and children.

When I landed there, that man, Mr. Goenka, was there to receive me - one single man. In three days when I was in Rangoon, where were about two or three hundred people from all the classes of Burma - all that high Government officials etc., monks, Burmese monks, Buddhist monks who had told people one year in advance that "on coming full moon day (which was Buddha's birthday) a great Yogi from the Himalayas is coming and all of you will have his Darshan, and he will talk to you etc., etc." It happened to be just that day (within those three days - one of those three days) that they found a Yogi from the Himalayas. The Buddhist monk who made this forecast brought all of his followers. They came in all their paraphernalia, (in a very demonstrative and costumed discipline.)

He took me round different places and told me the story that how he used to tell things one year in advance. We exchanged our hearts - exchanged our thoughts.

The basic thing in mind was that I know something, which is needed by every man, and it is so simple and natural - to whomsoever I talked, he would accept it.[82]

Here was a clear indication that Maharishi's teachings were capable of attracting people from outside the specifically Hindu world. After ten days of talks and initiations, Maharishi triumphantly returned to Rangoon Airport ready to embark on the next leg of his journey. A rousing send-off had been organized and a veritable sea of Burmese and Indians thronged the departure lounge to send him on his way, causing Maharishi jubilantly to consider the truth of an old maxim. 'Then it rang in my mind: "Well begun is half done."'[83]

So it was that he flew to Bangkok and then to the island of Penang. On Thursday, 22nd May 1958 *The Straits Echo and Times* carried an article in which Maharishi is quoted saying:

"Growing worries, anxieties and lack of mental peace in daily life of the people are a direct challenge to the validity of all religions everywhere. Everyone feels proud of his religion and every religion claims to bestow peace and happiness to its followers in this life and hereafter; yet almost all are suffering from the agony of mental unrest and it is found to be growing everyday. What is the reason?

Spirit of religion, spirituality, seems to have gone out of sight and people seem to cling only to the framework of ritualistic nature. Spirit of religion has to be lived if a man aims at peace and happiness in daily life.

As ritualistic religion or scientific and technological development have not conferred lasting peace and happiness to the society, spiritual regeneration of society of the present is urgently needed.

An effective means of bringing peace and happiness in day to day practical life of man is to lead him to experience the Divine Nature within himself- the bliss eternal.

It goes without saying the man attains peace and happiness and higher values of life by a flash of Divine Experience," said Maharishi.

"My system of meditation is a golden link to connect and harmonise materialism and spirituality." It is a direct process to integrate man's life on earth. He invites everyone to take the maximum advantage of his one week's stay in Penang.

The piece helpfully detailed the venues he had spoken at.

Yogi Mahesh, who comes from Uttar Kashi Himalayas, visited Sri Sivan Temple at Dato Kramat Road, Penang, yesterday evening and later the Sri Thandapani Temple at Waterfall Road. Last night he delivered a very interesting lecture at the residence of Dr. G.H. Yeang of the Theosophical Society, Penang, at Cantonment Road[84]

Indian expatriates clamoured to receive his message including many from the Sikh community, a group traditionally wary of Hindu doctrines. Speaking at both temples and *gurudwaras*, interested individuals would gather to hear of the blessings of 'Shri Guru Deva.'

After spending only a few weeks in Penang, he journeyed some 300 km south, to the city of Kuala Lumpur, the capital of Malaya. There he met with no less success than he had in Penang. Nevertheless, after staying only ten days there, the spur to travel on again found him garlanded and bidding goodbye with a '*Jai Shri Guru Deva*' to his new-found devotees.

The touring continued and by 14th June 1958 he had settled in Singapore. Whilst working there on plans for the establishment of a meditation centre, news came that a broadcast he had prepared during his stay in Kuala Lumpur, for Radio Malaya, was to be broadcast at 9 pm on Thursday, 24th July, and for five minutes the airwaves resounded to Maharishi's high-pitched tones.

> When we think about the joys of the world and try to locate the permanent abode of greatest happiness, we find that through our senses we are experiencing the charm of gross nature, and the charm of the subtler fields of nature are not being experienced ...
>
> The real joy of life lies in the field of subtle nature, beyond the field of sense perception ...
>
> It is the experience of thousands of people coming in my contact that they begin to feel calmness of mind, more energy and happiness in their daily life within two or three sittings ...[85]

Maharishi then returned to Penang where he set about establishing another Spiritual Development Centre and training more Spiritual Guides to continue his work. The Mayor of Penang performed the ceremonial opening of the centre, and the General Secretary of the centre gave a speech in which he referred to Maharishi's technique of meditation as a 'spiritual sputnik from the Himalayas'.[86]

The Russians with their Sputnik 1, and the Americans with their Explorer 1, had opened up the space race – so was it just coincidence that at the dawn of the space age, the realms of inner space were being newly re-explored too?

By mid-August 1958 the Singapore meditation centre was also ready to open, and the occasion was celebrated at the city's Victoria Memorial Hall. It was intended that the centre should take as its leader a newly appointed Spiritual Guide who for the past quarter of a century had been President of the Buddhist Union. The role of officiator at this inauguration was to be filled by no less a person than the Chief Minister of Singapore, Mr Lim Yew Hock.

From the *Beacon Light* conference onwards, Maharishi had shown a marked tendency to court the approval and sponsorship of the powerful and the rich, and at important functions he would ensure that he sat in the company of persons of high social standing. Of those who spoke at the opening on 17th August, the testimony of one speaker, a business magnate, is of particular note.

> Within three or four days of the initiation, I was able to enjoy unspeakable happiness, calmness, and peace. Now I always feel full of spiritual vigour and happiness. Maharishi is grand like the Himalayas wherefrom he comes, but humble like a child, great like truth but simple like love.[87]

Whilst in Penang Maharishi met with an Englishman named David Morgan, a former captain in the Royal Navy.

> Although David possessed good judgment, colleagues described him as having an almost other-worldly air, an unusual characteristic for someone in the hard-nosed world of investment banking. Perhaps this was partly explained by his association with Maharishi Mahesh Yogi, whom David met while working as a stockbroker for Charles Bradburne & Co in Penang in Malaysia in 1958. The Maharishi was fresh out of India and intent on making his Transcendental Meditation technique available worldwide. David, who by the Maharishi's account was the first westerner to learn the technique, then arranged for the Maharishi to travel to Hawaii and mainland US.[88]

Spurred on no doubt by much unwavering support, the lone *brahmachari* relentlessly pursued his quest to further publicize his teachings. The next trip was to be his longest yet; his destination lay in faraway Hong Kong. Again he met with a ready audience with whom he quickly set about forming a meditation centre, in this case to be called the Happy Valley.

> A Sikh community inhabits Hong Kong. All very good people. Highly sharp minded in business. Their Guru came from Bombay. This was after two months. I was staying in the same temple. He was also welcomed in that temple and because he was a Guru; lots of people used to come to listen to him and when he used to finish his talk, he also invited me to speak. He was a very good speaker. After a week, it so happened that the opinion of the community divided into two. Then one day the President of the temple came and asked me what I actually wanted. I said: "I am telling the people for the last two to three months to meditate and be happy." He replied: "All right, give us fifteen days; we will organize the inauguration of the Hong Kong Meditation Centre. "I said: "Fine. That is what I want." So, he organised with a big splash of publicity and it was a very successful inauguration of the Hong Kong Meditation Centre. That was the first inauguration. Immediately one came and said: "This is the hall of the Temple and we will divide it into two. Half the hall will remain as it is and half of it will be divided into 11 cubicles for meditation. "What appealed to them was my saying when they came to the Deity in the temple from the market, and when

they bow down before their Lord, their heads goes down but the mind goes behind into same market again.

I told them that was not the way to come to God to have His blessings. "You should have meditation first and then, when the mind is pure and in Bliss, so quiet and peaceful, you should bow down before your God and then your respect will be accepted. Otherwise, you bow down here and your mind is there and the Lord knows that something wrong is going on here. The display of surrender and the actuality - running away! This is no good." This appealed to people. In another two weeks, about three hundred people were initiated.[89]

At the Chinese Chamber of Commerce in Hong Kong, on Friday, 7th November 1958, a ceremony was held to mark the centre's inauguration. It was officiated by a local magistrate, Mr Hing Shing Lo. Following his speech Maharishi addressed the assembled crowd and confidently pointed out that 'everybody has the capacity for Deep Meditation'.[90] Clarifying the role of the centre, he told its staff:

It will be the sacred duty of the management to drum into the ears of the people that here is a place where everybody can get the key to all peace and happiness in life.[91]

Having spent just a little over a month in Hong Kong, the momentum of the tour caused Maharishi to move on yet again and this time not just a hop, but a huge bound, to the island of Hawaii, from where he intended to fly directly to America.

They advised me to stop on the way at Hawaii. It was a big crowd at the Airport to see me off. When the plane was just due to take off, someone asked me about the place I was to stay in Hawaii, I replied: "I don't know." He said "What! Why did you not tell us before that you don't know anybody there?" Then he went to enquire and returned back just when I started for the plane. He told me to remember Watoomal. (This was the name of a saint with whom I was supposed to stay). I was told to telephone him on arrival at Hawaii. When the plane landed in Hawaii I phoned Watoomal [Waterman?]. I said: "On the way from Hong Kong Airport somebody told me your name. I don't know you; you don't know me but I am going to San Francisco and I would like to stay here for a day or two" He arranged for my stay in a Hotel [YMCA] (it was a usual thing for him because every saint passing that way was staying in that hotel through that man). The hotel people knew the whole thing.[92]

In Hawaii Maharishi met with great success, and although he had planned to spend only two days in Honolulu he was prevailed upon to stay longer, one month longer as it happened.

On Wednesday, 31st December 1958 (one year after the formation of his movement), the *Honolulu Star Bulletin* told its readers about a visitor to the island.

He has no money; he asks for nothing. His worldly possessions can be carried in one hand. Maharishi Mahesh Yogi is on a world odyssey. He carries a message that he says will rid the world of unhappiness and discontent …

It seemed that the media had found itself a new celebrity, for the Hawaiian newspapers, radio and television stations all gave exposure to his message (although it is doubtful that many fully understood it). No longer was he preaching to the converted but to an ever-widening section of the populace, from diverse backgrounds, denominations and persuasions.

Back in India, devotees were kept abreast of new developments; they received hand-written epistles from Maharishi chronicling the movement's progress. In fact, the Madras mission took to publishing a newsletter, known as the *Torch Divine*, and in the absence of their teacher it played a vital role, not only in linking interested parties but in providing meditators with a mutual support system.

So it was that the Bal Brahmachari Mahesh who had toyed uneasily with the recurrent thought to 'go to Rameshvaram' had by now not only relinquished the role of hermit but in less than four years had assumed the position of Director of Operations in an organization that took as its goal the spiritual regeneration of the world.

I had one thing in mind – that I know something which is useful to every man; therefore no matter where I am people will find in me the commodity that they want. (laugh) With that confidence I left India and gradually I came to the States.[93]

4

—★—

FROM HAWAII TO HOLLYWOOD

Although confident of success, Maharishi appears to have had no real idea how his teachings would be received in the West. Undoubtedly he would have heard since childhood of the material advancements in economically go-ahead countries such as the USA and Germany and reasoned that these nations must be unusually receptive to new ideas. It appears he hoped to tap this tendency by presenting the system of meditation of meditation he taught as something new. In truth he was looking at the subject anew having brought the discipline of systematic enquiry (which he had become familiar with at college) to bear on the ancient teachings of his spiritual master. Having studied science, Mahesh was no stranger to experimentation and the subsequent need for verification and accreditation of discoveries. The young *brahmachari* had became convinced that amongst the spiritual practices his master taught were technique - simple, practical and easy-to-use - which might have a universal application. In his travels so far, Maharishi had found no lack of truth-seekers eager to learn and apply them, and after hearing the numerous glowing testimonies to the apparent efficacy of this meditation, he felt justified in forming the Spiritual Regeneration Movement.

For the most part, initiates were found amongst those already culturally predisposed towards Eastern teachings, but the time had now come to test the meditation on those who knew little or nothing of Eastern philosophies and still less about its practices.

So it happened that Maharishi, after a succession of short hops across South East Asia, finally arrived at his desired destination, the United States of America, on the western seaboard. There was no fanfare in San Francisco to greet him, for no herald of his arrival had been dispatched beforehand. However, the very appearance of this slight, foreign gentleman with his flowing mass of hair, billowing robes and graceful step, assured him immediate attention.

The two meditators who accompanied him from Hawaii saw to his immediate personal needs; and once installed at a small local hotel, visitors (mainly friends of meditators) came to visit him.

Then Maharishi began to speak at the local Cultural Integration Fellowship, and later recalled:

And then there was a good reception at San Francisco. By that time I was a professional speaker. People would call me to speak on all sorts of subjects. One man from Calcutta called me to speak on Cosmic Consciousness. When I spoke on Cosmic Consciousness he announced that next day I will again give a talk on Cosmic Consciousness because they wanted to listen more about it. Like that, for 29 different organizations, during those 29 days and the report was that wherever I spoke the membership began to fall in those organisations. I said: "I don't want to spoil my host. People invite me to strengthen their organization, this should not happen to the people."

MAHARISHI YOGI
Promotes meditation

Yogi To Talk At Church In Hub City

Gradually I started to become unpopular in San Francisco. Twenty-nine organizations and every one of them started to lose their memberships. It was tremendous. Then they rented a house and after one month they managed to purchase a big building.[94]

From that day I was speaking every day in one organisation in San Francisco, gave about 29 lectures and every evening the whole thing was full and because people found something which they thought can't be false …

And when they started to meditate, then they became propagandist about it. They spread it …[95]

He spoke too at the Jen Sen Tao Buddhist Association in San Francisco's Chinatown. It was during his stay in San Francisco that Maharishi received his first press coverage in the USA, but he was far from happy when he learned that this meditation had been dubbed a 'non-medicinal tranquilizer'. His comments are worth noting.

Cruel …! I feel like running away, back home. This seems to be a strange country. Values are different here.[96]

On Wednesday, 29th April 1959, Maharishi took leave of his friends and the rest of his new-found admirers in San Francisco, but he was not 'running away, back home', merely slipping away down the coast to spread his message further.

In Los Angeles he was met by a crowd of meditators' friends and their relatives, ready to bedeck him with floral offerings, and after briefly meeting with them he lost no time in moving on to the Ambassador Hotel where a press conference had been organized for him. Reporters from local newspapers gathered to hear of Maharishi's intention of bringing about a more loving society and eventually creating world peace. He told them:

> I have brought from the land of ancient sages to the modern man of this new world a simple technique of living in peace and happiness.[97]

An evening paper, the *Herald Express*, carried a report of the event with the challenging headline 'Yogi Has Cure for World Ills' above a picture of Maharishi holding a bouquet of roses. Beneath it they quoted him as saying, 'I will fill the world with love.'

The following weekend, on the back page of the Women's Section of the *Los Angeles Times* a small ad advised:

> Maharishi Mahesh Yogi
> Master from the Himalayas
> Valley of the Saints – Uttar Kashi
> Will speak at the Masquers Club
> May 1 to May 7 – Phone …

On the Sunday evening, 1st May 1959, at this Hollywood actors' club, he found an audience of several dozen interested individuals. The visitors seated themselves in comfortable armchairs that formed a semicircle around Maharishi, who initially sat for a period in silence, fingering a line of beads hung around his neck. One of those present, Mrs Helena Olson, later commented:

> His voice drew one's entire attention. At first it was almost without sound. The quietness of his speech seemed to direct ideas to the mind and not the ear.
> His voice became more audible and fell gently on the ear. The words were strong with authority. There was no thought of doubting what he said …
> He singled out a large, red rose and emphasized a few points with it. As the rose waved back and forth I noticed his hands … definite in movement, strong and beautiful. As I watched, he opened the palm and inclined it gently toward the audience.[98]

After this initial exposure to Maharishi Mrs Olson felt sufficiently moved to invite him to come and share her and her husband's house, on palm-lined South Harvard Boulevard.

On the evening of his arrival at 433 South Harvard Boulevard, Maharishi was shown his new quarters and after swiftly surveying the bedroom, set about removing the blankets from the bed. He then began to unfurl his mysterious carpet roll.

Then almost shyly, so as not to hurt our feelings, he said as he drew out exquisite silk sheets, pillow and spread: 'These have been provided for me by devotees in India.'[99]

From the carpet roll he also produced a brown cashmere shawl for extra warmth should it be needed and then proceeded to unpack the remaining contents of his most unusual form of luggage.

He lifted neatly folded pieces of silk from the rug, a small metal box of toilet articles, a little clock and a fountain pen – and our Yogi was all unpacked.[100]

In the evening, the Olsons invited Maharishi to join them in their family worship, which consisted of readings from the Bible followed by prayer and a period of silence.

When it was over, the Master who now sat with us in our family circle, said, 'A good silence, but I will add power to it. I will initiate you, in the morning.'[101]

The following day Mr and Mrs Olson prepared themselves to be initiated into the technique of Deep Meditation. Mrs Olson felt a strong desire to take along some flowers from her garden. Having picked a bunch of fresh white geraniums she handed a few to her husband in order that he too might have something to present to Maharishi. They found him ready and waiting for them.

He had us place our flowers on a small shrine. Very quickly we were given our technique, and told to sit with our eyes closed and practice it in his presence.
    In the first few seconds I felt my entire being quicken, and then a penetrating sensation of warmth. A flood of delight, of warmth.
    After some time, a soft voice whispered, 'Open your eyes.' Roland and I opened our eyes to look into each others'. I gasped at the sight of Roland's face. It was serene, yet glowing. All the drawn, serious lines seemed erased. His eyes were large and shining. I hoped mine were the same.
    Maharishi had fulfilled his promise of bliss.[102]

Bliss was not all Maharishi was offering, since he further whetted appetites by quoting the words of Jesus Christ: 'Seek ye first the Kingdom of Heaven within.'

The meditation technique the Olsons were that day taught centred on a word that 'has no meaning', and Roland Olson sought reassurance that the method of meditation Maharishi was teaching them did not conflict with

Christianity.

> These words were known many, many centuries before there were Christian words, and the effects of saying these words are well known. This is the ancient Vedic tradition that is passed down through our Masters.[103]

When it was thought necessary to take some pictures of Maharishi for publicity purposes, he surprised them when he offered useful suggestions regarding lighting – so perhaps as a young man he had helped set up portrait shots in his Uncle Raj's Jabalpur Photographic Studio?

Mr and Mrs Olson's home very soon became a hive of activity with visitors coming and going at all hours of the day and night. The presence of so charismatic a guest made Mrs Olson begin to seriously reappraise her lifestyle and even question continuing to work at her job in a local theatre. Maharishi, on divining her dilemma, offered her succinct advice: 'See the job. Do the job. Stay out of the misery.'[104]

Chance situations would occasionally provide insights into Maharishi's views on life, as for instance the time when one of Mrs Olson's Siamese cats, which freely roamed the house and garden, caught a bird. Whilst her cat received a scolding for trying to kill the defenceless feathered flyer, her guest looked on reproachfully, not at the cat but at its owner, Mrs Olson, who naturally defended her stance:

> 'Maharishi, this wretched cat would have killed the bluebird if we had not caught her. What am I going to do with her?'
> 'Nothing,' said Maharishi, 'that is the nature.'
> 'Why should it be the nature of a cat to kill when it is not hungry?'
> 'Mother Nature determines all these things, and the little animals cannot help but mind. Like when it is night all birds must sleep.'[105]

Most of Maharishi's basic needs were being attended to by well-wishers, including his being chauffeured about in a Karmann Ghia sports car by Richard Sedlachek, the man who had placed the small ad that announced the lectures at the Masquers Club. And from Hawaii came Sheela Devi, who saw to domestic duties such as washing silk *dhotis* and cooking the pure vegetarian dishes that formed Maharishi's diet. In fact the mere intimation of a whim or desire was usually enough to propel his converts into action, though there exceptions such as Maharishi's casual suggestion that someone might phone the President! In fact Maharishi was rather fond of the telephone, and having noticed the increase in calls for their guest, the Olsons even went so far as to arrange for a personal extension to be installed in his room. Again, when it was noticed that there was a lack of space for teaching meditation, helpers rolled up their sleeves to erect an outdoor centre in the garden. For many of the new converts, it appeared nothing was too much to ask of them.

Whilst talking about meditation Maharishi would often mention Christian teachings.

> When one dives within one's self and finds the Being, the perfect State of Being, his being living and thinking become infused with the Being, and then all good is automatic. You remember the Lord Christ has said, 'Seek ye first the Kingdom of Heaven within. And all else will be added unto thee.'[106]

With statements such as this, it is no wonder that the printed literature produced at this time referred to Maharishi as 'Rev.' or 'Reverend'.

Charlie Lutes, a local businessman, heard Maharishi speak at the Masquers Club and soon became a visitor at the Olsons.

> It was a few days after our initiation that Helen and I decided we wanted to help Maharishi spread his technique to others. We volunteered our services. Helen got involved on a daily basis, helping around the Olson house, arranging flowers, ushering in new meditators, and doing errands for Maharishi. I came whenever my work schedule permitted, mostly to offer my expertise in the construction of a meditation room that Maharishi wanted to build in the backyard.
> I was out there coaching some volunteers in building fundamentals one day when Maharishi walked up to me.
> "Do you like your meditation?" he asked.
> "Yes, Maharishi, I do."
> "Would you like to be with me?"
> "Yes, sure, Maharishi," I said, even though I didn't know what he meant.
> "Good," he said. "From today on you will be with me."
> With that he said to get my car, take his deerskin and put it on the passenger's front seat. As soon as I did, he climbed in and sat down on the deerskin.
> "Where do you want to go, Maharishi?"
> "We get some air," he said. "We see the city. We take drive."
> So off we drove. It was the first of many trips I would take with him..[107]

With so much activity being generated at No. 433, it came as no great surprise when the police came to investigate. Neighbours had found the constant comings and goings at the house a nuisance, and a police officer had been dispatched to confront the occupants about the extent of their nocturnal activities. Maharishi appeared unconcerned, openly sympathizing with the local residents. He resolved that a solution must be found.

Allegedly, operations transferred to the basement of the local church, Hollywood Congregational Church, where Maharishi would lecture. In measured tones and with absolute conviction Maharishi told the gathering:

> Anything that pleases the mind heals the mind. Anything that pleases the body heals the body.

Everything in the world has healing power, has the power of healing to some degree or the other.

Meditation has the greatest healing power because it leads to greatest happiness.[108]

A tape machine recorded his lectures for posterity.

What was really needed, however, was a meeting place that would serve as a permanent location for Maharishi's mission. . In the church hall the congregation had been expected to sit on creaking wooden chairs, but at length suitable premises were found in a local ballet school which had a large room, but badly in need of re-decoration. The room was given a fresh coat of paint, and because Maharishi had decreed that there was 'no need to suffer for the Divine'[109], fifty comfortable chairs were installed.

Although the newly acquired premises were much better suited to his needs, Maharishi still dreamed of creating a permanent centre in Los Angeles so his aides to be on the lookout for a suitable property. Meanwhile, 433 still remained the headquarters and heart of his expanding operation, though as a result of having somewhere to give lectures, the issue of excessive tide of visitors at the Olsons had been dealt with.

Although Maharishi appeared to have no interest in money, his devotees no doubt agonized over how they might meet the expenditure of hiring halls, printing literature and placing advertisements. Visitors had actually not been unmindful, and in addition to donating their time and effort in diverse ways, they had already been making monetary contributions which they placed in a basket outside the Maharishi's bedroom. But to him this was unacceptable as, in his eyes; it was tantamount to openly begging. So the question was raised as to how to generate sufficient funds for the spread of meditation, and the topic of levying charges for initiation was discussed but Maharishi's advisers, Roland Olson and Charlie Lutes, were concerned that if there were a compulsory fee, people on a low or no income would become debarred from learning to meditate. So, a compromise was eventually reached: and it was agreed that any money given in payment for initiation should be earnings-related.

Over a year had passed since Maharishi had bade farewell to the shores of Mother India and news came that some of his countrymen had decided to pay him a visit. Lachsman and Mata-ji (reputedly from one of India's wealthiest families) arrived from Calcutta in the company of Rama Rao, the President of a meditation centre in India. Mata-ji was intent on offering service to Maharishi and spent much of her time preparing specialities for him, such as peeling and crushing grapes in order to quench his thirst. She was relieved of this particular task when it was found that commercially produced fruit juices could be sourced locally.

For the newcomers, excursions to all the local tourist spots were organized, the highlight being a visit to the world-famous Disneyland, which provided an agreeable opportunity for Maharishi to relax from the relentless pursuit of his mission. The presence of Mata-ji and her companions stimulated a wave of interest in Indian fabrics, causing many of the American women to temporarily adopt the fashion of wearing colourful Indian *sarees*.

The Olsons proved themselves capable and thoughtful hosts. In fact, Mrs Olson even took it into her head to ask Maharishi whether his mother had been informed of his welfare and whereabouts. Coming from someone else, this might have appeared a strange thing to ask of Maharishi, but not from 'Mother' Olson, who had come to look on him almost as part of her family. He did not look up and answered her simply: 'Mother knows son is doing well.'[110]

One visitor to 433 who received particular attention from Maharishi was someone referred to by Helena Olson as 'Mr. H---', whom Maharishi spoke of as 'Rishi'. Mrs Olson described him as a writer and lecturer, as having a 'lean, ascetic face' and blues eyes. It is likely this was Gerald Heard, the British born writer and pacifist, friends with both Aldous Huxley and Christopher Isherwood, who was interested in Vedanta and the teachings of Swami Prabhavananda of the Ramakrishna order. Gerald Heard fits Mrs Olson's description of Mr. H--- and can be heard on recordings made at the Olson's house in June 1959.

Maharishi was in constant contact with his many centres by telephone, and in addition to maintaining links with his followers he was preparing the way for future endeavours. It appears that he was giving his mission his undivided attention. The preparation of publicity material, lectures at the University of California and daily meetings and initiations all tested his stamina, but found his energy undiminished.

In July 1959, one of his inner circle, Dr J.S. Hislop (formerly a pupil to another philosopher, J. Krishnamurti), organized an International Convention of the Spiritual Regeneration Movement, which was held in Sequoia National Park California. Seated on woollen blankets a loyal group of supporters surrounded Maharishi and listened as he unveiled his hopes and plans for the future. Contained within the highly optimistic package of ideas he presented was the proposal that an International Academy of Meditation might soon be started. After calculating the world's population, a man asked who was to teach all the new students to meditate. Maharishi answered him simply: 'I'll multiply myself many-fold.'[111]

As Maharishi announced his imaginative 'Three-Year Plan' it emerged that he intended to train a large number of teachers (25,000) and establish an equivalent number of meditation centres within the span of this plan! Even the most committed believers doubted his ability to fulfil this ambition, but the plan's strength lay in its power to motivate and galvanize followers into vigorous activity. Further justification lay in the fact that it provided the media with ready-made copy, thereby promising further potential for news coverage.

After the Sequoia Park convention Maharishi resumed touring, no longer clutching the curious carpet roll but now replete with a set of leather luggage, and a parcel containing tapes of his most recent lectures. This most modern of mystics was now headed for America's East Coast, to the cities of New York and Boston. Whilst staying in Los Angeles he had become thoroughly versed in dealing with the difficult questions such as, is it necessary to suffer in order to gain self-purification.

'We do not even think of giving up anything,' Maharishi would insist.

'We do whatever our needs demand, but we are regular in Meditation, and when we become filled with the Bliss, the Being, – the need is no longer there. There is no need to even think of it. Thinking of something we wish to give up drives the desire for it deeper into the mind, and we desire it more and more.'[112]

The topic of suffering proved recurrent and because the Maharishi's homeland was seen by many as being caught in the grip of dire economic problems, he was called on to offer an explanation.

If the people of India are starving and they are Meditating, then it is Karma [Law of Cause and Effect], but it does not mean that they are miserable. It is possible to have little to eat and still be happy. In America, where you have so much, people are found to be miserable. It is worse to be miserable in the midst of plenty, than it is in the midst of poverty.[113]

After almost a year in the United States, for reasons as yet unidentified (although it could simply be that his visa expired), Maharishi moved on. He prepared to take to the air again and on Saturday, 12th December 1959, he departed New York for London. During the trip he is said to have chatted to an English woman, Mrs Marjorie Gill, and convinced her of the value of his mission, and the two became friends.

When Maharishi arrived in London, the heart of the rapidly diminishing British Empire was undergoing the usual seasonal discomfort of winter and its inhabitants were busily preparing itself for the traditional festivities. At what better time of year could one with the outward appearance of a young but decidedly jovial Father Christmas show himself? The long journey of some 5000 miles would have had the average man pining for rest, but

Maharishi had energy enough to deal with a press conference. The BBC World Service also took an interest, booking him for a live transmission later that month. Eight hours after landing on *terra firma*, he was ensconced in the Howard Hotel in London's Bayswater district. Soon after that, readers of *The Times* saw an advertisement to the effect that 'Maharishi Mahesh Yogi has arrived'. Details of his whereabouts were also given and in time, after several days, someone responded.

Then the familiar pattern established itself and on 18th December he gave his first public lecture in London, at the Caxton Hall in Westminster. Within the context of creating a better, more peaceful society, he stressed the importance of the role of the individual, reasoning:

> If we want to make the whole garden green, it is necessary to make every tree green. Talks of the greenness of the garden will not help: every tree has to be attended to – watered, fertilised, and made green. Then with that process the whole garden could be made green.[114]

Although Maharishi possessed a rare talent for finding analogies to explain his theories, his audiences must often have been puzzled about their meaning. But for those who gained extended exposure to his line of thinking, their meaning became abundantly clear. Behind every analogy was a reference to the practice of Meditation, Deep Meditation or Transcendental Deep Meditation, as it was variously referred to. Not only was its learning highly commended, but the technique was made to sound indispensable.

On Wednesday, 30th December, Maharishi publicly announced his Three-Year Plan, to commence on 1st January 1960, and also told his followers that he would shortly be returning to India via Europe. But first, after a week of silence, the engaging Indian visitor moved just a few miles away in south-west London, to an apartment in Chelsea which soon became the centre of operations and remained so for some months to come. There he could lecture, initiate and direct his followers. And amongst the steady flow of people interested in his philosophy came the occasional journalist, and there was soon a smattering of articles in local, national and European newspapers.

Soon, as in Los Angeles, his followers advised their teacher to take time off from his work and enjoy the sights and surroundings, and Henry Nyburg, a wealthy businessman, even offered to chauffeur him on a trans-European holiday. So it was decided, and together they toured, motoring through Switzerland, Austria, France and Germany in a Rolls Royce car. Naturally, Maharishi took the opportunity to spread the teaching of meditation.

A lady from San Francisco had written to her friend in Germany. She gave me the whole programme for Germany. So that one single lady organized for ten places in Germany. She got the pamphlets and posters printed, arranged the display. Each day I would give lectures - three lectures in every place. So, I decided that I should change the policy to three days. The response that Germany showed in three days was unimaginable. Everyday I had to initiate hundreds of people. On the very second day in Germany - the first day for initiations - I initiated one hundred people in one day. A cave was founded there and I was initiating in that cave. It took me from 7:00 A.M. to 8.30 P.M. The audience was waiting in the hall from 8:00 P.M. The report was that everyone was very satisfied and quietly sitting in the hall waiting.

In about 6 weeks, ten centres came up in big cities of Germany, After the first initiation of a hundred persons, when I gave the talk people said that, that was the best talk - it must be due to radiance of a hundred people initiated. The people came to know that if you want to hear good of him, give him more people to initiate. More initiations mean more talk. This was very, very remarkable.

Then there was a story of a Yoga teacher. Four German Yoga teachers came. They wanted a private interview.

I said: "Alright, come privately." So, four of them came. As they were entering the room, one said, "Your Transcendental Meditation has put an end to Yoga in Germany."

I said: "You are feeling sorry for an end of Yoga in Germany, and for this I welcome you because if someone feels sorry for the end of Yoga he is my friend."

The other man said, "Your teaching is against Patanjali."

I said: "If someone teaches against Patanjali, and if you feel that it is wrong, then you are my friend, because I also hold Patanjali as the authority on Yoga. I welcome you."

The third man said (by that time they had entered half way into the room, all of them attacking me in their way, but I was always bursting with laughter). "No. Patanjali says eight steps and you say you can do just like that."

I said: "Oh! Just come and we will discuss that. In my opinion Patanjali did not mean eight steps for union, He only says eight limbs of union. When the limbs develop in the womb of the mother, the whole body develops with all the limbs simultaneously and not one by one." This appealed to them.[115]

The success of the European trip can be measured by the fact that another was planned very soon after.

When Maharishi was not busy becoming acquainted with the roads of the Continent, the London centre continued to demand his attention, and by the summer of 1960 an offer of a rather grand-looking property, in Prince Albert Road, north London, gave the impetus to the formal establishment of the Spiritual Regeneration Movement of Great Britain, with its own board of trustees. At about this time Maharishi took the opportunity to train about twenty followers as Spiritual Guides. To qualify for this title, it was necessary to have an understanding of how to 'check' the meditations of other initiates', and to be able to re-establish correct practice should it prove necessary. The training of teachers of meditation, as proposed in the Three-Year Plan, found its first phase in this teaching of Guides.

When Brahmachari Mahesh had taken the initiative to discover the 'active ingredient' that lay within traditional *yogic* practices, the problem of liberating these techniques from the trappings of Hinduism was a complex task. Though he was frequently referred to as a 'monk of the Shankaracharya Order', his lectures gave few insights into the 'monkish' side of his thinking, though the odd chance remark would inevitably surface. A promotional pamphlet formulated in Los Angeles had delineated the many benefits to be derived from meditation. For the singer came the promise of a sweeter voice, and for the salesman an increased capacity to convince prospective buyers. But for seekers of God Maharishi issued a challenge: 'As long as the mind is not steady on the name of God, the devotion has not begun.' From this it can be conjectured that the 'word without meaning' imparted to new initiates could perhaps equally well have been termed the 'name of God'.

The audience at his lecture at the Guildhall, Cambridge, on 11th July 1960, might well have missed the mention of the celestial sandwiched as it was amongst some fairly down-to-earth observations:

If we drop a stone in pond the ripples begin to move and they move over the whole pond.

Similarly, by every thought, word and action, every individual is setting forth influence in his surroundings and that influence is not restricted to any boundaries. It goes on and on and reaches every level of creation.

Every individual by his every thought, word and action shakes the entire universe. This is the status of the individual.

He shares the responsibility for the life of the whole cosmos. The entire universe lies in the individual.

Every move of the individual shakes the cosmos. The universe reacts to the individual action. Every individual has this power that shakes the universe and shakes and saves the gods and angels in heaven. Man has this strength that upholds the universe. The individual by his every action serves the universe and the great power of Nature is ready to serve the individual if the individual influences the universe for the progression of the process of evolution.[116]

But what importance, if any, should one place on this mention of celestial beings? Maharishi seems to have anticipated such a question for in the same lecture he stressed:

> We belong to the realistic age of science. Let us be sure that all we strive for and achieve remains realistic. Our age of scientific unfoldment does not give credence to anything shrouded in the garb of mysticism. Let us realise the Absolute Being through a scientific and systematic method of achievement where every achievement will be supplemented by the personal experience.[117]

Maharishi Bal Brahmachari Mahesh Yogi owed much, if not all of his spiritual understanding, to his teacher Shankaracharya Brahmananda Saraswati. But the outward impression that Maharishi gave was that he was going it alone, a self-made man, which probably made his relationship with the general public easier. But, for those who made the effort to gain greater familiarity with his views, things became much clearer; his master was far from forgotten.

Prior to instruction, prospective students were asked to bring a few pieces of fresh fruit, some flowers, a clean white cotton handkerchief and their donation of a week's wages. At the initiation these offerings were placed before a photograph or painting of an elderly Indian gentleman deeply absorbed in thought. Once the student was comfortably seated (the cross-legged posture was most strongly recommended), Maharishi would murmur a prayer of devotion) which the initiate would be unlikely to understand). Of course, if he or she happened to be a scholar of Sanskrit the content of this *puja* ceremony would be clear, but many students were blissfully ignorant of the content or meaning. In truth, the sonorous chant that was being offered is an invocation containing the names of those particularly famous in the annals of *yoga* tradition.

One verse of the Invocation of the Masters of the Holy Tradition can be translated as:

> Skilled in dispelling the cloud of ignorance of the people, the gentle emancipator, Brahmananda Saraswati, the supreme teacher, full of brilliance, on Him we meditate.

> Offering invocation to the lotus feet of the blessed guru, I bow down.

Only after the completion of this prayer, and the performance of a short ritual involving the offerings, is the new initiate taught how to meditate.

Having learned Maharishi's technique, new initiates were encouraged to attend follow-up meetings in which they were given further practical tips and additional information on the theory and philosophy of meditation. To those close to him, Maharishi would sometimes narrate stories concerning the life of his teacher, Swami Brahmananda Saraswati. Fortunately, much of the late Shankaracharya's life story had been preserved as his lectures were peppered with personal anecdotes. Transcripts of these talks were later published in the *ashram's* newsletter. Though Maharishi did not arrange for translation and distribution of these lectures in English, he wanted meditators to know and respect his departed teacher and exhorted them to praise him. He taught them to say the phrase, '*Jai Guru Dev*' meaning 'Hail the Divine Guru', which soon came to be used between meditators, and could be used even to say 'Hello' and 'Goodbye'. For some unaccountable reason the utterance of these words seemed to hold a certain indefinable magic for its users.

5

—★—

THE DIVINE PLAN, GOD AND SUFFERING

In the summer of 1960, after a spell at his disciple Henry Nyburg's luxurious home, the Old Manor in Wiltshire, Maharishi decided to resume his favoured policy to 'establish a centre and then go to a new country'.[118] The world tour had gone well, with centres established across South East Asia, in Hawaii, on the west coast of America and in England. And rather than return directly to India just yet, Maharishi decided to try for just one more triumph, the winning over of the people of Germany. The Rolls Royce and driving skills of Henry Nyburg were duly pressed into action.

After each of his lectures in his tour of Germany, Maharishi had the task of initiating the many dozens that heeded his message, and very soon he became a victim of his own successes, for the volume of initiations increased and on one occasion, in Stuttgart, he found himself giving over 100 people instruction. Since he had to check the experiences of all the new meditators in order to ensure that they had a proper understanding of the practice, his other commitments became delayed. However, when belatedly he arrived for the next introductory lecture, he appeared as fresh and vital as ever. His apparent indefatigability had his devotees in awe, but for the remainder of the German tour a revised strategy was put in place. Each lecture would be advertised prior to his arrival and then he would spend just three days in each location. The campaign more than fulfilled everyone's expectations and as days turned into weeks, and weeks into months, Maharishi found himself inundated with candidates eager to participate in his Spiritual Regeneration Movement.

With the increasing demand for initiation it seems it was increasingly more important to fulfil Maharishi's desire to 'multiply himself', and train others in the art of teaching the meditation method. He might have enlisted a fellow *brahmachari* from Jyotish Peeth Ashram, but instead he made the rather surprising decision to use the services of his travelling companion. In the shy, retiring, bespectacled, middle-aged Henry Nyburg, Maharishi found a clarity of intellect and speech which qualified him for training as a deputy, so he did not delay and before long the Spiritual Regeneration Movement had not one but two teachers of meditation.

During that visit to Germany, no fewer than nine centres were opened. It might have been a good time to return to India, riding upon the crest of a wave, but instead he headed back to London, to share the news of his triumphant journey.

Utilizing the new and proven tour strategy practised in Germany, Maharishi announced his next campaign, and lectures were arranged in all the major university towns, and he travelled as far north as Edinburgh. A lecture at the Guildhall in Cambridge found him in strident form:

> It's a pleasure for me to be here this evening, in the company of all of you, in this great seat of learning.
>
> What is needed today is a technique to harmonise the qualities of the head with those of the heart. The head alone going ahead leaving the heart behind, man is found tumbling down. This is what is happening today in the world. All advancements in the field of science and technology and all study of the various subjects in the world leading the man to what ...? Increasing state of chaos and tension in the world!
>
> The word meditation is not new, the gains from meditation are not new to be counted, but, the information that it is easy for everyone to meditate and experience the inner glories of life, this seems to be a new message. Although the message is a centuries-old message. The same age-old message of Buddha, the same age-old message of Christ, the same age-old message of Krishna. Get within, experience the Kingdom of Heaven, experience Nirvana, experience Eternal Freedom, come out with that freedom, live a life of freedom in the world, the same age-old message. Only for the past centuries it had been forgotten, as if forgotten, the technique forgotten. And that's why the life, the individual life seems to be suffering, seems to be increasingly suffering. So much so that centres which were responsible to lead the people to the Kingdom of Heaven within began to propound the theories of suffering.
>
> Essentially, life is bliss ...[119]

In this talk, Maharishi aligned himself with the leaders of three world religions, such that one might suspect that he was attempting to trigger a religious revival, that he might have Messianic tendencies. However, it is important to realise that in the tradition to which he belonged, for in India unlike the West, it is not uncommon for people to be accorded the status of saint whilst they are still alive. Likewise it is not unknown for such individuals to be identified with the Supreme, and as such given the title *Bhagavan* or *Bhagwan* (God); in fact Maharishi's own master was frequently addressed in this way. There is no getting away from the fact that Maharishi's words seem to imply that he had personally received the grace of God and experienced some sort of Heaven, but since he offered neither prophecies nor claims of divine revelation, he remained in relative safety from those who might judge him to be a false prophet, and such was the gentleness of his manner and the authority of his voice, that he encountered no real hostility. Far from being branded a religious fanatic, his predominantly conservative audiences found him reassuringly reasonable. After all, he appeared to be offering something much more than fine speeches, he claimed to be able to reveal the 'Kingdom of Heaven within', not just for the select few, but for **anyone** who wished it.

Let us examine how this miracle was to be achieved. Central to Maharishi's thinking lay his stated belief that the natural tendency of the mind is towards greater happiness. Therefore, he reasoned, that given the opportunity the mind would gravitate towards ever-greater happiness. To facilitate this expansion of happiness, he offered this method of meditation. Acknowledging that the mind is accustomed to entertain thoughts and that any attempt to instantly purge it of this habit might prove counter-productive, he offered to provide a 'vehicle' for keeping the mind occupied. He indicated that the selection of the correct 'vehicle' or 'word would likely be without meaning', maintaining that by the correct use of this word, the mind might easily 'transcend' (meaning to 'go beyond') the thoughts that prevent the mind from experiencing the 'Kingdom of Heaven'. For the cynic that would sound just too good to be true!

Plans were made to tour Scandinavia pushed away any imminent return to India. Before the tour had started Maharishi had been informed that the people of Sweden were more 'sophisticated' and 'conservative' than the British. To this he retorted:

> This is good. Conservative means they are self-sufficient, and they don't want any infringement from outside.[120]

In trying to understand the country he was to visit, he was assisted by one of his aides.

Then one Englishman, very noble, good and conservative as all the English people are, said: "If your Movement is established in Sweden, then I will think that you can really establish it through the world." I asked him to tell me something of Sweden. He replied: "Swedish people are proud of their culture. They think that they don't need anything from outside and that they are self-sufficient. They don't like the infringement of any other cultural activity in their private life." I asked him to tell me something about the Swedish Hospitals, whether the mental hospitals were increasing in that Country. Then he said: "Sweden has the highest standard of living and highest rate of suicidal tendencies. Then I said: "That is enough for my message to be accepted in that country." The first talk that I gave in Sweden was. "I am very happy this evening to be speaking to those fortunate people in the world who feel that they are self sufficient. Swedish culture in Europe - greatest standard of living, and I am very proud to give my message to such population."[121]

Maharishi in Sweden, December 1960

The tour commenced on Monday, 28th November 1960, and after the customary press conference, he lectured at Hoyres Hus Hall, Oslo, Norway, to a predominantly student audience. From Norway he moved via Denmark and on to Sweden. In the event, there was only enough time for a hurried taste of Sweden before returning to Germany to lead a Spiritual Guides course where, between 23rd and 29th December 1960 he instructed another twenty meditators as 'Guides'. This course was held in the Black Forest area, from where he travelled back to Stuttgart and Munich in order to resume his lecturing. He subsequently initiated several hundred newcomers.

Another busy year had come to an end, and to mark the occasion the boss of the Spiritual Regeneration Movement decided to take some leave, to be spent in silence at Henry Nyburg's chalet in Kitzbühel, amidst Austria's snowy Tyrolean Mountains.

The New Year, 1961, got off to a good start with Maharishi returning to Sweden in order to deal with a backlog of initiations there, before taking a flying visit to Italy and making a brief but very effective appearance in

Greece. The crowning achievement of Maharishi's visit to Greece came in his televized appearance at the Acropolis, which subsequently became a worldwide radio broadcast heard by countless millions.

He chose this moment to return home to India, not to a life of solitude but to make contact with his followers. As it happened though, he barely had time to look up old friends and catch up with the news before it was time to fly out again. But before leaving, he found time to meet with Dr Hislop, who had been nominated to look for a suitable site for a teacher-training academy.

> He [Hislop] stayed there three months. A man brought up in the American aristocracy, goes to the Himalayas and then stays there for three months, where there is no proper food ...
>
> It is Uttar Kashi, and the surrounding area is a place of poverty, not of luxury [122] ...

The reason for Maharishi's hasty exit from India was that a date had now been set for the First World Assembly of the Spiritual Regeneration Movement. Organized by the President of the School of Economic Science, in London, Leonardo Mclaren, this prestigious event was set to be held at London's Albert Hall on Monday, 13rd March 1961.

An advertisement was put up to advertise the Royal Albert Hall event, which appeared in copies of *The Times* on Friday, 10th March 1961

> DEEP MEDITATION—a practical method—Maharishi Mahesh Yogi from the Valley of the Saints, Himalayas, will describe a simple technique to enrich the life of every normal person. First World Assembly of Spiritual Regeneration Movement, Royal Albert Hall, Monday, 13 March, at 7.30 p.m. Tickets 20s., 10s., 5s. and 3s. 6d. (unreserved), from S. R. M., 4, Albemarle Street, W.1 (HYD. 6296), or Royal Albert Hall.

For two days prior to the big event, preparatory sessions were held at Caxton Hall, in Westminster. In those days Maharishi had as his constant companion and deputy, an Anglo-Indian lawyer named Philip Williams, who Maharishi renamed Brahmachari Devendra.

When at last the day of the assembly arrived, Maharishi is said to have found himself addressing a capacity crowd of 5000. Also speaking at this event was Henry Nyburg, who was there to propose a Declaration of the First World Assembly of the Spiritual Regeneration Movement. And following this appearance at the Albert Hall, Maharishi became rather attracted by the idea of world assemblies and proceeded to arrange a number of similar events across Europe and throughout India. Assisting him at these assemblies would be any of some several dozen meditators ready to testify to the merit of the practice of meditation.

**Addressing a capacity audience at London's Royal Albert Hall,
13th March 1961**

Back in India Maharishi had gained popularity and now enjoyed celebrity status, with government ministers eagerly endorsing his campaign. When a three-day assembly was convened in Jabalpur on 5th April 1961, Maharishi and his family had the chance of a brief reunion, but he had little time for idleness, for on average, 200 people were coming to be initiated each day. The finale of this 'assembly tour' was held on Wednesday, 12th April 1961 at Sapru House in New Delhi, some two years after the commencement of his successful world tour. Clearly, his capacity for strategy might, if he had so wished, have won him employment in virtually any major advertising concern.

In the West Maharishi's lectures were attended by people uninformed about India's spiritual heritage, but here in his homeland, he was addressing his peers. News of his fame was met with a mixed response amongst his fellow countrymen, where even the most unlettered villager could give expert information regarding his or her religion. India is a nation deeply steeped in traditional values, so Maharishi had his work cut out to defend his version, his reinterpretation, of age-old beliefs. To some it must have appeared audacious that anyone would presume to rework their most treasured beliefs, and they did not intend letting him off lightly. They demanded scriptural authority for his teachings, forcing him back upon the repertoire of quotations he no doubt learned from his 'Guru Dev'. Many of his critics were appeased by his responses, but others remained unconvinced. Perhaps it was just such entrenched attitudes, the clinging on to philosophies which depended on renunciation and self-abnegation, that first inspired him to court Western approval before, thus becoming more self-empowered before tackling the bastions of his homeland.

From Delhi Maharishi made his way northwards, towards Rishikesh, known as the 'Gateway of Uttarakhand', an area for time immemorial associated with the spiritual history of India, containing the towns of both Joshimath (Jyotir Math) and Uttar Kashi. . It had been decided to hold the course in Uttar Kashi, at Gyaan Mandir, and to that end several simple but capacious wooden buildings were constructed to house the course. But during Maharishi's previous visit, an alternate location had been found, a fifteen-acre site on which there was to be the International Academy of Meditation, but as yet there had not been enough time to get it ready for occupation.

> Dr. Hislop came to India in connection with the establishment on an Academy at Uttar Kashi. He faced many difficulties and sacrificed a lot of his health, But unfortunately the place which he selected for the Academy was taken by the Government to make District Headquarters. He was very much disappointed, Then I came to India and with the help of Swami Shankar Lal. I arranged the place for the Academy in Rishikesh after putting in lots of effort.[123]

> It is difficult to build in the mountains, especially in the Himalayas -everything has to come on horseback or muleback. Every little bit, stone and brick and all these things, so it is taking a little longer than I expected. Because in my mind everything should be easy and quick. But the buildings have gone up beyond my expectations.[124]

Whilst work was being carried out on construction of Dhyaan Vidya Peeth (the Academy of Meditation), the training course convened at a spot known as Ram Nagar, at Rishikesh, just across the river from the newly acquired plot. And from around the world came more than sixty meditators to study in conditions Spartan but tranquil. On moonlit nights the group would gather together to take part in communal meditation. During this course Maharishi found time to dwell upon his quest, of searching the scriptural texts in order to find material that would bear out his line of philosophy.

The prime source of inspiration for many Hindus is the *Bhagavad-Gita*, a scripture detailing a dialogue between Lord Krishna and his friend, Arjuna, an archer. Arjuna faces a weighty dilemma for his family has become divided by dispute and a decision has been made to settle their differences by armed combat. Though Arjuna is famed for his skill and prowess as an archer, he will not enter the fray, so Lord Krishna, who has volunteered to be his charioteer, counsels him to abandon all uncertainties and get on with the fight. Krishna advises him that any reluctance to engage in combat will be interpreted as cowardice. However, Arjuna's dilemma lay not in any lack of courage but in his concern that by wounding or killing his relatives he will suffer guilt and remorse forever. Lord Krishna, often identified as an *avataar* or incarnation of God, intent on freeing Arjuna from his indecisiveness, instructs him how to act from a level of inner balance.

Reviewing the verses containing Krishna's instructions, Maharishi found several references that appear to support his own philosophical contentions and so proceeded to test them on his captive audience of course participants and was not displeased with their reactions.

On Tuesday, 30th May 1961, eight years to the day after his master's death, the successor to the throne of Shankaracharya of Jyotir Math, Swami Shantanand Saraswati, graced the teacher-training course with his presence and was received there with all due ceremony. Arriving at the site where the new Academy was being built, he addressed Maharishi and the gathered meditators:

> Rishikesh is a place where so many saints and sages meditated with a view to attaining Self-realisation. Every grain of sand is vibrating forth the holy influence of saints and sages who have inhabited this part of India since ages past.[125]

Dr Francis Roles was very taken with the Shankaracharya, Swami Shantanand, and he later shared his impressions, concluding:

> I do think the combination of the Maharishi and the official Head of the Tradition is a very marvellous one. No question of the Maharishi being his pupil, or anything like that; no question of one being the pupil of the other; they were fellow pupils of Guru Deva. The Maharishi, with his brilliant brain and many-sided experience was trained in a certain way for a particular role. Of the two he was actually with his Teacher longer.

> This man, who is of quite different type, was trained in quite a different way for quite a different function; trained by the way of Bhakti; sent away as an ascetic and brought back to take over the post from his Master. So, no question of precedence; they simply agreed for the honour of the Tradition to conduct everything in this way, with the Maharishi doing honour to the living Head of their Holy Tradition. So by now, all Northern India knows (and many in the south as well) that the Maharishi has the official support and goodwill of his Tradition in everything he does.[126]

In expansive mood at a press conference in September 1961

Expounding his teaching to the press in London, September 1961

The Shankaracharya commended the practice of Maharishi's meditation, describing it as a 'master key to the knowledge of Vedanta' and added:

'There are other keys, but a master key is enough to open all the locks.'[127]

After staying for a while at Rishikesh the Shankaracharya announced his intention to move on and before leaving offered a parting message to those gathered there:

'We are ever at God's feet. Never forget that we are the sons of Sat Chit Ananda.'[128]

Swami Vishnudevanand, Swami Shantanand's closest aide, stayed until the end of the course, whilst Shantanand and his retinue, many of whom had also served the former Shankaracharya, departed. They came at Maharishi's request and it is clear that his position in India was strengthened by this support. Whilst at Ram Nagar, Maharishi also devoted time to a course for saints, *sadhus* and *swamis* interested in hearing his teaching.

Although sixty meditators had attended the teacher training sessions at Rishikesh, far fewer than that were ordained as teachers of meditation, but it was a good step forward towards the fulfilment of his Three-Year Plan. And soon the lure of touring drew him again, this time Maharishi flew to Africa, where on 23rd August he made an appearance in Nairobi, before moving on to Kenya, and then on to England for a brief meeting with meditators in London. From England he returned to the United States where, after a visit to his friends the Olsons at their home in Los Angeles, he embarked on a West Coast tour, before journeying northwards into Canada, visiting the cities of Vancouver and Victoria.

Maharishi was undoubtedly concerned that he had so far trained few teachers, therefore, as a preliminary measure towards the training of the '25,000 teachers within three years' for which he aimed, he set up a Meditation Guides' course on Santa Catalina Island off the Californian coast. This course, which was specifically aimed at providing an opportunity for extended meditations, occupied the last months of the year.

In late December he followed his custom of taking a few days off for silence, during which he undertook the composition of a devotional poem, entitled 'God', of which the following is an extract:

> *My Lord*
> *And I know*
> *When I begin, I begin so abruptly*
> *I know now*
> *When I began, I began so abruptly*

> *From the loudest note I began*
> *For I could not sing it low*
> *Thy Grace of Eternity*
> *The Glory of Eternity*
> *I could not sing it low*
> *The Glory of Eternal Life*
> *I know not how to sing it low*
> *So I blew my trumpet full!*
> *It echoed round the world*
> *How it sounded to Thee, I do not know,*
> *But to me it has been fun*
> *A real fun of greatest joy*
> *A real, good great fun*
> *Yes.*[129]

At the start of 1962, Maharishi was still in the USA, but he was now working on the East Coast, and though the rather optimistic goals of the Three-Year Plan were still far from being realized, interest in this meditation method increased daily. Though he believed that the use of pamphlets and literature was of little consequence in spreading his message, that did not stop a steady flow of publications emerging. In fact the new year was to yield a bumper crop of publications starting with *The Blessing That Awaits You*, a basic introduction to meditation, followed by the provocatively titled, *Discovery of 'Nuclear Life Energy' – Maharishi's Theory of the Absolute: The Fulfilment of Dr Einstein's Theory of Relativity*. Another publication, a guide to *yoga* postures, was released in March, and the genesis of this booklet is of some interest. It is told that a vexed and serious meditator asked Maharishi what would happen to an individual if the goal of the meditation, the permanent state of bliss, was not achieved in a lifetime. Uncharacteristically, Maharishi was rendered temporarily speechless, and when at last he found words to answer his enquirer, he recommended the daily practice of simple *yogic* exercises, in order to accelerate the process of expansion of consciousness. The exercises he chose were prepared by Professor K. B. Hari Krishna, of the University of Travancore, India. In the foreword to *A Six Month Course In Yoga Asanas* Maharishi said:

> For good health it is necessary for everyone to do something with the body so that it remains flexible and normal.
>   The advantage of YOGA ASANAS over other eastern and western systems of physical posture is that they do not consume energy. They help restore life force, promote health and maintain normal conditions in the body.[130]

And for those wishing to offer a 'prayer before taking food' Maharishi offered them these words:

> *Jai Guru Dev*
> *In thy fullness, My Lord*
> *Filled with Thy Grace*
> *For the purpose of union with Thee*
> *And to satisfy and glorify Thy Creation*
> *With thanks to Thee with all our hearts*
> *And with all our love for Thee,*
> *With all adoration for Thy Blessings*
> *We take Thy gift as it has come to us*
> *The food is Thy Blessing*
> *And in Thy Service we accept*
> *In all gratitude*
> *My Lord*[131]

In March 1962 a long-playing record of two of his early lectures, *Deep Meditation* and *The Healing Power of Deep Meditation*, was issued on the World-Wide Records label.

Although meditation was not being taught in a specifically religious Maharishi did make frequent references to the divine. He explained in a lecture, which was published at this time, that there exists a Divine Plan devised to assist mankind along the road of spiritual progress. But, according to Maharishi, as motorways become worn and need repair, so it is with the highway to the divine, and to facilitate travel, engineers must be sent out to assess and improve the route.

That Maharishi perceived himself as following a divine calling is implicit throughout, although not actually stated. In describing the function of the Divine Plan, he offered an insight into his perception of the purpose of life:

> The whole complex of the Universe is so designed that all must evolve -angels, man, animals, birds, insects, and all – must forge ahead on the highway of evolution and must reach the ultimate destiny in God Consciousness. But when man begins to act in a negative way, in a way which would lead him to suffering and misery in life, then the Divine Plan is disturbed.[132]

He furthermore indicated that the practice of the techniques he was teaching could reveal both the nature and the detail of the Divine Will.

According to Maharishi, the lineage of monks known as the Shankaracharya Order is the 'authentic custodian of the wisdom of the *mantras*'. Central to the teaching of this meditation lies the successful selection and application of these *mantras*. In explaining this, he drew a comparison between the choice of correct 'medium' and the assessment of blood groups, pointing out that a doctor could do untold harm by transfusing the wrong blood type. He continued in this vein, asserting:

> There are thousands of *mantras* and all have their specific values, specific qualities and are suitable for specific types of people.[133]

Having spent the early part of 1962 in the USA, by spring Maharishi was preparing another trip to India to put in an appearance at Rishikesh. In the event, the Shankaracharya was again on hand to lend his support. After another course for recluses (*sadhus* and *swamis*) Maharishi then undertook a brief tour of northern India.

Maharishi's mission to spiritually regenerate the world seemed, on the surface, to be going well, but in reality a divisive undercurrent was already starting to make itself felt. At least two of his prominent followers, namely Leon Mclaren and Dr Francis Roles, had became disaffected and were already branching out on their own. But perhaps this had been their intention all along? Dr Roles had been a follower of P.D. Ouspensky, who in turn had been a prominent disciple of Georges Ivanovitch Gurdjieff, a notable thinker of his time, and it is claimed that Ouspensky instructed Dr Roles to seek out a simple method of finding inner stillness and offer it to those living ordinary lives. In addition to finding such a method, Roles had discovered an unlikely, and very useful, ally in no less a personage than Swami Shantanand (the Shankaracharya had given a clue to his breadth of vision in his address to the participants of the teacher-training course the previous year, in which he had alluded to the many keys or paths to illumination). Roles found the Shankaracharya willing to offer his group the spiritual guidance it sought, but Maharishi, on discovering the existence of the breakaway group, made every effort to persuade the mutinous Roles to toe the party line, though Maharishi was eventually forced to accept the situation. According to Joyce Collin-Smith in *Call No Man Master* (Gateway, 1988) Roles 'announced that he had forged a link with a much greater master'. Joyce appears to have been a close personal assistant and chauffeur to Maharishi at this time. She confided that, in her opinion, Maharishi was not particularly enamoured with Roles but believed the meditation movement needed the organisational skills possessed by Roles and his associates from the 'Society for the Study of Normal Man'.

Maharishi's desire for the rapid expansion of his world movement fuelled more plans for training further teachers to teach this meditation. In the summer of 1962 Maharishi set up yet another course, this time in Hochgurgl, Austria, as course participant David Fiske recalls:

> I was fortunate to start TM and meet Maharishi Mahesh Yogi in 1962 (Hochgurgl Austria) when I was 23. He had a very easily understood and a very

convincing explanation of the nature of the mind and how, using this nature and the structure of awareness, deep meditation is, and should be spontaneous and easy.

I found TM worked well for me and on the 1962 course in Hoch Gurgl Austria Maharishi empowered me as a teacher of TM, probably one of the first dozen in the world. He asked me if I wanted "to spiritually regenerate Africa". I told him South Africa was a big enough challenge. [134]

And David Fiske recalls an awkward moment when he came to Maharishi's assistance:

In Germany at a conference hall before some function I went to the washrooms and was just finishing a pee when in comes Maharishi. It was strange to meet him in that place. I looked at the urinals and at his robes and said "I better put a coin in so we can open the toilet door for you." No pockets no money can be a hazard sometimes. [135]

Maharishi's ability to attract influential people continued, and now he made the acquaintance of Prince Giovanni Alliata de Montreale, a Member of the Italian Parliament, who thereafter took an active and high profile part in detailing the merits of Deep Meditation. At the conclusion of the course, Maharishi took another break at Henry Nyburg's country home in England, then with renewed energy he recommenced operations, travelling to Scandinavia, France and Ireland before returning to Los Angeles.

Whilst Maharishi vigorously pursued his worldwide campaign, his followers were not inactive, seeing to it that new publications, in the form of pamphlets and booklets, were published. Many of the Maharishi's lectures were transcribed and reproduced for public consumption; these generally focused on a particular theme but were united by essentially the same message: meditate and be happy.

Although, for the most part, Maharishi succeeded in steering clear of making any particularly contentious or controversial remarks, this sometimes proved unavoidable. For example, in a question and answer session he offered some radical, and therefore very provocative, comments on contemporary Christian thinking:

Questioner: Maharishi, why is, in the Christian circles, such an accent laid upon the suffering of Christ?

Maharishi: Due to not understanding the life of Christ and not understanding the message of Christ. I don't think Christ ever suffered or Christ could suffer. The suffering man from the suffering platform sees the Bliss of Christ as suffering. Green specks on the glass and everything is seen as green. [136]

6

— ★ —

TALKING BOOK

The time that had been set aside for the Three-Year Plan were almost up, and aware of the fact that his achievements had not matched his plans, Maharishi prepared his response, the Second Three-Year Plan. But before revealing this new initiative he decided that another short holiday was in order. Once at the quietly beautiful retreat at Lake Arrowhead, California, however, the ebullient master of relaxation could not restrain himself and threw himself into yet another project.

Although Maharishi had started writing his commentary on the *Bhagavad-Gita*, he interrupted this to work on a second book, intended as a textbook to his teachings. But since he was far better attuned to public speaking, he chose in the first instance to speak his thoughts onto tape, and then, whilst the transcriptions were being made, to revise and edit. The resultant book, *Science of Being and Art of Living*, was finished by late January 1963 and published (in English) soon after. On Saturday, 12th January 1963, his forty-fifth birthday, he wrote these words as part of the book's introduction:

> The *Science of Being and Art of Living* is the summation of both the practical wisdom of integrated life advanced by the Vedic Rishis of ancient India and the growth of scientific thinking in the present-day Western world.[137]

Readers would, for the most part, have had to take his word for the truth of this claim since the thinking of the Vedic *rishis* was unfamiliar to most of them. Included in Maharishi's introduction was an acknowledgement of his indebtedness to his Master, His Divinity Swami Brahmananda Saraswati, Jagadguru Bhagwan Shankaracharya, whose picture graces one of the opening pages, but, unaccountably, no photograph of Maharishi was included in this first edition.

Science of Being and Art of Living was no small achievement for it addressed a multitude of subjects and pointed to meditation as a practical means to their fulfilment, and for those who sought further justification for purchasing the book, what could have been more persuasive than the following declaration?

> This is a book of revival for the age. If the golden era is ever to dawn on human society, if the aquarian age is ever to be on earth, *The Science of Being and Art of Living* will provide a free way for it to come.[138]

Although Maharishi's Hawaiian followers had published a volume in his name, this was the first book about Maharishi's teachings available to the mass of meditators and it afforded a unique opportunity for them to gain a greater understanding of, and familiarity with, his philosophies. By the thoughtful inclusion of analogies and anecdotes, some relief was provided in what would otherwise have been pretty dry text. Maharishi's vocabulary, and that of the Spiritual Regeneration Movement, could pose difficulties for new aspirants, in particular the similarity between the words spirituality and spiritualism. Perhaps it was this confusion that caused Maharishi to offer his views on the value of spiritualism:

> There are some who try to make use of the supernatural power of creation by contacting the spirit world through a medium or through invoking spirits. That is on a very limited level of strength because no spirit is in possession of the total power of nature. There may be spirits who may be more powerful than man but invoking these spirits or behaving as a medium for them is not a practice to be encouraged because of two reasons. First, the power gained through these spirits is an insignificant, infinitesimal fraction of the power of almighty nature; second, in order to receive that portion of the power of nature, one has to give oneself completely to the influence of that spirit.[139]

Throughout *Science of Being and Art of Living* Maharishi seems to have been intent upon urging readers on, to a point where they would feel compelled to try out this system of meditation. This was an invitation to test the teaching of the Vedic *rishis,* the claim that 'I am That. Thou art That, and all this is That.'[140]

In striving to explain his view of man's position in the order of things, Maharishi asserted his vision of the scope of evolution:

> At the lowest end of evolution we find the inert states of creation. From there, the life of the species begins, and the creation changes in its intelligence, power and joyfulness. The progressive scale of evolution continues through the different species of the vegetable, the egg-born, the water-born, the animal kingdom, and rises to the world of angels. Ultimately, on the top level of evolution, is He whose power is unlimited, whose joyfulness is unlimited, whose intelligence and energy are unlimited.[141]

Stating his opinion that all human beings have the ability to share a close affinity with the very highest strata of evolution, he then focused his attention on established religion.

The true spirit of religion is lacking when it counts only what is right or wrong and creates fear of punishment and hell and the fear of God in the mind of men. The purpose of religion should be to take away all fear from man. It should not seek to achieve its purpose through instilling fear of the Almighty in the mind.[142]

One way of describing the meditation Maharishi promoted to achieve this union, was to say what it was not. In surveying the practice of emptying the mind, he warned:

All such practices of silencing the mind are wrong.

There are many groups in the world who sit in silence and try to hear their inner voice or the voice of God, as they term it. All such practices make the mind passive and dull.[143]

The then prevailing practice of psychoanalysis also met with condemnation.

If there could be a way to expand one's consciousness in the direction of more evolved states of consciousness, and if there could be a way to enlarge the present stage of consciousness to the unbounded universal state of cosmic consciousness, then the subjects of psychoanalysis would certainly be saved from the unfortunate influence of overshadowing their consciousness by digging into the mud of the miserable past – which suppresses their consciousness.[144]

It might have appeared to some that the benefits to be derived from Transcendental Deep Meditation were of a purely personal, even selfish, nature. Far from supporting this view Maharishi claimed that it could not only be useful for the individual, but could prove a valuable tool for creating world peace.

It has been brought out by Charak and Sushrut, the great exponents of medical science in ancient India, that as long as people behave in righteousness, the atmosphere remains full of harmonious vibrations.

Thus we find from every angle that in order to produce a good, harmonious and healthy atmosphere for the good of all creatures in the world, it is necessary that man live in happiness, peace, and abundance. Every man has a chance to live this way.[145]

Towards the end of *Science of Being and Art of Living*, Maharishi's vision of future possibilities is outlined, in which, including the provision of structures dedicated to the practice of meditation.

It seems necessary that sanctuaries of silence be constructed in the midst of noisy marketplaces of big cities, so that people, before going to their business, and after completing their business of the day, may enter into silent meditation rooms, dive deep within themselves, and be profited by undisturbed, regular, and deep meditations. Apart from the silent meditation centers in the noisy areas of towns, it seems to be necessary that such silent meditation centers also be constructed in the holiday resorts where people go on weekends to stay for one or two days. There they may have long hours of deep meditation and come home renewed in spirit, intelligence, and energy.[146]

In compiling *Science of Being and Art of Living* Maharishi must surely have hoped that by tantalizing the reader with page after page of positive assertions about the benefits to be derived from meditation, resulting in a hunger which could only be satisfied by a trip to the local meditation centre. Indeed, a coupon was attached to the inside of the back cover of the book giving the address and telephone number of the nearest contact. Unfortunately for those as yet unacquainted with his method of Transcendental Deep Meditation, the book yielded little information about the actual method of meditation, for in spite of the countless references to the technique; there was no attempt to give details of it.

Having created a textbook to his ideology, Maharishi was again free to resume his travels, and on Sunday, 27th January 1963 he flew to Hong Kong and then on to Rangoon in Burma, finally touching down on 5th February in India, at Calcutta Airport. He then made for Allahabad, bound for the *ashram* of Shankaracharya Swami Shantanand, which the former Shankaracharya, Swami Brahmananda, had secured in 1950 a few years before his death. There is an interesting tale told about this property.

> Once Pashupati Singh, Raja of Dilippur, offered to donate his Kothi [mansion] to the Peeth. The Kothi was situated in Alopi Bagh, Payag. Swamiji rejected the offer forthwith and instead proposed for the purchase of the Kothi on the market-price. The market-price of the Kothi was then Rs. One lakh. In no time, Swamiji arranged the money and purchased the Kothi. Nobody knows, from where such a huge amount dropped into his lap. Even those very close to him, could not solve this mystery. [147]

News that the Shankaracharya had been able to raise 100,000 rupees made tongues wag. How could one who forbade the offering of material wealth have access to such a vast sum – and in cash? When the people pestered him for an explanation, he maintained a stoic silence. However, eventually, in a bid to settle the matter, he declared:

> 'The coming of these *rupees* is not in the hands of any man.'

> 'At the time of the Mahabharata, when Draupadi's cloth became longer, then thousands of yards it grew. Where did the cloth come from? Another thing is this that, the *sari* that Draupadi was wearing, that very cloth came. It was not just some red, some green, some yellow. When Bhagwan (God) gives then he gives all, and gives the genuine real thing. If the work could be done at the time of the Mahabharata, that now also can be. The essence of Bhagwan always exists, in Him no end comes.'[148]

The converted palace at Allahabad was been named 'Brahma Nivas' ('Abode of Brahma'), and used Shankaracharya's winter residence, prior to the *ashram* passing to his successor.

Whilst in India, Maharishi sought to confer with Swami Shantanand Saraswati, his former fellow-disciple. Fortune smiled on him in that he received the *swami's* blessing for his new scheme, an All-Indian Campaign. The plan was to start in Delhi, continue across the northern provinces and then go on to central India, and it seems that Maharishi genuinely believed that he could offer something that would help alleviate the severe problems of poverty and suffering in his home country, a nation still beleaguered by superstition and caste-consciousness.

Maharishi claimed a close relationship with his 'Guru Dev', the former Shankaracharya of Jyotirmath, so it would be handy if a photograph of the two of them together could be found. Such an image was circulated at this time, and shared with the press, of the former Shankaracharya with Bal Brahmachari Mahesh seated close by him, but it was not genuine, being the one taken of the Shankaracharya in the company of the first President of India, doctored substituting an later image of the *brahmachari* for that of the President.

Interestingly, this episode provides unexpected and reasonably conclusive proof that as a *brahmachari* Maharishi had not seriously entertained thoughts of forming his own organization or mission, not at least until the very end of the Shankaracharya's life. Had he done so he would almost certainly have prepared himself for the event. In fact there is no evidence that Maharishi ever prepared for the growth of his Movement nor, more importantly, that he had the capacity for predicting its progress. This is not to say that he had no interest in the future, for after the *Beacon Light* lectures in October 1955 he is said to have consulted a *jyotishi* (astrologer), who offered an extremely favourable forecast.

Saturday, 2nd March 1963 was a red-letter day in the All-India Campaign for Maharishi had been specially invited to speak to Members of the Indian Parliament. In measured and self-assured tones he drew from his wealth of ideas, with the words flowing almost involuntarily from his lips. No doubt the politicians of New Delhi would have loved to have been able to equal Maharishi's eloquence; perhaps it was in the hope of acquiring such skills that some of them later asked for initiation into his meditation.

The All-India Campaign tour continued, embracing the predominantly Sikh cities of the Punjab, the distant north-eastern state of Assam, a couple of cities in central India and then to scenic Srinagar in Kashmir.

At the conclusion of the campaign, a forty-day Spiritual Guides' course was to be held at his Academy near Rishikesh and in late April he made his way there. The course, which was intended to train new teachers, laid a heavy emphasis on gaining greater familiarity with the experience of meditation. Accordingly, the course participants spent much of their time in silent inner communion. These periods of quiet were interspersed with lectures from Maharishi.

The course also provided a valuable opportunity for foreign visitors to better acquaint themselves with Indian culture, a chance to discover for themselves how the other half live. In keeping with local custom, only strictly vegetarian food was served to them; even eggs were banned from the Academy menu. For those brought up on 'meat and two veg' this must have been a dramatic culture shock. However, in the search for the 'untapped source of energy within', a change of diet was but a trifling matter.

At that time the Spiritual Regeneration Movement was virtually synonymous with its founder, Maharishi Mahesh Yogi, whose personal charm and volubility made him well loved. The meditation, in addition to its proclaimed efficacy, also offered followers a symbol of his presence. In attending courses with Maharishi, his devotees had a chance to bathe in his reflected glory. Whilst Maharishi was still in India, dates were fixed for courses in both Norway and Austria, and it was naturally assumed he would attend, but in this the organizers were to be disappointed, for Maharishi wanted to remain in India to preside over his All-India Campaign. He delivered something of a bombshell by deputizing his understudy Henry Nyburg to officiate in his absence. The news that he would not be overseeing the Scandinavian and European courses in person meant that, in order to show their allegiance, they must accept his will and settle for tuition from his right-hand man.

But there was some cause for celebration in that a gramophone record was released at this time.[149] On one side of the vinyl disc was a lecture, and on the other a poem, simply entitled 'Love'. Like its predecessor, 'God', it was anything but short, and with a dedication sung softly in Sanskrit. The poem itself is a series of impressions on the theme of love, with only one explicit reference to the technique of Transcendental Deep Meditation, though to the initiate the implicit references are many and various. For example, in this technique of meditation one is not required to dispel nor be held by the thoughts experienced during its practice.

The sun shines, and it shines forever in fullness. It may be that the clouds are gathering. Let them come and go, they go as they come. Take no notice of their coming; you go your way. Make your way through the clouds if they lie on the way. Do not try to dispel them; do not be held by them, they will go the way they have come. They are never found stationary, but if you like to pause to see them wither away, wait for a while. The wind is blowing anyway; it is to clear the clouds from your way. Just wait to see the cloud wither away, and the sun, the same old sun of love will shine again, in fullness of its glory.

In this poem Maharishi makes some profound and irrefutable observations:

When an ocean flows in love, it flows in peace within. When a shallow pond moves to rise high in waves of the ocean, it only stirs the mud at the bottom, and the whole serenity of the pond is spoilt. When a heart, shallow as a pond seeks to rise high in waves of love, it creates a muddle and brings out the mud that was so far gracefully hidden underneath. To enjoy the ocean of love, we have to improve the magnitude of our hearts and gain the depth of an ocean, unfathomable and full.

Also included in the poem is a prayer which is perhaps of traditional origin This was not the first time he had been known to offer up personal prayers for contained in *A Sixth Month Course in Yoga Asanas* is another, related to success in *yoga* practice and yet another, concerned with thanksgiving for food, is to be found in *Science of Being and Art of Living*. The prayer that lies within the 'Love' poem is by far the most devotional of the three (I heard something similar from a *yogi* I met one morning near Rishikesh):

My lord, in the temple of my heart, on the altar of thy glory, my God, my love is full, and thy love is treasured safely. My love for thee is safe and full in freshness and purity at the glory of thy altar. My lord, thy lordship is secured in the shrine of my heart, and when my love flows, it spreads the glory in thy creation.

The following passage appears almost autobiographical in content:

In love of God, the lover of life finds expression of the inexpressible. Cosmic life gains expression in his activity. The thought of cosmic life is materialized in his process of thinking. His eyes behold the purpose of creation; his ears hear the music of cosmic life, his hands hold on to cosmic intentions. His feet set the cosmic life in motion; he walks on earth, yet walks in the destiny of heaven. Angels enjoy his being on earth, this is the glory of unity born of love.

The main body of the poem is packed brim full with optimism, and it finishes in like fashion.

Love shall save us from wrong and guide our path in life. Love shall forever shine on our way and the light will guide our steps whether we go slow or fast. The light of love shall forever be with us on our way. Love shall forever be with us on our way. Love shall forever be the anchor of our life. We shall be in love and love shall be in us. We shall live in love, shall grow in love and shall find fulfilment in love eternal. Jai Guru Dev.

His plans in the meantime underwent a dramatic change; and instead of continuing his work in India, he left to join his followers in Los Angeles and later presented himself at a course in Canada. Meanwhile, the Norwegian and Austrian courses went on as planned.

Maharishi intended to fly to Britain but before doing so he showed his mettle by making an impromptu tour from the west to the east of Canada. Then on 1st October he set off for Britain where he met up with Henry Nyburg. Together they proceeded to Henry's country home, however, for Maharishi, holidays had a habit of turning into 'busman's holidays' and on this occasion he recommenced work on his commentary on the *Bhagavad-Gita*, enlisting the help of his devotees. With Dr Vernon Katz help in translating the Sanskrit text, others assisted in putting Maharishi's ideas into 'good' English. Then he was off again in search of new minds, on a whistle-stop tour which took him to Norway, Sweden, Denmark, Germany, Italy and Greece, and by Christmas he was back in India. In Delhi, facing a barrage of questions from the press, some topics he would answer with great patience whilst others he would give but scant attention, as if some self-imposed censorship were at work. For instance:

> Questioner: Why do you choose to propagate this system in foreign countries rather than in India?
>
> Maharishi: For India I went out! (laughter)[150]

Over the following months Maharishi curbed his desire to roam in order to catch up with paperwork. A renewed effort to complete his commentary on the *Bhagavad-Gita* took up much of his time until March 1964, when he was invited to appear at a three-day conference on *yoga*, in Calcutta, under the banner of the All-India Yogic Sammelan. The conference provided an invaluable chance for Maharishi to test his new interpretations of old and familiar teachings, for attending the conference were teachers from a diversity of traditions representing a wide range of philosophies and spiritual practices. Perhaps it was at just such individuals that Maharishi's commentary on the *Gita* was aimed, for after all, at this time precious few Westerners had even heard of the book.

In late May 1964, the news of the death of India's Prime Minister, Jawaharlal Nehru, provoked Maharishi to urge his followers to observe a meditation week in memory of this celebrated leader. Throughout the country, the days became marked by group meditations at centres of the Spiritual Regeneration Movement. Devotion to Nehru's memory was taken a step further when it was decided to dedicate a 'temple of peace' to him in Bangalore, India.

The organizers of the Norwegian summer Meditation Guides' course no doubt wondered whether events in India would again conspire to rob them of the presence of Maharishi. Their fears were confirmed when again they were requested to go ahead without him. However, in the event, he joined them after the first week of the course, but since the course was but a short one, it was just a matter of days before Maharishi was off again.

The 'movement' in London had its backbone in long-standing meditators such as Marjorie Gill, Henry Nyburg, Jemima Pitman and Vincent Snell, a surgeon. It is said of Vincent that he had a reputation for being somewhat volatile, but after learning to meditate he claimed the temperament of his colleagues improved immensely! Maharishi entrusted the work of running the organization in Great Britain to Vincent and with the assistance of Maharishi's devotees another tour of the country was arranged. As in India the greatest barrier to success was the established order of religion. Although much of what he said had a religious flavour, the road to God that Maharishi described sounded just a little too easy to be believed. Those who had dedicated most of their lives to attempting a union with God were sceptical of his claims. Furthermore there were those who doubted that the God he spoke of was the same as the one they were searching for. In order to muster popular support for meditation, Maharishi needed to establish himself as a man whose word could be relied upon. What was desperately needed was some endorsement for his methods, preferably from someone senior in the religious establishment.

A chance to address some of these concerns came in an offer for Maharishi to appear in a televized debate alongside a representative of the clergy, the Abbot of Downside, Abbot Butler, on the aptly named 'Meeting Point', broadcast on the evening of Sunday, 5th July 1964.[151] After a brief introduction, presenter Robert Kee asked Maharishi how he had acquired his knowledge of meditation:

Maharishi: I would say a very systematic teaching of my Master in India.

Kee: Who was your master?

Maharishi: He was Jagad Guru Shankaracharya Swami Brahmananda Saraswati, a very great saint in the Himalayas, hailed by all the people.

Kee: He is a Hindu saint?

Maharishi: Yes, a Hindu saint, but what I think is the essence of every religion, is really the same – to enable every man to rise above conflicts and anxieties and sorrows and sufferings in life, and to live a peaceful and joyful and harmonious life.

During the course of the ensuing discussion, Maharishi outlined the theory behind this system of meditation, after which Kee observed:

Kee: It seems to me though, really what you are saying is that by a simple almost mechanical technique I can show you God.

Maharishi: Very right, very right, mechanical, because now we are in the mechanical age, this mechanical age – and then these mechanics are easy, because at every step of the subtlety of thought, the charm is increasing, the charm is increasing. So this increasing charm draws the mind automatically. That's why we say to enjoy the grace of God we don't have to do anything, just begin to enjoy, because it is the grace of the Almighty and Merciful.

However, in Kee's opinion, the physiological change associated with meditation – the lessened rate of breathing – could just as well be brought about by the use of drugs or hypnosis.

Kee: And I'd like to ask I think the Abbot at this point, where really he sees the religious content in all this – if at all.

Abbot: Well, I think that of course the great difficulty that the Maharishi and I would find in discussing these matters is that we both have our separate vocabularies, and they come from the different traditions in which we've been educated and grown up. But I must say that I can only sympathize enormously with what he has to tell us about the importance of the recovery of what I suppose we, at any rate, would call the contact with God, which must be a union within us, and for that very reason our heart is restless until it comes to rest in God.

On the surface at least, it seemed that the Abbot and Maharishi had nothing but respect for what the other had to say, so they proceeded to while away the time in pleasant conversation. But the presenter couldn't let this state of affairs continue for too long, as there were points yet to be raised. Kee introduced the topic of Christ's crucifixion, and on cue Maharishi revealed that in his opinion Christ had not suffered on the cross. Whilst the matter was being debated the presenter played his ace card.

Addressing the Abbot, he asked: 'Would you regard the Maharishi as a heretic?' At home, glued to their television sets, Maharishi's followers must have been shocked and alarmed at this dramatic twist in the proceedings. So, were they to turn off their sets and avoid seeing their beloved teacher tarred, feathered or worse, or hang on with grim determination and hope for the best? But they needn't have worried, for the Abbot was in a relaxed and generous mood as he responded:

I don't think I'd regard him as a heretic, because, technically speaking, a heretic to us is one who has seen the Christian light and has rejected it either wholly or in part. Now, therefore, nobody who is faithful to his own lights should be called a heretic; and I would be far from suggesting (General laughter).

This episode of Meeting Point concluded with the presenter, Robert Kee, putting forward the view that at a time when the church was in the process of self-examination, 'all religions should come together, if only to find out how much they are apart'. That Maharishi's followers were pleased with his performance was amply demonstrated by the swiftness with which they produced a full transcript of the programme and published it under the title of *The Maharishi and the Abbot.*

Two courses had been arranged for the summer of 1964 the first of which was scheduled to be held in the Austrian Alps, at Hochgurgl, commencing on 12th July. During Maharishi's stay course participants were treated to his personal account of the inception and subsequent growth of the Spiritual Regeneration Movement. Having told of his success in southern India and the consequent decision to tackle the problems of the rest of the world. He then changed tack to reveal a fundamental weakness which he believed dogged his Movement's relentless motion. The problem that so concerned him was what he referred to as 'tension in the atmosphere'; the effect of which he attributed the lapses that sometimes beset meditators. It was uncharacteristic of him to dwell upon negative issues, let alone focus on something as nebulous as 'atmosphere'. He explained:

> A hundred people are initiated, and after a month only about 25-30 are found meditating, and after six months there will be only five, then no one. Even though experiencing peace and happiness out of meditation, the atmospheric influence is such that it takes the people away from meditation.[152]

From this statement it is clear that, whilst he never lacked an audience for his message, he was increasingly concerned over the number of meditators who strayed from the path during his long absences. So, many of his audience were thus encouraged to become 'checkers', whose task it would be to ensure that fellow meditators derived sufficient satisfaction from their practice. In turn, this would give them useful experience which could be built upon should they take the plunge and enrol for teacher-training.

The topic of tension in the atmosphere had Maharishi sounding decidedly gloomy, raising the question as to what were the chances of averting another world war, which might be brought on by collective tensions? He concluded his speech with a rallying call, exhorting the faithful to busy themselves in spreading the knowledge of this meditation:

> Give this message to people in whatever way you can, but to large numbers and quickly. Then only will you be able to save our present generation and leave a better world for the future.[153]

David Fiske

There is a photo of Maharishi and Henry Nyburg taken by one of the course participants, David Fiske.

> On the very left a woman who was among other things a lion tamer and who asked Maharishi when people should have sex. I think his reply [was that] after meditating everything is better.[154]

In the summer of 1964 Count Blucher took Maharishi to see a toyshop near his German home. Maharishi particularly enjoyed the radio controlled model planes. The store's owner who had answered many questions said that, as he was so interested, the club was meeting that afternoon and he could join them. Maharishi said he would most appreciate seeing them.

So after lunch we drove there. It seemed that the object of the participants was to get the planes to climb as high as possible before their little engines ran out of fuel. Then they could glide, gradually losing altitude. Maharishi said," No, No. Make them go like this." He demonstrated with his hands he wanted a steep dive and a skim just above the ground in full throttle. I could see the fun in that, more fun than circling up and up.

David Fiske

He chummed up with one of them and discussed importing planes to India. The man offered to come and see Maharishi the next morning, a Sunday. It was all arranged. Bright and early we all met in Maharishi's room. I asked Maharishi what he wanted the planes for. He said he wanted them to hover above the meditation academy all day. They make a dreadful racket so I said it seemed a horrible idea to do this in the quiet of the Rishikesh forest. He said," the saints would come from miles around to see the planes once they heard them."

So they discussed plans and Maharishi, as he can when he gets creative and full of fun, decided he would also like radio controlled motorised ducks that could skim across a pond. I imagined him crouching behind reeds controller in hand startling visitors. It might have even gone further in extremity but I sort of tuned out of the subject. Nothing, fortunately, came of the idea.

All this was discussed with as much seriousness and as much hilarity and bouncing on his bed as he applied to anything profound, such as commenting on the Gita etc.[155]

7

—★—

THE ONE AND THE MANY

If the tendency for new meditators to become tardy in their practice had begun to worry Maharishi, it had not prevented him from rewarding loyal practitioners. He achieved this with the introduction of 'advanced techniques'; given to those who were steady in their meditation. The advanced techniques were dubbed 'fertilizers', subtle additions to the existing method. Since the techniques were available only from Maharishi himself, those desirous of his company were given *carte blanche* to seek him out. A less than desirable spin-off from this situation was the inequality it created amongst his followers for possession of these 'fertilizers' distinguished the supposedly advanced adept from the ordinary meditator and thus created a situation where a sense of incompleteness might arise in someone who had previously experienced no such dissatisfaction. Nevertheless Maharishi continued to offer advanced techniques and there was no shortage of takers.

Following the courses in Austria Maharishi returned to Canada and the USA, stopping off in Scandinavia en route. In addition to his normal quota of lecture dates he dusted off the *Gita* project and seriously contemplated the formulation of as many as two-dozen commentaries, aimed at people in different states of consciousness. Of fundamental importance to his philosophy was the concept of differing states of consciousness. And in addition to the basic divisions - waking, dreaming and deep sleep – he declared the existence of a fourth state, known as 'pure consciousness, which he described as 'transcendental' to or 'going beyond' the other three states. By cultivating this state of pure consciousness, by going beyond the thought process, the meditator is then readied and steadied to arrive at the Absolute, the Being, or in religious terminology, God. And what Maharishi was teaching was that by the regular practice of his system of meditation, the nature of the practitioner would become sufficiently infused with Being to give rise to a fifth state of consciousness, which he termed 'cosmic consciousness'. In this cosmic consciousness, an awareness of Being is said to be maintained even after meditation and during one's everyday life. The promise of this fifth state is the promise of bliss as an all-time reality. A sixth state, termed 'God consciousness' is also postulated.

The more Maharishi talked of different states of awareness, the greater became his followers' yearning for them, and understandably, since Maharishi described these states, they assumed the lived an exulted existence. Believing that he was speaking from a high platform of consciousness, it was difficult for his audience to doubt his authority on even the most mundane of issues. Furthermore, his audience delighted in his unpredictability, his unexpected inspirations, as for instance the picnic he arranged at Big Bear Lake in deep snow.

Maharishi's interpretations of the *Bhagavad-Gita* inevitably gave rise to discussions on Indian philosophy and its inherent belief in *karma*, the allegedly inescapable law of cause and effect, which states that one reaps the consequences of one's own actions or inactivity. Maharishi likened this process to writing a letter and eventually receiving a response. Whilst he was addressing an audience in Los Angeles he gave another example of the process of *karma*, which was that apparently, of the few hundred initiated there, many had lapsed in their practice, but he stated that was their *karma*, their loss. But for those who were steady and had attended the meeting he had a reward.

> For those who persevere, when the leaves begin to appear, we add something to the soil, around the root. When the buds begin to show, we add something more.[156]

Maharishi was of course referring to the newly introduced advanced techniques or 'fertilizers'. The substitution of the word 'we' in the place of 'I' was used a great deal, both by Maharishi and his followers, and in some circumstances, such as teaching meditation, it sounded very appropriate, as in: 'When we meditate, we experience the finer phases of a thought'.

Maharishi had often made it clear to his students that the great distinction between man and other creatures was in man's free will. Early in December 1964, whilst still with the Olsons, the topic of animal behaviour reared its head again. He now reinforced this idea by stating his conviction that animals are incapable of producing pollution. He had much to say about the inordinately complex field of *karma,* and set about explaining the very origin of all actions, of creation itself.

> When the time of creation comes, it is held, almost in all religions, that the great Lord wishes the creation to be, desires the creation to be. Vedas also say, 'I am

One, maybe I become many.' *Eko-ham bahu-ssyaam.* In almost all religions they say, 'In the beginning was the Word and the Word was with God.'

When God desires or in other words when it is time for creation to begin, then in that silent unbounded ocean of life a stir is created. And how is that stir created? If you take water in a big flat dish and the water is all still and then you give a push from one side, with one little jerk the whole water moves, one wave goes over the whole water, hum-m-m-m, like that. That means the first subtlest vibration starts and that is the start of creation ... From that eternal silence a hum starts and hum is called OM.[157]

Om is thus the 'word of God' and also without meaning. It is of note that phonetically, *om* is found to be remarkably similar to other words of power, such as the Christian 'Amen' and the Islamic *'Amin'*. Furthermore, the nasal 'mmmm' or half-nasal 'nnnnnn', though commonly used as a means of expression, has no literal meaning.

All this is OM, that hum, which is the first silent sound, first silent wave that starts from that silent ocean of unmanifested life.[158]

According to Maharishi, not only does creation start with the monosyllabic, primordial sound, so too do all life forms and certain matter, including the Indian scriptures, the *Vedas*. The *Vedas* is the name given to a set of four texts which some believe contain the earliest records of human thought. Study has yielded some interesting evidence that goes a long way towards corroborating this assertion. A.C. Das, in *Rg Vedic India*, (Banarsidass) claims that studies of geophysical data contained within the *Vedas* accurately describe how the north-western region of India must have appeared during an epoch formerly relegated to prehistory. Prof. Das further asserts that the *Aryan* (Sanskrit for 'Noble') people were indigenous to this area. Thus the claim, that the *Vedas* are intimately connected with the act of creation, raises questions concerning the very origins of human life. Although Professor Das distances himself from this particular aspect, he does propound a theory that the Aryans of 'Sapta Sindhu' ('Seven Rivers' - modern 'Punjab', 'Five Rivers') had a direct effect the culture of the Western world. Indeed, the Sanskrit language is accepted as the parent of a vast array of languages, not least of which is Latin. But how did India come to affect such distant regions as the area now known as Europe? According to Professor Das, those who could not bring themselves to accept the religious and social customs of Vedic India were forced to migrate, and established themselves in neighbouring countries, in Afghanistan, Iran and beyond.

Maharishi explained how the *Vedas* are something more than historical records.

The Vedas are a very basic study of the fundamentals of life. That is the reason why, through Vedic hymns, it is possible for those expert in chanting those hymns to produce certain effects here, there or there. The universe is vast, so many worlds and all that. We do something here according to Vedic rites, particular, specific chanting to produce an effect in some other world, draw the attention of those higher beings or gods living there.[159]

Vedic *mantras* are in fact verses, poetic in content and with definite meaning, whereas the *mantras* used in the meditation technique are quite different. Although a code of secrecy governs the selection of suitable *mantras*, they are chosen from a limited palette of *bij* or seed sounds. So how were *mantras* discovered, and by whom? Maharishi's quoted a popular Sanskrit phrase in order to explain how *mantras* are cognised:

> *Risha yah mantra drishtarah.* Rishi is a word that means those who contemplate. Rishis [sages] are the seers of the *mantras* and maharishis are those who apply the knowledge for the good of the world.[160]

In other words the verses of the *Vedas* are not man-made, some might say they are of supernatural origin, indeed, within Vedic literature many celestial beings are described. The beings, the angels and gods, are seen as agencies of God. To those of us unfamiliar with such beliefs, the mention of gods elicits feelings of incredulity and prejudice. In fact Vedic descriptions of divine beings are commonly dismissed by Western scholars as being the poetic and fanciful imaginings of a primitive, aboriginal people. Nevertheless, mankind has yet to dispose of the belief in supernatural beings entirely, such beliefs still persists the world over.

It should be remembered that Maharishi had been a devotee of the Shankaracharya of Jyotirmath, one of the leading lights of the Hindu faith. The word 'Hinduism', which is commonly used to describe the belief structure many in India adhere to, including those who worship according to prescribed Vedic custom, are more properly termed followers of *Sanatana Dharma,* the 'eternal law' or 'eternal duty'. So, had Maharishi been addressing fellow Indians, many of them would have been only too pleased to hear him supporting traditional beliefs, but he was in Los Angeles and was thus treading on very thin ice.

It should be remembered that he wanted to promote his system of meditation as verifiable by experience and hoped to find acceptance within the scientific community. In fact, since his arrival in the United States he had been encouraging those with a background in the sciences to produce tangible proof of its effectiveness. So, with such an agenda, was this the time to be making pronouncements about the existence of gods? True, the naming of the days of the week after gods and their planets are reminders of a belief system that existed in the past, but in the jet age, what could

Maharishi achieve by reviving beliefs in the supernatural?

Of course, the work of the Spiritual Regeneration Movement had one specific goal, that was to get the world to meditate; and no second step had been suggested. But maybe, with his talk of eternal freedom, access to Nirvana and the Kingdom of Heaven within, Maharishi hoped and believed that everything would automatically work itself out. But if this were the case, how could he possibly hope to reconcile all the populace's religious differences? Well, he simply minimized the importance of any differences, which he did with alacrity; by likening the *Vedas* to a mango tree, and describing the various religions of the world as just like branches of the tree. Having delivered this graphic analogy he then placed meditation at the base, as the supplier of nutrition for the whole tree whilst claiming that meditation is not antagonistic to any religion but by its practice the truth of all the great scriptures can be revealed.

After expounding his belief that The Creation is the emanation of a divine 'hum', Maharishi then turned his .attention to society and its divisions. In India the division of labour is often determined by birth, with those of particular families performing specific types of work. This division by *varna* (caste) is attributed to the progenitor of the human race, whom the Hindus know as Manu. It might be presumed that Maharishi, being a well-travelled man, would have shied away from such extreme orthodox views about caste, after all, even in India there was a clamour for the removal of these restraints. But his statements on this sensitive and contentious subject were both assertive and unequivocal. The following is just one example:

> It is a very fine scientific discrimination of human values so that each man is allowed to have the maximum spiritual development and thereby the whole society is allowed to have the maximum in a combined manner.[161]

So, far from trying to soften or remove the distinctions that preordain the course of individual lives that prenatally decide that someone will be a peasant or a priest, a pauper or a prince, Maharishi endorsed the continuance of caste-consciousness. But was he not aware that educated people were generally opposed to such elitist values and were replacing them with altogether more liberal attitudes, as evidenced by the prevailing attitude that anyone might aspire to be the President of the United States. Many notions of class, and other divisive mechanisms, were being abandoned, and a new order was emerging where everyone could aspire to anything. Employees found themselves on familiar first-name terms with their employers; even the President and his wife were addressed in this way. It is therefore difficult to imagine that anyone would wish to establish a caste system similar to that practised in India. But then, Maharishi was something of an enigma, and therefore an exception. But the philosophy he espoused was essentially his own and was therefore separate from the teaching of the meditation technique. Therefore each new initiate was totally free to accept or reject Maharishi's worldviews. He had not created a club or society which required repeated attendance to derive the benefits of membership. The meditation was a voluntary activity, so it left the initiate free to continue his or her life outside the framework of the Movement. Largely speaking, only those who wanted to increase their understanding of his ideas, or who were simply desirous of his company, had reason to attend his follow-up meetings. Meditation was definitely gaining popularity, but it is hard to understand why Maharishi expected to be able to estimate the numbers of his followers by attendances at his meetings, since the technique of meditation he taught did not depend on any future contact with him for further guidance. It was therefore impossible to monitor the number of regular practitioners with any accuracy. In any event, rather than reformulate his relationship with his students and followers he chose instead to pursue a policy of reaching out to the maximum amount of potential initiates.

When the time came to again leave Los Angeles, he put in appearances in San Francisco and Santa Barbara before crossing to New York where, on 19th December 1964, he had the good fortune to meet the Secretary General of the United Nations, Mr U Thant. As has been noted, the cultivation of the powerful, rich and influential was a significant part of Maharishi's *modus operandi*. In *The Science of Being and Art of Living*, he had observed:

> If there is a fort, and the whole territory belongs to it, it is wise to go straight to the fort and capture it. Having captured the fort, all that is in the surrounding territory will naturally be possessed.[162]

This imagery evokes the mentality of a *Kshatriya*, the caste traditionally responsible for supplying warriors. Perhaps somewhere in Maharishi's ancestry there were military strategists? Uncle Raj thought his nephew to be beyond caste:

> Let me tell you, Maharishi is so spiritually evolved that he is raised above the worldly. He is free from bondage to caste and everything in the world.[163]

After his meeting with U Thant, Maharishi rejoined his followers, first on a course in Germany, then on another in Britain. In Germany, at BadMergetheim, a new wing of his Movement was unfolding. The new division was formed with a view to aiding the recruitment of young people and was therefore named the Students' International Meditation Society (SIMS). This gave Maharishi three principal organizations SIMS, the intellectually inclined International Meditation Society (IMS), and the original Spiritual Regeneration Movement (SRM).

By now, roughly seven years had elapsed since Maharishi announced his intention to spiritually regenerate the world. His efforts had brought the idea of meditation to a very wide audience, and of those who had enrolled for instruction, many proclaimed its benefits. Some reported a greater feeling of awareness leading to decreased anxiety; and some thought they experienced an improvement in memory. The strength of Maharishi's sales pitch still lay in promises of higher states of consciousness; any perceived benefit of meditation was hungrily seized upon and quickly worked into the Movement's propaganda machine.

Whilst waiting for Nirvana to become more than a fleeting experience, many dedicated followers organized themselves into local groups under national umbrellas. To keep everyone informed of the Movement's progress, newsletters were produced, giving details of forthcoming meetings and residential courses. Meetings involved listening to tapes of Maharishi's lectures, group meditations and occasionally a group *puja.* Weekend courses were intended to give initiates the opportunity to extend periods of meditation which, it was suggested, would accelerate their spiritual progress. Meditators came from diverse backgrounds, but the majority were from the white middle classes and many had no previous interest in or involvement with spiritual organizations. Those who had been with other teachers attempted to extricate themselves from their former beliefs, for Maharishi laid great emphasis on the fact that different techniques should not be mixed.

The tape recordings that were played at meetings at that time ranged from general spiritual topics like harmony, purity and fulfilment, to the theory of *karma* and practical dissertations on the subject of meditation, and some tapes were also used to check initiates' meditation. Every effort was made to maximize resources, to create an ideal atmosphere in which to learn and practise meditation,

Rightly or wrongly, meditators tended to ape Maharishi's habits, even down to his patterns of speech. But his example could not always provide answers to his devotees' problems. There were practical issues such as what to do about diet – were there certain foods that should be avoided? Maharishi answered them patiently, counselling them not to make any sudden changes in their lives and to avoid those things which resulted in any dulling of their meditations.

Some wanted to know whether they ought to follow his lead and abstain from alcohol and cigarettes. He had made passing references to these substances, advising those who derived financial gain from them to seriously consider making donations to charity. On smoking he had more specific advice:

If one smokes it is very difficult to quit smoking, but very easy to gain God consciousness and thereby not feel for smoking if smoking is bad. It is much simpler to attain God consciousness, much more difficult to go the righteous way.[164]

Importantly, he was suggesting that habits such as smoking are not enough to debar one from the attainment of higher states of consciousness, but he did not offer guidance as to what activities might best be avoided. So whilst Maharishi appeared very relaxed about his followers' lifestyles, they were left in a quandary about how best to spend their non-meditation time.

Many considered visiting Maharishi at his Academy of Meditation in India in order to delve deeper into the mysteries of meditation. Meditators from the world were attracted to studying the Academy which, in addition to offering instruction in teacher-training, also promoted custom-made courses for businessmen, ostensibly both to increase alertness and to improve performance levels. Situated close to the crystal clear waters of the River Ganges near the market town of Rishikesh, Shankaracharya Nagar had arisen out of a forested hillock amidst a vast swathe of verdant jungle. In truth, anyone incapable of finding tranquillity in this beauty spot, whether they practised meditation or not, was unlikely to find peace of mind anywhere.

When time permitted, Maharishi continued his work on his commentary on the *Bhagavad Gita*. Until it was completed, those wanting to read about his philosophy had to content themselves with his *Science of Being and Art of Living*, which was going into its second edition. As is frequently the case subsequent rereading of a work brings with it a desire to make additions and corrections. Since his words had not been etched in stone, Maharishi felt free to modify certain statements and generally to revise his terminology. Interestingly, the word 'Deep' was dropped from the term 'Transcendental Deep Meditation' and noteworthy is that the list of those who had helped in the book's preparation was cut. Maharishi was particularly careful to purge the work of any expressions which might lead readers to associate the meditation he taught with the philosophies of others. This he did in an attempt to distance himself from other practices, such as concentration, contemplation, self-remembrance, surrender and a whole host of other practices. In his bid to make crystal clear the view that meditation does not require effort, he stressed the futility of cultivating a mood of peacefulness on the level of the mind. In fact it is hard to find a single tradition with which he would ally himself, why the Tibetan Buddhism received short shrift.

Questioner: Are you the same school of thought of *yoga* as Milarepa that Evans-Wentz wrote about?
Maharishi: I haven't heard his name.
Questioner: A Tibetan.
Maharishi: Oh Tibet is far-fetched. All the Tibetan ideologies that you hear, they don't belong to this age.[165]

On Tuesday, 12th January 1965, in the comfort of Henry Nyburg's country home, Maharishi wrote part of the preface to his uncompleted commentary on the *Bhagavad-Gita* sharing his thoughts on this subject of alternative systems of self-unfoldment, remarking:

> Thus we find that all fields of religion and philosophy have been misunderstood and wrongly interpreted for many centuries past.[166]

But what of the Indian traditions of *yoga*? Surely others know the method of meditation he was teaching?

> You should also know that there are thousands of people all over the world who are aware of thousands of *mantras* written in India by writers of many books. Do not go by what they say about the *mantras* or about the meditation propagated by the Spiritual Regeneration Movement in different parts of the world ...[167]

Quite why Maharishi took up this position is hard to understand.

Let us consider the effect of all this on his followers. Having heard how easy it was to unlock the 'Kingdom of Heaven' within, they would be looking for signs of success. Having been made to understand that they would be wasting their time trying to cast off bad habits, and having been alerted to the dangers of 'mood making' (affecting an air of spirituality), they would need to see signs that his method worked for them. Since so many had already sung the glories of Maharishi's meditation, any inability to derive benefits would inevitably be construed as personal failure. A very real danger for those under pressure to succeed in this 'simple and easy' method was that they might be tempted to indulge in false eulogies in an attempt to hide their supposed inadequacy, which was something the world did not need.

It was natural that people should be cautious about Maharishi's claims; after all, nobody wanted to find themselves misled. His oft stated claim that his technique required no faith to make it work was not enough to convince the cynics, therefore, clear indicators of the real physiological value of his methods were sought. Scientific study into the practice of meditation was already underway; the first experiments involving the measurement of light emission from meditating subjects, had started the ball rolling. Those motivated by faith and spiritual convictions felt there was no need to convince unbelievers, but they kept their peace most loyally.

8

---★---

FLOWER POWER

Maharishi's outward appearance easily fulfilled people's expectations of a sage from the Himalayas, and the passage of the years only enhanced his image. Gone was the youthful countenance, his oiled jet-black locks had lost their spring and were fast becoming shot with streaks of silver. The first significant patch of grey facial hair had already begun to spread around and about his mouth. In fact he was beginning to look ancient, and this image served him well, since people were better able accept the teachings believing him to be of some age and to have spent many long years in study and quiet contemplation. The ability to remain fresh, calm and patient, yet retain a lively sense of humour, was rare. Presumably he had developed these traits in the decade and more he spent with his Master and the time he spent in silence at Uttar Kashi. Why therefore was he promising immediate success to his students?

> Questioner: You have been studying all your life, how can we possibly learn in a matter of so many minutes?

> Maharishi: I have not learned it in many years. I got it through the Grace of my Master.[168]

This response from Maharishi raises the question of how he actually gained this 'grace'. How much was due to his devotion and surrender to his Master achieved, and how much was the practice of meditation a factor in his progress? And, since his Master, Swami Brahmananda, was no longer alive, was it possible for his disciple, to confer this Grace?

The memory of the old Shankaracharya appears to have still burning strongly in the hearts of his devotees, and in 1965 came the publication, in Hindi, of his biography, compiled from *ashram* newsletters by his devotee Rameshwar Tiwari. Much of this work was in autobiographical, since the Shankaracharya had been eager to teach by example and would use instances from his life experiences to illustrate his spiritual discourses. The publication, *Shri Jyotishhpeethoddharak,* the Hindi story of the life of

Shankaracharya Swami Brahmananda Saraswati, came complete with various colour plates, including an artist's impression of Adi Shankara, a photograph of the aged and white-haired Swami Krishnanand, two of Shri Brahmananda and one of his successor, Swami Shantanand. Perhaps by coincidence, perhaps by design, Maharishi himself had also decided to publish an account of his master. In a small slim volume entitled *Love and God*, he offered versions of his two poems of the same names and a piece entitled 'Our Guiding Light', a tribute to his late master. Of great interest is his description of the process by which his master as a young *chela* had, through the aid of his *guru*, Swami Krishnanand, found enlightenment.

> To that realized soul, the young ascetic surrendered himself for being initiated into the mysterious realms of the spirit, whose key practices are attainable not from books and treatises, but only from perfect spiritual masters, who silently pass these top-secret practices from heart to heart.
>
> After some time, with the permission and order of his master he entered a cave at Uttar-Kashi with a resolve not to come out before he had realized the Light Supreme. His desire to attain the Highest knowledge was not merely an ideal wish or intention; it was a mighty, overpowering determination that burned like fire in his heart. It permeated every particle of his being and bade him not to rest or stop before the complete realization of the Bliss Eternal.
>
> Soon he arrived at the Heatless Smokeless Effulgent of the Self and realized the Divine Truth, the Cosmic Consciousness, the Ultimate Supreme Reality, Sat Chit Anandam, the Nirvana.[169]

Having attained this blessed state, what did Swami Brahmananda, as a young truth-seeker, do? Apparently, the answer lay in his destiny, for as Maharishi disclosed, 'his hour of nativity claimed him for the recluse order …'[170]

Though Maharishi was working on a commentary of the entire 24 chapters of the *Bhagavad Gita,* the initial publication was limited to just the first three chapters in which there are verses referring to a philosophy or method, aimed at gaining liberation. In the second chapter, whilst offering counsel to his friend Arjuna, Krishna postulates the existence of a state of existence beyond the reach of worldly energies, a state of purity and self-possession, a condition called *yoga* (union or completeness), which Krishna explains is a state of existence from which action can be undertaken in complete freedom. He thus advises Arjuna:

योगस्थः कुरु कर्माणि

yogastah kuru karmani

Established in *yoga*, perform action

In recent years a new order had begun to make itself felt within Western society. In the wake of a call for greater attention by their children, many adults began to re-examine their outlook on life. This reappraisal resulted in a gradual shift in the *status quo*, along with the coining of a new word, 'teenager'. Youngsters were demanding greater involvement in decision-making about education, choice of employment and above all their recreation time. After meeting with a certain measure of success, some took their newfound freedom yet further, feeling free to challenge inherited beliefs. Religion, which for so long had been largely responsible for dictating moral and social attitudes, could no longer demand unquestioning allegiance. For those who came to doubt and in turn reject the pre-digested truths of orthodox religion, the evaluation of right or wrong was becoming simply a matter of personal preference. Without the moral restrictions and injunctions imposed by religion, there was very little to stop the newly 'liberated' from gorging themselves upon forbidden fruits. Each successive year saw an increase of pleasure seeking, on a grand scale, and this was by no means limited to the younger generation. One consequence of this situation was a pronounced increase in interest in sense gratification.

In America black musicians had created a stir by developing a compulsive and exciting new dance music which they called rock 'n' roll. The outrageous and extrovert antics of its exponents, coupled with the music's sexually explicit lyrical content, had caused an uproar among the self-appointed guardians of public decency, who sought to restrict its performance. But there was no shortage of white musicians willing to ape the style, the most able of whom was Elvis Presley. Through radio broadcasts, the music of Elvis and other rock 'n' roll artistes reached the shores of Great Britain, causing a lot of teenagers to try their hand at the new craze. In next to no time, the youth market became saturated by groups of young musicians who, whilst they were in possession of no more than a rudimentary command of their instruments, were intent on success. Of these, The Beatles were to prove by far the most popular.

Maharishi acknowledged the youth revolution by offering young people their own separate organization, the SIMS, run by his trusted assistant, Jerome Jarvis. With his dark suit and conventional hairstyle Jarvis looked to be anything but a typical rock 'n' roll teenager, but since it was assumed that only the more serious types would be drawn to meditation, his appearance did not seem inappropriate.

The teenage craze for instant enjoyment did not confine itself to music, alcohol and sex, but found increased momentum in the ready availability of mood altering drugs. In their search for sensation and excitement teenagers were increasingly turning to stimulants, especially the so-called pep pills, which enabled partygoers to forgo sleep and stay 'high' all night long. In addition to artificial stimulants like amphetamines and barbiturates, some sought out marijuana, and its resin derivative, cannabis or hashish. With the use of these drugs, unusual experiences of altered states of awareness became fairly freely available. In time, some of the more studious drug-takers began to seek information on those cultures where drug-taking was prevalent. They found particular satisfaction in reading certain Eastern scriptures, particularly those which contain descriptions of altered states of consciousness. An increased interest in South American culture resulted from the discovery that it possessed knowledge of extremely powerful mind-altering drugs. By the ingestion of a certain cactus known as peyote, a state of otherworldliness was brought about, and although extremely unpleasant side effects, such as nausea and vomiting, are attendant hazards of such experimentation, for the serious experimenters this proved no great deterrent.

Whilst researching the circulatory problems of pregnant women, in 1938 by an Austrian chemist called Albert Hofmann undertook a study of fungi, which produced an unforeseen effect, the isolation of an acid known as Lysergic acid diethylamide or LSD. It is said that in 1943 Hoffmann accidentally touched the acid and through its absorption into his skin found that his perception of reality became greatly changed. He found the experience overwhelming. By the early sixties official studies into the effects of LSD resulted in a certain amount of the substance 'disappearing'; and before very long the drug was being experimented with by academics and their friends; the youth of America were interested in taking LSD trips. Those hungry for greater sensory experiences had found in it the active ingredients of the peyote without the nausea. LSD spread like wildfire and its users evaded apprehension as it had yet to be made illegal.

Some ardent users of the drug claimed that they encountered profound experiences whilst 'tripping' on the drug, making some wonder whether a direct path to enlightenment had been discovered. In their pursuit of greater happiness they had discovered drugs, which in turn stimulated them to question the very nature and existence of reality. Those who identified as users of LSD were termed 'acid heads', hedonists in search of a constant high, many of whom congregated together, sometimes living communally. The first outward signs of this phenomenon were identified in the city of San Francisco and to some extent spread down the Californian coast, which gave rise to 'flower power'. The 'flower children' or 'hippies' believed in free expression, which became evident in their individualistic, and frequently bizarre, clothing and their preference for wearing their hair long.

Maharishi, with his long hair, his obsession with flowers and his unusual garb, might well have been taken for the hippies' founding father. Indeed, it was not unusual for people to become confused about his image; he had on occasion even been mistaken for a flower-seller! But the hippies, with their predilection for drugs and the attendant quest for mysticism, had already found themselves a mystic '*guru*' – the writer, Aldous Huxley, who in had written of his experiences experimenting with the drug Mescaline (a derivative of peyote). A flavour of his writing is to be found in this extract:

> I took my pill at eleven. An hour and a half later I was sitting in my study, looking intently at a small glass vase. The vase contained only three flowers – full-blown Belle of Portugal rose, shell pink with a hint at every petal's base of a hotter, flamier hue; a large magenta and cream-coloured carnation; and, pale purple at the end of its broken stalk, the bold heraldic blossom of an iris. Fortuitous and provisional, the little nosegay broke all the rules of traditional good taste. At breakfast that morning I had been struck by the lively dissonance of its colours. But that was no longer the point. I was not looking now at an unusual flower arrangement. I was seeing what Adam had seen on the morning of his creation -the miracle, moment by moment, of naked existence.[171]

And Huxley was no drug-crazed hippie but a respected writer, and had more than a passing acquaintance with Indian techniques of meditation, concentration and contemplation. Huxley wrote in *The Doors of Perception*.

> My eyes travelled from the rose to the carnation, and from that feathery incandescence to the smooth scrolls of sentient amethyst which were the iris. The Beatific Vision, *Sat Chit Ananda*, Being-Awareness-Bliss – for the first time I understood, not on the verbal level, not by inchoate hints or at a distance, but precisely and completely what those prodigious syllables referred to.[172]

Huxley had written a second book on the experiences he gained through the use of Mescaline, entitled *Heaven and Hell*. The title was quickly used by the media to describe the scope of the altered states of consciousness which LSD supposedly induced.

Less than enamoured with the prospect of further brushes with hell, some LSD users set about achieving the experience of heaven alone, and the state of endless heavenly bliss they sought was precisely what Maharishi appeared to be offering. Maharishi therefore attracted many who saw a kinship between his teaching and their perception of eastern mysticism, of a culture where pleasure, drug-taking and the search for God all coexisted happily together. Since Maharishi made no explicit attempt to exclude drug users, the assumption was that they were welcome to join this meditation movement. It is likely that had Maharishi chosen to abandon the brightly coloured blooms he carried and taken on the appearance of his conservatively dressed associates, these new followers, being very image conscious and not a little suspicious of 'straights', might well have looked elsewhere for inspiration.

A fundamental ingredient in the hippie lifestyle was music, either to listen to or to play. Hippies were quick to latch on to Indian music, observing that it offered a ready-made and exotic aural tapestry to augment their experimentation with drugs. Amongst the available records of Indian artistes were those by sitarist Ravi Shankar, who shortened traditional *ragas* in order to accommodate the expectations of Western audiences. Soon Indian music was found filtering though to the mainstream of popular culture by way of incidental inclusion in pop songs. Jazz musicians, too, saw great promise in its use of melody as a vehicle for unlimited extemporization and one such musician, a flautist by the name of Paul Horn, went so far as to work with artists chosen by Ravi Shankar to produce some exceptional and inspired music. Working with Indian musicians had alerted Horn to other aspects of Indian culture, namely its philosophy and its *yoga* teachings. In response to this new stimulus, he became interested in the idea of learning to meditate and sought out a *mantra* from the SRM.

Another musician with $35 to spare was drummer John Densmore, who reasoned that a less hazardous path to peace than that offered by psychedelics might be the use of meditation. In the spring of 1965 he set off to find out more.

> Meditation sounded a less shattering route. We went to some preliminary meetings in LA's Wiltshire district and listened to a mellow man in a business suit. His name was Jerry Jarvis, and his eyes seemed to express a remarkable inner contentment.[126]

Densmore decided to take the plunge.

> They asked us to bring flowers, fruit and a white handkerchief. We would each receive an individual *mantra*, an Indian Sanskrit word that we were supposed to repeat mentally. Our teachers instructed us not to speak it out loud or write it down; it would lose its power if we did.[127]

He recounts how he became a little dizzy during his first experience of meditation and attended the second meeting eager to try and rectify the problem. Jerry Jarvis was again in charge.

> He talked about how the mind's nature was to have one thought after another. Mind-chatter. He said that the *mantra* was a vehicle to take a thought from the surface of our mind down to the source of thought below. Still, not too much happened when I meditated. There were no colored lights or explosions. Though I was expecting the same quick, startling effect as my LSD experiences ...[173]

But although he was initially disappointed, he did not complain. Rationalizing the situation he realized that it would probably be some time before he gained the full benefits of the practice and so decided to persevere. But one of his fellow meditators was not taking it so easily.

> During the follow-up meeting, a blond guy with a Japanese girlfriend by his side kept raising his hand and saying to Jarvis, 'No bliss, no bliss!'
>
> It was very embarrassing. He acted as if he had been ripped off. I think he expected to become Buddha on the first day. We had all hoped it wouldn't take too long, but he was especially impatient.
>
> After the meeting the same guy came up to me and said, 'I hear you're a drummer. Want to put a band together?'[174]

Soon after this event, a group of youngsters with interests in pleasure-seeking, music, 'mind expansion' and meditation, sprang up on the Los Angeles 'scene'. They called themselves The Doors after Aldous Huxley's book *The Doors of Perception* and John Densmore and the heckler from Densmore's meditation group, Ray Manzarek, were members. The Doors soon became one of the 'house bands' of the new culture, whose favourite buzzwords, 'bliss' and 'cosmic' were quickly adopted by the pop generation. Maharishi's directions on to how to meditate found their way into the group's songs: phrases like 'take it easy' and 'take it as it comes'. Maharishi and his brand of Eastern promise were daily gaining increased popularity amongst the youth market.

In 1966 Maharishi was still hard at work on his mission to spiritually regenerate mankind, and still travelling the world, lecturing. And in his spare time he still continued work on the unfinished *Gita* project. But nothing was going to keep him from the Kumbh Mela in Allahabad, India, a festival held only once every twelve years, is a rare opportunity for *sadhus*, *swamis* and other holy men and women to gather together. For the sake of meditators, Maharishi attempted to explain the difference between the thinking of the *sannyasi* (recluse) and the householder.

> *Sannyasis* don't have that advantage of full values of life, they negate the physical aspect of life. The whole basis of the recluse life is that engaged in the worldly affairs it is not possible to gain perfection in life.

> But that we don't accept from the SRM platform. It is not a method, it is a wrong understanding of life, because... see, the method of dyeing the cloth fast is, dip it in the colour and put it to the sun. Let it fade away to the extent it could fade away. Put it in the colour and put it to the sun. So putting to the sun is also a part of dyeing it fast. If you don't let the colour fade away, then you may think that it is dyed, but it may fade away any time you come out in the sun.

> So to be sure that the colour is fast you have to put in the colour and put it to the sun. The mind gaining the transcendental state of Being during meditation, coming out and acting in the world. The only difference in the life of a

householder and a *sannyasi* is that the householder indulges in the field of activity on the level of the senses. The *sannyasi* indulges in the mental activity. Activity has to be undertaken so that the transcendental state of consciousness maybe allowed to fade away in the field of activity.

Only the *sannyasi* takes a mental activity–he thinks and thinks and thinks. Thinks of the world in terms of *'nitya'* [meaning 'eternal' and 'unchanging']. He keeps on manipulating his mind that all that what is seen is just nothing like a mirage. It is like a dream which has no substance to it. During the dream it seems to be true, but later on it doesn't exist. So the world is like a dream, it is like a mirage, it doesn't exist, it exists only in the mind. All such thoughts of manipulations. It is a very hard exercise to see a tree and to see it completely as nothing [laughter]. It is like the hard activity of the householder, running in the market and getting tired and getting to sleep. That great physical activity of the householder is just like the tremendous mental activity of a *sannyasi*, who seeing the world as so concrete, he likes not to see it as anything concrete.

The thing is that just as the householder is advised to go into the market and dig deep this thing and do the physical labour and earn some thing and support the family–a great responsibility, a great pressure of activity. This pressure of activity is necessary after gaining transcendental consciousness during meditation in the morning. This is what Lord Krishna said *'yogastah kuru karmani'*. Bring the mind to the Self, that is *'yogastah'*, be a *yogi* and then come out to act. In the field of action there is a difference between the householder and the *sannyasi*. The householder indulges in the vigorous activity on the sensory level, *sannyasi* enters into the vigorous activity on the mental level. That is the difference.

That is his market, thinking and thinking. It is a strenuous exercise to think the concrete dream in terms of complete evanescence and not existing, a dream and just a thought and all, all sorts of vigorous mental activity.[175]

Writer Ved Mehta describes the scene at the Kumbh:

By the camp fires, beneath the open sky, were huddles of squatting *sadhus* and milling or motionless crowds of pilgrims. Now and again, I passed an elephant, festooned with flower garlands and embroidered rugs. All along the way, beggars held out their bowls, into which pilgrims dropped coins or grain. There were naked *sadhus* and *sadhus* opulently robed. There were *sadhus* wearing *dhotis* and marigolds, with horizontal stripes of ash on their foreheads. There were *sadhus* with ash-smeared naked bodies, offering *ghi, jaggery* and *sesamum* to a sacrificial fire that crackled in a brazier, and chanting *'Hare Ram. Hare Krishna. Hare Om.'*[176]

Amongst the endless sea of pilgrims attending the *mela* were exponents of the many sects, cults and disciplines comprising modern Hinduism. In addition to the smoke spiralling up from the campfires and ritual fires was that of the *ganja* (marijuana), used by many *sadhus* in their quest for a taste of heaven. Some pilgrims were camped beneath the stars whilst others sought the comparative comfort of a tent colony. Mehta met many *swamis*, saints and *yogis*, and he also met a follower of Maharishi.

> A man in a brown lounge suit and with a vermillion mark on his forehead comes up to me. He tells me his name and continues, in English, 'I am America-returned. I am MA and PhD in public administration from the States. Guruji has fifty-four *chelas* from distant foreign lands here at Kumbha. I myself am going to be initiated on this Amavasya, when Guruji will recite some *mantras* to me by the side of Mother Ganga, and I will recite them back. I met the Guruji only a month ago. After I set eyes on Guruji, I left my five children to follow him.'[177]

Western followers of Maharishi directed Mehta to speak directly with Maharishi, who he found him in his tent, surrounded by a group of disciples and no less than three tape recorders. Ved Mehta asked the silk-robed teacher about his philosophies, and after ascertaining the identity of the newcomer, he explained:

> All I teach is a simple method of meditation. We are all conscious on a mundane level, but beneath that consciousness, in each one of us, there is an ocean vaster than any in the world. It's there that most new thoughts originate. The bridge between the mundane level of consciousness and the ocean is meditation – not reading, because if you read you can have only second-hand thoughts.[178]

Maharishi further explained that the test of this meditation was in its utility, indicating that a result of its practice was increased material welfare and achievement. Emphasizing this point, that this meditation technique had a place in a world far beyond the *mela*, he added:

> As I said when addressing a meeting in the Albert Hall, in London, my technique does not involve withdrawal from normal material life. It enhances the material values of life by the inner spiritual light. My method is, in my London example, 'like the inner juice of the orange, which can be enjoyed without destroying the outer beauty of the fruit. This is done simply by pricking the orange with a pin again and again, and extracting the juice little by little, so that the inner juice is drawn out on the surface, and both are enjoyed simultaneously.'[179]

In spite of spending several hours with Maharishi, Ved Mehta claims he came out feeling dissatisfied with what he had heard. It was not so much the message of meditation that bothered him, but the attitude Maharishi adopted whilst speaking to his audience. According to Mehta the 'Guruji', in addition to being unreasonably dismissive of questions, also ridiculed the questioners. Perhaps this was true, and perhaps Mr Mehta himself had had a particularly rough ride. Rather than hearing stories of a cure-all formula, as yet unproven, he sought more tangible answers to the world's problems, and in that he represented the views of many people.

When Maharishi embarked on his seventh world tour, he returned to Europe and to North America, where he targeted university campuses in a bid to capitalize on the noticeable increase of interest in meditation amongst the young. In his lectures he would liken thoughts to bubbles rising from the depths of the mind, with meditation giving one an enhanced perception of thoughts at progressively more subtle levels. This would, he assured his audiences, enable meditators to think more clearly and more powerfully. Some students who already used this technique supported Maharishi's view, claiming they had gained an increased ability to study. When all was said and done, Maharishi was no longer particularly concerned about *why* people turned to his methods; any reason was good enough.

Towards the end of the year Maharishi set out to conquer new territories, specifically Trinidad and South America. Charlie Lutes, the head of the SRM in the United States, accompanied him on these forays. Arriving in Caracas, Maharishi was particularly happy; to friend Nancy Jackson, who had organized the South American tour, Charlie Lutes confided:

> He is radiant because he has left behind the heat, humidity, and low vibrations of Trinidad. He didn't like that place at all.[180]

The tour, on which he was billed as a famous philosopher, was relatively successful. It was arranged that he would meet some dignitaries, and his message was, on the whole, well received. But in Rio de Janeiro, he found himself being heckled by a French *yoga* instructor who ranted 'Don't listen to him! He is a fake! He is telling you nothing but lies!' When the Frenchman was finished the audience showed their disapproval, and Maharishi commented to his critic:

> You should call yourself a professor of exercise. *Yoga* means 'union'. You will never achieve union with God just by twisting the body.[181]

The tour continued with dates in Argentina, Chile, Peru and Colombia.

Of the many thousands who had so far been initiated into this technique of meditation, relatively few felt the compulsion to train to become a teacher. But amongst those who were tempted to get a little closer to Maharishi was flautist Paul Horn, who first became interested in meditation after working with sitarist Ravi Shankar. When given the opportunity to attend the Guides' course in Rishikesh, Horn fairly jumped at the chance.

> I met the Maharishi in September 1966. On his then yearly travels around the world, he came through Los Angeles to talk. He was such a beautiful man I really felt very strongly to be with him, to spend some time with him. I just

packed up and left it all behind. Unequivocally and without hesitation I can say that this was the greatest experience of my life. In the midst of relative success I was feeling empty and unfulfilled. I was at a major crossroads. The Maharishi gave me back my life. I was reborn. I became a teacher of Transcendental Meditation in April 1967 in Kashmir, India. Teaching such a beautiful technique for unfoldment and inner peace adds another dimension to my life. The balance between that and music is very rewarding.[182]

Whilst training to become one of the first twelve meditation teachers in the USA, an idea for a new musical venture offered itself to Horn. In a bid to find a balance between long periods of meditation, study and attending lectures, visits by local entertainers were arranged and soon plans were hatched for a recording session.

It just so happened that I had my flute along and joined them at Maharishi's request ... I mentioned to Maharishi my desire to make a record with these musicians and have the rest of the world hear their fine talents. Nothing more was said. Then one evening two weeks later I was called to Maharishi's room. There sitting on the floor at Maharishi's feet were the assembled musicians. He proceeded to plan an album with the insight of an experienced record producer.[183]

The result of this meeting was a recording session that resulted in the release of an album of material by World-wide Records entitled *Cosmic Consciousness*, with a colour photograph on the cover of the musicians performing before Maharishi at his houseboat on a Kashmir lake.

After this teacher-training course Maharishi embarked on what looked like being his last tour of the world. His original intent had been to give ten years to the founding of his worldwide movement, so he had only a few months left to put the last finishing touches to his handiwork. His lectures were showing no signs of any diminishing pace or energy, as he reworked and expand his teachings. An audio record, *The Seven States of Consciousness*, recorded live in Los Angeles at this time, shows him again delineating the various states of awareness accessible to those who practice Transcendental Meditation:

Those who meditate, they retire from the outside, they take their awareness from the outside and gradually go deep into the thinking process and eventually go beyond the thought. Transcend thought and then the thinking mind, the conscious mind becomes consciousness. When it goes beyond thought then it transcends thought and becomes consciousness. This consciousness is pure consciousness. The nature of this pure consciousness is bliss. It is non-changing sphere of life because we have transcended all the variable section of relative life and gone to the Absolute. This is called Being, Inner Being, Absolute Bliss consciousness.[184]

The relative order of the universe he termed the 'gross and subtle levels of creation'. He explained that the object of meditation lies in appreciating the 'subtler phases of a thought', and then in transcending thought, in order to arrive at the very source of thought.

> Transcendental Meditation is that process which has made the realization of the Absolute a scientific phenomena. Scientific phenomena means it can be explored in a very systematic manner and it is open to experience by everyone. It only needs taking our attention from the gross field of activity in the relative life to the subtle fields of activity in the relative life, eventually to the subtlest field of activity in the relative life and transcending the subtlest of the relative, we get to the Transcendental Absolute.

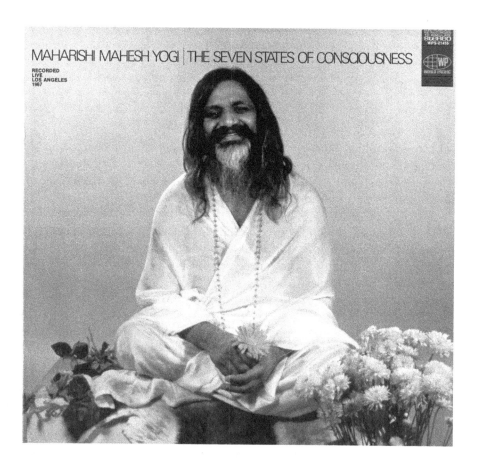

Maharishi was only too aware that other spiritual organizations used the word 'transcendental', and was quick to make fun of its alleged misapplication in the term Transcendentalism, pointing out in his lecture that 'the Transcendental field of life is that which is free from "isms"'. So he strived to establish the significance of his theory regarding the need to transcend thought in order to go beyond the realms of the waking state of consciousness. Having pointed out that this transcending would lead the meditator to discover pure consciousness, he then went on to identify other states of awareness accessible to those practising Transcendental Meditation. Apparently, in order to raise one's level of consciousness from the familiar 'waking state of consciousness', repeated contact with the Transcendental Absolute or pure consciousness is needed, and according to Maharishi, the result of such inner activity bestows 'cosmic consciousness', an enhanced mental condition with a corresponding physiological condition, brought about by the repeated lowering of the metabolic rate. This description could be applied to the sleep state, where suspension of thought and lowering of the metabolism are common occurrences; however, Maharishi refuted this notion, making the distinction that the meditator unlike the sleeper is in fact, wide-awake.

> As long as the thinking mind is experiencing a thought, so long the mind is a thinker and the thought becomes finer and finer, then the thinker becomes more and more alert in order to experience the finer thought, and then the thought becomes finer and finer, it becomes finest and when the thought drops off, the thinker remains all by himself and this is self-realization.
> What I have to do to realize myself? I have only to stop realizing things from within and see that I don't go to sleep.

To underscore his message that the condition he referred to was not a state of inertia, he added: 'How to be? Stop being active but don't become passive. This is how to be.' But whilst Maharishi's directions clearly refer only to the action of thoughts in meditation, to the less attentive it might be construed otherwise, with the result that some might believe that enlightenment was found merely by refraining from action.

Whilst Maharishi could generally talk very fluently, there was odd occasion when his delivery would be marred by an unexpected blip in the cosmic script, as in an instance during the same lecture, which found him momentarily uncertain of his facts: 'For thousands of years, maybe hundreds, self-realization has been declared to be a difficult thing.' His change of mind was quickly spotted, producing a peal of laughter from his audience. Although rare, such instances, in addition to providing necessary light relief for his students, served as reminder to Maharishi, if such was needed, that he was still human and therefore prone to faults.

Maharishi made extensive and imaginative use of colourful analogies in order to get his points across. He likened the process of meditation to visiting the bank where, having collected some cash from the bank, one would be in a better position to enjoy the market place. And he would liken the process of repeatedly targeting the state of pure consciousness to a traditional method of fabric dyeing, where cloth, once dipped in colour, is made fast by long exposure to the sun, and that by repetition of this process the colour becomes extremely fast. These and countless other analogies demonstrated a fertile creative function at work, which at times proved curiously informative.

Maharishi had set himself the task of enumerating and describing the various states of consciousness open for exploration clearly. Towards the end of this lecture, which lasted almost an hour, he explained:

> For about four years at the beginning of my Movement I was only devoted to establishing the value of the Absolute into the relative life, value of the Absolute into the relative. It's only from about the fifth or sixth year that I started to speak about the Light of the Celestial. And it's only since last year that I have started to explain about God consciousness in a systematic manner. And it's only from about this year that I have started to speak about that state of Supreme Knowledge. These things cannot be understood clearly enough to bring satisfaction on the intellectual level even without the experience. A few days of experience in Transcendental Meditation when the mind begins to retire in a very systematic manner from the gross thinking to the subtle thought to the source of thought, a few times one has known this, this march of the mind from out to inwards and a few flashes of inner pure bliss consciousness, then one is able to understand this whole philosophy of development of the realization of the self and development of self consciousness to become all-time reality and then from there glorification of cosmic consciousness into God consciousness and from there the rising to Supreme Knowledge.

Until this time, Maharishi had not talked about a seventh state of consciousness, so even meditators who were firmly established in their practice had heard nothing of this area of his thinking.

He now offered his audience his vision of a life lived in enlightenment:

> One could rise to that Supreme Knowledge beyond which there is no possibility of any more expansion of consciousness, beyond which there is no possibility of any development of life, and having risen to that most developed state of human life so that one lived that high state of life where everything is easy and one's life is fully supported by Nature, every thought will be materialized. Just, we don't do anything and enjoy everything. One should live life and enjoy life on *that* level.

9

—★—

TIME FOR A SONG

The purpose of Maharishi writing a commentary on the *Bhagavad-Gita* was presumably to win over his critics at home. It was therefore odd that he chose to write this work in English and arrange for it to be published outside India, as a commentary on another, more familiar work might have better met the needs of his Western devotees. He was asked to explain himself.

> One day a very sweet man asked me, 'Why you are writing a commentary on *Bhagavad-Gita*? What is your idea?'

Maharishi gave him this answer:

> If you hear a song of a good music sung by someone and if you have a good voice, when you are alone you'd like to imitate this song, wouldn't you? Some beautiful song heard some time and in your loneliness, if you have a good voice, you try to imitate that song and try to sing it and try to fill the whole atmosphere with that song. *Bhagavad-Gita*, it means the Song of God, the Song of Truth and the embodiment of truth, Lord Krishna, sung this Song of life and he sung the Song of Eternal Life. And in my loneliness I try to imitate or copy the rhythm of his song. Certainly I am commenting on *Bhagavad-Gita* for the joy of my own writing.[185]

Jerry Jarvis, typed up the completed commentaries of the first sixteen chapters, but in the event, Maharishi halted halfway through Chapter 17, leaving Chapter 18 untouched, but in the event, it was decided to publish only a fraction of this work.

In 1967 the SRM published Maharishi's commentary on the first six chapters of the *Bhagavad-Gita,* to a market almost wholly unfamiliar with the sacred writings of the East. A handsomely produced book, it contained two black and white photographs (one of the author and one of his 'Guru Dev'), the Sanskrit verses displayed in Devanagari text, transliteration and translation, and detailed a commentary of each verse.

In the Preface, readers were alerted to the existence of other commentaries and cautioned about them:

> Interpretations of the Bhagavad-Gita and other Indian scriptures are now so full of the idea of renunciation that they are regarded with distrust by practical men in every part of the world.[186]

In the *Bhagavad-Gita* a discourse is presented between the Lord Krishna (frequently referred to in the text as 'Keshava', the 'one with long hair'), and an archer named Arjuna, and Sanjaya, a charioteer with alleged powers of clairvoyance, clairaudience and perfect memory, witnesses their conversation. It soon becomes clear that Lord Krishna, far from being a mortal of common stock, is perceived as a superior being, insofar as he not only identifies himself with God but also wishes to be recognized as an *avataar* or godly incarnation.

The actual writing of the *Bhagavad-Gita* is attributed to an immortal sage called Veda Vyasa, who is also held to be the author of numerous other Hindu scriptures.

The Hindu concepts concerning time, reincarnation and the existence of gods take time, imagination and patience to understand, let alone accept. However, Maharishi spoke as one without doubts:

> Time is a conception to measure eternity. Indian historians base their conception of time on eternal Being; for them eternity is the basic field of time.
>
> To arrive at some conception of the eternal, the best measure will be the life-span of something that has the greatest longevity in the relative field of creation.[187]

To those educated in the West might guess that the longest life-span might be a tortoise, or a tree perhaps. But from a Hindu perspective, an altogether different answer would be forthcoming. Maharishi explains:

> This, according to the enlightened vision of Vyasa, is the Divine Mother, the Universal Mother, who is ultimately responsible for all that is, was and will be in the entire cosmos.
>
> The eternity of the eternal life of absolute Being is conceived in terms of innumerable lives of the Divine Mother, a single one of whose lives encompasses a thousand life-spans of Lord Shiva. One life of Lord Shiva equals the duration of a thousand life-spans of Lord Vishnu. One life of Lord Vishnu equals the duration of a thousand life-spans of Brahma, the Creator.[188]

According to this school of thought, measurement of time has as its fundamental units the life-spans of the principal Hindu deities, of Divine Mother and the trinity of Shiva, Vishnu and Brahma. Each life of Brahma (the god of Creation) is said to be 100 years long, and is broken into lunar months. Each day in the life of Brahma is known as a *kalpa* and is equivalent to fourteen *manus* or *manvantaras*. Each *manvantara* is equal to seventy-one *chaturyugin*, and one *chaturyugi* comprises a period of four *yugas*. These four *yugas* are not equal; *Treta-yuga* is three-quarters of *Sat-yuga*, *Dvapara-yuga* is half of *Satyuga*, and *Kali-yuga* is a quarter of *Sat-yuga*. This smallest unit, the *Kali-yuga*, is said to equal 432,000 years!

Maharishi was outspoken in his condemnation of historians who 'reject as non-history any series of events for which they fail to find a proper chronological order'.[189] Presumably he was referring both to the *Mahabharata*, from which the *Gita* is supposed to originate, and to the numerous other sacred Indian texts, which modern scholars either dismiss as myth or, at best, date within the last two millennia or so.

The mention of Hindu gods inevitably leads on to speculation about where such celestial bodies might dwell. They would presumably live in a heaven or heavens somewhere far beyond the reach of man's sensory apparatus. If this is so, it would not be unreasonable for people to hope that one day they might obtain entry to such regions, or at least to aspire to reaching planes higher than that on which they presently exist.

> When righteous people who have not been able to gain cosmic consciousness die, they enter one or other of these planes, for human life is regarded as the gateway to them all. Here life is longer and very much happier because these planes correspond to higher levels of consciousness. The highest level of consciousness is absolute Being, which has eternal life. At the other end of the scale, where purity is least, life is infinitely short.[190]

But what about those who had not yet gained the state of awareness referred to as cosmic consciousness? Do they not have a chance of this higher life? Although understandably reticent about sharing his own beliefs on the rather touchy subject of re-incarnation, he was not completely silent on the subject. In offering his alternative reading of the word 'birth', he cleverly redirected the reader's thoughts from the subject of the soul's transmigration into countless forms, back to his favourite topic of meditation:

> The Lord says: 'perfected through many births'. By this He means perfected through the continued practice of repeatedly gaining transcendental consciousness and thus being re-born to the world many, many times until cosmic consciousness is gained.[191]

Although Transcendental Meditation might be described in such terms for some people, it left the topic of the afterlife unanswered, though elsewhere, he came closer to committing himself.

> The result of being engrossed in worldly desires is that one remains in the cycle of birth and death. For the joys of the senses can never satisfy; they involve man

more and more and thus keep him in bondage. There being no chance of lasting contentment, the cycle of birth and death continues.[192]

This would suggest that the whole of humanity is caught up in a process that can only be interrupted by the loss of worldly desires, but this concept is seemingly tangential to the main thrust of Maharishi's stated philosophy, which sees no problem in man having desire so long as it finds its way to satisfaction. Perhaps he was suggesting that without the experience of transcendental consciousness, bondage to worldly desires ensues, which hampers success and in consequence leads man to repeated worldly experiences until he finally gets the message! For those who are inextricably caught up in worldly affairs, who have not seized the chance of attaining cosmic consciousness, Maharishi offered some reassurance:

> Death as such only causes a temporary pause in the process of evolution. A pause like this is no real danger to life because, with a new body taken after the pause, more rapid progress of life's evolution becomes possible. A greater danger will be something that actually retards the process of evolution.[193]

In attempting to understand the message of the *Bhagavad Gita*, one must also consider the peculiarly Indian concept of *dharma*. Although *dharma* is most often translated as 'duty', a fuller definition is needed. Maharishi, in fact, preferred to use the expression 'guiding principle'. In practical terms one could interpret *dharma* as living one's life to the best of one's abilities, being a credit to one's family and friends and of use to society as a whole. Conversely, to live a life of selfishness and greed, to be inconsiderate and heartless, or worse still, to live a life of delusion, would all be termed *adharma*. These concepts of *dharma* and *adharma* offer a basis to establish a value system, a self-imposed framework of reference in order to determine right from wrong.

The problem of defining and providing a clear moral code has always posed difficulties, and laws and rules which were held to provide absolute frameworks of reference have found themselves reviewed, amended and repealed because of their incompleteness. Could there ever be a set of laws that hold true in all situations, at all times? Maharishi offered his perspective:

> If, in the absence of any scriptural authority or tradition, a criterion of natural duty has to be found, it may be said on the basis of common sense, that an action which is necessary and does not produce any undue tension or strain in the doer and his surroundings is his natural duty.[194]

Maharishi proposed that in the technique of meditation can be found the means to live a life in harmony with all the laws of Nature. This suggestion, that by using a technique of relaxation, the practitioner of meditation might spontaneously gain the ability to perform only right action, might seem extremely far-fetched at first sight. But, when all is said and done, the idea is also very attractive since it would be wonderfully reassuring to know that one might be able always to take the right decisions and make all the right moves. But who is to say that such an ideal condition could ever be attained? Was Maharishi not in danger of offering his followers to create self-fulfilling, self-gratifying, fool's paradises for themselves? Indeed on what basis did he make this extravagant claim? Where was the evidence? The theory he advanced was that by transcending the relative states of thought, by going beyond the *gunas* (the three aspects of relative energy), one becomes free of all impurities and 'freed from duality'. In his commentary to Verse 45 of Chapter 2 of the *Bhagavad-Gita*, he pointed out what Lord Krishna's message was:

> … wants to assure Arjuna that this state will always prove right, in accordance with dharma, ever furthering the process of evolution for the good of all. Nothing wrong can possibly result from it, because that is the state of fulfilment.[195]

This facility to be able to perform only right action spontaneously would, on its own, be a tremendous incentive for anybody to take up the practice of meditation. Imagine a life free of criticism and dangers!

Of the many alluring benefits promised to those who would take up meditation that must rate especially highly, was that of access to a world of the gods, and Maharishi was offering just that, explaining that meditation is also a *yagya* (offering).

> When, through the practice of transcendental meditation, activity is realized as separate from the Self, then all of life's activity is said to have been given over as an offering to the gods. This means that activity continues in its sphere of relative life, over which the gods preside, while the Self remains in the freedom of the Absolute. This is the way to please all the gods through every activity at all times. A situation is created in which every activity automatically becomes a yagya.[196]

Maharishi's assertion that not only do higher beings or gods exist but that they can be contacted is, to say the least, quite astonishing! Who are these gods he refers to and what activities are they supposed to perform?

> They are powers governing different impulses of intelligence and energy, working out the evolution of everything in creation.[197]

If we were to accept this notion that gods do exist, then we would want to know more about their characteristics and personalities. For instance, are all or any of the gods Asian in appearance or Hindu by religion? What language do they speak and how do they get about? If all this is not already perplexing enough, there is also the question of how they can live multiple existences, as claimed by Veda Vyasa. Are they, along with the rest of creation, also involved in a cycle of transmigration from one life to another? If this is indeed the case, then the various names of the gods and goddesses are but job-titles, positions that in the fullness of time, *all* could hope to aspire to. If this is so, then the position becomes further complicated in that the lure of celestial status would, in itself, provide new snares for a mankind already caught up in too many worldly desires.

Whether Maharishi conceded it or not, his attempts to find in the verses of the *Bhagavad-Gita*, any direct reference to the *mantra* meditation he advocated, were unsuccessful. Notwithstanding this shortcoming in his work, he did provide many thought-provoking insights into Hindu thinking and much that is of interest to practitioners of his technique. However the overriding self-evident message of the *Bhagavad-Gita*, that Lord Krishna extols us to perform his worship, is all but overlooked. Perhaps Maharishi secretly acknowledged this for he wrote:

> Only when he has become himself can he properly surrender to the Great Self of the Lord. If he remains in the field of the three gunas, in the many sheaths of gross and subtle nature, then it is these sheaths that prevent direct contact with the Lord.[198]

10

—★—

THE BLESSING OF THE BEATLES

There could have been few people, including his strongest critics, who actually wanted all of Maharishi's pronouncements to be discredited. For if he was correct about nothing else, his assertion that no one really wants to suffer seems to hold true, for ironically, even those who deliberately indulge in suffering do so only in a search of greater enjoyment. But as for his claims regarding higher states of consciousness, nobody had yet appeared on television claiming to have entered into the cosmic consciousness that Maharishi spoke of. The race was now on to see which of his followers would be the first to proclaim and demonstrate the existence of these elusive states of awareness that Maharishi spoke of. Speculation as to the existence of gods and 'counting the number of angels that can dance on a pinhead' could wait, indefinitely if necessary.

Meanwhile, whilst Maharishi had been travelling the world propagating the teachings of meditation, a pop group called The Beatles had been enjoying unprecedented success, performing to sell-out audiences around the world, their records selling in ever greater quantities. The inevitable pressure of so much acclaim had pushed them to always want to better their last achievement, and in order to meet the ever-increasing expectations of their public they concentrated on their recorded material. Out of the glare of publicity that surrounded their tours they were free to indulge themselves in whatever way they felt inclined. They dabbled with new ideas as a means of finding new material and alternative directions for their music. . The public had begun to see them as spokesmen for the new generation and attached ever-greater importance to them as 'thinkers'. Experimentation with drugs opened new avenues, leading to altered states of mind, stimulating fresh ideas

The making of *Help*, in 1965, The Beatles' second feature film, though primarily intended as a showcase for their new material, also gave The Beatles a chance meeting with Indian culture. The film's lightweight plot has as its theme the story of an Indian cult in pursuit of a ring indispensable to their rites. In an effort to reconcile the actors' comic escapades with The Beatles' music, the soundtrack includes occasional passages of their songs played on Indian instruments. From then on George Harrison's appetite and interest for things Indian burgeoned. His liking of Indian music led him to try and master the sitar, under the guidance of Pandit Ravi Shankar. Through his familiarity with a wide range of 'new' sounds, George was able to make an increased contribution to The Beatles' music. He also developed an avid interest in Indian philosophy, and when given the opportunity he would devour any Indian spiritual literature he could get his hands on. In these pursuits he had the support of his wife (former model Pattie Boyd), who shared his enthusiasm for the magic of the mystical East. Mrs Harrison, who had by now discovered that marriage to a wealthy celebrity frequently left her with more than enough time for herself, on hearing of meditation was determined to find out more about it.

> **TRANSCENDENTAL   MEDITATION**   of
> Maharishi Mahesh Yogi; for further infor-
> mation regarding this technique write to
> Spiritual Regeneration Movement Founda-
> tion, 20 Grosvenor Place, London, S.W.1.
> BELgravia 8994.

In February 1967 Pattie attended a lecture on meditation at Caxton Hall in London, and subsequently went, with a female companion, to Maharishi's meditation centre in fashionable Belgravia to be initiated. Although the volunteer helpers there warmly received them, she must have sensed a certain disapproval of her clothes. The problem lay less in the fact that the young women were inappropriately dressed for winter but that they wore high 'Jesus' boots which consisted of long strips of leather thong plaited neatly up the leg. A precondition for initiation, with its roots in Indian tradition, is that shoes must be removed. The mini-skirted women struggled long to disentangle themselves from their footwear, before being allowed entry to the *sanctum sanctorum* of the shrine-room.

George was also interested in *yoga* meditation. When Barry Miles of the *International Times* in London interviewed George, he spoke readily about his passionate interest in matters Eastern. He was especially eager to espouse the cause of Paramahansa Yogananda, and his autobiography.

> It's a far-out book, it's a gas. Through *Yoga*, anybody can attain; it's a God-realisation; you just practise *Yoga* and if you really mean it, then you'll do it. You'll do it to a degree … there's *Yogis* that have done it to such a degree that they're God, they're like Christ and they can walk on the water and materialise

bodies and they can do all those tricks. But that's not the point; the point is that we can all do that and we've all got to do that and we'll keep on being re-born because for the law of action and reaction; 'What-so-ever a man soweth, that shall he also reap'; you reap when you come back in your next birth, what you've sown in your previous incarnation.[199]

When in June 1967 The Beatles launched *Sergeant Pepper's Lonely Hearts Club Band*, their latest record, the cover was festooned with the faces of the famous, the infamous and the less familiar. Included amongst those in the mock 'class photograph', are a selection of pictures of Indian mystics whose deeds and exploits had been immortalized in the fascinating book written by Indian *guru* Swami Paramahansa Yogananda.

In an interview with Alan Aldridge, Beatle Paul McCartney enthused:

Those Indian people have amazing stories. There's one called Yogananda Para Manza, who died in 1953 and left his body in an incredibly perfect state. Medical reports in Los Angeles three or four months after he died were saying this is incredible; this man hasn't decomposed yet. He was sitting there glowing because he did this sort of transcendental bit, transcended his body by planes of consciousness. He was taught by another person on the cover and *he* was taught by *another*, and it all goes back to one called Babujee who's just a little drawing looking upwards.

You can't photograph him – he's an agent. He puts a curse on the film. He's the all-time governor, he's been at it a long time and he's still around doing the transcending bit.[200]

In *Autobiography of a Yogi*, by Paramahansa Yogananda, the book to which Paul McCartney referred, the principal interest for many people is the inclusion of innumerable tales of miracle working. Although the author makes a commendable effort to explain away such phenomena, and cautions readers against becoming distracted and therefore obstructed in their search for spiritual experience, he none-the-less fuels the desire to witness such miracle workings. Yogananda's work has elicited much interest and praise in academic and spiritual circles for its attempt to provide rational and scientific explanations for mysticism and *yoga* practice.

The Indian instrumentalization that had surfaced on The Beatles' previous two albums continued on this their latest offering. The sounds of *sitar*, *tabla*, *tanpura* etc had become ubiquitous and formed a swathing sympathetic texture behind some of their songs. On the subject of self-realization, George Harrison had even penned an all-Indian piece, entitled 'Within You, Without You'. Paul McCartney explains:

I think George's awareness has helped us because he got into this through Indian music-or as he calls it, 'All India Radio'. There's such a sense of vision in Indian music that it's just like meditation. You can play it for ever; there's just no end to what you can play on a sitar and how good you can get.[201]

Wherever The Beatles ventured their fans tended to follow, they were trendsetters. News that the group had lately been dabbling with psychedelic drugs had only recently broken, giving fans the impression that The Beatles endorsed the taking of recreational drugs. And already it seemed that The Beatles might be tempted to go beyond such induced ecstasies by pursuing the road of *yoga* philosophy. Would hordes of fans be joining the growing number of people eager to share the teachings of Swami Paramahansa, Sri Yukteswar Giri, Lahiri Mahasaya and Babaji? Interviewer Alan Aldridge asked Paul McCartney more about these *gurus*.

Aldridge: These are all George's heroes?

Paul McCartney: Yes. George says the great thing about people like Babujee and Christ and all the governors who have transcended is that they've got out of the reincarnation cycle: they've reached the bit where they are just there; they don't have to zoom back.[202]

Clearly, had Paramahansa Yogananda still been alive he could have counted on The Beatles to seek him out, but in his absence they tried to make the best sense they could of his ideas. Admittedly, his book was no substitute for the man himself and the search was on for a living, breathing, blissful, miracle-working *yogi*.

The Beatles had long been aware of the existence of Maharishi, having seen him on television, and through George's wife Pattie, had some impressions of his philosophy. But there was something that upset John Lennon about his teaching.

I didn't believe it at the time. She said: 'They gave me this word but I can't tell you, it's a secret'. And I said: 'What kind of scene is this if you keep secrets from your friends?'[203]

When the opportunity arose to hear Maharishi in person, The Beatles made sure they would attend, and by some inexplicable coincidence or quirk of fate, it transpired that this was to be the very last public engagement Maharishi was intending to make.

Maharishi Mahesh Yogi

Lecture
at the Hilton Hotel, London, W.I.
Tonight at 8 p.m. **ALL TICKETS SOLD.**

Public Lectures
Wednesday, 30 August, at 8 p.m.
John Phillips Lecture Hall,
Normal College, Bangor, N. Wales.
Admission Free.

Friday, I September, at 8 p.m.
Concert Hall,
Amsterdam, Holland.

All enquiries to :—
S.R.M. Foundation of Great Britain,
20, Grosvenor Place, London, S.W.I.
Telephone: Belgravia 8994.

On Thursday, 24th August 1967, almost three months after the release of *Sergeant Pepper*, three of The Beatles, John, Paul and George, arrived at a London hotel (Ringo was otherwise spoken for, visiting his wife who had just given birth to their son, Jason, a few days before).

Arriving at the Park Lane Hilton, where the maharishi was residing, The Beatles found an overflow crowd in the ballroom. Indians in garish Terylene suits and nylon saris rubbed shoulders with drably attired British folk. The Beatles were ushered to the front of the assembly, where a flock of earnest devotees sat in lotus position, holding their hands cupped upward with their eyes cast down. The holy one came onto the stage dressed in Indian robes that contrasted sharply with the dark business suits of his British disciples. Seating himself on a deerskin in the center of a semicircle of straight-backed chairs, the Maharishi called for five minutes of silent meditation. As The Beatles looked on self-consciously, consciously, embarrassed by the *sotto voce* gossiping of the old ladies about them, the suspense built, until, at last, the *guru* spoke.

Talking in a high-pitched voice, interspersed with odd little giggles, he launched into an endorsement of transcendental meditation. 'This practice,' he warbled in a high reedy voice, 'will alone bring one to the complete fulfilment of one's life.' Demanding but 'one half hour a day', transcendental meditation's effect could be detected immediately. 'Rejuvenation is there!' enthused the monk. 'Within two or three days, the face of a man changes.' The maharishi's claim must have made every Beatle zoom in on the old man's face. God knows, he wasn't any beauty. His complexion was dusky, his nose broad, his hair long, greasy, and unkempt, his beard a cotton boll stuck on his chin. Yet the man was right! He *had* a glow in his face.[204]

John and Cynthia Lennon, Paul McCartney, his girlfriend Jane Asher, Mike

McCartney (Paul's brother) George Harrison, wife Pattie Boyd and her sister Jenny Boyd, watched and listened attentively.

Pattie Boyd:

'Maharishi was every bit as impressive as I thought he would be, and we were spellbound.'

George Harrison, to journalist Peregrine Worsthorne:

'That's the first time anybody has talked about these things in a way I understand.'[205]

And after Maharishi's farewell appearance, he found himself in demand.

Maharishi -

'Now in that lecture I found quite a lot of questions about drugs, here and there and there .. And I, I replied as I reply.

Then when the lecture was over, and the whole thing stopped, some man came from behind the stage and said, "The Beatles were listening you, and they want to hear you, they want to meet you".

I said. "Tomorrow morning I'm going to Wales, and it's already eleven in the night, there won't be any time."

But he said, "It's very important they should talk to you".

I said, "When they can talk to me?"

Then he said, "Can't they come on the stage?"

And I said "Alright, then draw the curtain". The curtain was drawn; I sat again on the stage. They came - I had been hearing some, some word "Beatle", from California, and I thought they may be boys, may be ten years, twelve years. (laughter)

But here came, they came, the boys, moustaches and all that.

And then the man who came before, he introduced, "These are The Beatles", one, two, three, like that. Then I sat and talked to them for about fifteen minutes, and I said "You have created a magic attraction in your name, so you should do something for the youngsters."

They said, "We want to do, tell us to do, and we'll do."

When I said, "First you experience this meditation and then try to become teachers."

They said, "We'll do everything, we want to experience. Tell us now."

I said, "Now is twelve o/clock you must be feeling sleepy. I'll be in Wales for three days, and .." But I said "You don't have to come there, there are about twenty teachers in London, here is healthy centre."

They said "No"; they want to learn from me.

I said, "Then come there."

There were some pressmen, listening to our talk from behind the curtains, and the news went around the Press that The Beatles will be going [with] Maharishi, to Wales, to start meditation.'

Paul McCartney:

We'd seen Maharishi up North when we were kids. He was on the telly every few years on 'Granada's People and Places' programme, the local current-affairs show. We'd all say, "Hey, did you see that crazy guy last night?" So we knew all about him: he was the giggly little guy going round the globe seven times to heal the world.'[206]

John Lennon:

'We thought, "What a nice man," and we were looking for that. I mean, everyone's looking for it, but we were all looking for it that day. We met him and saw a good thing and went along with it. Nice trip, thank you very much.

The youth of today are really looking for some answers - for proper answers the established church can't give them, their parents can't give them, material things can't give them.'[207]

In his eagerness to 'capture the fort' of the younger generation, Maharishi was prepared to overlook a great deal. Having gained the attention and support of such celebrities he must have been very pleased for he told them:

'You have created a magic air through your names. You have now got to use that magic influence on the generation that look up to you. You have a big responsibility.' The Beatles, all twiddling red flowers, nodded agreement.[208]

So, at Maharishi's invitation The Beatles decided to join him next day at a 'Spiritual Guides' course in Bangor, Wales. The group seem to have been of one mind in having their interest in meditation publicized, for instead of travelling to Wales by limousine they took the unprecedented step of using public transport.

The 'Mystical Express', the 3:05 train from Euston arrived at Bangor bringing with it The Beatles, singer Mick Jagger, his girlfriend, singer Marianne Faithfull, and Maharishi. It is said that Maharishi thought the waiting crowds had turned out to see him; perhaps it hadn't dawned on him how extraordinarily famous the group.

After everyone was settled in at the University of Bangor, a lecture was given by Maharishi, with The Beatles as the honoured guests, sitting up on the platform. Naturally enough, the Press lost no time in relaying the details of The Beatles' meeting with Maharishi.

> For more than an hour they sat cross-legged in a semi-trance listening to an old man from the East expound his theories. Earlier The Beatles had sat with 1,500 other people for more than two hours at a Think-In, a lecture on transcendental meditation – given by Maharishi Mahesh Yogi, leader of a Kashmir cult.[209]

Another report gave a little more information:

THE BEATLES FOLLOW THE HOLY MAN

> The Mystery shrouding the background of His Holiness Maharishi Mahesh Yogi, who preached his doctrine of meditation to the Beatles this week, deepened yesterday.

> Each of his names means the same thing in India - "The Greatest" or "Great Saint."

> Maharishi, 56, white-robed and bearded, founded the International Meditation Society nine years ago - in Britain. He started in humble surroundings when he first decided to teach the Western world of the simple life - a small flat in Knightsbridge.

> Five years later he was at the Piccadilly Hotel, where he gave a lecture to 900 people, each paying 2s. 6d. This week he was staying at the Hilton Hotel in Park Lane, where 1,500 people, including the Beatles, paid 7s. 6d. each to hear his theories.

> After making his "farewell public appearance" last night he was travelling by train to Bangor Caenarvonshire - with the Beatles and Rolling Stone Mick Jagger - for five days of lecturing.

> He claims that he now has a following throughout the world of some 100,000 people, each of whom contributes a week's salary to the cause. Sometimes the people are poor - sometimes they are Beatles.[210]

Suddenly, Maharishi was very much in demand by the Press, who wondered at the attention he commanded.

> Interviewer: People think of you as a saint. What is it that you preach?

> Maharishi: I preach a simple system of transcendental meditation which gives the people the insight into life and they begin to enjoy all peace and happiness, and because this has been the message of all the saints in the past, they call me saint.

> Interviewer: You seem to have caught the imagination of the pop stars in this country.

> Maharishi: What is this pop stars ...? You mean The Beatles? I found them very intelligent, and young men of very great potential in life.[211]

The prospect of wealthy pop-stars contributing to the cause begged the question of how their money would be used. Maharishi was openly defensive:

> It goes to support the centres, it does not go on me. I have nothing. But my wants are simple. I do not drink or smoke. I have never been to the theatre or to the cinema.

Quite why The Beatles and their companions received the 'red carpet' treatment is something of a mystery, after all, they did not easily fall within Maharishi's 'Vedic' worldview (Vedic being the word given to the body of early Indian Scriptures, another word is Hindu). Far from having followed their fathers' professions, The Beatles had taken their lives into their own hands and in doing so had become the very antithesis of this philosophy. They were children of the *laissez-faire* society, rebels against orthodoxy. It could not have escaped Maharishi's notice that whilst he spoke with the group, McCartney felt no compunction at lighting up a cigarette.

The Beatles' stance on drugs had stirred a considerable amount of controversy recently, what with their signatures included on a petition for the legalization of 'pot' and the admission of at least one of the group that he had experimented with LSD. Under the influence of Maharishi, perhaps, they decided to clean up their image and John Lennon made a surprise announcement:

> We don't regret taking drugs but we realise that if we'd met Maharishi before we had taken LSD, we would not have needed to take it.[212]

In truth, disenchantment with the effects of drugs had already set in before they met with Maharishi. A trip to San Francisco's hippie community earlier in the year had quite upset George, who was appalled at the squalid conditions of the Haight-Ashbury district. He made a conscious decision to rethink his views on the hippie ideology, centred as it was around drug-taking in general and the use of LSD in particular. John Lennon explained:

> We'd dropped drugs before this meditation thing. George mentioned he was dropping out of it and I said: 'Well, it's not doing me any harm, I'll carry on.' But I just suddenly thought, I've seen all that scene. There's no point and if it does anything to your chemistry and brains? Then someone wrote to me and said that whether you like it or not, whether you have no ill-effects, something happens up there. So I decided if I ever did meet someone who could tell me the answer, I'd have nothing left to do with it.[213]

After lessons, The Beatles and their womenfolk returned to their dormitories in the appositely named Normal College. Most course members at Bangor were a far cry from the hippie set, and the strongest drugs most of them took were tea and perhaps the occasional aspirin, so there was going to be no temptation for The Beatles to break their resolution to abstain from mind altering chemicals.

Whilst at Bangor Maharishi wrote a message for a new teen magazine, positioning himself in such a way as to capitalize on his association with The Beatles.

> The interest of young minds in the use of drugs, even though misguided, indicates their genuine search for some form of spiritual experience.
>
> With the interest of The Beatles and the Rolling Stones in Transcendental Meditation, it has become evident that the search for higher spiritual experience among the young will not take long to reach fulfilment. But it is for the older generation to provide facilities for the teaching of Transcendental Meditation.
>
> It is an indication of progress that The Beatles are thinking of having their own academy for teaching, in London to start with, and I congratulate the Archbishop of Canterbury who has expressed his satisfaction with The Beatles' interest in Transcendental Meditation.
>
> The youth of today need the support of their elders and I hope they will extend their grace.[214]

Both The Beatles and the Rolling Stones were renowned for their self-opinionated attitudes, so were they really going to subdue and surrender their personalities in order to bathe in purity and righteousness? How were the fans to respond to their idols' sudden switch in ideology? Where would meditation and its surrounding philosophy fit into the fans' lives?

Alarm bells started ringing in certain quarters of the media; the satirical magazine *Private Eye* lampooned the rising interest in Indian mysticism with outright cynicism by introducing a character named Veririchi Lottsa Money Yogi Bear.

After only a couple of days of the ten-day course at Bangor, came the shock news broke that The Beatles' business manager, Brian Epstein, had died in mysterious circumstances, whilst under the effects of barbiturate drugs and alcohol. Epstein was more than a business associate of the famous foursome, but a close friend and confidant. Privately, the group tried hard to make sense of the loss of their friend and mentor, and naturally they sought advice from their host and meditation teacher, Maharishi. From habit he shied away from any mention of negative topics, but in this situation he was forced to speak out and counsel his protégés in their time of need. When at last The Beatles emerged from their meeting with him, their comments underlined just how far they had travelled in the direction of their new teacher.

John Lennon told the waiting journalists:

> He told us not to get overwhelmed by grief and whatever thoughts we have of Brian to keep them happy because any thoughts we have of him, they will travel to him wherever he is.[215]

Thus it appeared that Epstein was still alive, and sensitive to the thoughts of his departed friends. George Harrison echoed John's sentiments:

> There's no real such thing as death anyway. I mean it's death on a physical level but life goes on everywhere and you just keep going. Really! But... So the thing is, it's not so disappointing ... it is and it isn't ... you know? And the thing about the comfort, is to know he's ... okay![216]

It seemed The Beatles were reasonably calm and relaxed about the situation, so perhaps meditation was helping them at this time of need.

Though many people became interested in meditation, there were many, many more who were left totally confused as to what The Beatles had become involved in. To the watching world they appeared to have surrendered themselves as disciples to an unknown ageing Indian and worse still might yet find themselves caught up in a make-believe world of mumbo-jumbo mysticism.

At a press conference Maharishi tried to clarify his message.

> Maharishi: One sits down comfortably in a chair or wherever one wants, and he uses a thought that he has been given specially for himself and he starts experiencing the subtler state of thought.

> Interviewer: Are you experiencing this subtler state of thought at this moment?

> Maharishi: No I am out in the gross field.

> Interviewer: What do you have to do in order to obtain this state of thought?

> Maharishi: Just a few instructions from a trained teacher and one begins to experience it.

> Interviewer: How long does it take?

> Maharishi: About half an hour.

> Interviewer: But how do you know when it's happened?

> Maharishi: Ah, one begins to feel relaxed right from the beginning one begins to enjoy some improved level of well-being.[217]

A few days' earlier, seasoned journalist and Malcolm Muggeridge had interviewed Maharishi. The recorded discussion had as its subject Muggeridge's assertion that in order to grow in spirit one has to abstain from temptations of the flesh. Muggeridge himself confessed to having a 'greedy sensual nature' and believed that if he were to follow this nature he would be 'like a pig in a trough'. He thus decried the popular trend towards self-indulgence as alien to spiritual growth. Muggeridge saw the advance of American and Scandinavian cultures as wholly unwelcome, describing them as 'bestial and degraded'. He opened the way for debate by stating his belief that the story of spiritual teaching, in both the Christian and Hindu traditions, had their basis in practices of abstention from desire and self-control. Unlike its predecessor, 'Meeting Point', this discussion promised to be altogether more sparky and contentious.

Maharishi responded to Muggeridge, agreeing that 'greediness' needed controlling but that that control should be natural, cultivated by his method of meditation. Muggeridge wanted him to clarify the precise formula used in meditation and asked whether the *'Uuuum'* syllable might be used. Maharishi indicated that whilst he instructed people to use a specific sound, he favoured syllables other than *om*. Muggeridge thought he detected elements of the 'pill doctrine' in Maharishi's teaching and flippantly suggested that this meditation might therefore be likened to taking a 'spiritual capsule', cynically putting forward the recommendation: 'Take three drops of the *swami's* essence and you'll be in tune with the infinite.'

Far from taking offence at these comments Maharishi readily agreed with his line of reasoning, but went on to point out that the injunction to shun or turn one's back on the world should be understood in the context of meditation. He pointed out that to permanently shun the world gave satisfaction only to those few who had chosen the reclusive life, whereas most people need only set aside a few minutes to meditate. He claimed that 100,000 people had already derived enormous benefits from its practice, and went on to say:

> The thing is it's just not possible to check the increasing fast tempo of modern life. It's just not possible. What is possible is to supplement this fast life of the outside activities in the world by the inner silence, by the inner bliss consciousness. And this will not only give man stability in his outer life but give him ability for greater progress. This is the need of the modern age. [218]

The mention of 'progress' had Muggeridge interrupting, saying 'The idea of any more progress fills me with unspeakable horror.' But the progress he seemed to be referring to was the erosion of values, the casting out of the old world and the replacement of conservatism with suspect and untried new philosophies. Maharishi answered in bubbly tones.

> I want to make progress more fulfilling and more useful to life by the impact of inner silence and increased energy at the same time. We want peace, but not at the cost of progress and life, but peace that will be the basis of greater activity and yet life in greater fulfilment and more joyfulness. This is what the Spiritual

Regeneration Movement has brought -this philosophy – and this is not a new philosophy, I count it to be just the interpretation of the original text of the philosophy of life contained in the books of every religion.

And he went on to say that he believed it was hard, if not impossible, for a modern man to entertain concepts of abstention and detachment. However, in these words, Muggeridge found more fuel for his argument.

That is maybe why modern men of action have made such a disgusting mess of the world. Isn't that so?

Maharishi, in stating his position on the need to prioritize inner values, pointed out a basic dichotomy, observing that even those who advocated the path of renunciation had, of necessity, need to abandon their lifestyles in order to come out and speak. Muggeridge did not want to debate this point, preferring instead to lay down a challenge, asking whether the kingdoms of the outer material world are not those of the devil. Maharishi, careful to avoid conflict, chose to pursue a comfortable middle ground:

So what we want is to regenerate the spiritual value of the devil and then all the kingdoms are fine. And … yesterday I was very happy to see The Beatles; they were so deeply interested in this deep thought of inner life. I was just surprised to find their interest in this Transcendental Meditation.

Muggeridge, a past master in the role of interviewer, used the change of topic to launch an attack on the use of drugs, questioning the view that the nature of God could be understood by taking a drug, as one of The Beatles had allegedly remarked. He was openly contemptuous, saying: 'But do you imagine that sucking a drug is going to, is going to produce the result? No, no, no, no, no.'

It is strange how this lively debate had so soon gone aground after mention of The Beatles. Evidently, he had mentioned their name in order to impress, but in this he had failed, for his host held no brief for the permissive society in general or for the use of recreational drugs in particular. But now Muggeridge too let himself down, for this linking of Maharishi and meditation with young people's use of drugs was spurious in the extreme.

Demonstrating his capacity not only to deal with opposition but also to turn a situation to advantage,

No. But then we must supply them with some tangible, simple, natural means to glorify all aspects of their personality and life. If the religious people and religious practices and churches and all that goes with it, if they are not able to satisfy the need of the youngsters for that experience of higher consciousness then they must fall into this and into this, into this. But what is important there for us is the desire in the youngsters for some experience of higher nature or experience of some bliss consciousness. If Christ has said that Kingdom of Heaven is within you, a young man of today wants to verify where is that Kingdom of Heaven within me.

Deep in the Himalayan foothills lay a small dry cave, a cave that Maharishi had left in order to follow a thought, a thought that had in time led him to leave India and take his brand of philosophy to the people of the West. The time he had allocated for his mission had almost expired. Somewhere, in the recesses of his mind he knew that one day soon he might return to that cave. Perhaps the memory of that cave was a part of the unfathomable source of strength that kept the erstwhile *brahmachari* empowered in his public speaking, and whilst carefully befriending his adversaries.

***

It seemed to have become increasingly fashionable to be seen as a 'deep' thinker, and since John Lennon had now taken to meditation, it was not surprising that he should borrow ideas from Maharishi, especially those that sounded rather profound. He would dazzle acquaintances with concepts such as the one imperfectly lifted from Maharishi's commentary on the *Bhagavad-Gita:* 'Time is a concept by which we measure eternity.'[219]

Such was John's commitment to his new interest in meditation that he envisaged The Beatles playing a substantial role in recruiting new converts, and he addressed his fellow musicians on this topic.

'If we went round the world preaching about transcendental meditation, he said earnestly, 'we could turn on millions of people.'[220]

Peter Hazlitt reported a meeting he attended with Maharishi and The Beatles, after which Mick Jagger observed:

What the Maharishi teaches is this. When a man's mind is not peaceful, whatever he does or thinks creates vibrations in the atmosphere. The sum of these tense vibrations finally explodes into calamities like war. There is only one way to neutralise the atmospheric tensions, he believes, and that is to reduce them at source – in individuals.[221]

But was the method of meditation all that it was claimed to be? How could anyone really answer that? For the moment the world would have to take at face value the words of 'His Holiness' and his devotees. John Lennon, seldom at a loss for words, some weeks later conveyed his feelings about meditation with admirable clarity and succinctness:

You just feel more energetic, you know, just simply for doing work or anything. You just come out of it and it's, 'who-o-oaah let's get going.'[222]

11

— ★ —

INDIAN SUMMER

The East was well and truly 'in' with the 'in crowd', and Indian garments, crafts, incense and accessories were selling like the proverbial hot cakes, in face a few months before The Beatles met Maharishi they were invited to become involved in the world's first international satellite transmission, and performed John Lennon's song-with-a-message, 'All You Need is Love'; they appeared wearing Indian *kurta* shirts, their necks strung with love beads.

Following The Beatles interest in Maharishi and meditation, the re-release of Maharishi's 'Love' poem, with the addition of a sensitive and lyrical accompaniment on sitar by Amiya Das Gupta, could not have been better timed. The cover of the American release boldly proclaimed 'Maharishi Mahesh Yogi, The Beatles' spiritual teacher, speaks to the youth of the world on Love and the untapped source of Power that lies within.' The record opens with a Sanskrit prayer, a fragment of the *Guru Gita*, an excerpt from the TM *puja* ceremony [223]

आज्ञान तिमिरान्धस्य ज्ञानाजन शलकया ।

चक्षुरून्मीलितम् येन तस्मै श्री गुरवे नमः ॥

aagyaana timiraandhasya gyaanaajana shalakayaa .
chakshuruunmeelitam yena tasmai shri gurave namah ..

Which translates as:

> The blinding darkness of ignorance has been probed with the ointment of knowledge.

> The eyes have been opened by Him, to the Blessed *Guru* I bow down.

The verse refers to Swami Brahmananda Saraswati, Maharishi's 'Guru Dev'.

The word *guru* was an unfamiliar one with Beatles' fans, and there was much speculation about how the alliance between The Beatles and their 'spiritual teacher' would affect their music. Would they turn their skills to creating a eulogy to the marvels of meditation, or in praise of a *guru*, or Maharishi? No doubt Maharishi was hopeful of this, perhaps envisaging a 'Top Ten' million-selling paean to Transcendental Meditation. As it was, The Beatles were commendably cautious about making such a move, and instead went on to weave their 'magic' spells in their own inimitable way, by pooling their creative energies in a film project entitled *Magical Mystery Tour*. However, as individuals they were pleased to endorse meditation.

A popular British television host, interviewer David Frost, succeeded in persuading John and George to make their first appearance on a chat show, in order to present their case for meditation. The *Frost Report* of Saturday, 30th September 1967 also included an interview with Maharishi, which Frost had fitted in earlier that day at Heathrow Airport whilst Maharishi awaited a flight to Scandinavia.

Frost showed himself to be a reasonable and capable interviewer, unafraid to ask the questions that just begged to be asked. He started with the more obvious. Why did Maharishi always surround himself with flowers? What was the power of the flower?[224]

> Maharishi: Flower also presents my message. The message is – enjoy all the glories of outer life and also enjoy the honey of life present in the inner being. Bliss consciousness should not be lost when enjoying, when one is enjoying the outer material glories of life.
>
> Frost: And how does a flower sum that up?
>
> Maharishi: The outer beauty attracts the honeybee and it knows the technique of going deep; enjoys the honey and goes out.

Frost then dug a little deeper and asked what the difference was between Maharishi's meditation and 'just sitting around and thinking'? The answer came clear: 'Other methods try to concentrate, control the mind.' Expounding on this idea Maharishi went on to brand such control as unnatural, and therefore undesirable, explaining:

> Transcendental Meditation uses a natural faculty of the mind to go deep and that natural faculty is to go to a field of greater happiness.

Still pursuing his question, Frost asked for further elucidation on the actual technique that was being proposed.

> Experiencing the subtler state of a thought takes the mind to the source of thought. Here thoughts start as an air bubble from the bottom of the sea and coming up it becomes big enough to be appreciated on the surface.

A discussion of the nature of the teaching given to new initiates then ensued, with Maharishi then explaining:

Someone one day started to meditate and next day he came for checking and he said: 'I feel wonderful, I slipped very deep and the whole thing is good but tell me what you have taught me?'

I told him: 'Nothing, because the process of thinking has not to be learned.'

His comments drew forth a great deal of mirth from Maharishi himself, and from his associates, and rightly so. It would have been an interesting line of thought to pursue but Frost instead raised another issue entirely. He wondered whether, if this meditation could confer greater power of thought, it might not be possible for this additional power to be misused. Maharishi usually preferred to side step the subject of morality, and by habit he avoided explicit negative vocabulary; adjectives such as bad, evil and the like he expressed in terms of lesser happiness. But Frost wanted straight answers.

Frost: Do you, to the people that come to you, say that certain things are right and certain things are wrong?

Maharishi: No, nothing, nothing. Only we tell them just start experiencing the subtler state of thought, and experiencing the source of thought which is a tremendous reservoir of energy and intelligence. When I say that the source of thought is a reservoir of energy and intelligence, what I mean is ... See a thought has energy due to which it flows and it has intelligence due to which it takes a direction. So the source of thought must be a tremendous reservoir of energy and intelligence. Conscious mind going to that field becomes filled with greater energy and intelligence and this is what makes a man more efficient in life.

Frost got the message, quickly suggesting that the message was that one should meditate and therefore, automatically, act rightly – and to this Maharishi readily agreed. Perhaps it was Frost's Methodist upbringing that made this formula a little hard to swallow, and on detecting Maharishi's reluctance to offer clear moral guidance, the otherwise easygoing interviewer began to despair of committing him to even 'just *one* example of wrong doing'. Undeterred, Frost persevered and was at length rewarded by this rather hesitant offering from Maharishi:

I think, if a man ... if a child is very careless and the mother takes his book and puts it somewhere else – it is stealing.

Since the interview was destined to be seen by countless thousands of television viewers Maharishi would have done better to explain his beliefs further. Why was he being so openly evasive on the topic of crime? Some crimes are obviously unacceptable, and his avoidance of admitting it made him appear somewhat ineffectual. There seem to be two main reasons for his reticence on the subject: 1. That he wished to maintain an image of forgiving saintliness; and 2. That he wanted to avoid any risk of identifying with others' misdeeds. This sort of thought avoidance is often referred to as 'sticking one's head in the sand', and in this case might be seen as superstitiously avoiding 'bad magic'. But years of habituation to this practice were not going to be overturned in a moment of pressure.

In an effort to keep the interview going, Frost moved on and asked Maharishi more about the actual technique of meditation, asking how many *mantras* there are. This question also seemed to make Maharishi uneasy, but when pressed, he answered somewhat evasively: 'You could say thousands.' But he did go on to elaborate and explain that the 'sounds' or *mantras* were chosen 'to accord with the rhythms or impulses of the individual'. By repetition, the initiate would resonate in harmony with the 'sound', and a state of fulfilment would be gained.

In addition to being a capable *agent provocateur*, Frost was a gentleman, and having got the interview that he had come for, he allowed Maharishi the last word, a statement of his claims for the efficacy of his system of meditation.

After a brief commercial break The *Frost Report* continued, with John Lennon and George Harrison in the studio. Frost quizzed them both about Maharishi's claim that meditation can provide serenity and increased energy, to which John replied that he had now learned to tap his energy and reassured viewers that 'the worst days I have on meditation are better than the worst days I had before, without it.'

When asked to comment, George showed a powerful grasp of the subject:

> The energy is latent within everybody. It's there anyway... meditation is a natural process of being able to contact that, so by doing it each day you contact that energy and give yourself a little more. Consequently, you're able to do whatever you normally do just with a little more happiness maybe.

In his evaluation of the meditation process, George demonstrated a little of his ability at Maharishi-speak, contrasting with John, who was speaking in everyday terms, who continued to do his level best to show just what meditation might mean to ordinary people:

> You just sort of sit there and you let your mind go wherever it's going. It doesn't matter what you're thinking about just let it go and then you just introduce the *mantra*, the vibration, just to take over from a thought. You don't will it or use your willpower.

Thereupon George came in:

> If you find yourself thinking, then at the moment you realize you've been thinking about things again, then you replace that thought with the *mantra* again.

Sometimes you can go on and you find you haven't even had the *mantra* in your mind, you've just been a complete blank. But when you reach that point, because it's beyond all experience, then it's down there and that level is timeless, spaceless so you can be there for five minutes and come out. You don't actually know how long you've been there.

Though George spoke with evident enthusiasm and obvious sincerity, there must have been viewers who felt uncomfortable at the prospect of deliberately creating such feelings of disunity with time. But for anyone who felt the burden of having already experienced an excessive amount of experiences, 'switching off' for a while would have appeared a very welcome option. But were these descriptions of a Kingdom of Heaven within, or Nirvana that Maharishi had promised his audiences?

As John and George continued and the subject unfolded, it became evident that the benefits of meditation were not to be expected within the actual process, but would show in the quality of the meditator's outer life.

Frost asked what evidence they had of any tangible benefits since they had started the practice of meditation. Again it was George who answered.

We've only been doing it a matter of six weeks maybe, but there is definite proof I've had that it's something that really works. But in actual fact it'll take a long time to arrive at the point where I'm able to hold that pure consciousness on this level or to bring that level of consciousness into this level of consciousness.

Frost discussed other topics with them, ranging from their views on taking drugs, to questions about morality and religion. He asked whether they had come to revise their views about religion in the light of their meditations? From their answers, it appeared that they had, and it was now John's turn to indulge in a display of Maharishi-speak in order to discount the proposition that meditation necessitated a change of religion. But Frost pressed them about their *own* personal religious beliefs, asking what difference they saw between Jesus Christ and Maharishi, to which John Lennon was extremely quick to reply:

Well I don't know, you know. Maharishi doesn't do miracles for a kick-off. I don't know how divine or how, you know, superhuman or whatever it is, he is at all.

George shared his belief that certain spiritual leaders, such as Buddha and Krishna, were born as divine incarnations of God, whilst others acquired realization of their divinity having had only ordinary birth. John, the ready wit, could not resist interrupting him: 'So Maharishi's one of *them.* He was born quite ordinary but he's working at it!'

His remark was greeted by a storm of applause. It was evident that John, far from having succumbed to a cult whose mind-numbing practices would bring the downfall of The Beatles, was still a jolly, good-humoured chap and a long way from losing his grip on reality.

It might have been a good moment to begin winding down the show, but Frost was still in pursuit of answers to the questions about morality he had posed to Maharishi. In particular he wanted to know if the effects of meditation were always positive. John retorted:

> We don't really know what would happen to a sort of a killer or something that did it [TM]. You know maybe he'd change his mind. You can't ... we don't know about that, you know, you should have asked him that side of it. But it's for the good you know, it's simple, that's the main bit about it, so, they're bound to be a bit better than they were.

He had rightly put Frost in his place, but one sympathizes with the interviewer in that Maharishi had been seemingly unwilling to discuss the matter at any length. Overall, John and George had put in a sparkling performance, proving themselves on top form. For meditators of only a few weeks' standing they represented Maharishi's philosophy extraordinarily well. George Harrison, once known as the 'quiet one', was now almost loquacious, whilst John Lennon seemed uncharacteristically attentive and self-controlled.

Immediately after the broadcast they withdrew to the recording studio to spend the night recording 'I am the Walrus' with its message about the unity of all: 'I am you, as you are me, as we are all together.'

The following Wednesday John and George re-appeared on television on a successful follow-up show for Frost, and entered into a debate about meditation with invited guests, including a convert and a sceptic.

One might have expected Beatles' fans to follow their lead and turn out with week's earnings (or pocket money) and a bunch of flowers to pick up the *mantra* that would assist them to reach untapped levels of energy and serenity within. Certainly some did just that, but the majority remained ignorant of the mysteries of meditation and not a little suspicious of The Beatles' aged Indian friend.

The sovereign right to determine one's own life and think one's own thoughts is fundamental. For many, the very idea of surrendering oneself to a teacher, least of all a mysterious Hindu monk in order to receive lessons in how to think was singularly unacceptable. In addition, unlike their idols, most fans had had relatively little experience of the sensory overloads that had precipitated The Beatles' involvement with meditation. Some were still enjoying the experiences, excitement and personal prestige that drugs promised, and didn't want anyone to come and straighten them out.

It is true that newspapers in general tended to emphasize and sensationalize the negative side of drug-taking, but the degenerative effects had also begun to become apparent to users, even amongst the flower-power hippies. The time was right to rethink the pivotal force that drugs had become amongst the young. Richard Neville, founder journalist of the 'underground' organ Oz, put the situation like this:

> A generation took LSD having discovered that the values of the world they inherited were bankrupt. (Later, some took to the Maharishi, having discovered that it was not the world which was spiritually bankrupt, but themselves)[225]

So, was Maharishi's meditation just for the burned out, for the disillusioned 'druggies'? To say so was to ignore ten years of Maharishi's activity. Nevertheless, in view of his current influential position with The Beatles, the press now felt free to adopt an altogether more sceptical attitude towards the man and meditation.

Earlier that year, at the beginning of August, Maharishi had visited Sweden to conduct that country's first summer course at Holmsby Brunn. Then, after his extraordinarily successful stay in Britain, he flew on to Bremen, Germany, to be present at the inauguration of the newly built Academy for Development of Personality. Then he returned to Sweden, spending the autumn of 1967 at Falsterbohus, which became the temporary European headquarters of the Movement.

It was at Falsterbohus that Maharishi received a visit from Beatles Paul McCartney and George Harrison, in order to sort out a minor misunderstanding. The story goes that, having gained the interest and attention of the group, Maharishi had counted on their willingness to do his bidding, and had committed them to media appearances without their consent. The task that now confronted Paul and George was to inform Maharishi that his making claims on their time without prior arrangement, was not acceptable. As aide Peter Brown recalls, George put the situation all down to his teacher's unworldliness.

> I went to Malmo again, this time with Paul and George in tow. We met the Maharishi and tried to explain to him that he must not use their names to exploit his business affairs, and that they definitely would *not* appear on his TV special, but the Maharishi just nodded and giggled again. 'He's not a modern man,' George said forgivingly on the plane home. 'He just doesn't understand these things.'[226]

> Towards the end of the year Maharishi was on the move again, this time on a trip to Paris where he joined up with John Lennon and George Harrison.

On Monday, 18th December Maharishi attended rehearsals for a concert at the Palais Dc Chaillot, in aid of UNICEF, at which sitarist Ravi Shankar was due to appear. The American group, the Beach Boys were also due to perform at the benefit, and their drummer, Dennis Wilson, arrived in time to see John and George in the company of their Indian teacher watching Ravi Shankar's recital.

> Dennis shook the Maharishi's hand. 'All of a sudden,' Dennis said, 'I felt this weirdness, this presence this guy had. Like out of left field. First thing he ever said to me [was] 'Live your life to the fullest.'[227]

Wilson became very smitten with him and before long had assembled the rest of the Beach Boys, intent on having them all initiated into meditation.

> And then I got my *mantra*, and as the Maharishi was giving them to us he said, 'What do you want?' I said, 'I want everything. Everything.' And he laughed and we meditated together. It was so wild.[228]

It seems that John's friend Pete Shotton was also in town. At a private audience with Maharishi, he claims he heard John ask the teacher what could be done to bring a halt to the American war in Vietnam.

> He delivered his reply in the soothing tone of an over-indulgent parent to a wayward child. 'You're all very fortunate,' he said, 'to be living under a democratically elected government. You have every right to voice your own opinion, but in the end you must uphold your country's democratic system by supporting your government, which represents the will of the people.'[229]

Also at the meeting with Maharishi was an associate of John Lennon's, Alexis Mardas, whose father is alleged to have worked for the Greek secret police.

> 'I know you!' he exclaimed suddenly. 'Didn't I meet you in Greece, many years ago?'
> 'No, no,' the monk tittered. 'I've never even been to Greece.'
> 'I *know* I've met you,' Alex persisted. 'Only you didn't call yourself the Maharishi then. You were travelling under another name, doing something completely different from what you're doing now.'[230]

Pete Shotton asserts that Mardas continued with his accusations:

'I'm *positive* I've met him, John,' Alex insisted. 'He's *not* what you think he is. He's just an ordinary hustler. The man's only in it for the money.'[231]
It seems that John's friend Pete Shotton was also in town. At a private audience with Maharishi, he claims he heard John ask the teacher what could be done to bring a halt to the American war in Vietnam.

> He delivered his reply in the soothing tone of an over-indulgent parent to a wayward child. 'You're all very fortunate,' he said, 'to be living under a

democratically elected government. You have every right to voice your own opinion, but in the end you must uphold your country's democratic system by supporting your government, which represents the will of the people.'[232]

Also at the meeting with Maharishi was an associate of John Lennon's, Alexis Mardas, whose father is alleged to have worked for the Greek secret police.

'I know you!' he exclaimed suddenly. 'Didn't I meet you in Greece, many years ago?'

'No, no,' the monk tittered. 'I've never even been to Greece.'

'I *know* I've met you,' Alex persisted. 'Only you didn't call yourself the Maharishi then. You were travelling under another name, doing something completely different from what you're doing now.'[233]

Pete Shotton asserts that after the meeting Mardas continued with these accusations:

'I'm *positive* I've met him, John,' Alex insisted. 'He's *not* what you think he is. He's just an ordinary hustler. The man's only in it for the money.'[234]

On Boxing Day, Tuesday, 26th December 1967, The Beatles' *Magical Mystery Tour* film was aired on television, and the group found themselves subjected to unexpectedly hostile criticism. Just why the reviews were so disparaging is not clear, for the television film and the music it contained were very much products of their pre-meditation personas, and the fooling and surrealism were very much in keeping with the times. The explanation most likely lies in the fact that this was the first opportunity since the release of the 'psychedelic' *Sergeant Pepper's Lonely Hearts Club Band* album that the establishment had had for giving the group a good dressing down. No longer did they qualify for instant and unconditional approval; instead they were to be chastised for their flagrant use of drugs and involvement with mysticism – the principle of action and reaction, the law of *karma*, perhaps?

In January 1968, whilst Maharishi was in America, George Harrison flew out from Britain to Bombay (Mumbai); to the EMI Studios to work with Indian musicians on the soundtrack of a film he was scoring called *Wonderwall*. A by-product of these inventive sessions was the music for a composition entitled 'Inner Light', a song with a meditative feel based on a poem from the Taoist scripture *Tao Te Ching*. On his return to London he recorded the lyrics with George and Paul adding harmony. The Beatles also worked on a track called 'Across the Universe' (later to become a personal favourite of John's), with the repeated refrain: 'Nothing's gonna change my world – *Jai Guru Deva Om*'.

With the endorsement of his teachings by pop 'royalty', Maharishi then found it particularly easy to woo the youth of America. When he arrived for a short visit in January, he was given a hero's welcome, being greeted by a couple of thousand people at Los Angeles International Airport. He gave a lecture at the Santa Monica Civic Auditorium, which was full to capacity, and he is said to have met prominent musicians there, such as Mick Jagger and members of groups, such as Grateful Dead, and Jefferson Airplane. Everywhere Maharishi went, he spoke to packed houses, extolling the younger generation to turn the world on to meditation. His face was even to be found for sale on mass-produced posters alongside pop stars and folk heroes such as Che Guevara. But not everyone was caught up in the adulation; some wanted to dig a little deeper before committing themselves.

In a particularly revealing interview, Maharishi had spoken out against the politics of Communism, claiming that they sounded like 'weakism'. On reading this, and hearing also that Maharishi equated poverty with laziness, 'beat' poet Allen Ginsberg felt impelled to go and see him. Having gained a personal audience with him, Ginsberg alarmed Maharishi's aides by so being far from starstruck and sycophantic; as to appear positively hostile. He harangued their teacher for nigh on half an hour, quizzing him about his attitudes to the US involvement in Vietnam, the use of the military, and specifically the compulsory drafting of young people into that war.

> Maharishi hadn't covered the problem satisfactorily. He said Johnson and his secret police had more information and they knew what they were doing. I said they were a buncha dumbells and they don't know and his implicit support of authoritarianism made lots of people wonder if he weren't some kinda CIA agent. He giggled 'CIA?' His devotees began screaming so I said it was a common question so it should be proposed and they shouldn't stand around silent and fearful to speak. [235]

Maharishi's answer to virtually any problem that Ginsberg presented was that everyone should meditate. And to a question about LSD, Maharishi responded by claiming that meditation was stronger, but it is unlikely that he had himself taken the drug, for had he any detailed knowledge or personal experience of the overpowering sensory effects experienced by those taking it, perhaps he would have been more careful about making such comparisons, and if this was Maharishi's way of enticing a wider interest in meditation then it was doomed to fail. To the user of drugs, stronger means more intense, and the drug-user was thus being misinformed. Maharishi went on to warn that LSD could damage the nervous system and mentioned that some half a dozen hippies had visited him in a room in Los Angeles and had smelled so bad that he had had to take them into the garden. Ginsberg was outraged.

I said *WHAT*? You must have been reading the newspapers. He said he didn't read newspapers. I said he likely had a misconception from his friends (at that point, I guess I said acid hippies were the largest part of the day's audience). He insisted that hippies smelled.

So Ginsberg was left with mixed feelings about Maharishi views.

Judging from voicetone of his business manager – a sort of business man western square sensitive – sounds like he is surrounded by a conservative structure and he would come on unsympathetic in relation to social problems.

But although far from won over by Maharishi, this ambassador of hippiedom was not completely dismissive. He concluded his report by saying:

The main burden that everyone should meditate half hour morning and night makes sense. His blank cheque claims that his extra special meditation form is more efficient than any other is something I haven't tried so I can't judge. His high powered organisation method of advertising meditation is getting, like Pyramid club of people meditating and massive enthusiasm application which would certainly tend to accomplish general peacefulness if it caught on massively and universally. His political statements are definitely dim-witted (and a bit out of place).

Maharishi was gaining a reputation for being unwilling (or unable) to offer useful guidance on contemporary issues, appearing to prefer to dwell in a comfortable bubble of neutrality. Perhaps a clue to the situation lies in his own definition of his responsibilities:

'Maharishi's are those who apply the knowledge [of the *mantras*] for the good of the world.'[236]

This seems to imply that those seeking guidance on mundane matters would do better to look elsewhere, and that each and every individual would have to determine his or her path through life. The situation was not improved by pronouncements which frequently antagonized and alienated potential converts. The problem lay in the assumption that because he *looked* like a saviour, he was expected to speak and act like one.

The donations of a week's salary, and the $35 a head paid by students, were still coming in. So, viewed in a purely material light, Maharishi undoubtedly possessed the Midas touch.

12

— ★ —

RETIREMENT PARTY

The last weeks of January 1968, some sixty or so meditators were preparing to embark on a sort of magical mystery trip, to the Academy of Meditation, Shankaracharya Nagar, in the Himalayan foothills of north-western India. The plan was for them first to go first to Delhi, in order to attend a conference there, and then to travel northwards towards the Himalaya Mountains, then, having reached the town of Rishikesh, to cross over the River Ganges via the Lakshman Jhoola suspension bridge. They all had one purpose in mind – to meet with Maharishi and under his guidance to train to become teachers of his Transcendental Meditation.

For flautist Paul Horn, who was planning on filming the three-month course for posterity, additional excitement came with the news that, according to the *cognoscenti*, it was likely that The Beatles might also put in an appearance.

When Maharishi flew out of New York on his journey home, he was accompanied by a female admirer, the estranged wife of entertainer Frank Sinatra, actress Mia Farrow, whom he had earlier spent time in Boston, Massachusetts. The flight took first to London's Heathrow Airport where, on 24th January, a waiting photographer snapped a shot of them alighting. Maharishi later flew to Bombay and from there, made a belated arrival in New Delhi on the eve of the Eighth World Congress. The congress, which was held on Sunday, 28th January, with a line-up of speakers who commended meditation to solve a variety of problems including health, education, social behaviour and world peace.

Many Indians arc suspicious of prominent holy men, and, since Indian culture is steeped in stories of the lives of simple hermits, there is particular contempt reserved for religious leaders who appear to be too comfortably off. During a guest appearance by Maharishi at the University of New Delhi the following day, a portion of the audience appeared openly sceptical of Maharishi's message and, on this occasion, he had his work cut out to deal with the unwelcome hecklers and their loaded questions. But he was a veteran campaigner with a rare talent for keeping calm.

Before leaving Delhi Maharishi made one more appearance, this time in a particularly public place in the open air, and to the surprise and consternation of his Western devotees, addressed the many thousands of assembled Indians in Hindi.

The following day Maharishi journeyed to Rishikesh, where for three months he would be running a teacher-training camp. The building programme at Shankaracharya Nagar had by now come a long way, and the small patch of land on the wooded hillock boasted many new buildings. Allegedly boosted by a $100,000 donation from a wealthy heiress, Doris Duke, Maharishi's devotees had planned and constructed a residence in which it was intended he should stay. Surrounded by trees, the purpose-built residence had, on the ground floor, two fair-sized adjoining rooms and a comfortable veranda lined with pillars, with a further two rooms, ventilated by fanlights, in the basement. On the flat roof of the white building was an additional room surrounded by a low-walled terrace and overlooking an ornamental pond and beds of flowering plants. Canadian actor Jerry Stovin recalls that Maharishi's first instinct was to spurn the use of the new building in favour of the grass hut he usually occupied whist in Rishikesh.

Up the hill from the bungalow, on the western perimeter of the Academy, six stone dwellings had been built which were for the exclusive use of guests. Adjacent were several other buildings, 'blocks', single-storey whitewashed residences for other students. Some distance from these was the spacious subterranean lecture hall, accessed via wide pathways which connected the various buildings. And a certain amount of landscaping had been effected too. Access the site and through a pedestrian gateway, lay a sub-post-office and a branch of a national bank. Motor transport was supposed to come along a track that had been cut through the dense surrounding jungle, which terminated at a double gate to the rear of the site

The overcrowded, dilapidated black taxis negotiated the final part of their journey, the short passage through the jungle track, during which the excited travellers were able to catch glimpses of the broad River Ganges snaking its way past the *ashrams* and temples of nearby Swargashram village, and to hear the calls of local wildlife. From the drivers and from the bearers of their luggage, the foreign passengers found themselves gaining faltering familiarity with a few words of the Hindi language. As they approached Maharishi's academy or *'ashram'* as many called it, they could see festive bunting hanging from the trees. They arrived to find Maharishi's staff waiting there to greet them. The air rang with the sound of constant and repeated chanting. Pervading the thoughts and ears of all were but three magic words: '*Jai Guru Dev.*'

Many of Maharishi's students must have worried that the climate in India would be far too hot for them. Naturally, they were relieved to discover that although the sun shines brightly throughout the day, the air can be fresh and cool. But the nights however can be really cold, which explains the fireplaces that newcomers discovered in their rooms.

Every bedroom was simply furnished, with bedstead, bedding, a chair and a table, shelving and a mirror. All basic facilities were laid on and there was even hot water, which was heated up in disused oil drums by servants.

The main reason that such a diverse collection of people had come together at this remote place was of course to learn to become teachers of meditation. In addition to meeting many like-minded people, course participants could also indulge in ever-increasing periods of meditation. But for many the great attraction was to be able to be with Maharishi, who was to hold lectures twice daily, at 3.30 and 8.30 pm. At these sessions the audience was encouraged to recount their experiences of meditation, thus providing reference points from which Maharishi could expound his theories.

The *ashram* breakfast was definitely not to be missed, comprising as it did of cereal, porridge, toast with jam or marmalade, fruit juice, coffee and tea. In general main meals consisted of generous helpings of simple, strictly vegetarian dishes. Guests were expected to eat the same food as Maharishi – traditional north Indian fare of rice, *dhal*, curds (soured buffalo milk), boiled vegetables, *puris* (small flat breads) and fresh salads. This fairly basic diet could be supplemented by anything the visitors wanted, orders being processed through the *brahmacharin* or made directly to the servants. It seemed that everything had been thought of, and that a good time was going to be had by all.

As everyone settled into their new environment and became better acquainted with their fellow students, they began to look forward to the period between noon and mid-afternoon when they were free to do as they pleased, although there were some restrictions. There were wire fences to keep out unwanted intruders, constantly patrolled by guards, both day and night. No one was allowed to wander beyond the confines of the *ashram* and the adjacent riverbank. One thing Maharishi (and indeed, the Indian authorities) did not want was an incident with the locals, so those who wished to bathe in the chill, snow-fed waters of Mother Ganges were to be watched over by conveniently positioned soldiers. Maharishi's Uncle Raj was also about, and from his residence in the quarter set aside for Indians, he dispensed homeopathic medicine and turned out oil paintings of 'Guru Dev' for the new teachers.

Amongst Maharishi's assistants were two men who had once served Maharishi's teacher, namely Brahmachari Shankarlal, and Brahmachari Satyanand (formerly Satyanand Gaur). It is interesting to hear Satyanand's recollections of meeting Maharishi.

> "When I became a disciple of the Shankaracharya, naturally it was my desire to get acquainted with all the intimacies of the Shankaracharya. I gained acquaintance with all the Brahmacharis and Sadhus who were living there. I would sit with them and talk to them and exchange ideas.
>
> There, I came to meet a Brahmachari with unshaven face and long hair, but he would not pay any attention, just stayed all by himself. He appeared from one door, he exchanged greetings, and the moment I wanted to talk with him, he would disappear from another door. I said 'Who is this Brahmachari who would not pay any attention, for not even a moment's time?' And for two or three days after I inquired people, 'After all, who is this Brahmachari?' I had been able to talk to everyone to know that people came to do here, but he is not allowing just even a moment's time. Some people told me that he was a Brahmachari that was in the service of Guru Dev. He was always busy. Therefore he gets practically no time to talk to others.
>
> When I came to know that he was very close to Guru Dev, he was always in the service of Guru Dev, my curiosity to talk to him, to be with him, increased. I would deliberately force him to talk, to talk to him something. But, again, I found he was always in a haste, not to mix with the crowd assembled there, but would disappear with his own work. But somehow, I don't know, it came to my mind, that among all these men of the Shankaracharya, he has the greatest affection for me. And I was, every day, developing my highest respect for him.
>
> This thing became more manifest, when all of a sudden, one night Guru Dev asked me to accompany him to Calcutta on some work. That was the first occasion, some time in 1947, when I got an opportunity to be with him, for a period over three months. To be with him in the closest contact, to work together and to know exactly what he was. And then I found that for him food and sleep, rest and thirst had no meaning. His whole intention was to carry out what Guru Dev had asked him to do, and so long that the work was not done, he had no rest, he had no sleep, he had no food. He would not talk of it. He would not care for it.
>
> His one-pointed attention was to carry out the wishes of Guru Dev. In that I found I had my greatest respect merging on devotion for this man. And that respect for him and his affection for me is intact until today. And that Brahmachari is today called Maharishi Mahesh Yogi."[237]

Mia Farrow was accompanied by her sister Prudence, and there were the 'ordinary' people, the housewives, the hairdresser, the nurse, the railway signalman, the pilot and the German physicist taking time off from work on the American space programme. But it was not long before Mia Farrow developed a yearning to travel, to visit other places in India, so she was permitted to come and go at will, going off for jaunts to a game reserve and as far away as Goa, a place made famous for being a hippie resort.

A couple of weeks into the course, the 'jungle telegraph' carried news that gave meditators at the *ashram* cause for speculation. Seems that one of Maharishi's principal *brahmacharin*, Swami Satyanand, had been seen leaving for New Delhi by car, something he would do in order to welcome new visitors and accompany them back.

The rumour that circulated was that he had gone to meet The Beatles. When Satyanand returned John Lennon and George Harrison, along with Cynthia Lennon, Pattie Boyd, her sister, Jenny Boyd accompanied him, and the group's road manager, Mal Evans. After a welcome by Maharishi, the new visitors spent their time settling into their quarters and meeting fellow meditators. It was to be some days before the rest of the group joined the course.

The presence of The Beatles in India brought the world's press to the *ashram* gates in droves, hopeful of getting the photographs, footage and interviews that their paymasters had sent them for. Without the fences and guards, the course would almost certainly have ground to a halt. Eventually, Maharishi responded to this invasion by issuing instructions that no one should enter the Academy without his express permission and barred the use of professional film cameras. In a bid to outwit this strategy, the journalists were forced to attach powerful telescopic lenses in order to photograph their prey, and they were thus able to convince their public that they had been allowed in. In her book *The Way to Maharishi's Himalayas*, Swedish author Elsa Dragemark recounts what it was like to be on the receiving end of this unwelcome attention:

> After a few days of zealous waiting outside the gates without any result, the journalists took matters into their own hands and forced down the three gates towards the Ganges and stormed into the area. Without respect for people's integrity, they stormed into The Beatles' rooms, chased by the despairing guards, who were now forced to be a little tougher.
> Maharishi knew what to do. Rather than letting them stay in the area, Maharishi went out to them, while we had lunch, and had a press conference under the large trees in the open space near the post office and the guesthouse. Maharishi tried to calm the excited men by saying: 'The Beatles are meditating and can't be disturbed.'[238]

In a piece of interview footage, Maharishi is recorded as saying:

See. In the midst of all these activities and the world's interest for Transcendental Meditation, I don't get a moment to think of silence.[239]

But the hounds of the world's press were less than satisfied with his parsimonious offerings and took revenge by dispatching cynical and disparaging reports.

> The music reporters, whose jobs depended on promoting The Beatles, were properly respectful, but the general press ridiculed the goings-on at the camp as hokum and struggled to expose the maharishi as a crook. The Beatles defended their saint, John remarking, 'They had to kill Christ before they proved He was Jesus Christ.'[240]

The futility and expense of maintaining surveillance on the *ashram* could not be endured forever:

> The days soon became calmer on Shankaracharya Nagar's hill and the days passed as usual with lectures, meditations, meals and an enjoyable co-existence.[241]

In an evening lecture, Maharishi spoke to his students about Patanjali, who is said to have created a Scriptural text known as *Yogadarshanam*, popularly known as the *Yoga Sutras*:

> Maharishi: - 'Patanjali provides a systematic vision of the whole thing, that means he brings out the philosophy of the whole.. Principles of *yoga*. This is a clear vision. Our procedure is, we respect Patanjali, but.. and the teachings of the philosophy of *yoga*, but doesn't much do any practical good to us. Theoretically we feel, in our own meditation we experience that the body becomes still, and the *prana* becomes still, and the senses return inwards. And the mind goes in, and the state of being results. All these different phases, which Patanjali describes, we are experiencing. And therefore, there is not much of inspiration from Patanjali. We are in the grip of the direct teachings of Lord Krishna, to rise to Cosmic Consciousness, and then take some of the teachings of Lord Shiva, rise to God consciousness. This is our relation with Lord Shiva, Lord Krishna, Patanjali.'[242]

John Lennon's wife, Cynthia, was particularly happy with life at the *ashram* and later wrote her account of those 'blissfully happy days':

> As one day merged into the next, the weather altered dramatically. The sun shone and the heat created a marvellous feeling of well-being. Meditation and its effects began to show on us all. The Maharishi was a wonderful teacher. His lectures and talks were humorous and enlightening and provided truly halcyon days. John and George were in their element. They threw themselves totally into the Maharishi's teachings, were happy, relaxed and above all had found peace of mind that had been denied them for so long.[243]

On Friday, 15th March Beach Boy Mike Love had the pleasure of hearing 'Happy Birthday to you' sung by the all-star scratch band, led by Paul McCartney. The 'Happy Birthday' lines were delivered in the style of the Beach Boys, with extra verses dedicated to Maharishi's teachings.

> We'd like to thank you Guru Dev
> Just for being our guiding light
> Guru Dev, Guru Dev, Guru Dev
> We'd like to thank you Guru Dev
> For being up through the night
> The Spiritual Regeneration Worldwide Foundation – of India
> A-B-C-D-E-F-G-H-I. Jai Guru Dev.[244]

George Harrison's twenty-fifth birthday, on Sunday, 25th February, was also celebrated, with partygoers being entertained by a local band of performers, featuring a man attired in turban and a costume of shimmering crimson, and everyone was treated to a specially prepared cake.

The Beatles were dressed in pyjama-style Indian clothes (*kurta* shirts and elephant trousers) and the women in colourful saris. Maharishi presented his famous follower with a plastic globe, inverted so as to confuse the polarity, and by way of explanation he told George:

> This is what the world is like today – upside down. It is rotating in tension and agony. The world waits for its release and to be put right. Transcendental meditation can do so. George, this globe I am giving you symbolises the world today. I hope you will help us all in the task of putting it right.[245]

George: 'I had my twenty-fifth birthday in Rishikesh (a lot of people had birthdays while we were there), and they had lots of flowers and garlands and things like that. Maharishi made me play my sitar.'[1]

In addition to boasting the presence of the world-famous Beatles, the Academy also played host to other musical talents, so it soon found itself with a house band, comprising the famous Fab foursome, the Beach Boys' vocalist Mike Love, and flautist Paul Horn, augmented by folk singer Donovan Leitch.

According to Donovan, on hearing 'Isle of Islay', one of the singer's recent compositions, Maharishi turned to him and observed 'You are a transcendental musician then?' Donovan also recalls an incident offering an insight into the difficulties faced by adults going 'back to school':

You see, Maharishi was quite a relaxed guy, but there was an embarrassed silence in the room. It was the four Beatles, Mia Farrow and myself, or was it Mike Love? We'd all just arrived and nobody was saying anything we were all wondering what to say.

John was so funny and so direct that to break the silence he went up to the Maharishi, who was sitting cross-legged on the floor, patted him on the head and said, 'There's a good little *guru*.' We all laughed. It was funny. John was very funny and he always said exactly what he felt.[246]

A film exists which shows course participants enjoying some community singing of 'When the Saints Go Marching In', led by John Lennon.

John Lennon's 'good little *guru*' proved a thoughtful host, sparing no effort in attending to his guests' needs, and making sure that they were not only comfortable but also suitably entertained. No chance for 'a bit of a do' was missed; if anyone had a birthday, and there were many, it was turned into a big celebration.

Maharishi was not slow in recognizing the need for other diversions and arranged singsongs by the River Ganges, a moonlight riverboat trip and a day trip to the nearby town of Dehra Dun.

An additional distraction was provided by the comings and goings of a helicopter loaned by industrialist K.S.Khambatta.

One of Maharishi's students, Richard Blakely, noted the occasion.

'While we all watched, Maharishi stood near the helicopter laughing, just out of range of the still revolving blades. Standing there with a big yellow dahlia in one hand and fingering his beads with the other, he looked like a child waiting for his first ride on a pony. Finally the blades came to a standstill and Maharishi started towards the cockpit, accompanied by two brahmacharis. Despite his dangling dhoti he managed to climb in unassisted on one side, while John Lennon climbed in on the other.'[247]

But for those hungry for higher experience, Maharishi's suggestion, made during the course that everyone should prolong their sittings, was met with enthusiasm. He told them:

'Now go to your rooms and meditate as long as you can. For the time being we will cancel all lessons, but remember one thing that is important – if you want to talk to me about anything, come to me, even in the middle of the night.'[248]

This suited most of his dedicated followers, but more recent converts found the discipline a little demanding, as Mal Evans recorded.

The students gradually built up their periods of meditation with Maharishi explaining at discussion sessions what our various experiences meant and how we might progress from there to the next stage of the course. John and George were meditating for anything up to eight or nine hours each day. The record for the course was a non-stop forty-two hours! Then as the course drew towards its end, the idea was to decrease the length of time spent in deep meditation so that everyone would come out of India ready to return to routine life at home.[249]

Ringo and his wife stayed only two weeks before deciding to return home to England, on the grounds that he missed his family and that the diet did not agree with him. Maharishi himself said that no one should suffer for the divine; and that it was only necessary to meditate for a few minutes morning and evening.

For the most part, students were happy to sit for longer periods in meditation, but the temptation to 'play hookey' could not always be suppressed. Truancy took various guises, with some simply idling whilst others wandered beyond the *ashram* grounds, only to be brought back by pangs of conscience. But the main source of distraction was with the stars and the impromptu music sessions up on the flat roof of the lecture hall. These work-outs were highly productive, with Donovan coming up with new ditties including one to George Harrison's sister-in-law 'Jennifer Juniper', and another to Maharishi, an ode to meditation, 'Happiness Runs'.

Of course Paul McCartney also worked out new material, such as 'Back in the USSR' with a little help from Mike Love, and 'Everyone's Got Something to Hide Except for Me and My Monkey' which dwelt on the carnality of the local species. John Lennon was working out several new songs, using his verses to challenge 'Dear Prudence [Farrow], won't you come out to play', and to mock 'Bungalow Bill', who had come on the course with his mother, and in fact a song sung to his own mother, 'Julia'. Of the many songs composed at the *ashram* were some directly inspired by Maharishi, like Paul's 'Mother Nature's Son' and 'Cosmic Consciousness'.

It is difficult to visualize well-known entertainers becoming a teacher of meditation, least of all chart-topping pop phenomenons, or a highly attractive film star like Mia Farrow. During her brief sojourns at the *ashram*, it had been observed that she received favoured treatment from Maharishi, and her disappearances caused many a tongue to wag. But Mia was not training to be a teacher, nor did she complete the course, and eventually flew to London where she threw herself into a new film production.

By now John Lennon, George Harrison and Paul McCartney were by now sporting full growths of facial hair; the prolonged electricity cuts at the *ashram* inspired many to dispense with shaving.

Neil Aspinall, another of The Beatles' close associates, flew out to spend a little time at the *ashram*. He had been entrusted with the business end of a projected endeavour to produce a feature film on the life of 'Guru Dev', starring Maharishi. Another Beatles associate, Peter Brown, recalls:

> Neil expected to have a hard time explaining the business arrangements to the spiritual man, only to find the Maharishi employed a full-time accountant. For a long while Neil and the *guru* haggled over an additional 2½ per cent. 'Wait a minute,' Neil thought, 'this guy knows more about making deals than I do. He's really into scoring, the Maharishi.'[250]

Perhaps it was Neil's visit, and the discussions about business, but Paul McCartney decided to get back to London. When he arrived at London Airport he gave a brief interview.

Reporter - 'So you feel better after your vacation of meditation in India?'

Paul - 'Yes. Yes. Except for the flight. That's quite a long one, so I'm a bit shattered... but the meditation? It's great!'

Reporter - 'What exactly have you been doing? How do you meditate?'

Paul - 'You sit down. You relax. And then you repeat a sound to yourself. And it sounds daft... but it's a great system of relaxation. We meditated for about two hours in the morning and three hours in the evening. And then the rest of the time we sun bathed and had fun.'

Reporter - 'Paul, what about the extreme poverty in India? Presumably you saw some of this while you were there.'

Paul - 'Oh yea. The Maharishi's idea is to stop the poverty at its root. You see, if you just give handouts to people, it'll stop the problem for a day or a week, you know. But in India there's so many people that you'd really need all of America's money poured into India to stop it. So you've got to get at the cause of it and persuade all the Indians to start doing things... because their religion is very fatalistic. They just sort of sit down and think, "God said this is it, so it's too bad. We can't do anything about it." The Maharishi is trying to persuade them that they can do something about it.'[251]

Cynthia Lennon thought she understood why Paul and Jane left India ahead of the rest of them:

They had missed the early stages of the course, and the growing feelings of friendship that we had all gained, they were very much on the fringe of activities.[252]

The prolonged bouts of meditation took their toll on some of the course members, who found themselves suffering some unwelcome side effects, and in particular the phenomenon of waking the 'sleeping elephants' of the mind. As a meditator became acclimatized to long periods of silence, there would be unexpected moments of distress, explained as being the 'unwinding' of accumulated deep stresses. Sometimes these were fairly easily dealt but at other times the effects could be more difficult. One such instance - a sort of 'collective calamity' - is worth noting, and to deal with the situation Maharishi convened a lecture in which he explained to the students that what was disturbing their meditation was just the process of inner purification. After the lecture, Maharishi sent his followers back to their rooms so that they could see the process through for themselves. But soon after they had re-entered the silence, the sound of hammering rent the air. If anything was designed to upset the students, it was this! How could they be expected to attend to the absolute when the relative came incessantly battering at their senses? A delegation was dispatched to try to deal with the noise.

It seemed the noise was coming from the direction of Maharishi's bungalow, so picture their amazement when they looked up and saw Maharishi fiddling on the roof with hammer and tacks. So they were left to assume that in some inexplicable way Maharishi was passing on a message.

The experience of unwinding continued, leaving many students temporarily oversensitive and potentially moody. Cynthia Lennon too noticed these unwelcome effects.

> Meditation practised for long periods renders the meditator truly sensitive to any overt or strong vibrations.[253]

Cynthia mentioned her concern in order to convey the state of mind her husband slipped into in the latter weeks of the course. His mind was additionally distracted by his attempts to keep his relationship with Yoko Ono. He had hoped she would accompany him to India, but apparently she slipped away to Paris instead.

John's enthusiasm for meditation was very real and nothing mattered to him more than the chance to become enlightened – to be bestowed with the vision of cosmic consciousness. So he worked surprisingly hard but became increasingly frustrated in his ambition. He wanted more than just a handful of songs for the next Beatles album; he likely wanted nothing less than the spiritual equivalent of promotion - Enlightenment! Paul McCartney explains:

> 'John thought there was some sort of secret the Maharishi had to give you, and then you could just go home,' Neil Aspinall says. 'He started to think the Maharishi was holding out on him. "Maybe if I go up with him in the helicopter," John said, "he may slip me the answer on me own." '[254]

John wanted some of the spiritual powers he had read about in the Swami Yogananda's book, so both he and Paul impressed upon Maharishi just how much they would like to see some transcendental magic, a bit of levitation perhaps. On this subject Paul McCartney points out:

> When we were out in Rishikesh, that was one of the things we were interested in ... We were almost throwing in the Indian rope trick too. It was all part of a new thing and we would ask him, 'Did they do that? Was that just a magic trick? Do they really levitate, Maharishi? What about levitation, is that actually possible?' and he said, 'Yes it is, there are people who do it,' but he took it as, 'Oh, you wanna see levitation, well there's a fellow down the road, he does it. We can have him up, he'll do a little bit for us if you like,' and we said, 'Great,' but he never actually showed. I say, 'Give me one photograph and I'll have you on *News at Ten* tonight and you'll be a major source of interest to the world and your organisation will swell its ranks.'[255]

The balmy days of what the press dubbed the 'love-in' wafted on. George continued to explore his passion for Indian music ever further, experimenting with a range of unusual instruments, whilst his wife toyed with her *dilruba* (a stringed instrument for accompaniment). George would write down ideas, penning such lines as 'Looking for release from limitation? There's nothing much without illumination' for a song he was writing about Transcendental Meditation, titled 'Sour Milk Sea'.

Having found something to believe in, George and John were determined to succeed in it, and their support for Maharishi and the spread of meditation was total. There was even talk of putting on a concert in Delhi with the remaining Beatles, the Beach Boys, Donovan and Paul Horn.

Remarkably, though The Beatles were arguably one of most famous entertainment acts on the planet; they had no one to keep an eye on them since Mal Evans their Road Manager had returned to London with Ringo Starr. And whilst Neil Aspinall had spent a short while at the *ashram*, he also had left, with Paul McCartney.

Though John wanted Yoko Ono to come out to India and attend the course, she kept her distance, busying herself in London, but, midway through the course, their mutual acquaintance, Alexis Mardas, turned up instead. John seemed to hold Alexis in high regard, having the impression that this personable blond Greek was a magician of sorts, calling him 'Magic Alex'. Alex was therefore free to air his views with impunity.

> 'An ashram with four-poster beds?' he demanded incredulously. 'Masseurs, and servants bringing water, houses with facilities, an accountant – I never saw a holy man with a book-keeper!'[256]

The longer Mardas spent at the *ashram*, the more outspoken he became, allegedly criticizing Maharishi for organizing the 'class photograph' earlier in the course, in which The Beatles figured prominently. In fact, reading Peter Brown's account, it appears Alexis seemed to find fault with Maharishi in whatever way he could.

> After a week he heard that the Maharishi expected The Beatles to donate 10 to 25 per cent of their annual income to a Swiss account in his name. He reproved the Maharishi for this, accusing him of having too many mercenary motives in his association with The Beatles. He claims the Maharishi tried to placate him by offering to pay Alex to build a high-powered radio station on the grounds of the ashram so that he could broadcast his holy message to India's masses.[257]

Alexis settled in and took up with one of Maharishi's students, Rosalyn Bonas.

> 'About three to four months [more likely a couple of weeks] after I had arrived at the retreat, we were attending a lecture given by the Maharishi. Also present was an American teacher, whose name I now know to have been Rosalyn Bonas. I remember the Maharishi saying that this lady had an "iceberg" in her brain and was unable to understand what he was saying. In the presence of everyone there, he told her that she should come to his villa after the lecture for private tuition.

On the evening of the following day or the day after (I do not remember which) John Lennon and I were sitting outside John Lennon's little house. The teacher came up to us and told us that the Maharishi had made sexual advances to her while she was in his villa. She also told us that, despite the fact that we were all supposed to be strictly vegetarian, the Maharishi had offered her chicken to eat. She told us that she had been invited back to the Maharishi's villa the next evening.

During the next evening, John Lennon, George Harrison and I were curious and went to the window of the Maharishi's villa at the time that the nurse was supposed to be there. We looked inside and saw that the Maharishi was trying to hug the teacher. Both of them were fully clothed.

All of us were very upset about what [we] had seen. We had complete confidence and trust in the Maharishi and this confidence had now been severely dented. [258]

To resolve the matter, an all-night discussion was convened, and when George's steadfast convictions appeared to waver, John's doubts deepened. So at first light, John led a deputation down to the bungalow and announced their collective intention of leaving the *ashram*. Alexis takes up the story.

> On the next morning, John Lennon and I went to see the Maharishi about what had happened. John was our spokesman. He asked the Maharishi to explain himself, I remember the exact words that the Maharishi used when answering, namely: "I am only human". John said that he was disgusted with what had happened.'[259]

When Maharishi pressed George and John to explain their sudden decision to leave, John responded by turning the question around, saying:

> 'If you're so cosmic you'll know why,' because he was always intimating, and there were all these right-hand men intimating that he did miracles, you know.

And I said 'You know why,' and he said 'I don't know why, you must tell me' and I kept just saying 'You ought to know.'[260]

At first sight, John's attempt to assert himself appears somewhat childish, but on closer inspection it turns out to have been rather clever, for his real concern was not whether or not Maharishi had succumbed to the pleasures of the flesh, but about how superhuman he really was. If Maharishi could show himself capable of any higher power now was the time to signal it.

In the eleventh chapter of the *Bhagavad-Gita*, it is said that Arjuna, after hearing the elaborate philosophical arguments set out by 'Lord' Krishna, asks to witness his *swaroop* (divine form). It is recorded that he was rewarded with a vision so awesome as to leave him with hair standing on end. But perhaps Maharishi was not the Lord, and John Lennon was definitely not a confused launcher of arrows. Nevertheless, by John's account, it would appear he had a vision of sorts:

> He gave me a look like 'I'll kill you, you bastard,' and he gave me such a look and I knew then, when he looked at me, you know, because I had called his bluff, because I said if you know all, you know. Cosmic consciousness, that's what we're all here for. I was a bit rough to him.[261]

Disgruntled and disillusioned, George and John left Maharishi alone, and went off to sit in the communal dining area. Cynthia Lennon recalls:

> The real turning of the knife came as we were about to take our leave. While we were seated around the dining-tables waiting for the taxis and conversing in whispers, nerve ends showing, the Maharishi emerged from his quarters and seated himself not a hundred yards from our agitated group of dissidents. One of his ardent followers walked across to us and asked us to please talk things over properly with the Maharishi. He said he was very sad and wanted desperately to put things right and to convince us that we should stay.[262]

Jerry Jarvis dutifully passed on Maharishi's request, but it was ignored and the party filed past Maharishi without a sound. The tension and disquiet was too much for Cynthia.

> To me it was tragic – hearsay, an unproved action and unproved statements. The finger of suspicion was well and truly pointed at the man who had given us all so much in so many ways – the Maharishi. Alexis and a fellow female meditator began to sow seeds of doubt into very open minds.[263]

> I wanted to cry. It was so sad. The Maharishi was sitting alone in a small shelter made of wood with a dried grass roof. He looked very biblical and isolated in his faith.[264]

Mike Dolan, a young Liverpudlian who had hitchhiked to India with a friend, was working in the kitchen as chef, and had become firm friends with The Beatles and their womenfolk. Mike recalls:

'I noticed Cynthia had been crying. Nobody looked happy. Patty and Jenny smiled meekly. Rhaghwendra [Brahmachari Raghvendra[265]] the lovely man wore the gray ashen mask of the defeated. I noticed Maharishi sitting alone on a rock just outside of his garden the rain the night before threw up a light mist giving the scene a theatrical effect. Rhaghwendra told me that something had happened, there had been meetings all through the night, that John and George were upset and that Magic Alex was insisting that they all leave. Which of course they did. Rhaghwendra was given the job of transporting them all to New Delhi, they were very upset when they got into the several taxis the girls were sobbing still trying to persuade them to reconsider, they were fighting back tears as they drove away.'[266]

Just then Nancy Jackson returned, after walking with her son:

'A taxi stood at the ashram entrance and George Harrison was loading suitcases. His shiny, long hair hung over his flushed face a result of his efforts.
He paused to greet us, "Well, you're just in time to say a fast farewell."
"What do you mean? Where are you going?"
At that moment, a teary-eyed Patty Harrison joined her husband. Patty, delicate and pretty, was usually serene and friendly. At this moment she was obviously distressed. "We have to leave because of a misunderstanding."
"'But only a few nights ago we were discussing all your plans for making the movie of Maharishi's life. You had definitely decided to go to Kashmir with the group and finish the course. Will you still meet us there?"
As I asked this, an angry John Lennon strode up to the car, "We're not going to join Maharishi there or anywhere - we've 'ad it."[267]

Peter Shotton, John's friend and confidant, offers an alternative version of the departure:

According to John, the Maharishi – for just one instant – turned purple with rage, in effect blowing his cover. It was only then that John made his irrevocable decision to leave the ashram.
A few hours later, the Maharishi materialized in the distance as John and the others loaded into a couple of taxis that Alex had commandeered from the nearest village. 'John, John,' the *guru* called out mournfully. 'Please don't leave me! Come back, come back!'
'Even then,' John told me, 'he sent out so much power that he was like a magnet, drawing me back to him. Suddenly I didn't want to go at all, but I forced meself to carry on before it was too late.'[268]

2 more Beatles quit ashram

Hardwar,. April 11 (UNI)—Beatles George Harrison and John Lennon quietly left for home yesterday two weeks ahead of their scheduled departure date.
According to the previous programme they were to leave at the end of April after visiting Srinagar where they were to conclude their ten-week course as teachers of meditation. The other two Beatles had left Rishikesh a few weeks ago.
The ashram sources did not say why the Beatles left before completing the full course.
Meanwhile, Maharishi Maheso Yogi is getting ready to leave for Srinagar on April 15 where he will continue the meditation class for another two weeks. Then he leaves for Europe for a week's stay in Holland, and the Scandinavian countries before he flies to the United States for a three-week tour. He will return to India in the last week of May.

A lesson for his Indian students

**According to Maharishi, it is possible to become spiritually fulfilled
whilst living in the material world**

Swami Krishnanand Saraswati, *guru* to Maharishi's *guru*

Shankaracharya Swami Brahmananda Saraswati, *guru* to Maharishi

Maharishi in Paris, October 1962

A press conference to inaugurate the establishment of the
International Meditation Society as a registered charity

Maharishi's mission was often misunderstood;
he was even mistaken for a flower seller

Maharishi envisaged his message of meditation
passing from generation to generation

About to board the 'Mystical Express' train to Bangor, Wales, 25th August 1967

Maharishi finds approval with the 'pop royalty'.
Seen here with Beatles John Lennon, and George Harrison (in the background)

**David Frost is presented with a flower after interviewing Maharishi
at Heathrow Airport London, 29th September 1967**

Receiving devotees in New Delhi, India, November 1967

It was Pattie Harrison who first introduced The Beatles to Transcendental Meditation, seen here attending a concert in Paris, 18th December 1967

To the right stands Charlie Lutes as the 'giggling *guru*' meets well-wishers in New York, 20th January 1968

Maharishi accompanying actress Mia Farrow en route to India, 24th January 1968

Seated before a portrait of his master Shankaracharya Swami Brahmananda Saraswati, Maharishi presents a birthday gift to Beatle George

A walk in the grounds of his *ashram*
at Shankaracharya Nagar near Rishikesh in Northern India

Maharishi in Kashmir, April 1968

Maharishi on a riverboat ride, Kashmir, April 1968

Everywhere Maharishi went followers would present him with flowers

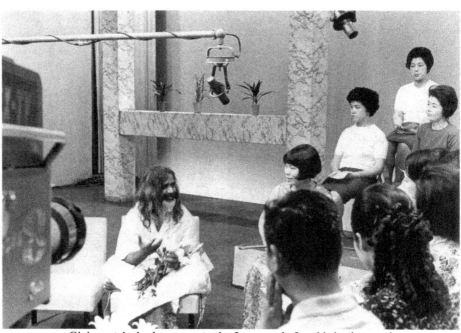
Giving a televised message to the Japanese before his 'retirement'

Back in the USA,
pictured in the company of mayor of Los Angeles, Sam Yorty, May 1968

The master of meditation taking a rare moment alone

Swami Satchidananda, Maharishi Mahesh Yogi, Tat Wale Baba
Gerd Hegendörfer, Charlie Lutes, Jerry Jarvis

13

— ★ —

THE COMEBACK TOUR

The Spiritual Guides' course in Rishikesh, India, had been in the process of winding down when John Lennon and George Harrison hurriedly left, and Maharishi's students were preparing themselves for a change of location. But before the course transferred to Kashmir, some distinguished holy men visited the *ashram*, amongst them Tat Wale Baba, and for Paul Horn, one particular visitor stood out from the rest.

> Now this man came to visit us at the Academy. He's just beautiful – 115 years old with pure white hair and very firm skin. He couldn't speak English, only Hindi, but through an interpreter I remember him saying, 'the Almighty created only Bliss, man created everything else.'[269]

From Shankaracharya Nagar, a long straggling motorcade soon made its way to Palam Airport, New Delhi, and from there Maharishi and his students flew to scenic Kashmir. For Westerners finding it difficult to acclimatize to the now soaring temperatures, the chill and drizzle of high-altitude Srinagar promised to be more conducive to study. The remaining weeks of the course were to be spent at Dal Lake where both accommodation and shopping facilities bobbed and swayed upon the surface of the waters. Maharishi made himself comfortable at the grand-sounding Green View Hotel but chose to hold court on an adjoining covered barge. As at Rishikesh, occasional excursions were arranged. There were boat trips around the lake and surprisingly, a riding expedition where Maharishi demonstrated his skill on horseback whilst clutching a bouquet of flowers and later allowed himself to be drawn across the snowy slopes of Gulmarg on a toboggan. These exploits were for the benefit of the attendant camera crew, who were still collecting footage for the forthcoming documentary.

But not all was well with Maharishi, who was showing signs of strain. One evening he said to his followers:

> I am now a bad example to you. Because of too busy a schedule, I have not tended to my own body's strength. You must let nothing in life interfere with your meditation; there will always be a force trying to keep you from it.[270]

For Maharishi to make such an admission indicates something of the graveness of his condition, and one of his aides insisted that a doctor check him over. The diagnosis was alarming:

> He has double pneumonia and should be in hospital. That man can't do anything for two weeks at least; it would kill him.[271]

However, in the event, he made a remarkably speedy recovery and was able to host the graduation frivolities, after which the course members returned to Delhi and, bidding fond farewells to their teacher, they then departed for their various futures.

Maharishi must have puzzled over the loss of his most famous pupils, The Beatles. It is likely he had hoped that the unpleasantness would blow over and that they could all be friends.

What of all the plans, the movie, the all-star concert?

The world at large was, as yet, still blissfully unaware of the rift, and there was therefore still time, before the news broke, to reaffirm his standing in the world community. However, this would mean abandoning his stated resolve to remain in India.

The venerable *guru* was distressed, but he didn't creep back into his expensive bungalow. Instead, he flew to New York, hired himself no less a public relations firm than Solters and Sabinson and installed himself at the Plaza, coincidentally the first New York hotel to accommodate The Beatles.[272]

Some months earlier, Mike Love suggested to Maharishi that he join The Beach Boys on their next tour of America. He agreed by apparently on condition his requirements regarding the provision of appropriate diet and on-stage floral presentations had been met, Maharishi was lined up to appear at no less than seventeen venues, and on Friday, 3rd May he joined the group in their private plane. But unbeknown to him, the Beach Boys had by now passed the peak of their fame, and it is said they were starting to have problems attracting large audiences. In New York the show was promoted as 'the most exciting event of the decade', but, all told, what with many dates cancelled, the tour was not a success. Audiences stayed away in their droves and those who did turn up were, for the most part, not interested in hearing Maharishi.

> There was a date at the Spectrum in Philadelphia where quite a few people showed up to see the Beach Boys, but when the Maharishi came on, they all left. No one cared, which is what everyone told Mike would happen. You can't slug your audience around like that and ask them to pay a high-priced ticket to hear this guy talk.[273]

Of course, other reasons could be postulated for the public response to Maharishi. Perhaps word had got round that the meditation was not quite what some had thought, not as powerful as they hoped. This was the time of the 'now' generation and things that required too much patience and commitment were definitely out. On the surface at least, however, the tour left Maharishi his normal bouncy self.

> 'Maharishi laughed,' said Duryea [the Beach Boys' road manager]. 'He was laughing all the time. He got his money.'[212]

Whatever the reasons for the failure of the Beach Boy tour, Maharishi had sampled the unwelcome taste of mass rejection, and he high-tailed it back to his *ashram* in India to take stock of his situation. Allegedly he declared: 'I know that I have failed. My mission is over.'[274]

So, it now looked as though the robed crusader was finished, the 'unlimited source of energy within' had run dry. Had the world heard the last of his particular brand of optimism? But this was a toughened, veteran campaigner, who could take his fair share of brickbats and abuse, and in his search to rediscover his 'bounce', he had only to reflect on the life story of his master Swami Brahmananda, for he too had not been a total stranger to the all-too-human conduct of mankind. Apparently he had to contend with deliberate attempts to drag down his name and reputation:

> Having given a prostitute a drug to lower her awareness, they made ready for her to go near to Maharaj Ji in the night. She was to attempt shaking his fixed position (of celibacy). Prostitutes are very greedy. She arrived there at 10 or 11 o'clock at night dressed in the clothes of a man along with the people who had devised the plot, and they flowed in to go for *darshan*, and to have *satsang*. After *satsang* all the people then left and went downstairs, but the *veshyaa* (prostitute) stayed seated there. Because she feared the energy of Maharaj Ji she did not speak but nevertheless she sat there for some time. Downstairs all the people who had been plotting this conspiracy were waiting below wondering what would happen. Upstairs, the *veshya* was suffering such great stomach pain that she screamed out loud and ran away.

> Below, the people who were standing waiting became frightened. They asked, 'What happened?' and they all listened as she told them the news of her suffering. Then, having heard her story all the people were very sorrowful and remorseful. They expressed regret that they had given distress to Maharaj Ji.[275]

On another occasion a 'sadhu-looking man was calling him names, loudly criticizing him, and uttering a lot of obscenities'. What should a *swami* do in order to uphold his reputation, should he resort to retaliation and put such a man in his place? The *guru* thought otherwise telling his disciples:

> 'By little conversations you have learned all about *yoga samadhi*, but the chapter on enduring insults has not been read. It is by the grace of Ishwar (God) that today this opportunity has become ready. You should practice the quality of endurance.'[276]

A debate then ensued with his followers, during which the *guru* observed:

> In the spiritual community slanderers are put on a par with excellent devotees, because faithful devotees then, by means of worship, *aarati* (ceremony), service and attendance, by way of grace, share the accumulated ultramundane energy of the *mahatmas*. But the people who censor do not want anything for themselves, but in doing this scorn they share their sin. Therefore the very same are excellent devotees and they are really a means of advantage. You shouldn't make any effort to stop the passage of *ninda* (scorn) but you should do your own work and allow them to do their work.'[277]

After a further hour of insult-slinging the intruder then took a rest beneath a tree, at which time the *guru* spoke:

> 'You have spent a long time addressing these insults, you must have become weary. Please take some refreshment.'

> The attendants of the *ashram* went to satisfy him with sweetmeats etc. and when it was time for him to go, at Maharaj Shri's order he was given two *rupees* for a carriage.

Later it transpired after he chatted with his associates, that he had gained a very good impression of the *mahatma* and that he very much regretted babbling the abuse. The next day, having come in front of the *ashram*, he declared, 'Swami Ji *ki jaya ho* (Victory be to Swami Ji). Swami Ji, please excuse me. A big offence has been by us,' etc etc., and for a long time he talked words of atonement and implored forgiveness.[278]

The news that The Beatles no longer held him to be their *guru* had yet to become public. When interviewed they still upheld his practices, as such meditation was still in fashion. The continued clamour in the West for things Indian boded well for the sales of Maharishi's books and records. In May 1968, Bantam Books had published the very revealing *Meditations of Maharishi Mahesh Yogi*, containing reprints of three of his more compelling early lectures. And he received useful publicity from some of his celebrity fans. On Donovan's boxed set album *A Gift from a Flower to a Garden* was included a photograph of 'His Holiness Maharishi Mahesh Yogi and the Author'. Donovan had written a song called 'His Hippiness, Maharishi Mahesh Yogi' which was mooted as his next single release. The first verse goes like this:

> When the sun is tucked away in bed
> You worry about the life you've led
> There's only one thing to do
> Let the Maharishi straighten you

> Maharishi, Maharishi, Maha-rishi, Ma-ha-rishi
> Maharishi, Maharishi, Maha-rishi, Ma-ha-rishi[279]

During the course in India Donovan and Paul Horn had played a lot together, much to the enjoyment of course members. And amongst the songs he composed on the course was one for a guitarist friend of his, Mac Macleod (who had a group called Hurdy Gurdy), 'Hurdy Gurdy Man', about a 'hurdy gurdy man singing songs of love'; later stating it was about Maharishi.

After Paul Horn's plans for filming the Rishikesh course ended unsatisfactorily, he took a break with some of the crew, taking his golden flute to one of India's most beautiful buildings, the Taj Mahal, putting the inherent acoustics of the structure to dramatic effect, recording the tapes which were later released as the *Inside* album.

The 'love and peace' flag was still waving freely amongst the young; and the Bear, the hirsute, happy, generously proportioned singer of Los Angeles-based blues band Canned Heat, was commanding listeners to 'sit back and meditate as Maharishi said'.

The Beatles had been getting on with recording their new songs, and putting their energy into trying their hands at becoming businessmen. In mid-May John Lennon and Paul McCartney flew to New York, to attend a press conference, convened in order to announce the opening of their own corporation, Apple, and on Tuesday, 14th May 1968, at New York's Americana Hotel, journalists took the opportunity to ask John and Paul about their association with Maharishi.

John - 'We made a mistake.'
Reporter - 'Do you think other people are making a mistake to go see him now?'
John - 'That's up to them.'
Paul - 'We thought....'
John - 'We're human, you know.' (laughter)
Reporter - 'What do you mean he was a mistake?'
John - 'And that's all, you know.'
Paul - 'We thought there's more to him than there was, you know, but he's human. And for a while we thought he wasn't, you know. We thought he was, uhh...'
Reporter - 'Do George and Ringo feel the same way about the Maharishi as both of you?'
John - 'Yes, yeah. We tend to go in and out together. I mean, with a few spaces. So, yeah.'
Reporter - 'Are the Beatles still meditating?'
Paul & John - 'Yeah.'[280]

When Charlie Lutes told Maharishi of the allegations that had precipitated John and George's decision to leave him, he responded: 'But, Charlie, I am a lifetime celibate, I don't know anything about sensual desires.'[281] Allegedly, Maharishi had given Charlie a special *mantra* to meditate with, one supposed to ensure his celibacy.[282] So, if Maharishi was able to prescribe such a *mantra* for Charlie, surely it follows that he was capable of being self-restrained himself?

Over the years, Maharishi would be asked hundreds of times to talk about his past. Reporters were especially curious. But his answer was always the same: "Once you take the vows of the monk, past life is forgotten."
He told me long ago that when you become a brahmachari, or monk, you no longer relate to your family or to any of your background.
Once an Indian newspaper said that his father was a tax collector for the British colonial government and that Maharishi as a young man once had been employed in an ammunition factory. Maharishi would say little more than that he came from a large, cultured family and graduated from Allahabad University with a degree in physics.[283]

Whilst in New York, John Lennon and Paul McCartney also appeared on the American chat programme *The Johnny Carson Show*, hosted by Joe Garagiola, who asked them about meditation and Maharishi:

> John: 'We believe in meditation, but not the Maharishi and his scene. But that's a personal mistake we made in public. So, to explain that to these five million and ten people.. '
> 'But I wouldn't say, "Don't meditate" to them, a lot of them would get a great deal from it.'
> 'I think it's just that we're seeing him a bit more in perspective, you know, 'cos we're as naive as the next person about a lot of things.'
> Paul: 'We get carried away with things like that, though, you know, I mean we thought he was.. uhh pheeww.. magic, you know.. just floating around and everything, flying.'
> 'The system's, you know.. but the system's more important, than Maharishi.'
> Joe Garagiola: 'Are you saying, "Meditate, but not with the *yogi*"?'
> Paul: 'Yeah. I mean, he's good. There's nothing wrong with him. But I .. We think the system is more important than all the big personality bit, you know? Cos he's, you know he gets sort of treated like a big star, you know, and he's on the road with The Beach Boys, it's all that scene.' (laughter)[284]

In view of the damage these remarks might have on Maharishi's reputation and on the public perception of the value of Transcendental Meditation, it must have been tempting to make a public statement, in order to dispel the mixed messages. But Maharishi thought otherwise, telling Charlie Lutes:

> We do not recognize the negative. We just keep on working, putting one foot in front of the other. If we refuse to resist untruth, it will fall on its own. By resisting it, we give it support.[285]

Maharishi flew to Australia, and in June 1968 came the news that he had given up on his mission to spread meditation.

Yogi Admits Failure To Save Beatles

SYDNEY, Australia (Reuters) — Indian mystic Maharishi Mahesh Yogi, who set out eight years ago to convert the world, admitted failure Friday and said his mission is over.

Sitting on a calf-skin rug at Sydney airport on his way to India from the United States, Maharishi said his failure even extended to his most famous pupils — the Beatles.

Of the Beatles, he said:

"They are not a great success for me because they were too unstable — and they weren't prepared to end their beatledom for meditation.

"Perhaps if they were older, and more stable, they would have been better."[286]

I shall now explain
what makes an airline
Transcendental!
AIR-INDIA

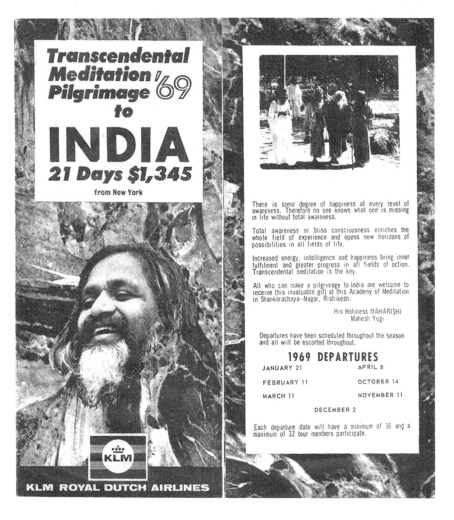

PART II

— ★ —

Maharishi Upanishad

An Audience With Maharishi

David Fiske

14

— ★ —

EVOLUTION TO IMMORTALITY

Of the sacred texts of India, the ones relating to the sharing of spiritual knowledge are the most cherished by teachers of *yoga* and meditation. The *Upanishads* are ancient records of the teachings of some of India's most famous wise men. It is recounted that in the past, men retreated to the forests and jungles in order to pursue a hermit life of contemplation, attempting to unravel the mysteries of life and discover its meaning. Stories abound of such *vanaprasthas* (forest dwellers) becoming absorbed in their meditations to such an extent that sufficient time elapsed for anthills to grow up and engulf them. It is said that many became imbued with a deep wisdom which they attempted to impart to sincere disciples and visitors. These wise men, known as *rishis* (seers), resided in hermitages situated in the midst of forests of bewildering natural beauty. Some dwelt alone whilst others lived their simple existences in the company of their disciples and in some cases, their families. All classes of society revered these forest dwellers as knowers of reality, and the *rishi's* guidance was sought in matters both religious and secular. To these *ashrams* truth-seekers would journey in order to receive *darshan* and to hear of the higher truths of life.

The word *upanishad* means 'to sit down near', which is what those truth-seekers eager to improve themselves did. In their quest for liberation and enlightenment, the *rishis* not only took to meditation but also spent time in contemplation, attempting to formulate a scientific understanding of Nature. As reference material they studied the four *Vedas*, therefore the *Upanishads* accordingly contain numerous references to epochs long since past. Attempts to pin down the age of extant *Upanishads* have divided scholars – as some contend that the works are no older than about 2,000 years, whilst others date them back as far as about 1,500 BC, and there are those who contend that they are far older even than that.

The contents of the various *Upanishads* vary considerably, from complex theorizing, to verses of devotional worship. The most accessible are those which narrate the *rishis'* attempts to enlighten their students. In the following example, from *Chandoga Upanishad*, the disciple is Shvetaketu, the son of Rishi Uddalaka Aruna. After hearing from his father an account of the creation, he urges him to tell him more of this knowledge.

> Very well, my son. When the bees collect nectar from many different plants, blending them all into one honey, the individual nectars no longer think, 'I come from this plant', 'I come from this plant.' In the same way, my son, all creatures when they contact Being lose all awareness of their individual natures. But when they return from Being they regain their individuality. Whether tiger, or lion, or wolf, or boar, or worm, or fly, or gnat, or even mosquito, they become themselves again.
>
> And that Being which is the subtlest essence of everything, the supreme reality, the Self of all that exists, THAT THOU ART, Svetaketu.[287]

Thais Rishi Aruna goes on to give many further colourful examples of his point, repeating time and again that all creatures are but emanations of one basic supreme reality, caught up in identity crises. And in *Mundaka Upanishad* is to be found the clue as to how one might conquer the inability to unite with 'That':

> Taking the great weapon of the Upanishad as your bow. Place upon it the arrow of the mind, made pure and sharp by meditation. Draw it back with a will made strong by contemplation of the Eternal. Then, my friend, release the mind, let it fly from the bow and swiftly find its target.
>
> Meditate with the *mantra* as your bow, consciousness the arrow, and Brahman still the target. Free from distractions of the senses, take aim, release the mind, let it fly with Brahman, and be oned with It as the arrow is oned with its target.[288]

Naturally, Maharishi had more than a passing acquaintance with these works and would sometimes quote verses from the *Upanishads* in support of his thoughts. If further proof were needed of his familiarity with these writings, we find in his descriptions of his master, the following lines:

> His Darshan made the people feel as if some ancient Maharishi of upanishadic fame had assumed human form again, and that it is worthwhile leading a good life and to strive for realization of the Divine.[289]

The 1969 teacher-training course in India was a little less exciting than its predecessor; insofar celebrity partying was quite definitely off the agenda. The focus was firmly on students acquiring greater intellectual understanding of meditation and its attendant philosophy. And lined up for the course were some bright and enquiring minds, less interested in soaking up the good vibrations, much more intent on posing the questions that might define the very limits of Maharishi's capacity to explain himself.

The course participants knew little of the Indian tradition to which he laid claim. However, something of Maharishi's gentle manner and appearance spoke quietly of a noble past.

As the students listened to the flow of their teacher's thoughts, the scents of the jungle would waft on the breeze with the scattered sounds of monkeys, peacocks, parrots, crows and stray dogs breaking their attention from time to time. In this setting, with time far from mind, notions of a bygone golden era were easy to contemplate, and the faintly audible whirring of tape recorders reassured that this *maharishi's* outpourings would be forever accessible and that these lectures would not become but scattered images across the fabric of memory.

Maharishi's lectures were fairly informal affairs and being only loosely sequenced and structured, there were many chances for impromptu discussions. But there was so much ground to cover before the actual process of teacher-training could commence. One thing that he needed to impart to them was the significance of meditation in the quest for self-realization, and he provided his students with this thumbnail sketch:

> Every generation has realized people, lots of them here and there. Coming to realization by that 90 ... I ... 2 ... 3 ... 4... 99 and 100 per cent - gradual realization. Realized people are found everywhere in all the generations, but this wisdom of natural integration, this system, this completeness of wisdom of what we speak – this is not brought to light in such utter simplicity and natural level ... before.[290]

Here then was Maharishi's basic claim – that the goal of realization was not in itself something new, only that his knowledge of 'natural integration' had not previously been available. But if, as Maharishi maintained, his teachings were ancient and to be found in the *Vedas* and *Bhagavad-Gita*, how could they have become overlooked?

> What is lost is the correct expression. The correct expression of the wisdom gets lost. It's there in the scriptures, it's there. What gets lost is the meaning of the expression, that gets lost. And it is this meaning that gets revised, generation after generation, according to the current language.[291]

It was Maharishi's opinion each age has it's own language, religious, scientific, political, economic or of some other kind. Accordingly, if the prevalent feeling of an era had a particular slant, a vocabulary would be espoused that clearly transmitted those ideas. But regardless of what vocabulary was adopted, the language must be able to describe a path to realization. In his 'Beacon Light' lectures of 1955 Maharishi had chosen to strike a balance between the languages of religion, mysticism and science. Even after arriving in the West, he still sometimes referred to the goal of meditation in religious terms, referring to 'the Kingdom of Heaven within', but he generally preferred to describe the inner peace to be found using meditation technique, in broader terms, using words such as 'Being' and 'Absolute'. This terminology, however, had an altogether less graphic quality about it.

Maharishi raised the point about language changing over the millennia to support his argument that such changes accounted for periodic lapses in the understanding of realization. Perhaps this is a valid point, nevertheless it is interesting to note how well one can understand the following words, a translation of a verse from the *Rig Veda* which suggests a procedure for obtaining the bliss of realization, made all the clearer by its devotional context:

> O God, do thou cut off all our shackles of mind and body and free us from worldly bondages! 0 Eternal Being, by faithfully obeying Thy commands, we shall be freed from all sins and thus enjoy eternal bliss.[292]

It is not difficult to understand the composition of a poet who lived in the Vedic era:

> Our thoughts wander in all directions
> And many are the ways of men;
> The cartwright hopes for accidents,
> The physician for the cripple,
> And the priest for a rich patron.
>   For the sake of Spirit, 0 Mind,
>   Let go of all these wandering thoughts!
>
> With his dry grass and feather fan
> And his tools of fashioned stone,
> The blacksmith seeks day after day
> The customer endowed with gold
>   For the sake of Spirit, 0 Mind,
>   Let go of all these wandering thoughts!
>
> I'm a singer, father's a doctor,
> Mother grinds flour with a millstone.
> Our thoughts all turn upon profit
> And cowlike we all plod along.
>   For the sake of Spirit, 0 Mind,
>   Let go of all these wandering thoughts!
>
> The horse would draw a swift carriage,
> The entertainer a good laugh,
> The penis seeks a hairy slot
> And the frog seeks a stagnant pond.
>   For the sake of Spirit, 0 Mind,
>   Let go of all these wandering thoughts![293]

Notwithstanding these examples, the *Vedas* are on the whole, abstruse in the extreme, owing to the obscure nature of their content.

The hymns of the *Vedas* are more properly sung rather than spoken, the sound allegedly having the power to affect the listener in a profoundly positive way.

The power and beauty of verse was not lost on Maharishi. His lectures were frequently punctuated with poetic observations:

> Action is the language of Nature. Through action Nature manifests its desire. Nature of man manifests man's desire through action.
>
>   Action speaks much louder than words and leaves its footprints on the sand of time much longer.[294]

But Maharishi's concern about the changing use of language is not enough, of itself, to explain why he found it necessary to amend his vocabulary. This tendency to refine his language seems to have been in order to meet the differing persuasions of peoples in disparate parts of the world, thus facilitating the spread of meditation. But behind the superficial changes in vocabulary lay many age-old (some might say Hindu) beliefs. A keen observer could detect, even in relatively innocuous statements, skeletal traces of traditional Indian wisdom, even though they were usually stripped of references to faith and devotion. This is not to say that Maharishi had no use for these aspects of spiritual unfoldment, only that he did not commend the devotional path to his students. However, many was the time he let his guard slip, coming out with veritable show-stoppers. In discussing the loss of wisdom over the ages, he mentioned in connection with the changing *yugas* (epochs), the presence of immortals! He named one immortal in the *Treta Yuga* as Vashishta, and when questioned as to whether an immortal might exist in the present *Kali Yuga* he answered: 'Vyasa is another immortal.' Vyasa, it will be recalled, is credited with the writing of *Bhagavad-Gita.* If what Maharishi was saying is true, there is a man living somewhere (presumably in a Himalayan cave) who has been on this planet countless centuries! Did Maharishi seriously expect his students, people of the modern age, to believe in such immortals?

One inspired questioner asked that if an immortal did exist on earth, then why was the spread of meditation not being undertaken by such a soul. After a significant pause Maharishi responded, his answer evasive but none the less revealing:

> I think he must be whispering to me when I am commenting on *Brahma Sutras* or on *Gita* and things. He must be in the air ..., around.

According to Maharishi, not only was it possible to postulate the existence of immortals, he even asserted the presence of life in apparently inert material; in the same lecture he had expounded this theory, explaining that material substances were but lower life forms, of which sand and stone were the least evolved. On the premise that destruction of the least evolved living matter would result in the minimum upset to Nature, he recommended to his pupils a vegetarian diet.

Maharishi's students had primarily come to India to learn how to teach people how to meditate and as such they must sometimes have wondered at his flagrant attempts to indoctrinate them into Hindu beliefs. When anyone was bold enough to probe or question their teacher's wisdom too deeply, a mocking murmur of disapproval would arise from the other devotees. But fortunately, this was not enough to deter the rare individual breaking through with an awkward question or two.

Having placed rocks at the bottom of the evolutionary ladder, Maharishi then pointed out that certain stones were exceptions, that precious stones – gems such as diamonds – are more evolved and that each has its own distinct vibration. According to Maharishi, the power of such precious stones can be harnessed to benefit an individual, suggesting that one just needed a competent jeweller to select the correct stone and offered to bring one in on the course.

One of his more questioning students sought to explore this issue further and chipped in:

> Certain stones that man can make in the laboratories now, like sapphires and diamonds and emeralds and things like that. Is man helping out somehow in the evolution from the rock material to the evolution of matter, through making precious stones, or do they have a different significance to the ones you find in the rocks and caves?

Had he found a flaw in the precious stone business? Apparently not, for Maharishi answered coolly: 'Depending on how near the truth is the imitation!'

A recurrent topic was the problem of how knowledge about meditation can disappear, yet from age to age finds revival. In acknowledging the greatness of past spiritual giants Maharishi made particular mention of the Buddha:

> Somebody told me that during the lifetime of Buddha 500 people got Nirvana, 500. So he must have made a great impact on the masses during his lifetime, otherwise he wouldn't survive till today. Must have made.

Maharishi appeared to be saying that the teachings of the Buddha have survived, but this would argue against his contention that the message had become lost; more likely that he was pointing out that some of Buddha teachings survives but that this is not enough. If the Buddha's success in bringing 500 people to Nirvana were due to the use of a secret teaching, then it is easy to see how it might have become lost. By the same token, however, if Maharishi's movement continued to keep the finer details of its teaching secret, so perhaps fate would deal with it unkindly. But Maharishi thought otherwise:

> We are obliged to these jets flying twenty-four hours around the world. Jets – quick, quick. This was in favour of our movement, quick communication, quick.

But whatever the advantages of modern technology, they were surely as nothing in comparison to the living presence and example of an illumined master, seen by some to be prerequisite in acquiring any great success in *yoga* practices. Maharishi himself freely acknowledged his debt to his own 'Guru Dev', so by what method old Swami Brahmananda had prepared his pupil for the world mission undertaken in his name?

> Oh he must have known. He never said to me, otherwise quite a long time would have been wasted in planning. He saved us from that waste, just of planning. It just blossomed and blossomed and blossomed and blossomed.

It should be noted that during the last years of the Shankaracharya's life he appears to have initiated quite a number of people (both recluses and householders) into the mysteries of spiritual development.

One of the course participants was intrigued as to whether 'Guru Dev' had taught the same techniques of meditation as his disciple, such as the use of single-syllable *mantras*, or whether he deployed the use of long *mantras* of many syllables.

Maharishi replied a touch whimsically: 'Must be using better techniques than I am using!' But this was not the time to be deflecting questions and he knew that, so he tried a different tack:

> It's very difficult for me to find out what he was using, because initiation is all in private ... and I was never interested who was given what *mantra.* I was interested in myself...

This lack of knowledge about the formula his master had used in his teaching had evidently not deterred Maharishi from applying himself to the task of unravelling the mysteries of *mantra* selection for himself, before offering them up for mass consumption. To the casual observer his remarks might seem to indicate a certain irreverence and lack of respect for his *guru*, but this must surely have been far from the truth, for, speaking of his master, Maharishi explained that Guru Dev was:

> ... full of divine radiance. People don't have to do the *mantra* and meditation in

his presence. The transformation was in his air, so full of life ... Out of that
fullness I started to teach. At least by practice people could raise themselves up.

Whilst many of Maharishi's followers must have wished that they too could
have met 'Guru Dev', in his absence they put complete trust in Maharishi,
believing him to be capable of conferring a deep understanding and
experience of the union with being that he spoke of.

David Fiske

David Fiske, who had first met Maharishi in Austria in 1962, was on this
teacher training course in Rishikesh in 1969, and recalls meeting a local
baba (holyman).

Above Maharishi's ashram in a cave lived Tatwalla Baba [sometimes written
Tat Wale Baba]. In the army, during a dispute, he had allegedly killed a man
with a blow to the head. Maybe that was the spur to his search. He lived [and
was] looked after a by a devotee in a cave heated with a wood fire and spent
most of his time in meditation. Maharishi invited him to talk to us explaining
that Tawalla Baba often criticised him for being so active and not meditating
more. He is a large, strongly built man, with long matted locks, either tied
around his waist or carried by a devotee when he walked. He came with a sort of
loin cloth, what I call a coffee bag, kept up by what I believe is a gold chain. He
carried a stick. He gave his discourse with his eyes shut as though he was
looking at another reality. He told us that truth is like a river. Everyone is happy

where they swim and describe their river from their point of view. He said the world is as you are. There is no difference. Later someone asked him whether he thought the world was getting better now that there were movements like Maharishi's and how he saw the future of the world in that light. He replied," I have already told you; the world is as you are. As you are so is the world. That is the answer to your question. There is no question of the world getting better."[295]

David Fiske

Of the many things Maharishi's students had to learn, the complex ritual of initiation was not the least. All were eager to hear Maharishi's view of the subject as he pointed out to them that the 'body of the effect [of initiation] is from the sequence of instructions, but the sanctity of the whole situation is contributed by this [ceremony]'. The 'sequence' of the ceremony or *puja*, requires the initiator's 'one-pointedness' of mind, and involves the offering of various items such as rice, water, cloth, fruit and flowers. The ritual offerings are accompanied by the singing of Sanskrit verses sung in praise of the 'Holy Tradition' - those listed in these verses are said to be teachers of meditation from way back in time.

> The growth of Being in the field of activity is the direct result of words being spoken, hands moving and the mind floating in meaning and getting serene and serene and serene and serene and serene. By the time we have done so many things, moving the hands and words coming out and mind on the meaning, item after item, there are about sixteen items. By the time the whole thing goes, the whole mind is settling down deep and by the time we just prostrate, the mind gets to that deep state of silence within and it sings ... 'Good initiators'.

The new initiate is only a witness to this ritual and is not asked to become involved. At the conclusion of the ceremony, the initiator becomes silent for some moments and then begins to intone the sound or *mantra* that is to be used by the initiate. Maharishi tried to explain this process:

> Just in that one momentary bowing down, just sink into That. And the deeper they are to pick up the *mantra*, more effective is the *mantra* and then they speak the *mantra* and then they lead that *mantra* back to the same situation, the same depth from where it was picked up and this circle being complete is called 'initiation'.

This last statement is very revealing in that it yields a deep insight into aspects of *mantra* theory. Maharishi seems to have been contending that beyond the boundaries of our limited range of hearing there exist certain subtle sounds, and these sounds are those which are given as *mantras*. These sounds are perceived as somehow more blessed than ordinary sounds and are thus highly effective at settling the human nervous system. So, to some extent, the *puja* ceremony is conducted in order to attune the initiator's mind to 'pick up' these sounds. Having done so, the clear and effective communication to the new initiate of the chosen sound, or *mantra*, is possible. Interestingly, this leads one to wonder that anyone whose mind is sufficiently purified would have the capacity to recognize these *mantras* and to impart them to others. But in reality, initiators are not expected to hear or intuit the *mantras*, but are given a list of them along with formal instructions regarding their correct choice and pronunciation.

Maharishi was ever eager to emphasize the benefits of performing the ritual *puja*, and he stated:

> This is the gain to the initiator: that he gains the value of cosmic consciousness, rising to cosmic consciousness when he is leading someone else to transcendental consciousness. It's very scientific! It's very great! It's very beautiful! It's beyond words!

15

CELESTIAL CONNECTIONS

Ideally, in order to be really effective in teaching the practice of Transcendental Meditation, the initiator would have to be permanently in the state to which he or she was attempting to guide the initiate, that is the fifth state of conscious, known as cosmic consciousness. The fourth state of consciousness is to transcend thought and experience pure being; the fifth state is to experience that pure being even whilst going about one's everyday life. Trainee teachers did not claim to experience this fifth state, but despite this, Maharishi had decided to press on with his initiative to spread the news of meditation, and for this he would need many more trained teachers. According to him, all that was necessary was that the teacher's awareness become purified before starting to instruct anyone in a *mantra* or its usage. This purification of the initiator was to be achieved by the conducting of the *puja*. During the *puja*, the initiator directs the initiate to look towards the portrait of Swami Brahmananda and states:

'We receive this teaching of meditation from him...'

Whatever the stated reasons Maharishi gave for the performance of the *puja*, some observers felt uncomfortable about its religious connotations, since *puja* is customarily regarded as a purely Hindu ritual, an act of worship to a Hindu god or gods, whereas Maharishi had attempted to liberate the meditation technique from its religious associations. And by presenting his beliefs without religious terminology, he was able to address a far wider audience that he might otherwise have done:

It is I who gave it the present expression, but I learnt it from him (Swami Brahmananda) in the traditional way ... through very old expressions of religious order. Every religion has its own vocabulary; Hinduism has its own vocabulary; *yoga* has its own way of expression of the reality; Vedanta has its own approach. He taught me in the traditional way of *yoga* and Vedanta and Indian religious language. I gave it an expression in the universal way...[296]

Despite the *puja*, therefore, new initiates were therefore reassured that meditation would involve neither a change of religion nor conflict with any existing religious beliefs they might have.

With the rise of interest in meditation, traditional methods of *yoga* were also being reappraised; the core teachings of Indian thinking were entering the scientific age, the rational age, and were found to be no less interesting as a result. It is quite possible that even in prehistoric times, Indians were not the superstitious idol worshippers we are led to believe, but that their religious rituals were based on some kind of logic and that they had developed methods of self-improvement on the basis of good sound ideas. If this is so then there is no reason why the 'active ingredients' of their practices cannot be isolated.

Some believe that there is much knowledge of great value hidden within the supposed superstitions of indigenous peoples, as the following example from Africa demonstrates:

> The Pedi, in South Africa, believe that infection can be cured by eating grain that has been chewed by a cross-eyed child and hung for three days in a gourd shaped like a snake that is suspended from a particular tree that grows near the water. And they are right, because under these conditions the grain grows a mould like *Penicillium*, with antibiotic properties, but the child's eyes and the gourd's shape and the species of tree do not necessarily have anything to do with the cure. In just this way, alchemy stumbled on some great truths but produced theoretical structures in which the line of reasoning between cause and effect was cluttered up with all sort of irrelevant mystical and magical red herrings. This has discouraged modern science from investigating the source material, which is a pity.[297]

Let us assume, therefore, that Maharishi had been successful in prising a self-help technique from the inaccessibility of its custodians, said to be the order of the Shankaracharya Tradition. But, having dropped the religious language that surrounded the teaching, was it also necessary that he should dispose of his own religious beliefs? Surely not, for if Maharishi's followers were entitled to pursue their own faiths, so too was he. And from references (apparently poetic) to gods and angels in his works, it would appear that this was the case – but that he neither could nor wished to shake off his religious habits. We should give him the benefit of the doubt in this, but his religious beliefs cannot be ignored, as there were times when his beliefs became merged with his claims about meditation.

As **the** authority on this meditation technique, Transcendental Meditation, Maharishi's word was frequently taken as definitive, yet there were instances in his teachings when his beliefs would predominate, in fact it is quite likely that his unassailable faith in the meditation technique was in part due to a broader philosophical commitment.

But, meditation aside, where did his concepts of celestial beings fit into the scheme of things? In the following explanation, Maharishi used his style of oratory, of repeating himself, often, often words and phrases, and sometimes whole sentences. Although this clearly served to help his followers to catch his drift, in all probability the main reason was simply to give himself more time to think his subject matter through, as when he shared his thoughts on the 'celestial strata of existence'.

> The fine strata of creation is everywhere, underneath every existence uh? And taking this logic further on, the celestial strata of existence is everywhere, everywhere, everywhere, everywhere, everywhere … uh? Celestial strata of existence, everywhere. And … now, there is also a range in the region of the celestial – gross celestial and subtler celestial and subtler celestial. Supreme, most supreme celestial, one with the Absolute, almost one with the Absolute till eventually it ceases to he and gives way to absolute Absolute alone. So this … when the cognition of the celestial will become at home with the celestial field of life, then this question of the details of the field of the celestial brings to us all these which we may call 'presiding deities', of different elements, of different gunas also.[298]

From this it appears that Maharishi not only believed in the existence of divine beings, but also considered that 'cognition of the celestial' was also a real possibility. He seems to have believed that one can experience a finer objective reality and have the chance to meet with inhabitants of a celestial realm.

> There are two aspects to life, the objective aspect and the subjective aspect. There are gross levels of objective aspect; there are gross levels of subjective aspect. There are subtle levels of objective aspect, subtle levels of subjective aspect. So in all these, both, two, both fields of life, subjective and objective the creation runs parallel.

If Maharishi was prepared to postulate the existence of celestials, did he therefore rule out the presence of one absolute God, as worshipped by the many faiths? It appears not:

> Gross and subtle and subtler and subtlest and transcendental. Eventually in the Absolute transcendental, both merge and the distinction of both is no more found. It is one. There is a teaching in the Upanishads somewhere and they say: 'God created the world and entered it' and therefore the world is permeated with God. Creation, he created creation and then entered the creation and it's not that the personal God is everywhere, it is that the celestial field of life which is the field for gods to roam about is permeating the whole creation, underneath creation all are running about here and there and there and there.

Maharishi made heaven sound quite a busy place! In his explanations of the celestial he identified various personal deities by name, but cautioned that the quality of the god was more important than the name.

On Saturday, 15th February 1969 a *pandit* visited Shankaracharya Nagar and explained the significance of the festival of Maha Shivaratri (the Night of Shiva - the night before the new moon, the darkest night of the month) to Maharishi's students. The god Shiva is the austere *yogi* sometimes identified with Being, and at other times perceived as the irrepressible Nataraj (King of the dance). His consort, Mother Parvati, is worshipped as Shakti (spiritual energy).

Maharishi pointed out that 'during these four nights [of Shivaratri] inner awareness is maintained'. The reason is that during these four nights a state of 'most intensified ignorance' is at play. During this same dissertation he also mentioned that:

> Even in the most intensified structure of ignorance, then one is awake, one is in union with Shiva, one is in union with Vishnu one is in union with the Mahashakti. A very great significance of a practical nature, in all this. And Shiva is supposed to be ... he is not supposed to he ... he is ...! He's so merciful

Later, Maharishi spoke of the places where the energy of Lord Shiva is most pronounced and easiest to contact, citing both Cape Comorin and Shankaracharya Nagar as examples.

Maharishi's enthusiasm for discussion of the celestial had not lessened when he came to speak at an outdoor lecture the following day. According to him the principal Hindu deities can be identified with the elements. Obligingly he listed the following:

Space	– Vishnu
Air	– Surya, Sun god
Fire	– Devi, Mother Divine
Wisdom	– Ganapati, Ganesha
Earth	– Lord Shiva

Whilst imparting this information he allowed himself to be recorded singing, in a melodious recitation of an excerpt from a *bhajan* (reverential or devotional song) to Ganesha (the god of wisdom depicted with the face and trunk of an elephant).

Maharishi was not at all bothered that his lectures were being recorded. Only when something confidential was discussed would he request that the tape machines be switched off. Otherwise he was tolerant, probably flattered, that people would wish to record his lectures. When the courses were over, many of the tapes, often varying in speed and audibility would become the focal point of meditation group meetings conducted by the new teachers.

Maharishi's students had only a rudimentary academic grasp on matters celestial, and they struggled hard to spell the names of these Hindu gods. Crows loudly squawking their responses and local labourers continuing their work on the building programme interrupted the lecture, held as it was in the open air. Apparently unmindful of the din, Maharishi continued with his discourse:

> Between human species and these [gods] ... finest level of creation, the celestial level of life, gods. Huge number of angels and gods, and they are different species, that's all, different, different species.

One of his devotees asked him to enumerate the celestials:

> Below man's species there are 8,400,000 species and then coming up to man ... and then between man and God there is no record. Because we don't have to keep the record of all that we are going to by-pass. That's the whole thing.

The crows, perhaps sensing the momentousness of this statement, screeched so loudly as to be almost deafening, and Maharishi paused while the crows quietened down. Naturally, what he was telling his students would in turn be passed on to others. At a meeting of meditators in Philadelphia, Charlie Lutes, outlined this teaching about the celestial:

> Top of creation are five gods, Shiva, Vishnu, Mother Divine, Ganesha and Surya, Surya is the sun god. There are also five elements, earth, water, air, fire, space, which is *akasha*... Now each person on earth is a combination of these five elements. However, one of these five elements predominates in each and every individual. So there are five channels of creation – space, air, fire, water and earth in that order, each channel is a channel of creation. So you have at one end the unresolved creation and the other end you have perfect creation. At the top of creation are five gods all at the same level. Each individual is connected to one of these five gods according to which element predominates in that respective individual. The spirit of Mother Nature is always rising upwards. As human having free will is free to act according to his own desires. You can rise upwards step-by-step or swiftly to the top by use of a *mantra*. *Mantras* are pertaining to the gods at the top of creation. Medium of the almighty has taken; each god has a thousand names. Now, a name now is not taken at random, a name is taken that has a special meaning which again means has a very special vibration, the most useful vibration for us. The vibration that has a most specific effect that can take you from the grossest aspect of life to the finest subtle aspect of creation, and transcend it. This is why the effects are very rapid. So there is the devotion to the personal god as well as to the intellectual aspect. We have both the personal and the impersonal aspect together. Therefore we can by-pass the personal god and go to the impersonal.

According to Maharishi there is included in the Vedic Scriptures is literature which deals with the subject of communication with deities.

> *Karma Khand* that is the section on action. *Upasana Khand*, that section of activity which is devoted to the highest attainment in the relative; communication to these gods. When I say gods, goddesses are naturally included, gods and goddesses, because we can't ignore Mother Divine otherwise we will be in trouble. And the third section of the *Vedas* is called *Gyan Khand.* G-Y-A-N means knowledge. *Upanishads* are the expressions of *Gyan Khand* the knowledge section of the *Vedas.*

For those without the time or resources to delve deeply into the *Vedas*, Maharishi had some good news, that the essence of the Vedic teaching is to be found in the relatively compact work of the *Bhagavad-Gita* (itself sometimes considered an *Upanishad* – certainly, some verses recorded in the *Bhagavad-Gita* bear an uncanny resemblance to verses of the *Upanishads*).

The Shivaratri festival proved a memorable occasion for all concerned and left Maharishi's followers with a greater understanding of the remoter aspects of Maharishi's thinking. But with all the talk of celestial beings, there must have been some who ached for the simple truths of their own upbringing and for the reassuring comfort of familiarity.

One query that was persistently raised concerned the optimum period practitioners should sit in meditation, and a common misunderstanding amongst new initiates was the belief that longer meditations would necessarily equate to increased bliss. Whereas it is true that at one time a stint of one hour was not been seen as excessive, the recommended periods became lessened to half an hour and then further reduced to just 15-20 minutes. The principal reason for reducing the recommended time for meditation was that experience had shown that meditators did not always derive increased benefit from longer sittings – indeed sometimes the contrary was the case – thus providing support for that old adage that 'sometimes less is more'.

Nonetheless, whilst attending residential courses meditators were encouraged to spend long periods 'rounding', spending much of their time absorbed in inner meditation. The theory was that greater exposure to the pure consciousness or Being is likely to accelerate the initiate's evolution towards higher states of awareness and consequently confers increased happiness. In reality, however, the increased time spent in meditation would often throw meditators into a state of confusion, occasionally causing depression and even temporary mental imbalance. Maharishi explained that this was just the outward symptom of the nervous system becoming purified.

For committed students, therefore, these experiences were to be expected and tolerated, even welcomed. In rare instances this 'purifying' process not only affected individuals but also seemed to affect everyone *en masse*. At such times, they sought out their leader in the hope that Maharishi might offer some explanation and reassurance, and he did.

> Where all the senses are witnessing that horrible scene, ears are hearing something horrible, eyes are seeing some horror. All the senses of perception, the whole field of experiencing machinery is being wound up, twisted up in great stress and strain and all that is happening at a time. And… huh? It took you so many days of constantly rounding, rounding – that means giving the system, giving the nervous system deeper and deeper rest every day through these rounds, through these rounds. So by tomorrow the system was rested deeply enough to give unwinding influence to all those deep-rooted stresses. And it's started. And as such are outbursts of these deposits of stresses. You are absolutely right to see clearly that at such a overwhelming and overpowering misery in such a collective way, nothing can help except love for God or love from God, some … only God could help.

Maharishi's hypothesis, that anxiety experienced in meditation is not so much a result of incorrect technique as of numerous accumulated stresses becoming neutralized, is most interesting. By way of explanation he maintained that the release of stress was an indication that real progress was being made, that, having released the stresses, the nervous system was now better able to support the experience of pure Being. The stresses Maharishi spoke of seem to refer to the accumulated impressions of past experiences, both good and bad, but most specifically physical shocks, jolts and the like. The argument is that if one were to narrowly miss being run over by a car, in all probability one would at least sustain shock to the nervous system, if not prolonged tensing of the muscles. The effects of multiple shocks could, in theory at least, accumulate and conspire to produce a condition whereby an individual is permanently stressed. Some might say that these stresses need not even have a gross physical origin, that they are more frequently incurred by subduing one's feelings and responses when the mind attempts to override instinctive reactions. But there are times when stress is occasioned by less direct means, as for instance when someone feels a sense of personal failure or rejection. Further, it could be argued that all or any of these examples could contribute to the accumulation of 'knots' of stress in the nervous system.

But even if we accept Maharishi's theory of stress release, apparently he did not give his students advance warnings about these experiences of 'overwhelming and overpowering misery'. Trainee meditation teachers were there to experience the bliss of the 'Kingdom of Heaven within'; but, whether they liked it or not, were now discovering a new meaning to the old maxim about there being 'no gain without strain'. Anyway, Maharishi discouraged his students from seeing these upsetting experiences as wholly negative situations to avoid; practitioners were encouraged to view them positively, as evidence of progress.

There can be no doubt that accumulated tensions can hamper one's ability to be at peace with oneself – after all, the whole realm of psychoanalysis has as its basis this belief. But since Maharishi held that meditation differs entirely from psychoanalysis, it is interesting to note how he distinguished between the two processes. Importantly, unlike those involved in psychoanalysis, meditators are actively discouraged from analyzing past experiences which might be responsible for any discomforts suffered during rounding. This is because whilst some stress might be experienced during the meditation, the thoughts that accompany this 'unwinding' process are considered to be unworthy of consideration. Actually, meditators were counselled not to place particular importance on thoughts that might arise in meditation, for these are deemed as results of 'unstressing', not as causes. This theory has been taken so far as to suggest that if one experiences *any* thoughts in meditation it is evidence of the effectiveness of the technique!

Having expounded the basis of his theory of 'unstressing', Maharishi further amplified his case with the use of an analogy:

> [It] depends on how much one is anchored to the eternal stable factor of life, the Being. How much one is anchored and what is the strength of the cyclone. How much one is anchored. If one is permanently established in the eternal Being, fine, any amount of gain in the relative, it will shake and it will just shake but it won't break it down. That is the reason why we are here, to get as deep contact with Being as possible, as soon as possible. And that's the reason why we are not doing anything other than digging deep into ourselves ... uh? And when we dig deep well, very deep, sometimes when the rocks come, we have to blow them out through dynamite. See there we have ... we are putting up dynamite against the rocks that are coming on our way to clear the whole situation – for full reflection of the omnipresent Being. That's the idea.

The fact that Maharishi showed such understanding, and familiarity, with the problems of stress release leads one to assume that at one time or another he himself had experienced this phenomenon of unwinding and had come through it unscathed. But whatever the reason for the phenomena of 'unstressing', is there nothing that can be done to minimize its impact?

Fortunately for the meditators, there is something that can be done and that was to 'feel the body'. This sounds like a physical exercise but is in fact a mental process whereby the meditator moves his or her attention from thoughts that provoke discomfort, and instead focuses on the body. This technique is also advocated for those who are sick or ill, as a means of healing or at any rate subduing symptoms long enough for the meditator to continue with his or her practice.

The subject of *karma*, the science of action, is central to Hindu philosophy, and it isn't surprising to find the subject raised in connection with meditation. This theory, that for every action there is a corresponding reaction, is a familiar one, and, apparently, a scientific fact. Surprisingly, therefore, it has yet to find universal acceptance. Many people stand firmly by the belief that one may get away with all sorts of misdemeanours, but Hindu faith has no place for such concepts and actively promotes the understanding that the law of *karma* is irreversible (notwithstanding the aid of divine intercession). The scope of the topic of *karma* is further widened when it is considered in connection with another Hindu doctrine, that of reincarnation.

And when Maharishi spoke of past actions, it is unlikely he was alluding merely to just one lifetime but to an immeasurable legacy built up through successive reincarnations. If it is true that human beings have had previous lives, previous forms, then how long would it take to remove the incalculable adverse effects of such pasts?

> This line on the board, and it seems to be such a long line. We can make it short without touching it, by drawing a much bigger line along... uh?
>
> If we have done some ... we have taken some loan, some loan, some loan and we make a big, big income now. That loan becomes tiny, little, little, small, small ... uh? Whatever *karma* we have done, whatever action we have performed, that is imprinted in Nature, we can't reduce it or enhance it. What we can do now is, do a better *karma* than that and let that better *karma* dominate, so that that becomes small ... uh? A $500 loan now, next moment 5 million gained, and that 500 loan seemed to be tiny, if it doesn't seem to be at all. Like that, if some bad has been done, something has been done, it can't be undone. But it can be complicated by a bigger action of a good nature.

Practitioners of Transcendental Meditation are asked merely to witness the thoughts and sensations experienced in meditation, but it is contended that meditation is not a state of passivity but an action, albeit an inner one, which can dispel or neutralize the results of stored *karma* in the individual. It is believed that meditation can ward off illness and sometimes even cure it.

Since good *karma* relates to life-supporting actions, which assist evolution, *karma* is not necessarily a byword for disaster; first one must establish the quality of the *karma*. The complexity of calculating the possibilities of causes and their effects is enormous, not to say unending, and potentially brings into question even the act of breathing, one's very existence in fact. But Maharishi assured that an intellectual appreciation of the laws of cause and effect is not necessary, only the ability to take one's mind to a level of such deep rest that transcendental consciousness becomes established. Having attained this stage of restful alertness, one is better able to emerge imbued with the capacity to act in accordance with Nature. Maharishi contended that, quite automatically, quite spontaneously, that by virtue of a simple natural innocent process - Transcendental Meditation - meditators are able to act rightly and enjoy life to the full.

David Fiske

16

THOSE WHO SPEAK DON'T KNOW

For those attending courses with Maharishi, the major objective was to achieve experiences of states of higher consciousness and thereby enjoy the delights of increased happiness. But this entailed that students first pass through the inner turmoil frequently associated with longer periods of meditation.

Whilst on the course trainee meditation teachers had to come to terms with dimensions of Maharishi's philosophy that they had hitherto been only dimly aware of. To a backdrop of steady chirruping from the jungle blending with the ticking of a clockwork timepiece, Maharishi braced himself before divulging a fuller understanding of the term 'unboundedness', one of the chief gains claimed for the practice of Transcendental Meditation.

> Now, from our own experience we know that we have to go beyond the finest activity and then that ... awareness which even for myself is without any boundaries, unbounded. Now, this unboundedness with reference to myself, how can I attribute that this is here also? That is the question. No? But because this experience of unboundedness with reference to myself has been gained by going beyond the finest experience. And there what we conclude is, beyond the finest strata of material existence is the non-material unboundedness which is myself. And because the entire manifest or material universe has layers of existence, layer after layer, layer within the layer, layer within the layer, from gross to the subtle layers ... uh? And therefore, every little bit of material universe deep within is nothing but unmanifest awareness which is this, what I myself am.
>
> And therefore I am all that I am without a second. Huh? I am the monarch of all I survey and more than that![299]

This is the declaration of *upanishadic* wisdom, *'tattwamasi'* ('Tat Twam Asi'), 'Thou art That" or 'I am That, Thou art That, All this is That'.

So, is the state of unboundedness a state of enlightenment or an intellectual state, or a temporary condition brought about by autosuggestion? The words enlightenment and illumination both suggest an increased presence of light, so perhaps this explains why Maharishi is said to have wanted to measure light emission from meditators.

In order to clarify the difficulties likely to be encountered on the way to an unbounded state of awareness, Maharishi chose to use an analogy focused on light. It went something like this: a mirror's ability to reflect is largely dependent on available light and as such would easily reflect the sun, which is a source of light in itself. However, any dust or dirt on its surface would impede the mirror's capacity to reflect the image of the sun. Similarly, according to Maharishi, an individual's ability to reflect the light of the Supreme is considerably lessened by his or her impurities.

> Sun ... water ... reflection, which is a combination of the two. Reflection, and that is small self, self is the reflection on this nervous system and the reflection of omnipresent Being. So the original thing is Being, but when it is reflected, then full value of Being is not reflected, it is small self. Now this self lingers on three relative states of consciousness, waking, dreaming, sleeping, waking, dreaming, sleeping, waking, dreaming, sleeping. But with the modification of the reflector nervous system the quality of the small self begins to shine more and more in the value of the big self the cosmic. And eventually the value of the reflection the small self gains the value of Being, then we write it with big S ... the Self. So it's just the transformation of the self small into Self big, by virtue of the modification of the nervous system from its stressed and strained condition to its normal functioning level.

Continuing this contemplation on reflections of light, Maharishi noted that in the process of reflecting the sun, the colour of the water inevitably affects the quality of the reflection. A green hue to the water would impact on the clear light of the sun, thus colouring the reflection green, giving an image of a green sun. The message is clear: those who still have *karmic* impurities cannot be adequate conductors of the light of the Supreme.

The word evolution was often used by Maharishi, yet seldom if ever defined. The evolution to which he referred was applied in a specific way, to progressive levels of personal consciousness, and accordingly it has little or nothing to do with Darwin's evolution of the species. Maharishi did not seem to support the notion that the human structure is in a state of evolutionary flux, that one day it might give rise to another species. His vision of evolution was very different in that he saw individuals as having an incomplete awareness but believed that with guidance this incompleteness can be addressed. In other words, those who acknowledge and rectify their shortcomings can hope some day to achieve optimum consciousness and in so doing become 'normal'. That is to say that, those who aspire to reaching the goal of meditation are likely to become normal and any difficulties that impede their progress on the 'pathless path' can be ascribed to physical or psychological abnormalities.

To those who perceived Maharishi's philosophy to be only catering for the mentally fit and physically able, he stated that this practice of Transcendental Meditation can be undertaken by anyone, just as long as they can think.

Maharishi often had to repeat himself to get his points across, and lecture after lecture found him covering the same ground from different directions, restating his points again and again, hoping to make himself understood. Many of his philosophies are difficult to grasp by virtue of their abstract content, so he frequently resorted to the use of analogies in order to offer a clearer understanding.

Speaking about the distinction between self and Self he further explained:

> I don't see any damage of logic in presenting this explanation of Being and transformation of the quality of the nervous system in order to live full Being. I think this reflection analogy is most accurate and it explains the whole idea in a very concrete and picturesque way ...
>
> Because the Absolute is attributeless we cannot explain it through language or remaining in the field of the attribute. What we say is, because the absolute Being is attributeless therefore it is not possible to speak the language of that field and if it is to be explained it can only be explained from the field of the attribute and therefore we say and we explain it. Because it in itself is attributeless and in that sphere of the no attributes, the language, the speech is mute ... uh? The words don't come out and that is why, from its own level, it cannot be spoken of. From its own level it cannot be explained. Therefore we explain it from the level it can be explained. And that's why we are talking about it. We are talking, not because we can't talk about it, but because we can talk about it. We can't talk about it because it can only be talked about on the level of speech. It in its own level cannot be talked about. We don't have a language of the Absolute value but we have a language that can enumerate the Absolute value and therefore we are open to talking about.

Ancient texts can often offer up clear descriptions of lives and events of the past; but in the province of matters metaphysical the power of words becomes strained. The topic of emotions places enormous demands on the skills of lovers who wish to communicate their feelings, so it is likely no less difficult for those who wish to speak of subtle spiritual realms. Maharishi continued:

> Once we start living the Absolute and therefore the speech is running through the Absolute, the sight is running through the Absolute and in this case we can really speak of the Absolute from the level of living it. In [the] other case – from

the level of guessing it, guessing about it. But from this level by living it. Huh
…?

Whilst many mystics of the past signalled their faith through poetry, yet
others chose the language of silence, communicating only by their
presence. So what is the truth of those oft-quoted words: 'Those who speak
don't know'? Well, it seems that anyone who speaks out on matters of
extreme depth is destined to be challenged, and sometimes dismissed. This
no-win situation puts such a person in an unenviable position. It is clear,
from the following remarks, that Maharishi had given very serious
consideration to this subject, enabling him to raise some significant
questions and offer some novel insights:

> Those who *know* it, they only can talk about it and it's … it's … it's … it's wild
> to say that those who know don't talk about it. Then who brings the knowledge
> from generation to generation… uh… if the talking is to be only in the field of
> ignorance? Then we say just 'Those who … those … they don't know about it.

> Now, there are some such passages in the *Upanishads* somewhere, that 'those
> who know it don't talk it'… beautiful passage. It means that those who know it
> have realised cosmic consciousness … huh? By being it and those and those
> who live it in life, whatever they speak, they are only a witness to their speech
> and they are not speaking that. They are only a witness to whatever they are
> speaking, So if they are speaking 'God', they are not speaking not speaking
> 'God', they are just witness to that speech. So those who know it, those who live
> it, don't speak it. But speaking, they don't speak it. Speaking they don't speak it.
> Huh? Not speaking, they don't speak it, but not speaking they don't speak it. So
> it is also right that they don't speak it because not only it they don't speak but
> the fact is that they don't speak anything. Because, just because by their own
> status they are a witness to things, whatever they are speaking they are a witness
> to it.

Maharishi's torrential outpourings, and his outbursts of laughter when
pausing to witness to his words, left his devotees in no doubt that he
understood his subject. Certainly, even if he couldn't confer the immediate
exaltation of an expanded consciousness, he could certainly stimulate his
students' intellects.

> So the knowers of reality don't speak it, but certainly they speak it. Otherwise
> how will this wisdom be transferred from generation to generation? It would
> have ended long ago if they had not spoken it. But because established in that
> reality they are a witness to whatever they are speaking, so speaking they don't
> speak, in this sense knowers of reality don't speak about it otherwise they do.

> Supreme knowledge speaks. It speaks. It speaks. When a knower-man in
> supreme knowledge speaks, it speaks, the Absolute speaks, and that's it. And no
> matter about what it speaks, but it is its speech. *Shruttis* are speech, and any man

in supreme knowledge is It personified. It personified. All this perception, experience, activity, are the activity of it, and therefore, it's not that the knowers of reality don't speak about it or don't speak it. But the fact is that only they can speak it out or only they can speak about it. It is only the knowers of reality that can speak, the ignorant can make gestures about it.

Maharishi had in his explanation done what surely few could do, to take this commonly held notion and review and revise its understanding, completely, remarkably. But who are the ignorant people who 'can only make gestures about it'? Other than Maharishi, are there no other teachers that could point a way to inner peace and greater health and prosperity? For the most part Maharishi's disciples convinced themselves that his way was the best, so they simply weren't interested in the rest.

Interestingly, Maharishi was very open to the idea that other techniques of meditation could work as well as Transcendental Meditation, and he offered a formula by which any other method of meditation might be measured, and that was to ask whether its technique became transcended by its practice. If the vehicle of meditation diminished to a point where it disappeared and yet the practitioner was found wide awake and in a state of fullness and bliss, then that meditation also qualified as Transcendental Meditation. So what of the other forms of *yoga* available in India, many of which promoted the use of *mantras* are they as effective as Transcendental Meditation?

> The state of *yoga* brought about by a *mantra* – this is *Mantra Yoga*. The state of *yoga* brought about by a *mantra* – *Mantra Yoga*. But we refrain from using that term because so much wrong understanding about that science of *Mantra Yoga*, very very deeply mixed up and therefore we don't categorize our system of meditation in any systems of *yoga*.

An example of a *mantra* thought to be suitable for meditation is '*OM*', though also popular are those *mantras* adopted by those desirous of spiritual awakening, and favoured amongst *bhakti* (devotional) groups, are *mantras* in praise of the gods or their *avataars*. Frequently, those practising *japa* (repetition of *mantras*) make use of a *mala* (a rosary sometimes having twenty-seven, fifty-four or 108 beads), to 'count' the chants. The chant of '*Hare Rama, Hare Krishna*' is claimed by its exponents to be transcendental. Since devotees of this *mantra* often sing or dance while chanting; one wonders how they can continue to stand if they indeed transcend their thinking? Maharishi distances himself from such practice, asserting that this style of meditation tires the mind, and that the real gain to be had from its practice lies in the silence that follows the chanting. The instruction given by the *bhaktis,* of 'chant and chant and chant' is in stark contrast to Maharishi's teaching of 'take it easy, take it as it comes'.

Maharishi's own teacher seems to have taught different people different techniques of meditation. Maharishi's Uncle Raj was apparently taught to use a *mala*.

> He gave him a rosary. An Indian rosary has mostly 108 beads. Guru Dev told Dr. Varma to close his eyes and repeat the *mantra* and with every *mantra* touch a new bead so that the rosary would go forward in his hand with each *mantra*.

> Then he told him to only think the *mantra* easily without speaking it any more while his fingers moving forward touched the beads. The rosary has one extra bead attached to it where you start and where eventually you finish the round of 108.

> When Guru Dev saw that Dr. Varma had reached the end of the round at the extra bead, he told him to stop thinking the *mantra*. After some time he told him to open his eyes slowly. He asked him how he felt.

> Dr. Varma said he felt very good and happy. "Very good," said Guru Dev, "now you go home and sit in your room and do three rounds. Then come out slowly, have breakfast and then open your shop and do your work. In the evening after closing your shop go to your room and again do three rounds. Come out slowly and have some food and then you can come to me and tomorrow morning before sunrise come again to me and report your experiences. So the next morning Dr. Varma was most happy to report all the beautiful experiences he had had during the day, business was so good, customers were so friendly and told him he looked so good, he managed to do so many things.
> But as to his meditation he was not quite happy. He said: "I felt so happy with my *mantra*, but I kept forgetting it while my fingers were moving automatically. In each round this happened! What can I do about it?!"

> A wonderful smile was on Guru Dev's face. "FOUND!" he exclaimed. "You have learnt to transcend the *mantra*! Excellent! You transcended the *mantra*, which wants to go back to the source. The best thing that can happen! When you are aware of having forgotten the *mantra* you quietly pick up the *mantra* again and continue happily. This was very good meditation. Continue meditating like that now and tonight and report to me tomorrow morning." [300]

It would be interesting to know what other *yoga* teachings Maharishi's *guru* embraced. Swami Rama is of assistance here, for in recalling his meeting with Swami Brahmananda, he remembered the *swami* showing him a Sri Yantra (the visual equivalent of a *mantra*), its geometric design of superimposed triangles made entirely of rubies.

Of the organizations which also teach *mantra* meditation, there is evidence that a few are extremely similar to Transcendental Meditation, but are taught within a specifically religious framework. Some initiates of TM have gone on to wonder whether a more 'difficult' practice might not yield greater satisfaction. Maharishi was adamant that TM is complete in itself:

> A system which produces the synthesis of benefits gained by all the systems of *yoga*, collective benefits of all the systems of *yoga*. Uh? The spontaneous purity of the system is the achievement aimed by the *Hatha Yoga*, so many systems of purification, so many systems of purification of the body, bring about all kinds of purification which are contained in, in the purification brought about through Transcendental Meditation on both levels, material and structural. Huh?
>
> Experiments have been performed by German meditating medical people to show that the chemistry of the system changes. And naturally these stresses and strains are released. So structural and material changes brought about by Transcendental Meditation are aimed through these various practices of *Hatha Yoga*.

Many spiritual aspirants see the exercises of *Hatha Yoga* - the *asanas* (*yoga* postures) - as preparation for a more 'serious' spiritual discipline, and *yoga* teachers advise that a seeker with an out-of-condition body, with bad habits of diet and habits of 'unspiritual' behaviour, is impure and therefore unable to attain higher experiences. Having established a more wholesome body and mind, by exercises, and with spiritual tuition, the advanced student only then is given permission to perform techniques of *kundalini*, the raising of *shakti* (serpentine energy).

Predictably, Maharishi saw the situation rather differently, citing that the various forms of *yoga* are not to be seen as steps to progress, rather that they are 'limbs' or branches of *yoga* philosophy, and he further contended that all the advantages claimed by the different schools of *yoga* are gained by the practice of Transcendental Meditation, quite automatically and without further study.

But it is difficult to understand how the practitioner of Transcendental Meditation, sitting virtually motionless, can hope to derive the muscular strength and flexibility gained by those practising *yoga asanas*, without taking regular exercise. Indeed, a common experience amongst meditators is a temporary stiffness of the body, presumably brought about by inactivity.

Perhaps this is why Maharishi had Professor Hari Krishna prepare a course of *yoga* postures and *pranayama* (systematic breathing exercises) for meditators. The inclusion of *asanas* in rounding makes a lot of sense, for these exercises provide the much-needed 'outward stroke' of meditation, the chance for the mind and body to resume contact with external reality before continuing with further inner meditation. Maharishi's suggested prayer for those commencing *asanas*:

> *In Thy presence O Lord!*
> *filled with Thy Grace*
> *I am starting Yoga asanas.*
> *Grant me good health energy*
> *and efficiency in life.*
> *I feel Thy Grace,*
> *Thy Divine Presence.*

One of Maharishi's favourite analogies helps illustrate the concept of inner and outward strokes of meditation. It is of a cloth being placed in dye (meditation) and then being hung in the sun to dry (the outward stroke), with this process being repeated until the dye is fixed. According to Maharishi, it is the repetition of this process that makes the dyeing, and the meditation, successful.

Maharishi's basic criticism of the various *yoga* systems was simple, that they had been misinterpreted, and the use of 'control' was being advocated instead of utilizing the 'wandering nature of the mind'.

The 'limb' of *yoga* known as *kundalini* or *Laya Yoga*, is defined as the raising of serpentine spiritual energy, which is said to exist in a dormant state at the base of the spine. It is held that through proper guidance this energy can be awakened and distributed through to the various spiritual centres or *chakras* of the body. This is a highly esoteric subject, the practice of which should only be undertaken under expert supervision. Whereas Maharishi suggested that this raising of the *kundalini* is but another by-product of the practice of Transcendental Meditation, and he let it be known that he believed tall his students had experience of it:

> *Laya Yoga* which deals with *kundalini.* We are experienced; everyone experiences the rising of *kundalini.* So all the effects desired through the practice of *Laya Yoga* are naturally gained without bothering about any one of them.
>
>   The practice of *Raj Yoga* aims at making permanent the state of transcendental awareness. The range of *Raj Yoga* is from the level of transcendental consciousness to the level of cosmic consciousness. This thing naturally results through Transcendental Meditation without taking into account any aspects of the practice of *Raj Yoga.*

After lecturing on the classic schools of *yoga* Maharishi found the wandering nature of the mind all too evident in his students, as one of his devotees asked him about the presence of life in human form on other planets. After some preamble Maharishi dealt with the question:

> Life in other planets? We would say nothing can be useless in creation. If something is created it must have some use. There may be planets without life but the majority of planets should have life in it. Lots of planets may be without life but the very existence shows that they can't be without life. Must be some life.

This answer elicited a certain amount of amusement from those gathered around Maharishi, but the question remained unanswered.

Time was getting on and even those who practised meditation found their energy sometimes waned. After working through several more topics, Maharishi then delivered his views on sleep, for many the closest they ever came to the deep rest and freedom of which he spoke.

> Due to habit the fatigue overtakes and one has to sleep. But the time comes when one doesn't much sleep. Sleep is a nuisance to life but it is inevitable nuisance, a waste of life. But it is inevitable waste. We can't say it.

The nights and days of the three-month course continued, spent alternately listening to lectures and meditating. For some the course was their only opportunity of getting close to Maharishi and hearing his teaching at first hand. But in addition to understanding the way their enigmatic Master thought, they also had the task of learning how to teach his method of meditation. This entailed not only learning the instructions to be given at initiation but also developing the ability to engage in public speaking. Not all the students were equally able, but they all did their best to absorb their lessons.

Those who succeeded in their training would also be expected to perform the function of salesmen for the organization. It was this 'business' side of their responsibilities that posed particular difficulties for new recruits, for how could they ever equal Maharishi's talent for presenting his teachings to new audiences? Like all those new to the field of selling, they needed a pep talk, and the sales manager obliged, outlining the role of those who were to take the news of this technique to the masses.

> This is the purpose of the Movement; we take delight in bringing the light to the other people, making them happy. That is our joy, which lies at the basis of our participation in the Spiritual Regeneration Movement. It's very simple. We are very selfish people, we don't want to see anyone unhappy and therefore for our joy for not seeing any unhappy face around us, we are busily engaged in teaching meditation. It's for our joy.

> 'Tell the people that they are born with that ocean of happiness – come on take a dive!'

Having found fresh converts to whom the technique of meditation could be taught, new teachers were forewarned about the overwhelming gratitude they were likely to encounter from new initiates.

> The teacher of Transcendental Meditation flows in all love and happiness for everything everywhere around him. And in order to set much higher and tidal waves of love in his heart, he is entertaining other people and giving them meditation. If a man says 'I am very thankful to you and you have done so much to me', say: 'Ah, you have brought me such great joy with these experiences, and you deserve more happiness, you deserve more thanks. Because all these expressions of yours bring to me such great joy in my heart and that is the reward that you have given me so I must thank you for that.' And then he feels more and then you feel more.

Once the course was over it was believed that Maharishi would retreat from the limelight and disappear from sight, possibly returning to his cave at the temple in Uttar Kashi, and Maharishi confirmed that it was still his intention to withdraw.

> And then when I go in silence, then our activity will have much more far-reaching effects. Then I'll be with the root and watering the fruit. That also for greater success to all the coming generations. These are the two reasons, basically two reasons.
>
> Once I have successfully established this training of teachers programme in all the countries then the work is done, then it will continue and continue and continue and continue.

Maharishi shared with his students his delight that, even if he had not yet achieved all his objectives, he had been reasonably successful at communicating his basic philosophy – that there are two aspects to life – inner and outer, spiritual and material. He had long been speaking of this concept in terms of a life where 200 per cent of life could be lived, 100 per cent inner and 100 per cent outer. Clearly he believed that this philosophy had gained considerable acceptance, promising a very real chance for the success of his movement, which now had centres dotted right across the free world, where people could avail themselves of his teaching. Also available through the movement were publications, records, tape recordings and films of Maharishi's lectures and discourses, not to mention the opportunity to attend further courses to gain a better intellectual understanding of his philosophy.

But although he had gained much ground he had yet to establish a teaching force sufficient to fulfil his ambitions. Part of the problem was that he demanded a strict uniformity in the pattern of his teaching methods, hence the need to school his students personally. The *ashram* at Shankaracharya Nagar was sufficient only for the training of a few dozen or so at a time. To make matters worse, only a percentage of the course participants were destined to be invested with the power to teach, and fewer still would become active on behalf of his mission. He certainly saw his teachers as a sales force, with a strong marketing strategy. The teachers were expected to work as part of an organization distributing a product, Transcendental Meditation.

> So having manufactured the ice-cream, ice-cream, and having found a beautiful label and then advertised and accepted its value in the market, now I have to see that every generation receives those beautiful packets in their purity.

Maharishi's long-term goal was to develop an organization which would outlive him, and there is strong evidence that his intention was not merely to gratify his own desire to see the spread of all the benefits of his methods, but to secure the possibility of those as yet unborn being offered these 'packets in their purity'. He said: 'Our efforts in this generation may go on for thousands of generations and all the world will enjoy.'

> So now whereas you are taking upon yourself to spread, I am taking upon myself more to consolidate. So the consolidation at the root and spreading on the level of the branches and leaves, both will simultaneously go on...
>
> It's such a joy to have so many, many good people to just spread and spread and ... take care of expansion, expansion. Then the root should be secured and I must keep it secured.

David Fiske

17

WATER THE ROOT AND ENJOY THE FRUIT

As a preparation for the time when some of his students would be speaking out as authorities on the Transcendental Meditation method, Maharishi paid close attention to the topic of public speaking. To pave the way, he addressed the several issues that had consistently created controversy amongst his audiences. Concern was voiced that his teaching might be a form of self-hypnosis or worse, self-worship. Others feared that Maharishi was engaged in an operation of Hindu missionary work. But by far the most common criticism concerned the fees levied for the teaching of meditation, for few could feel comfortable about parting with a week's wages on a whim.

> Religion is a big thing! Very huge ... big! It covers all phases of life and leads all the phases towards highest attainment, that is a religion. Religion covers the individual, family, nation, international, world, God, Creator, Almighty, Omnipresent. All these things are covered by religion.[301]

Religion does more than provide a place for worship and ritual; it also deals with the development of attitudes, offering such help as moral guidance – which might account, at least in part, for Maharishi's reluctance to offer firm guidelines of conduct to his devotees. But some must have doubted whether the teaching of Transcendental Meditation is entirely free from any form of indoctrination that could be interpreted as religious. Consider for a moment the view that the goal of meditation is to contact Being, otherwise known as God. It could be interpreted as an invitation to participate in prayer. Indeed, it is worth noting that some years earlier, when Maharishi had been asked whether meditation was in fact prayer, he answered that it was indeed a 'most refined' and 'powerful' prayer.[302]

The assertion that this meditation is not a religion seems to be rooted in the conviction that even Maharishi's own religion, Hinduism, has failed to lead people to a life of happiness. So his claims that meditation can lead to fulfilment even for the non-religious is encouraging. It is particularly reassuring to note that he advocates the cultivation of individuality, a seemingly liberal approach, quite the opposite to a system of mass conversion to a particular style of religious thought.

> So this [meditation] is useful to man to develop his individuality and then the fully developed man will find his God through his religion. Christians will realize God through Christianity; Muslims will realize God through Islam. But they will become fully developed Christians and fully developed Muslims and fully developed Hindus. So this we say is a technique and not a religion. Useful to the people of all religions.[303]

Maharishi wished meditators to recognize the distinctions between the various aspects of their lives. He cited the responsibility for earning a living, and the role of making purchases, as quite distinct from the responsibilities of a churchgoer or a meditator. Even at home, apparently the separation of activities should not be overlooked:

> When I go to the kitchen, then I look for some delicious dishes and this ... then I don't think of Shakespeare in the library. Then I have some good food before me and when I go to my library I don't think of sweet dishes in the kitchen. Then the Shakespeare and the Milton and Wordsworth and this is my concern in the library.

Established religions have a recognized tendency to create a degree of exclusivity for their adherents, leading some followers to become prejudiced against the followers of other faiths. Disarmingly, Maharishi made light of these potential antagonisms:

> And just as when we feel headache we go to the doctor and then we don't see whether the doctor comes from my church or not. He is a doctor and he gives us aspirin and then we don't see whether this has the label of my church or not.

In order to determine whether or not Transcendental Meditation can be classified as a religion, one would have to take many other factors into consideration, and this would require open access to the method of its teaching, the surrounding philosophy and its attendant belief system.

Much easier to counter is the charge that Maharishi's meditation is self-hypnosis. His commonly-used defence was that self-hypnosis is the result of introducing an idea and maintaining it even in the face of its absurdity, giving the example of a poor man proclaiming 'I am a king, I am a king.'

The teaching of this meditation requires that one focus on a sound 'without meaning for us' (as Maharishi put it), and let other thoughts slip away. In a state of 'no thought', there is obviously no room for thoughts of ownership, status or anything else and one could conclude that there is also no room for self-hypnosis. Commentators have presumed that because his basic philosophy could be used as a tool for self-hypnosis, the practice of this meditation must necessarily employ such a strategy, but Maharishi reassured his devotees otherwise:

> Self-hypnosis means self-delusion, hypnosis – putting oneself into the unrealistic state. But in Transcendental Meditation the effects that we gain, in the process of gaining those effects, we don't think of those effects. We get peace without thinking of peace. We get happiness without thinking of happiness. We get energy without thinking of energy.
>
> So here we enjoy the state of more energy, more intelligence, more happiness. And in hypnosis we place ourself deeply sunk in the thought of these things and that is why Transcendental Meditation is completely opposed to what self-hypnosis is.

Maharishi also condemned hypnosis for its role in breaking the co-ordination between mind and body, pointing out that with Transcendental Meditation co-ordination was improved.

The task of convincing his students about the merits of charging for initiation had also to be dealt with. It might be remembered that before the decision to fix the fee (euphemistically referred to as a 'donation'), contributions were made voluntarily. As if it was not difficulty enough to go out as envoys of Maharishi, the newly trained teachers had also to cope with the embarrassment of asking for money. Their teacher offered advice about how they might tackle this issue:

> We want to announce the charge but we want to announce these words also: 'We are a charitable organization… SIMS is a charitable organization'

Sensing his apparent hesitation and seeking to assist their Master in his explanation, students suggested words and phrases that might be of use to him and gradually a statement was prepared:

> 'Non-profit is the word. Non-profit char- Non-profit education corp-organization.'

Maharishi explained that it was in Los Angeles that the decision to standardize 'donations' had been made:

> People had made a rule, that they put some basket there so that people when they come and when they go, they put something in the basket. And I felt very ashamed with that basket on the door and people coming and I said 'It is like begging on the door', because it was too odd to me to put a basket in front of my room.

An alternate strategy might have been to move the basket elsewhere, however, at that time, Maharishi had many prosperous visitors so he must have wondered why a regulated pattern of financial support could not be made available. Anyway, it was his suggestion that a move be made towards a fixed 'donation', a proposal that was discussed at length. Initially the figure had been set at a week's wages per family, and later, in certain countries, it had become modified, with fixed individual rates being introduced.

Certainly money was needed. How else were his followers to book halls, print leaflets and publish books? But the insistence on compulsory 'donations' ran contrary to his professed doctrine, outlined in his message to the people of Kerala, that the 'path is straight and entry is free'.

Maharishi explained his current thinking:

> We are not ashamed to talk of money, to ask money or to accept money and to spend money. Because more money we have, more quickly we will spread this meditation. Money is needed for quick expansion of the ideology and if we can afford to be very slow then we don't need anything.

Recognizing that his students needed help in coming to terms with this extra responsibility, he offered to make their task easier by teaching them a selection of his winning one-liners:

> Say, 'This is such a great gift to life that it can't be evaluated in terms of some dollars or what or what', like that. That is a good expression to it.
>
> We can always say, 'It can't be repaid, the teaching of Transcendental Meditation can't be repaid, but this is how the organization runs and money is needed more and more' and ... like that.

Traditionally, spiritual organizations have relied on the goodwill of their supporters for funds, and no amount of explanation could conceal the fact that the 'donation' was in fact a fee. And Maharishi angered many of his countrymen who felt that spiritual teaching should be free of charge. Maharishi's own *guru*, Shankaracharya Swami Brahmananda Saraswati, had demonstrated his views on the subject quite unambiguously, having gone so far as to prohibit people from making any material offerings to him whatsoever. The tale is told that on one occasion a follower sought to share some newfound wealth and concealed a few gold coins amongst some flowers close to the Shankaracharya. He received an unexpected response in that he found himself temporarily banned from access to the old *swami*. According to the Hindu belief system, all objects have their own *karma* and evidently he who was hailed as 'infinitely bestowed' had no wish to share the influence of this man's *karma*, golden or otherwise. It is surprising that Maharishi should have taken such an apparently opposite view. He tried to explain:

> The organization needs money, but the method of receiving money has been so constructed, the style of accepting money and giving money. The word donation

provides that structure, the man feels contented in his heart: 'I am giving a donation for some pious work, for some good work.' Now he can give money in this way, feeling good about giving, or he can give money feeling that 'it were better if I had not to give' and yet giving it. Now the money is received by the organization but in one way, as far as the receiving is concerned, the value is the same for both .

That element of the heart and of this ... it's completely missing, it's a matter of the cashier recording it and finished. There is no pious or holiness attributed to it to culture the heart in the act of giving.

[the donations] which we have fixed for ourselves in all these countries, international standards. We just follow that, easily and comfortably.

Before someone can learn the method of Transcendental Meditation, they have first to follow a sequence of preparations. The first step is to attend an introductory talk, the second a follow-up preparatory talk, and the third a personal interview. The object of the introductory lecture is to outline Maharishi's basic philosophy and indicate in general terms what the practice of Transcendental Meditation entails. Having won the confidence and interest of the audience, the second lecture can be mentioned. The need to make a decision as to whether to attend the second lecture or not, filters out anyone who has no real desire to further their knowledge of the subject. So only after attending the second lecture are members of the audience invited to make arrangements for a private discussion with a teacher and be considered for initiation.

The success of the introductory talk is crucial in gaining fresh converts. In the early years, Maharishi had taken sole responsibility for all the introductory, preparatory and private talks, and he was determined to pass on to his wealth of experience to his task force.

Not only were the lecture topics to be carefully prepared beforehand, so too were the answers to the questions most frequently posed. It was perceived that greater gains were to be made by the use of more than one speaker.

That three, four speakers appeal to the people more, someone is charmed by someone, someone is charmed by someone, someone is charmed by someone ... something like that.

So if one speaker failed to appeal, for whatever reason, another might come over better. At any rate, the goal was to persuade the highest proportion of the audience to attend the preparatory lecture: 'Maximum initiations have come from many speaking in one lecture, many.'

All those who embarked on the teaching-training programme were encouraged to note any topics, phrases or anecdotes that they might find useful when lecturing. Students were to make sure that they could speak on issues such as education, health, religion and world peace, but the mainstay of the introductory talk is the preamble outlining Maharishi's basic philosophy. Although this could be presented in diverse ways it can be effectively stated in just one sentence. 'Water the root to enjoy the fruit', that society can be likened to a forest in which all the trees had to gain nourishment. In order to stay healthy and fruitful, each tree needs to be watered separately, so by supplying the needs of all the individual trees, the needs of the whole forest are taken care of.

> Meditation is like watering the root and supplying nourishment to all the aspects of the tree. 'Watering the root' can be defined in terms of the growth of leaf, also 'watering the root' can be defined in terms of the growth of the branches, also in terms of the growth of the flower, also in terms in the growth of the fruit. So 'watering the root' can be defined in numberless ways with respect to the effects it produces in all parts of the tree. Now, like that Transcendental Meditation can have innumerable definitions because it produces effects in all the phases of life.

But Maharishi was swift to acknowledge that, no matter how much work had been put into planning the introductory lecture, there might still be difficulties in getting the message across.

> Only speaking is not the responsibility of the speaker. He should see that whatever he is speaking reaches the ears first and then the mind and also pierces through the heart.

A pretty tall order! But what can be done to ensure that the speakers are not only heard, but also properly understood?

> There could also be a technique of capturing the attention of the people and that is, raise a question sometime. Some question. Maybe you don't wait for the answer from the audience and you answer it yourself, but raise the question and wait ... Five seconds waiting and your silence will awaken the minds and make them all alert.

> Even if one man comes we want to inform him all these four points, so that at least he, who had time to receive the message, could get the benefit of our presence. Because if we have gained one man, through him, his friends, their friends, it progresses like snowballs.

He gave some indication of his fascination with numbers by asserting that four speakers would have sixteen times the impact of a solo appearance. He argued, fairly persuasively, that the presence of a diverse panel of individuals, differing in age and drawn from both sexes, would enhance the chances of successfully imparting the message. One of Maharishi's students was perplexed that it might also be necessary to have so many speakers at the preparatory talk. He was reassured:

> That could be given by single individual, once the man has come for the second time; he is more or less drawn to the thing. Then you could breathe a little easier.

Having elucidated the means of gaining success in public speaking Maharishi then issued a salutary warning to his followers. Of paramount importance to the success of his Movement, he insisted, is solidarity amongst the ranks, and he cautioned his students against indulging in any open contradiction of one another. He explained that any evident lack of mutual respect amongst his initiators would only serve to detract from their status and in turn spread confusion about the meditation:

> Initiator carries an aura of all-knowingness around. The aura of all-knowingness. People like to believe an initiator because they hear that they have been trained.

> We never in our thought or speech or action ever depreciate the value of another initiator. Absolutely, we always hold him high in our mind, in our heart and ... in public. Very very very important, it's absolutely important.

He could have left the subject there, but he also had the responsibility to 'reach the ears first and then the mind and also pierce through the heart' of his students. So instead he chose to entertain them into submission.

> What happened once upon a time.., two *pandits* started from home and they went into a new village and then they were entertained by a very hospitable host. And he went to one and wanted the introduction of the other and then he said, 'Oh, he's just a bull, no intellect, just a bull.' And he went with all respect to the other one and he wanted the other wise man, *pandit.* So he said, 'Oh, he's just a horse, absolutely idiotic, nothing.'
>   When the dinnertime came, he prepared the dish for a bull and he prepared some good grass, very nicely cut, for the horse. And when the two dishes came each started to look to each other – 'Now what to do?' And then he requested them to start on their delicious dish and they would not eat. They just looked at each other.
>   He said, 'I asked you about him, so you said, "He is a bull", and you said, "he is a horse" and this is the food beautiful, delicious food for the bull and for the horse.'

Seemingly Maharishi's concern with integrity was not limited to his teachers; he made it clear that he was concerned with his own reputation too:

> One initiator holds the other initiator down, either in his thought or speech or action, in public or in private, then what he is doing openly is misjudging the value of the founder who had trained him.

Not only was there to be no antagonism between initiators but they were also expected to live up to pretty high standards generally. Maharishi felt inspired to list the qualities that an initiator should possess, what the 'man in the street' might expect from them:

> He expects from the initiator something more laudable, more remarkable, more ideal than he would expect from any other man, naturally.
>
> Friendly and loving and appreciative of each other is ordinary human value, the members of the same club at least.

> People feel that a man who has the ability to give peace to the people and some spiritual experience and raise the level of consciousness, his level of consciousness would naturally be, if not much, at least a little higher than the normal and he would behave a little more humanly at least, if not divinely than other people.

But in order to cover this topic completely, Maharishi also offered guidance as to what should be done if differences of opinion which created ill-feeling did occur. One recommendation of his was to 'feel the body', a mental exercise involving sensing an area of anxiety within the body, and neutralizing it with calmness and patience. And Maharishi warned against the contemplation of wrong thoughts or actions, holding that the same erroneous behaviour becomes inculcated in the beholder. This advice gives an insight into Maharishi's own behaviour, and explains the method by which he avoided confrontations and prevented discord. In an interview back in 1967 he was asked if he ever became angry, and answered:

> I am concerned with the suffering of the world, but I don't become angry with those who are suffering (laughter – shrieks) because I know through love I could make them happy. I could make them meditate and love. And if I feel angry with them then they are suffering – they will suffer out of my anger more. So there is no reason for me to be angry on any account.[304]

So Maharishi had now to devise ways to stop his initiators from becoming angry, or at the least prevent them from letting off steam and expressing their anger. He made no mention of the potential consequences of suppressing anger, which would likely add to accumulated stress, but chose instead to share an appropriate old Indian proverb:

> The sword will fail to serve where the needle will accomplish the goal. A big sword will prove to be useless and the needle will do the trick.[305]

In a bid to protect the teaching of Transcendental Meditation from distortion, Maharishi had devised a set of instructions to be learned parrot fashion by his students. It seems he believed this pre-formulated approach to instruction and checking would ensure the correct experience of meditation. The instructions are known as the 'checking notes', and have a series of numbered points which are supposed to cover every contingency that may arise. By memorizing the points, the initiator or checker uses them as a method for faultfinding. If the answer to a point is 'yes' then the checker can proceed to another numbered point. If the answer is 'no' then a different point is indicated. In this way a universal procedure was instituted which would, theoretically, prevent personal variations finding their way into the teaching of meditation, to keep the system of teaching free from impurities, to prevent his students 'getting ideas' about themselves.

Maharishi stated:

> 'With all these thirty-eight, thirty-nine points of checking, training of checkers has become very easy and mechanical.'

After the cloning process was successfully completed, Maharishi would then decide who most closely resembled the original. To these chosen students he would disclose the vehicles of meditation (the *mantras*) and the means of their selection. It might be presumed that possession of this knowledge of the *mantras* would in itself be enough to instruct someone in the method of this meditation, and since there are many who are deeply curious about the *mantras* and the method of their selection, why should they not have their curiosity satisfied? This would surely be a very direct method of fulfilling Maharishi's desire to produce a significant increase in those who knew how to meditate.

But Maharishi looked at the situation of teaching meditation from the completely opposite viewpoint. His concern was to ensure that the new initiate would know exactly how to use the technique he or she was given:

> 'Use of the *mantra* is one technical thing which is the central core to the whole training programme.'

According to Maharishi, this ability, to be able to train someone in the correct use of the *mantra*, is acquired before the specific details of the *mantras* are given. And another reason for confining information about the *mantras* just to trained teachers was that if the *mantras* were communicated in any way other than orally, then mispronunciation would most likely result.

Even with such precautions, there was still room for misunderstandings. Amongst those taught under the auspices of the Movement, there were situations of some confusion, a fact which Maharishi guardedly acknowledged:

> With experience it was found that some steps which were thought to be useful were no more useful. Better they leave them. So, some little change in the

expression of instructions but that does not change the basic thing.

As an example of this confusion, he cited an occasion when one initiate asked to have her *mantra* checked by a novice initiator, and the matter later came to Maharishi's attention.

> Her *mantra* became very subtle, then it expanded, naturally it became lonnngggg... like that. And experiencing that long drawn *mantra* of two or three syllables, she thought that her *mantra* is changed and she took her *mantra* to be that lengthened state of the *mantra* which naturally was more charming. *Mantra* in its finer state – much more charming, and it came out to be two or three syllables, whereas her *mantra* was one syllable and because it happened to be more charming she picked it up.

But the novice teacher had been unable to offer such a clear explanation, which all adds credence to Maharishi's claim that in order to teach meditation, it is necessary to first become thoroughly familiar with both the practical and the theoretical aspects of the teaching. Knowledge of the *mantras* is vital information that turns successful students into *bona fide* teachers of Transcendental Meditation.

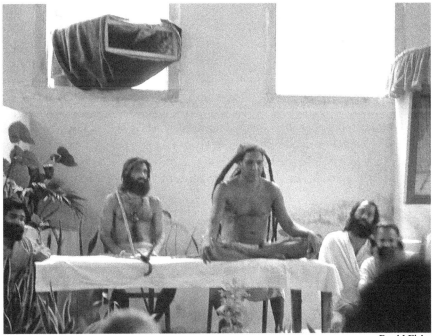

David Fiske

18

— ★ —

FREE WILL OVER DESTINY

Although his training courses usually conformed to a structure of sorts, this did not inhibit Maharishi's tendency to follow his own inimitable and spontaneous flow of ideas. Having proposed the basic topics, his lectures would usually develop a life of their own. Sometimes he would tell a story, share an anecdote or quote from Indian scriptures, but mainly he would focus on the fundamental issues of meditation and it's teaching. Themes would be examined and repeatedly re-examined, and through this process, a thorough revision of the basic vocabulary resulted. Students attending the three months of lectures were eager to remember all that they had heard, but not all could afford the luxury of a tape recorder, and even those who had brought one, had not foreseen the need to bring many dozens of blank tapes with them. The problem was remedied in an old-fashioned way, with the students taking written notes, and the *ashram* had thoughtfully provided hard-back exercise books for this purpose, with a picture of Maharishi on the front cover and the course date and location too.

There was so much to write about - the theory of *mantras*, the information regarding the Holy Tradition, and about 'Guru Dev', the celestial connection and philosophical concepts such as free will and destiny, not to mention the basic techniques of lecturing and teaching. Each time a subject was discussed, different facets of Maharishi's thinking would emerge.

Of the broad array of Maharishi's topics, by far the most intriguing was that of the mysterious and seemingly magical *mantras*. These were the vital ingredients that set Transcendental Meditation apart from other mental exercises.

Continuously dwelling on a particular sight, smell or sound would seem like an act of concentration, but Maharishi steadfastly maintained that concentration is not a part of the method. So, perhaps the benefits of meditation are achieved by first saturating one's mind in the sound of the *mantra* and then slipping into a state of blissful ease, devoid of thought? The poet Tennyson is said to have discovered a similar phenomenon, in that he found that if he repeated his own name sufficient times he would be transported into a beatific state of mind and freed from anxiety. So how does Tennyson's experience compare to the use of the 'meaningless sounds' and the practice Transcendental Meditation. If it comes to free choice then not sounds of another religion, or, come to that, why not just choose *any* sound of one's own preference? The answer seem to lie in the belief that the *mantras* offered in Transcendental Meditation have been passed from teacher to teacher over many thousands of years, and that they sprang from an unbroken tradition of masters who possessed the correct knowledge concerning their selection.

> They are passed on from the master to the disciple in every generation and this is the teaching that concerns very fine levels of the whole creation. The theory of the *mantras* is the theory of creation. As from the unmanifest, manifest comes. So the basic structure of individual life is considered as a whole and the vibrations or the sound waves which would create soothing influence on the existing vibrations of the individual. A *mantra* may be just a word or a sound for one man, and that sound may become the *mantra* of another man. So the sound becomes a *mantra* by virtue of its quality to resonate with the existing impulse of the individual.[306]

So, not just any sound is suitable as a vehicle for meditation; it would appear that an individual resonates best with a specific sound or sounds.

> Physics tells us everything is nothing but vibration, bundles of vibrations, specific permutations and combinations of the impulses ... That is what makes the individual life. A sound that will resonate with some other sound. See, if we play a tuning fork and a wire is strung on a particular tension starts ... huuuummmm. So this quality of resonance makes a sound, a suitable *mantra* for the individual.

This reasoning would be new to most initiates, that a solid body can be made to resonate merely by the inaudible inner chanting of a *mantra,* at a level of internal existence, but far too subtle to be appreciated or measured by external means.

If a different *mantra* were to be specified for each individual, knowledge of an incalculable number of different *mantras* would be needed, but Maharishi taught his students that humanity can be grouped into categories, and that one can with confidence specify the same *mantra* for anyone within each category. He illustrated this principle with an analogy:

> When the doctors infuse blood, transfusion of blood, they tally the sample with the specimen of the body. If the two samples match or correspond with each other, then that is the blood that will be transfused in that body, that's it. So the

harmony between the vibrations of the body and the vibrations of the *mantra*, the harmony between them decides the suitability of the *mantra* to the individual.

Through long practice of usages of these *mantras* for different types of people, certain universal formulae have been obtained and using those formulae of judgement the selection of a proper *mantra* is brought about on a very mass production level. Everything has been made easy, nothing is so much difficult.

It is commonly held that some words can reasonably be described as meaningless, but can the same be said of thoughts? But it seems that what counts is the effect.

And when we have to experience the subtle states of a thought, then we must consider what quality of a thought we should take, what kind of thought we should take. And then we are very careful to select the suitable thought, suitable thought.

The suitability of the thought lies not so much in the meaning of it, but more in its physical quality. And therefore the knowledge of the suitability of a thought for an individual is a very expert knowledge for which we depend on the tradition of our masters. What thought will suit what man? The tradition of masters is the most authentic place to take these suitable thoughts from. Authenticity from the tradition is the only measure which will give us some confidence about the absolute suitability of the *mantra*, of the thought.

If the *mantra* is right it means 100 per cent favourable effects will be multiplied millionfold as the *mantra* becomes finer and finer. If the *mantra* is not proper, not proper means maybe 5 per cent less than suitable, 10 per cent less than suitable, 50 per cent less than suitable, 1 per cent less than suitable and when *mantra* becomes very fine then 99 per cent suitable effect will become million times great. At the same time 1 per cent unsuitable effect will become million times great. That effect we certainly don't want.

By reinforcing time and again how highly technical and scientific this process is, Maharishi was gradually preparing his students for the time, in their turn had to deal with questions about the choice of *mantras*. He cautioned them:

We don't mention it from our side, but if asked, we ... are not in a position to say, 'We are not going to speak', so we speak about it and this is the point that we speak. It is in our favour to say, 'The correct choice of the *mantra* is highly necessary.'

And then we say, 'For this reason we must have 100 per cent suitability of the word that we want to use during meditation.'

We can also say one more thing: 'The value of gaining the contact with the Absolute is one value and until the mind has transcended the increasing power of the *mantra* to produce all good effect is another value.'

The assertion that those of the Shankaracharya tradition were the custodians of the *mantras* sounded remarkably plausible, in that it is highly probable that a monastic community would have amassed a number of secret disciplines, and passed them on through a succession.

Along with the memorising of the checking points, Maharishi's students had also to learn a get to grips with a sequence of Sanskrit verses commonly referred to as the Holy Tradition. The intoning of these verses is an integral part of the initiation rites of Transcendental Meditation.

If the new initiate asks about this part of the initiation, he or she is likely to be reassured that it is only a list of previous masters of meditation. But, it is curious that in all the available transcripts and translations of this *puja*, the name of Swami Brahmananda's *guru*, Swami Krishnanand, is not listed.

An extract from the Holy Tradition is given in the Appendix to Maharishi's commentary on the *Bhagavad-Gita*, Chapters 1-6, and the verses quoted are an invocatory prayer addressed to both Hindu divinities and celebrated spiritual teachers of antiquity. Listed are Lord Narayana, Brahma (the creator God), Vashista, Shakti, Parashar (son of Shakti), Vyasa, Shukadeva, Gaudapada, Govinda, Shri Shankaracharya (disciple of Govinda) and Shankara's disciples (Padma-Padam, Hasta-Malakam, Trotakacharya and Vartikkar). The name of Brahmananda Saraswati is also included, and as a part of the *puja* ritual, the initiator bows to all of them.

To confirm the suspicion that the *puja* is not just a listing of spiritual teachers but a devotional prayer, one need only take a ferry ride across the River Ganges from Shankaracharya Nagar to Swami Sivananda's Divine Life Society *ashram*, complete with *ayurvedic* dispensary. In his lifetime Swami Sivananda, a retired doctor, was highly regarded for his many good works and his writings, including a commentary on the *Bhagavad-Gita* and the *Brahma Sutras*. His devotional sect worship the *gurus* of their tradition and in their *Guru Vandana*, several verses are similar if not identical to those that were being memorized by students at Dhyan Vidhya Peeth, Maharishi's *ashram*. These are quoted below:

I prostrate myself to Lord Narayana, Brahma, Vasishtha, Shakti, his son Parashara, Vyasa, Shuka, Gaudapada, Govindapada, his disciple Sri Shankaracharya, his disciples Padmapadacharya, Hastamalaka, Trotaka, Sureshwaracharya, the commentator, and all other Brahmavidya *Gurus*.

I salute Sri Shankara Bhagavatpada, the bestower of peace and auspiciousness to the world at large, the ocean of mercy, and the seat of all learning inculcated in the Shruti, Smriti and Puranas.

I adore, again and again, the Lord Siva who is Shankaracharya and the Lord Vishnu who is Badarayana [Bhagavan Vyasa], who wrote the Sutras [Vedanta] and the commentaries.[307]

Indeed, there are many different communities who lay claim to belonging to the Shankaracharya tradition.

The absence of The Beatles or any other famous musicians on the 1969 teacher-training course was not enough to deter Maharishi's students from occasionally lifting their voices in song. Accompanied by some tidy strumming on guitar, a group of students performed devotional songs of their own composition (mainly in praise of Maharishi and his teaching), and with zealous fervour they recited chosen verses of the Holy Tradition. Amongst the verses offered up, the name of one individual predominated, that of Maharishi's 'Guru Dev'. Excitement ran high when it was learned that a film of the former Shankaracharya had come to light:

> Jerry got Guru Deva's very deteriorated film renewed and revitalized. Yes, it has come and we will see it some day. It's very beautiful. It's just five or ten minutes film but it gives some shots of 'Guru Dev', so beautiful. Something very precious, beautiful, that you feel like it was yesterday.[308]

The subject of destiny looms large in the teachings of Swami Brahmananda. So, how did Maharishi interpret this aspect of traditional Hindu thinking, and the notion that mankind has free will?

Some years earlier Maharishi had deliberated on this very subject, suggesting that unlike other species, man has freedom of action. But how could he reconcile this view with the apparently opposite view of man bound by destiny, a slave to fatalism? So, freewill, or destiny?

> Actually these are the two names for the same thing. Two names for the same thing and what lies between the two names is some time distance. Some difference of time, some distance of time. With the time difference taken off, destiny and free will are the same thing.

Expanding on this statement, Maharishi went on to say that destiny is the direct result of actions taken in the past, actions undertaken in a state of free will, and that the influence of those past actions create circumstances in which further action is to be undertaken, also in a state of free will. He summarized this philosophy and at the same time offered his students a little Sanskrit tuition, using a verse from Patanjali's *Yoga Sutras*:

> Destiny may influence, but we are not compelled to be overthrown by the force of destiny. *Heyam dukham anagatam* – it will be good to remember this in the original Sanskrit.
> It means: Avert the danger that has not yet come.

To reinforce the meaning of this saying, Maharishi pointed out that it adequately portrays 'the play of free will against the force of destiny'.

Evidently, by carefully predicting the effects of past actions, one is better able to assess what action to perform in the present, thus ensuring potentially negative effects are minimized and positive effects maximized. So, if before deciding a course of action, sufficient thought is given to its likely outcome, one might free oneself from any unexpected reactions.

As with any topic to Maharishi talked spoke about, some mention of meditation was never very far away. In this case he framed the practice of Transcendental Meditation - TM - as an action that could avert the unwelcome dangers that had not yet come:

> TM is absolutely conducted by cosmic intelligence, by the nature of life. Nature of life is to move more and more towards infinite. This nature of life pushes the mind on and on to the infinite. So most spontaneous action of minimizing activity which is Transcendental Meditation is the technique of living. That means, now here is the technique of living which is capable of raising man above the influence of his own doings of the past. Most spontaneous, most natural action of Transcendental Meditation which puts an end to activity, is the technique of action which cuts asunder the bondage of action in the past for the doer and establishes him high above the reach of his own doings of the past. This is free will over destiny. That's it!

So, with respect to past actions, this meditation technique was being prescribed as a 'karma-buster'. According to Maharishi, not only is past *karma* destroyed, but also any need to mention destiny: 'Only those who do not meditate complain against destiny in their laziness to rise.'

Maharishi had said that by repeatedly gaining transcendental or pure awareness, a state of cosmic consciousness is developed. He postulated that if this higher state of consciousness could be brought about by the individual mind repeatedly submerging its identity within the cosmic mind, then one could naturally arrive at a state in which the heart becomes sufficiently expanded to give rise to a condition where cognition of the celestial can be achieved. One assumes he wasn't speaking of an increase of the heart's actual physical size but of the capacity for love. This suggestion, that a person both hearty and loving has the innate ability to comprehend a world of angels and gods, is a revelation indeed.

> The atmosphere about angels is so pretty that even though they have principally, and practically also, greater ability of performance and action, but their free will is hampered by the great prettiness of the atmosphere. Here in man the atmosphere is just enough to keep him hoping for more and more and more.
>
> Greater free will in the life of the angels is hampered by the much more valuable and more fulfilling environment of the angel world.

This suggestion, of a heaven inhabited by angelic forms, immediately raises questions concerning entrance to such a sphere. Those whose belief system encompasses the doctrine of reincarnation are likely to hope that at some time they too might enter such a divine world. How did Maharishi feel about such ideas? What news had he of the 'great beyond'?

> The suffering at the time of birth and death is tremendous. That suffering is great, that's why there is no fun in getting to the pool of suffering over and over again. Very great suffering at the time of death and at the time of birth. And therefore even though the life of angels seems to be very alluring, but this is path to the angelic life, through so many births and deaths, simply horrible. It's just unbelievably horrible.

From these and the following remarks that Maharishi had vivid memories of a life before his birth in Jabalpur:

> Now imagine a house in darkness and you have to feel around every door and every bedroom and bathroom and everything and everything and just all in darkness, darkness. That is how terribly miserable will that state be, until you have located everything that there may be, and then you start living it. All that period of tremendous ignorance and trying to establish in that darkness, this is what happens when one enters the body.
>   Then the faint, fragile, almost incomplete structure is there, the eyes are there, but they don't open, the ears are there, but they don't ... nothing. And then the sense of sight has to enter this dwelling house and then it has to find its place and proper ... sense of hearing and sense of smell, and then the breath begins to flow and the lungs and all. Every aspect of the subjective personality has to feel its way and establish its new home in that lump of flesh.

Now, was Maharishi speaking from experience? The intimacy with which he described the period before birth might lead one to think that he was drawing on personal recollections, but in an interview some two years previously, when asked whether he could remember anything before his present birth he had not been forthcoming, other than giving this cryptic remark:

> 'I can find out if I want ...'[309]

It is of note that on many a sensitive issue he would avoid offering a direct response, apparently preferring to retain an air of mystery about himself. This could be interpreted in a manner of ways; perhaps that since his goal was to promote greater understanding about this meditation he chose not to confuse the issue by being drawn into a discussion of personal matters.

Having warned his students of the suffering involved in birth and death, Maharishi had to some extent quelled their eagerness for knowledge of reincarnation. Nevertheless, the inevitability of death has to be faced and his students wanted to know whether he believed that by practicing

Transcendental Meditation one was better prepared for the 'very great suffering' of death, he spoke of? In Sanskrit and in Hindi a word most closely connected with death is *prana*. Although this word is commonly used to mean 'breath' it has other, finer, definitions. Maharishi had this to say about it:

> *Prana* ceasing to function! Now, disease here and there is a grosser explanation, but *prana* ceasing to function is the phenomenon of death.[310]

Maharishi had stated that in meditation the rate of breathing becomes shallower and upon entering the state of transcendental consciousness breath becomes minimized, and, very occasionally, suspended. He thus contended that by habituating the body to entertain states of little or no *prana* the experience of giving up one's life breath is made that much easier. This sounds reminiscent of the Christian thought that one should 'die daily'.

It was Maharishi's habit, to show how every new topic raised had some relevance to this practice of Transcendental Meditation, so he then showed his disciples how to harness this perception of death to their teaching practice.

He chose to share another anecdote.

Several years before, at a three-three-day camp in Varanasi, an elderly physician had come to him. In the course of his work this doctor had witnessed the deaths of many people, and through their pulse he had sensed the great agony that their deaths seemed to entail.

Maharishi recalled the elderly doctor saying to him:

> 'Now it is my time, very near. I have come to you because you are the disciple of a very great master. Can you help me in dying in such a way that I don't suffer death?'

> I said, 'It's very simple.'

> He said, 'What?'

> Just this one thing I said. 'If your body is habituated to maintain itself, even for a moment, without *prana*, and if this maintenance of the moment is a pleasant, blissful state of experience, then when your mind will go, when your body will start going out of the influence of *prana*, then you will really enjoy. It's only a matter of giving the body a habit of maintaining itself without *prana*, and this will happen if you can gradually minimize *prana*, if you can minimize *prana*, minimize *prana*, minimize *prana* and then come to a normal state of *prana* and minimize *prana*. This habit will give you the stand in that state where the *prana* is completely gone and the body is surviving.'

> That was the question of him and I gave him Transcendental Meditation, but, on

the level of his demand. Where is this question of death and where is Transcendental Meditation? But in five minutes I connected him with his needs, which is the fulfilment of his needs. That's all!

This is what a teacher has to do, just the salesmanship. You sell your product to someone who needs it, or to someone who doesn't need it. An intelligent businessman gains profit whether the rates go low or high in the market. He wins, whether the market is rising high or falling low. It doesn't matter, but he makes a profit.

Maharishi instructed trainee teachers to keep copious notes on all aspects of lecturing, for future reference, and to record any useful points made by their fellow students:

This is the time to be 'bee'. We have been talking of being 'Being', now we are talking of being bees. One flower and pick up something nice, and the other flower and pick up something nice, and the other and pick up something nice.

By sharing their material Maharishi felt that his students would find lecturing easier.

Maharishi explained that the main role of the lecturer was simply to make the audience crave the chance to be taught Transcendental Meditation:

We don't have even to create hunger, the man is hungry already. We just let him know that he is really hungry. Just information that there is Being and then information that it is possible to experience. Everyone knows the Being is there. Fine. But only he doesn't know how to get on to it. But just this one information that it is available by nothing else other than its own nature. Nature of the mind and nature of the Being, one glides into that, and this is enough.

You can't imagine what a shock he gets. In all that you speak for ten minutes, you have been giving him ten shocks. Every information that you relay is a flash of knowledge to him.

David Fiske

In David Fiske's autobiography, *Stalking Personal Power and Peace*, he describes his arrival at Maharishi's *ashram*:

'To get to the Rishikesh ashram they had rented, they were going to use taxis. But Maharishi, after long, heated bargaining, decided the price demanded was too much and said "Come on we're walking". Most of the participants would have preferred to pay the high fee than carry their suitcases the fair distance.'

David Fiske

PART III

— ★ —

The Enlightenment Business

19

———★———

NOTHING BUT THE SWEET TRUTH

As the spring 1969 Spiritual Guides' training course drew to a close, Maharishi's students looked forward to a brief extension of their stay in India, a visit to Kashmir. As if the shocks they had received during the course were not enough, their teacher now announced that he wished to see them at their best. They took him at his word and dozens of bemused devotees cast off their jeans, sweatshirts and tennis shoes, and scrabbled through their luggage to find the most formal articles of clothing they could lay their hands on. Evidently Maharishi wished to distance himself from the contemporary trend towards individualism and free expression; and so regain the respectability his Movement had lost by his free association with The Beatles, the celebrities who had clearly contributed to his rise to fame.

Whilst in Kashmir Maharishi met with Swami Lakshmanjoo, a teacher of Kashmir Shaivism and propounder of the benefits of *112 Ways of Transcending, the Vaighan Bhyghan Tantra* of Lord Shiva.

As fate would have it, Maharishi also met with Acharya Rajneesh, a fellow Indian spiritual teacher who, like Maharishi, hailed from Jabalpur. Rajneesh recalls the meeting:

> I have met him, just by chance, and in a strange place - Pahalgam. He was leading a meditation camp there, and so was I. Naturally my people and his were meeting each other. They first tried to bring him to my camp, but he made so many excuses: that he had not time, he wanted to but it would not be possible.

> But he said, "One thing can be done: you can bring Bhagwan here so that my time and my scheduled work is not disturbed. He can speak with me from my stage." And they agreed.

> When they told me I said, "This is stupid of you; now I will be in unnecessary trouble. I will be in front of his crowd. I don't have to worry about the questions; the only problem is that it will not be right for the guest to hit his host, especially before his own crowd. And once I see him I cannot refrain from hitting him; any decision I make not to hit him will be gone."

But they said, "We have promised."

I said, "Okay. I'm not bothered, and I am ready to come." It was not very far, just a two-minutes' walk away. You just had to get in the car, and then get out again, that was the distance. So I said, "Okay, I will come."

I went there, and as I had expected he was not there. But I don't care about anything; I started the camp - and it was his camp! He was not there, he was just trying to avoid me as much as he could. [311]

So Rajneesh spoke to the assembled group of teacher training students, openly challenging the very basis of Maharishi's teachings.

Really, there can be no method as far as meditation is concerned. Meditation is not a method. Through technique, through method, you cannot go beyond mind. When you leave all methods, all techniques, you transcend mind. So meditation itself is not a method. Truth cannot be achieved through method. Method is our own invention. We, who are ignorant, have achieved knowledge through methods constructed, created, projected, in our ignorance. Through method you can achieve a sort of self-hypnosis, a sort of auto-hypnosis. Any method, whatsoever it's name, can only give you an illusory kind of peace. Through method you cannot go beyond yourself, because the method is yours, and it will strengthen you, your ego, your state of mind. If you leave all methods and all paths, and all ways, and remain in a total vacuum, doing nothing, thinking nothing -- only then what we call meditation can be achieved.

But if you are following some method, some path, some *guru*, then you are going nowhere...

(many people laugh loudly in disbelief.)

... because it cannot lead you anywhere.

It can only lead you into an illusory state of auto-hypnosis. [312]

Somebody must have told him because he was staying in the hotel just nearby. He must have heard what I was saying from his room. I started hitting him hard, because when I saw that he was not there, I could hit him as much as I wanted to, and enjoy doing it. Perhaps I hit him too hard and he could not stay away. He came out giggling.

I said, "Stop giggling! That is okay on American television, it won't do here with me!" And his smile disappeared. I have never seen such anger. It was as if that giggling was a curtain, hiding behind it all that was not supposed to be there. [313]

But Maharishi was ready to debate with Rajneesh, and fortunately the meeting was recorded.

Maharishi: Transcending on the verge of the finest perception is of the immediate. That can be gross perception or, if one has arrived at the finest perception that one has, then he experiences. And ..... he experiences eventually in a very systematic manner the awareness reaches the pure awareness -- it transcends. Transcending is applicable from the level of gross perception, through all the subtle perceptions, to the subtlest perception. Transcending, one has to take one's awareness, and this is the method. What can be refuted is the practice of meditation if I have already achieved cosmic consciousness where the pure awareness is already established. But if I know I am not living in this consciousness, then something has to be done to live it. And if you can say there is nothing to be done, fine. Nothing is to be done and the ..... can be achieved.

Rajneesh: The very achieving mind, the mind which longs for achievement, the mind which seeks achievement, the mind which is after achievement, is the hindrance. This longing to achieve is the hindrance. So God cannot be made an achievement. The enlightenment cannot be made an achievement. You cannot make it an achievement. It is the non-achieving mind which achieves. The non-achieving. It can never be an achievement, because that which has been achieved has been always with me.

It has never been lost.

Questioner: But how do you know it?

Rajneesh: This knowing, in that knowing, you also know this: that this has been with you, and you were not knowing it. But nothing has been achieved.

Questioner: But you know it afterwards.

Rajneesh: You have simply awakened that which was asleep then that when you try to go through safe, secure, systematic methods, your mind is a mind which longs for serenity, safety, systems. All that you gain is a big ego.

Maharishi: The state of enlightenment is not inertia. It is an achievement. God-realization, when we say you have god-realization, it is an achievement from the state where you have not achieved it. Enlightenment, the very word enlightenment, means "I was so long in ignorance, and now I am in light"; so this, in the common language of ignorance, is called enlightenment. In the language of the enlightened people it has ever been, it is ever; nothing has been realized. If you have lost the awareness of your glasses and then you begin to be aware of the glasses here and here, you have the glasses on, but yet you are searching and somebody says it is there, it is lost. It is lost in the awareness. It was present there certainly. If achieved, it is realized. It has been there, but I have lost it; without really losing it I have lost it, and without really gaining it, I have gained it.

It is there. So this is the achievement of the already achieved. Omnipresent is that thing, and eternal is that thing. And it is nothing that I was never not it, or it is nothing that I would at one time be it. From this level of ..... state of awareness, nothing to be achieved, nothing to be done, nothing to be done. And, therefore, if there is need of achieving it, there is need of being that we achieve it quickly through a technique. It happens, it happens, and then it will happen at all, at all, at all.

These are different ways of expressing. There is a story in some Upanishad with three or four very good seekers of truth come to an *acharya* and said, "We want to ask some questions." He said, "Questions to ask? All right. Remain in my *ashram* for a year, and after that I'll give a chance, and if I know the reality, I'll tell you." he doesn't give a guarantee that even after the year he will tell them actually where ..... are. He just says, "Remain in my *ashram*, and after a year." With preconditions, with a devotional attitude -- service to the Master, obedience. What is the relevance? If someone knows a thing, if you ask in good faith, but it is necessary to get acquainted with the language of a teacher. It is to the expression that we can go. And if you live with him for some time, then you know what he means by what. The Indians feel you have to be near a teacher to know what he means by what expression.

Otherwise he has his usual way of expressing; you have your usual way of understanding. There may not be any connection between the two. You may not be understood by him. He may not be understood by you. There will be a lack of achievement...... That is why familiarity with the teacher, familiarity with the way of his expressing, what he says when he says something, what he means when he says something; that is why nearness to the teacher is necessary. You have been exposed (?) to a phraseology with which you were not familiar. And once you hear Acharya Rajneesh a few times, you will know what he means. So it is (?) exposing yourself to familiar expression. [314]

At length, Maharishi made ready to leave the assembly.

Naturally it was too much for him, and he said, "I have other things to do, please excuse me."

I said, "There is no need. As far as I am concerned you never came here. You came for the wrong reasons, and I don't come into it at all. But remember, I have got plenty of time."

Then I really hit him because I knew he had gone back into his hotel room. I could even see his face watching from the window. I even told his people: "Look! This man says he has much work to do. Is this his work? Watching somebody else work from his window. He should at least hide himself, just as he hides behind his giggle."[315]

After the teachers' training course in Rishikesh and Kashmir, Maharishi had the time and space to fulfil his plans of retirement into a life of silence. The announcement that one of his *brahmacharin*, Swami Satyanand, was to undertake a world lecture tour in his place. It looked as though the present crop of students might well be the last Maharishi would instruct, for it seemed that he had nominated his successor and could now disappear from sight.

With Maharishi no longer the subject of media attention, his disappearance into silence would have gone virtually unnoticed.

In August 1969 a hirsute and denim-clad George Harrison gave an interview, published by the *International Times*, in which it sounded as though he still very much supported Maharishi and Transcendental Meditation.[316] It appeared that lapse of communication between The Beatles and Maharishi might yet be remedied, but George stressed that having already involved himself in giving publicity to meditation, he now preferred to stay out of the limelight:

> You can't say that going on the television and speaking to the press and doing things like that is a bad way to tell people about meditation. On the other hand, after being through all that, it was part of our everyday life. I wanted it to be quieter, much quieter. Anyway, the main thing was you asked whether it had ended or not – it's just that we physically left Maharishi's camp – but spiritually never moved an inch. In fact, probably I've got even closer now.

Not only was Beatle George still meditating but also he was still very active in his advocacy of its attendant philosophies. However, that said, he might have raised eyebrows amongst some of Maharishi's henchmen on account of his style of presentation:

> Well, again I'll quote Maharishi, which is as good as quoting anybody else, and he says 'For a forest to be green, each tree must be green', and so if people want revolutions, and you want to change the world and you want to make it better, it's the same. They can only make it good if they themselves have made it – and if each individual makes it himself then automatically everything's alright. There is no problem if each individual doesn't have any problems. 'Cause we create the problems – Christ said 'Put your own house in order', and Elvis said 'Clean up your own backyard', so that's the thing. If everybody just fixes themselves up first, instead of everybody going around trying to fix everybody else up like the Lone Ranger, then there isn't any problem.

According to Harrison, the Christian Church had failed to provide him with Christ consciousness and that only through his contact with Indian thinking had he gained a proper understanding, a spiritual awareness:

> Donovan said a great thing a while back, he said 'I never went to church much, but since I found the temple in my own mind I visit it very often.' Which is great. That's what all the meditation thing is about.

George Harrison seemed to enjoy sharing wise quotations:

> Vivekananda, who was one of the first swamis who came to the West, said 'Don't believe in anything, if there's a God we must see him, if there's a soul we must perceive it – it's better to be an outspoken atheist than a hypocrite.'

He was evidently up to his eyes in Indian philosophy and happy with it. But

why had he opted to take a lower profile publicly, when he obviously had
so much to say?

> The more I know about it, the more pointless it is to say anything because I
> realise how ignorant I am about the whole thing. There's so much there to know
> that it's ridiculous.

The role of Maharishi's organisations, printing leaflets, flyers and posters,
in order to reach out to those who had not yet received the message about
meditation, continued. Over the page from George Harrison's interview,
sandwiched between advertisements for sex magazines, films and toys,
appeared the following small ad:

Transcendental Meditation

Transcendental Meditation is a simple technique which takes the attention
naturally from the ordinary thinking level to the source of thought, the Inner
Being. This automatically results in the expansion of the conscious mind.
STUDENTS INTERNATIONAL MEDITATION SOCIETY
Founder MAHARISHI MAHESH YOGI
for information write to SIMS ... London SW6[317]

In many circles the Transcendental Meditation technique was fast being
dismissed as yesterday's fad, and had it not been for certain developments,
Maharishi's organizations might soon have fallen into disarray. But
whatever plans Maharishi entertained for his retirement, they were soon to
evaporate. Whether it is true, as rumours circulated by his detractors had it,
that he fled from India to evade inspection of his tax returns, or whether he
merely wished to revitalize his ambitious teacher-training programme,
plans were being made for his return to the West.

This bold U-turn provoked a degree of gossip, for how could he say one
thing and do another? One has only to look at Maharishi's perception of
non-attachment:

> The art of gaining self-consciousness and rising to the state of cosmic
> consciousness is the art of remaining free from the binding influence of
> speech.[318]

In an age increasingly dependent on the opinions of 'experts', major
companies frequently enlisted the support of a white-coated scientist to
endorse their products. And Maharishi, who was reputed to hold a degree in
physics, had long hoped to highlight the scientifically demonstrable aspects
of his teaching. But scientists are not easily persuaded by unproven systems
of belief, so if Maharishi's teachings were going to find acceptance by
scientists, it followed that the vocabulary would need to be purged of any

allusions to topics of a mystical nature. This was almost impossible, for how could he even begin to prove his claims about reincarnation, the existence of celestial beings and magic powers? Nevertheless, the belief that Transcendental Meditation might yet receive scientific verification and acceptance contributed a new impetus to his mission. Henceforth his students would have to familiarize themselves with radically revised terms of reference.

The scene was being set for the introduction of Maharishi's new brainchild, the restructuring of his philosophies under the banner of 'The Science of Creative Intelligence (SCI)'. The idea was, that by de-emphasizing the religious connotations of his teaching, Transcendental Meditation would gain greater acceptance and an increase in initiations would follow.

In February 1970, at Stanford University in the United States, the very first SCI course was held, not by Maharishi, who was holding another teaching-training course at Shankaracharya Nagar, but by his deputy, SIMS boss, Jerry Jarvis. And by March 1970 a scientific paper on the effects of the practice of Transcendental Meditation was being published in the journal *Science*.

In June 1970, a summer course was convened at a hotel in the wooded location of Poland Springs, Maine, and to their surprise, students discovered that in order to meet with Maharishi, they had first to dress in their best evening wear! As with previous camps, the emphasis of the programme was on gaining increased familiarity with longer periods of meditation, and an extensive programme of rounding was therefore commenced. Lectures again found Maharishi offering reasoned explanations for experiences of 'unstressing', along with tasters of his new Science of Creative Intelligence. He declared that henceforth expressions of a religious or spiritual nature should be set aside in favour of scientific terminology. To some his attitude might have appeared somewhat dictatorial, but for many of his American students, news of an academic bias was not at all unwelcome.

The desire to focus his followers' attention on his new approach resulted in Maharishi's involvement in a succession of advanced meditators' and teacher-training courses. After Poland Springs, he moved on to Humboldt State College in Arcata, California; Since plans to present his ideology in exclusively scientific terms were not yet firmed up, it was difficult for Maharishi to resist the temptation to revert to past patterns of speech. Though 'God' now became renamed as 'the source of creative intelligence' and the state of 'supreme knowledge' had become 'unity consciousness',

'God consciousness' and the 'celestial' still received the occasional mention. Those attending these formative 'scientific' lectures at Humboldt participated in an uneven struggle to forge links between the old SRM style of presentation and the new, streamlined 'science'.

Since the latter years of the 1960s the interest in things Eastern had stimulated a brisk trade in Indian artefacts, and also created openings for purveyors of various forms of *yoga* and meditation. Accordingly, Maharishi found himself under ever-greater pressure to explain why his followers should accept only his interpretations of *yoga* philosophy.

The earliest known definition of the word *yoga* is to be found in a Sanskrit work of some antiquity entitled '*Yogadarshanam*' and commonly referred to as the '*Yoga Sutras* of Patanjali'. The second verse reads: '*yogash chitta-vritti-nirodhah*' '*yoga* [is] mind-activity-restraint'. Since *sutras* are succinct statements made with least words, a clearer reading would read: '*Yoga* is the state of consciousness brought about by choosing to slow the mind's thinking process and bring it to a halt'.

Citing the *Yoga Sutras* as the authoritative text on *yoga*, Maharishi put forward the view that the 'eight limbs' (*ashtanga*) of *yoga,* referred to in the *Yoga Sutras,* need not be understood as steps, as has been commonly suggested, but as different systems. Maharishi claimed that by the practice of Transcendental Meditation, the benefits of all the different systems can be derived simultaneously:

> With all these experiences on our personal level we understand Patanjali to have advocated only Transcendental Meditation, the soul of all the *yogas.* This is *yoga* philosophy. We are not responsible for the misinterpretations of *samadhi*, and if misinterpretations have become common everywhere, we can deplore the whole situation and start refreshing the whole atmosphere. If everything has gone wrong ... Someone in India said to me, in open lecture like this, and he said 'You mean to say that all these saints who have gone by were wrong and you only are right?' I said, 'When I see your life, I am only concluding that this new voice only is right and all the old voices from wherever they came, they must have come from the field of ignorance!'[319]

> Whosoever advocated concentration, control, the need of detachment, renunciation for enlightenment, whosoever he was, he didn't know what he was talking about. Whosoever he may be, he may be God, he may be God's incarnation speaking from heaven, but we'll say 'Please stop! Let us hear the voice of the earth.'[320]

Yet a fellow disciple of Maharishi's Guru Dev, whilst championing Transcendental Meditation, also commended the role of renunciation. Shankaracharya Swami Shantanand Saraswati stated:

Whatever one sees in creation, all that lives and moves – one should use it fully and enjoy the Absolute in everything, but one should enjoy it with renunciation.[321]

In the same lecture, the Shankaracharya shed further light on the topic of renunciation:

The creation is such that everything has a purpose and must fulfil its function; so it must keep circulating, it must be used. Use everything, and give up the idea that you are renouncing. Don't hold on to anything in this creation; that can only be done by this final renunciation of giving up the idea that you have anything.[322]

Many other Indian teachers who aroused the interest of Westerners, were predisposed in favour of *mantra japa*, the chanting of auspicious *mantras*. In spite of the popularity of other *yoga* teachings, Maharishi resolutely stood by his claim that they are all based upon misunderstandings.

The differences between Maharishi's teaching and the other systems were such that the subject was destined to become contentious. The predicament was increased by George Harrison's decision to make public his association with the Radha Krishna Temple, a devotional cult which promoted the repetition of their free 'transcendental *mantra*', '*Hare Rama, Hare Krishna*'.

In a bid to reaffirm his position and make his opinions abundantly clear to his followers, Maharishi restated his views on this particular practice:

The principle of these chantings, long hours in continuous chanting, the principle of this is that the mind is wandering by nature. It is like a monkey jumping from branch to branch all the time. When we want to control the monkey it's very difficult to control the monkey because it always jumps off, always jumping on. If there could be a way to get the monkey tired very much, give him such fast running that he gets tired and then he sits in one place ... Mind is a monkey, we want the mind to be not wandering, mind wants steady. What we do, give it such heavy work, one word keep on repeating, '*duun, duun, duun, duun*', all the time all the time all the time. The tongue becomes tired, the lungs become tired, the mind becomes tired, the whole thing collapses.[323]

His explanation greatly amused his followers and provided them with much-needed ammunition with which to launch a broadside at anyone daring to suggest that their way was better than Maharishi's. According to their teacher, not only were these other paths relatively ineffective but they also spread confusion. Further, Maharishi suggested to his Humboldt audience that as a result of an incorrect understanding of spiritual existence, his countrymen in India had fallen prey to a philosophy which opposed material advancement:

Such a beautiful country, the source of all knowledge, where the *Vedas*, the truths of existence, are preserved. But look at that country, what has become of it? All lethargy and this and this and this. It's waking up now, but it should have not fallen into that tragedy of ignorance.[324]

Harsh words from a man of love, peace and flowers, though perhaps this foray into the arena of mud-slinging had unsettled him, for he then softened, adding in the sweetest of tones that the chanting of the 'Hare Krishna' *mantra*, whilst having 'good meaning', was 'not very comfortable'. Meanwhile the 'Krishnas' and their elderly leader Swami A.C. Bhaktivedanta were, for their part, busy running down Maharishi and his claims. The matter was additionally complicated in that Bhaktivedanta's organisation, the International Society for Krishna Consciousness, ISKCON, also laid claim to a tradition of masters going back to Lord Krishna, and claimed that their *mantra* is transcendental and can bring the initiate to higher states of consciousness.

Maharishi had the habit of illustrating his ideas by reference to any object to hand, and in his explanations concerning differing states of consciousness; many a bloom had been toyed with, scrutinized and dismembered before being scattered about. Using the anatomy of a flower he postulated, in the language of his Science of Creative Intelligence, the difference between outer and inner reality:

> Beautiful golden flower, but if we put it to analysis what we find is every fibre of this is nothing but colourless sap. Beautiful light green stem, if we put to analysis, every fibre of this will be nothing but colourless sap. All the various things will be found, nothing but colourless sap, all the various colours. Now, on the surface it is beautiful golden colour, underneath, colourless sap. This we say when we don't appreciate the colourless on the colour, we only see yellow, see the colourless on the surface, but because every fibre of this is nothing but the colourless sap, therefore the colourless sap is even on the surface. It's not only at the depth; it is also on the surface. This is the reality of this, that even though we don't see the colourless sap we see only the golden colour, but the reality of all the golden colour is that, even when we see it's golden, the colourless is there, even on the surface and even at the depth. When our vision is dominated by the golden then we don't comprehend the colourless, but if our vision is cultured enough or refined enough to cognize the reality of this golden colour, it will cognize golden colour and colourless sap, both on the surface of this. Because that is the reality.[325]

Continuing his tireless, timeless explanation, Maharishi asked, concerning the colourless sap: 'Where do we find it?' And those who had been paying proper attention should have immediately answered: 'On the surface and at the depth!' But this would be to assume that they already enjoyed familiarity with the state of unity consciousness.

> We go to the root and there is a root and then the finer root and finer root and finer root and finer root. At end of the finest hair of the root there is that drop of pearl, a pearl, a dewdrop-like colourless sap, a crystal colourless sap which has not yet become the root, but is now ready to become transformed into a root. It has separated itself from the soil it has not yet become the root.

In introducing the idea of 'the colourless sap' as a metaphor for divinity, Maharishi was likely setting the stage for future discourses on the abstract. He wished to communicate exactly what it was like to be established in the state of consciousness beyond God consciousness, that which he had dubbed 'unity'. The capacity to live this state of consciousness would come, he promised, when meditators' nervous systems became 'modified', a condition brought about by the removal of 'impurities'.

For many meditators the race was on, to experience higher states of consciousness and see the sap on the surface, and to this end they closely scrutinized Maharishi's daily routine in the hope of finding clues to help them accelerate their evolution. Those who had not already taken to a strict vegetarian diet, thought about it. Those who smoked tobacco, drank alcohol or used non-prescribed drugs were keen to clean up their systems. But in this desperate bid to root out impurities, hidden dangers lurked, for in trying too hard one ran the risk of losing interest in the material charm of life and become colourless, sapped of individuality and personal initiative.

On occasion, Maharishi gave the impression that the path to illumination is easy to comprehend, using the analogy of a darkened room being lit by the mere flick of a 'switch' (the practice of this meditation) and the 'light' (of higher consciousness) making the entire realm of forms and phenomena clear. In his use of this analogy he followed a time-honoured method of teaching, the tale of the snake and the stick. In a darkened place, fear might well ensue from the belief that a snake has been seen in the grass, but with light the snake may well be found to have been nothing but a stick. Maharishi wanted his students to realize that the material world can only be fully understood when spiritual illumination is gained and that the diversity of creation is then found to be just the emanations of the eternal Absolute (the source of creative intelligence). His contemporary, His Holiness Shankaracharya Shantanand Saraswati, also used this light and dark analogy to convey his essentially religious message:

> If a coiled piece of rope is lying where there is not enough light, one may think it is a snake. Then with the thought that it is a snake there comes a fear of death, but that can be removed by a flood of light – this knowledge that it is not a snake.
>
> When by the light of discrimination one understands that this is not real, and that it is all a manifestation of God himself – the Lord Almighty – then one

knows that everything is God himself. All that we can see is not the world but God himself.[326]

Maharishi had frequently described truth as being like an iceberg, with only a small fraction of the whole visible and the rest hidden deep below the surface. He himself adhered to a policy of using 'iceberg' truth in being fairly selective about what he made public. For this attitude he most certainly had scriptural support, for in the *Bhagavad-Gita* lies the message:

> Those deluded by the qualities of Nature are attached to the functions of the qualities. The man of perfect knowledge should not unsettle the foolish one who is of imperfect knowledge.[327]

The sentiment embodied in this verse of is not without parallels; the same principles seem to be embodied in *The Bible*: 'Cast ye not your pearls before swine.' But since truthfulness is one of three prerequisites for becoming or remaining a Hindu (the other two being harmlessness and a sincere desire to know God), it is unthinkable that Lord Krishna was offering a defence for dishonesty.

At Humboldt Maharishi offered his followers a formula by which they might better understand truth:

> Many people say, 'I am truthful and that's why people dislike me because I say something on their face.' Truth is not characterized by whips. If you say a truth, fine that the truth is there, but it should have some sweetness to it.
>
> Manu said – Manu, the first law-giver to human race – Manu he said, about speech he said '*Satyam bruyaat, priyam bruyat, na bruyat satyam apriyam*' – 'Speak the truth, speak that is sweet, don't speak the truth that is not sweet.' Not that you can take liberty with truth and massacre the whole field of behaviour. The truth, simple, natural which is supporting life, which is nourishing life. Truth is always life-supporting if it is really truth but it must come from a melted heart and not from a very unconcerned mind.[328]

But this definition of truth statement would not be admissible in the courts of justice where truth is frequently revealed which is far from sweet.

But ironically, Maharishi, had himself told only half the truth about this very verse in that he omitted part of it:

In the Penguin Classic version of *The Laws of Manu*, this verse (in its entirety) is translated with an altogether different emphasis:

> 'Priyam cha na anritam bruuyaat esah dharmah sanatanah.'
>
> A man should tell the truth and speak with kindness; he should not tell the truth unkindly nor utter lies out of kindness. This is a constant duty.[329]

The translators of this verse ascribe this work (known variously as *Manu*, *Manusmriti* or *Manu Samhita*) to no one author:

The Laws of Manu, like all other works we have from the ancient period of India, was composed by members of the social class (*varna*) called Brahmins or 'Priests'. Indeed, the text is not only *by* priests but to a large extent *for* priests.[330]

Central to any attempt to understand Maharishi is the need to identify his definition of truth. It is evident from his remarks about the need to speak the 'sweet truth' that he himself felt the need to practise a form of self-censorship; but just how far this process impeded his message is less clear. The demand that truth should always be 'sweet' could present some very real barriers to effective communication. For instance, how could one relate news of a misdemeanour so as to prevent its recurrence? Maharishi was adamant.

> If the wrongs of some other people come out, that means the wrong was stored inside. It just tells the structure of the heart, what is contained inside there. So if someone never speaks ill of others, that means he has a pure heart, doesn't have the wrong.
>
> Someone does some wrong, something wrong was done by some man...Why should I bring that wrong through thinking or remembering and try to keep it in my heart? And if I speak, that means I had stored something of that and if wrong is stored then the heart is not pure. It just indicates what kind of storage is there, whether purity is stored or impurity is stored or what is there. Speaking ill of others means first, transplant the wrong of his heart in our heart, transplant the wrong of his mind to our mind and then let that plant grow into a tree till it comes out, manifold it comes out.
>
> The whole process is dragging to evolution, it drags us down. That's why amongst all the things Lord Krishna said to Arjuna is 'I know you are a good recipient or deservant of this knowledge, because I haven't known from you any wrong of anyone.'[331]

The philosophy of speaking sweetly and never doing anyone down has a certain appeal, but it presumes that the individual concerned is already living an exalted state of consciousness where others' wrongdoings do not impact on him. Or were his students to take his ideas on truth as implicit spiritual instruction, and believe that by speaking nicely they would quicker evolve?

And there is the question of how one can ascertain whether or not one has attained a state of higher consciousness, or does one need confirmation?

> Maharishi: It's just not possible to know that one is cosmic consciousness or not because, from nothing this could be known. Absolutely nothing.
>
> Questioner: But you must know, Maharishi, whether any of us are cosmically conscious or not, because this is your job to know!
>
> Maharishi: That is my profession and I am good at my profession..., but.............

a doctor maybe very famous to cure diseases, he may be suffering himself. What could be the proof that he is absolutely normally healthy?

Questioner: So that doesn't make you 'Irish' Maharishi?

I don't want to get out... but when you look into the picture, the doctor maybe absolutely sick and he would be writing prescriptions, which would be, could be useful for others. The situation could be that![332]

Maharishi was also pressed further about *mantras* and the meditation methods taught by Swami Brahmananda:

Questioner: Are all *mantras* known?

Maharishi: No, knowledge of all *mantras* could produce effect on any level of evolution. We know some here and there. The knowledge of all would almost amount to omniscience.

Time of dissolution and creation is just cosmic night and day. The time of writing of the *Vedas* is entirely a matter of conjecture.

Many in India are using the same *mantra* as us but they have no 'T' in 'TM'.

About *mantras* it is always safe to learn from the tradition. Taken from a book we do not know of possible side effects. Especially we who know how to repeat *mantras* at deep levels should be careful. We should not wield power in ignorance.

Yantra isn't a game. Do not read in books and do not experiment; it is too risky. The science of contacting different regions of creation by *yagyas* and *yantras* etc. is by resonance and is very powerful. This is easy to understand for *mantras*. On a different aspect *yagyas*, an aspect of Shiva that is detailed. We excite to love of us and to anger elsewhere etc.

As human behaviour has different aspects so the properties of the gods have excitable aspects. *Yantras* are part of *yagyas*, the exact positioning of parts and *mantras* is systematic procedure for the invocation. Very exactly detailed. It is held that these *yantras* are liked by the gods - one for each aspect; although the basis were scientific it is now reduced to superficiality and superstition. All these are in the *Yajur Veda*.

Our *puja* is not an initiation *yagya*.

Questioner: These *mantras* are without initiation - can one transcend on them?

Maharishi: Only after initiation is the method taught to use *mantra* in such a way as to transcend.[333]

Questioner: Did Guru Dev give all the disciples the same?

Maharishi: From my observations I think he gave the basic technique and then the advanced techniques.[334]

20

RESEARCH AND DEVELOPMENTS

B ut for the shortage of trained teachers of Transcendental Meditation, Maharishi might well have been passing his time in the seclusion of some silent cave in Himalayas of northern India. His *ashram*, a symbol of his success, had been left in the hands of his closest devotees and *brahmacharin.* Those wanting an interview with Maharishi were advised that he was presently in the United States of America, and in the absence of Maharishi it fell to those who served him to undertake the duties of lecturing and teaching meditation.

In late October 1970, a two-and-a-half-month teacher-training camp was held at Estes Park, Colorado. The basic components of the course remained largely unaltered: checking points to memorize, familiarization with material for lectures, learning the *puja* ceremony, and of course receiving knowledge of the *mantras.* Course participants were presented with copies of the *Orange Book* a booklet containing a full rendering of the Holy Tradition (in Sanskrit and English) and a commentary on its content. Having perfected their pronunciation and presentation of the *puja*, trainee teachers looked forward to receiving instruction about the *mantras* from Maharishi himself. But before that they had first to complete one last piece of outstanding business, the signing of a pledge. The pledge amounted to an oath of silence concerning the hidden aspects of Maharishi's teaching.

Although Maharishi was said to be working on the remaining chapters of the *Bhagavad-Gita*, rumour had it that he had also started work on the commentary of another Hindu scripture, the *Brahma Sutras.* It had been some years since the publication of his last book and speculation was rife as to when a new one would be launched. Whilst he was spending time on these projects his national leaders directed the administration of his organizations, dealing with publicity, the co-ordination of courses, and the routine task of running the numerous national centres. As supplies of his commercially released lectures dwindled, followers had no choice but to attend meditation meetings in order to hear Maharishi's voice on coveted audiotapes of uneven sound quality. But so long as it was Maharishi talking, nobody was likely to protest about the quality or content.

Information regarding Maharishi's whereabouts and plans were becoming increasingly hard to come by, and only communicated in hushed whispers amongst the privileged *cognoscenti.*

All of a sudden Maharishi was back in the news when it came to be known he had been mentioned in an interview with Beatle John Lennon in December 1970. John Lennon had been going through Primal Therapy - a trauma-based psychotherapy created by Arthur Janov, who argued that neurosis is caused by the repressed pain of childhood trauma - a process known as Primal Scream. *Rolling Stone* magazine quoted John as saying:

> There was a big hullabaloo about him trying to rape Mia Farrow and trying to get off with Mia Farrow and a few other women and things like that.[335]

And John explained that The Beatles' song *'Sexy Sadie'* was in fact about Maharishi.

> That's about the Maharishi, yes. I copped out and I wouldn't write 'Maharishi what have you done, you made a fool of everyone,' but now it can be told, Fab Listeners.[336]

The Beatles still had a lot of influence on public opinion, and fans who had become meditators were caught in a confusion of loyalties, which a timely denial by Maharishi might well have averted.

Instead of tackling the rumours head-on, Maharishi's supporters, at least in private, attempted to discredit John Lennon, pointing out his much-publicized use of drugs and his discontent with life in general. It was easy for them to put such outbursts down to severe 'unstressing'. John complicated the situation further by claiming he still, albeit infrequently, practised meditation.

With Maharishi making few public appearances, his organizations were taking ever-greater responsibility for the spread of this meditation technique. Within the Movement, the pyramid of power, which had begun with the training of teachers and checkers, was by now spreading to encompass the ranks of volunteers who manned the typewriters and telephones. The emerging hierarchy was based roughly on two criteria – how long a person had meditated and their age – whilst additional merit points were awarded to those who had received personal instruction from Maharishi and to those in possession of the rare advanced techniques.

As the months passed, it soon became clear that Maharishi had more important things to do than involve himself in the day-to-day business of his centres, so for those with no inclination to become teachers of meditation, the way to his presence seemed to be permanently barred. If a meditator had the time and the money, the most likely way to meet him was to apply for a place on a teacher-training course. But these courses might be anywhere, since Maharishi appeared to be always on the move; sometimes he was in the USA, sometimes in Europe. It was difficult to guess where he would be next.

With the decision to press on with the SCI initiative, those meditators with scientific backgrounds suddenly found themselves very much in demand and given ready access to Maharishi. But their job was not easy, for no objective criteria had been established which could distinguish the various states of higher consciousness from each other. His scientists were therefore in the unenviable position of looking for quantifiable effects of meditation.

Westerners has long been intrigued by stories of the feats of mystics from the East: tales of *fakirs* lying on beds of nails, of *yogis* with the ability to suspend their breath and be buried alive for days at a time. And there was a rumour that Maharishi had himself at least once offered to demonstrate the skill of walking on water. It seems he had a change of mind, but the idea that he had miraculous powers stuck, and had students looking for evidence of his abilities. At least one teacher reported their conviction that he could disappear, that he had 'vanished', only to reappear moments later. But could scientists prove such powers, and connect them to meditation?

At the Guru Purnima celebrations at Amherst, USA, on the night of the full moon, Friday, 9th July 1971 Maharishi narrated a short tale about his master. Whilst talking about him, he assured the assembled disciples that his 'Guru Dev' had lived a 'life in unity' (the highest state of consciousness of the seven referred to by Maharishi). He then confided that it was he who had coined the expression 'His Divinity', in favour over 'His Holiness', as a means of glorifying his master. At the appropriate time, those attending the celebrations were invited to make offerings to the departed master, in the belief that they might partake of his rare state of purity. Attempting to explain how it was possible to derive such a blessing from someone who had cast off his body, Maharishi asserted: 'Exceptional is always to any rule.'

'But the great impact of Guru Dev, in his lifetime, in bringing out so clearly and in such simple words this technique of TM. And his blessing for this movement, which came out much after he left his body, because there was no occasion during his lifetime for any of his intimate blessed disciples to go out of his presence and that's why this any such movement to bless the world couldn't have started during his time.' [337]

At the First Symposium on the Science of Creative Intelligence, conducted at the University of Massachusetts in Amherst towards the end of July, scientist R. Buckminster Fuller proclaimed:

Our young world at first manifested great abhorrence for the non-truth, the superficial misleading information about customs, and now that young world has gone beyond just being dismayed and being disapproving of the non-truth, but is demonstrating in this wave of inspiration by Maharishi, demonstrating its yearning and its determination for humanity to survive on this planet. Very deep forces are operative here, the forces of the great intellect of the universe itself. This is the news. It's not easy to report in the newspaper this kind of news, but this is the news![338]

In addition to being the creator of the geodesic dome, Buckminster Fuller was also well known as a scientist, architect, mathematician and philosopher. It was a great coup for the Movement to have him onstage for two whole days.

Maharishi told him: 'You are a great inspiration…. The message Mr Fuller brings is the message of fuller life.'[339]

Buckminster Fuller declared:

What makes Maharishi beloved and understood is that he has manifest love. You could not meet with Maharishi without recognizing instantly his integrity. You look in his eyes and there it is.[340]

At a second symposium on SCI, a month later, held at Humboldt State College, Nobel Prize-winning biochemist Melvin Calvin's dissertation on atoms and his explanation that 'stereospecific autocatalysis means that molecules are capable of inducing their own generation in highly geometrically specific fashion', was presented. Then Maharishi proclaimed with some enthusiasm:

It's so beautiful. One expression of an outstanding scientist innocently reveals the essential nature of creative intelligence … The functioning of creative intelligence is such that under similar circumstances, similar results occur. Just this phenomenon explains why there is harmony in creation, not chaos. The apple tree grows only into apple fruit; it doesn't produce guavas. But if the circumstances changed, grafting could produce guavas. The infinite flexibility of creative intelligence maintains its stereo-specific quality.

There is something definite; nothing is random, and it is this specific value of creative intelligence which automatically carries out evolution everywhere.[341]

As part of the renewed thrust for credibility, moves were being made to institutionalize the Science of Creative Intelligence and in September 1971 Maharishi International University was founded in Goleta, California. But it was obvious to everybody; the writing was on the wall, that the spiritual orientation of the movement was fast being superseded by a drier, altogether more intellectual approach. A polarization of attitudes ensued with some members thinking that a great loss would result from the changing ethos, whilst others, who had formerly felt a little uncomfortable with Maharishi's mystical leanings, allowed themselves a sigh of relief. The revised vision of possibilities no longer contained any hint of esotericism (a word frequently used by meditators as a term of derision).

The publication in Britain of Anthony Campbell's scientifically oriented perspectives on TM reaffirmed the new direction and alerted those outside the organization to the change in emphasis.

Maharishi and his followers all too often encountered the objection to meditation – that it appeared to be a selfish activity centred solely on personal gain. Jokingly Maharishi would agree with this view, but contended that only by first taking care of the self can one attend to others. Notwithstanding this rationalization, his students still found themselves targeted for criticism. At a European course held at Kössen, Austria, in the autumn of 1971, Maharishi is alleged to have made the following observations:

> Naturalness is the basis of effectiveness. If one poses to be something else, one loses the charm of naturalness. The result is that one accumulates stress. We do not think of life ... we live it. We do not think of others too much. We do not think of ourselves too much. We just behave in a natural way. Don't make moods ... wondering what anyone thinks of us.

> We do not live life on the remarks of others. It is enough that we are naturally helpful to others. What others think of us is not our concern... it is their concern. If we are weak, we will always put ourselves at the whim of others. We do not base our lives on the opinions of others. But if we are not clear in our conscience then we will always be weak and will always mind the looks and remarks of other people. It is the weakness of individuality if it always looks to others. It is important only that we radiate life. Every individual must be a joy to himself, to his family and to his society.[342]

On 8th January 1972 Maharishi proclaimed the New Year the 'Year of the World Plan' and at his new base in Mallorca, Spain, worked with a selected batch of initiators to oversee the World Plan's implementation. At this time there were no more than 1000 people trained to teach this meditation, so with an estimated world population of approximately 3.6 billion, it was calculated that he needed to train 3.6 million teachers and to create a total of 3000 'World Plan Centres' for them to use.

The World Plan outlined its seven major objectives:

1. To develop the full potential of the individual
2. To improve governmental achievements
3. To realize the highest ideal of education
4. To eliminate the age-old problems of crime and all behaviour that brings unhappiness to the family of man
5. To maximize the intelligent use of the environment
6. To bring fulfilment to the economic aspirations of individuals and society
7. To achieve the spiritual goals of mankind in this generation[343]

During early 1972 Maharishi spent a prolonged period of time in Italy, at the resort of Fiuggi Fonte. Although the world's press continued to give coverage to the topic of Transcendental Meditation, Maharishi himself had, to all intents and purposes, gone underground.

The SCI symposia continued, with Maharishi flanked by an impressive array of speakers eminent in their respective fields. In addition to Buckminster Fuller and Melvin Calvin, the speakers included Marshall Macluhan, Nobel Prize-winner Donald Glaser, an Apollo 9 astronaut, Rusty Schweikart, and many others. On a personal note, those who attended the symposia could hardly have failed to notice the onset of age in the face of Maharishi. Some even suggested that he was beginning to resemble his aged master. Whether or not he was losing any personal vitality, his proven ability to sustain torrents of words and ideas remained largely undiminished. The fact that his lectures were becoming increasingly abstract in content was generally regarded as evidence of his ability to present his 'Vedic knowledge' in a scientific manner.

The symposia attracted considerable interest and support. There was definitely a will to see Transcendental Meditation in terms of science. To start the ball rolling, researchers set about gathering data related to physiological changes in meditators. Reported observations appeared extremely encouraging; decreased respiration leading to decreased consumption of oxygen, lowering of the metabolic rate, reduction in cardiac output, decrease in the arterial concentration of sodium lactate, specific EEG changes, increased skin resistance to electricity and faster reaction time, all of which were seen as indicators of greater relaxation. Although these findings led to much rejoicing amongst Maharishi's followers, the findings were not exactly earth-shaking, and were a long way from establishing evidence that meditators experienced any altered state of perception. Nevertheless Maharishi and his movement, eager to capitalize on the findings, advanced them as scientific evidence that TM worked.

Of those who were researching the effects of TM, not all were committed practitioners of Transcendental Meditation. The research which was most quoted had been undertaken by Dr Keith Wallace and Dr Herbert Benson, and the latter was quick to dissociate himself from some of the claims. Interestingly, Benson's research had shown him that the benefits gained through the practice of TM might as well be gained by the use of a word other than a TM *mantra*. He was not alone in feeling that the preliminary findings were far from conclusive. But the science was in its infancy and steps were still being taken to accumulate supportive data.

Although the Transcendental Meditation movement's attempts at scientific validation stimulated a renewed interest in meditation, the introduction of TM into schools was another matter entirely. Opposition was mounting with some people openly hostile to the scheme, fearful that the TM technique and the teaching of SCI were back-door attempts at conversion to Hinduism.

In August 1972, Maharishi confided something of the difficulties he had met with over the years.

I'll tell you my experience.

I was thinking, "Why responsible people in society are not coming to the movement?" in the beginning days of the movement, and this remained the situation for about four, five years. I was going around the world, many times, twice a year, but responsible people, higher level of society were not responding. And the reason - I came to know after about seven or eight years of the movement, about three years ago - that the people were not coming to my lectures, they were not inspired by me, *because I was an Indian*. And what India can offer? We can't take care of our own children, and all that, all that. What Indian culture, or Indian religion, or what Indian nation can offer?

But when the movement kept going, year after year, year after year, and they were hearing from some paper, from some television, from some friends of theirs that "It's good, it's good, it's good, it's good". It's only about three years back that some responsible people started to come in, and come in, and come in, and come in, and come in. And on this explosion of world publicity, when The Beatles came here and there, and the serious minded people withdrew from this, they said "No". Because that was the time when the responsible society, responsible people in society had been responding to the movement, feeling the effects around and they thought: "Seems to be something genuine, something nice, something". But then The Beatle explosion was a setback for the movement; serious-minded people just come to "*that*" [much less interest]

It was talked about more in the papers, it brought publicity to the movement, but it discouraged the serious minded people.[344]

Clearly, Maharishi was glad he had gained the attention of the *'more serious people'*, especially scientists, who were happy to assist him present Transcendental Meditation in scientific terms.

… when I started the movement, I couldn't bear to come out in terms of *"yoga"* or "Vedanta", because the whole Vedanta faith is so misinterpreted, Veda, *yoga,* so misinterpreted. *Yoga* means somewhere standing on the head, or somewhere sleeping on the thorns, (audience laughter) or nails, or walking on water, or walking on fire, some such ridiculous things in the name of *yoga*…[345]

The year 1973 was hailed as the 'Year of Action for the World Plan'. Certainly, it looked like being a bumper year for the promotion of Transcendental Meditation, with General Franklin Davis, Commandant of the US Army War College, and his successor Brigadier-General Robert Gard advocating the introduction of TM into the army and insisting that the force should also pay for the privilege. Other prominent dignitaries were also found supporting Maharishi's cause. The State of Illinois even passed a resolution encouraging a feasibility study on courses in TM and SCI. The list of those eager to spread the word appeared endless. Maharishi, never tiring of his mission and with a distinct flair for originality, even held a World Conference of Mayors in Switzerland.

In May 1973, from a course in La Antilla on the southern coast of Spain, were dispatched the latest batch of newly trained teachers of Transcendental Meditation, and these 1500 teachers were set to promote knowledge of Maharishi's World Plan and to improve his public image. Their first task was to ensure that the Movement's centres were kept abreast of the changing approach to presenting the teaching of Transcendental Meditation. A novel initiative was that Maharishi's World Plan would be presented along with his Science of Creative Intelligence, as a educational course, to be available as a set of pre-recorded lectures

At this time there was a concerted attempt to call in all private recordings of Maharishi's lectures in order to 'fill in the gaps in the archives', to ensure that new initiates only heard the new 'expression of knowledge'. And early IMS and SRM publications were soon to share a similar fate in that most became unavailable. And Elsa Dragemark's book *The Way to Maharishi's Himalayas*, which was rumoured to have met with his disapproval, was not made available within the Movement and had to be sought from sellers of esoteric books.

The World Plan tour-de-force lay in its masterful harnessing of emerging technology. The prohibitive costs of producing and copying film stock had previously placed severe restraints on mass dissemination of audiovisual material. Innovations in the realm of magnetic media had now produced a system that overcame these problems and was becoming increasingly compact and affordable. The Movement purchased scores of video machines, and courses were arranged for those wishing to become tutored in Science of Creative Intelligence - SCI. For those prepared to pay the not inconsiderable course fee, thirty-three specially prepared lectures were made available. For many this was their first chance to see lectures of Maharishi, and was preferable to committing themselves to a six-month residential course in some distant location. To complement the video lectures, recommended readings were chosen from Maharishi's two available works, *Science of Being and Art of Living,* and his commentary on the opening chapters of the *Bhagavad-Gita.* Accordingly, these publications enjoyed a massive sales boost.

Held in various local centres, the SCI courses were overseen by teachers of Transcendental Meditation who would take each videocassette from a secure hiding place, insert it in the machine and let Maharishi do the rest. Sitting locked in the crossed-legged lotus position Maharishi would rock gently to and fro, in his hand a fresh bloom which he waved this way and that. Sometimes the coral necklace he wore would click against the microphone as he extrapolated his teachings:

> Proceeding toward the subtler layers of the expression of creative intelligence within the mind, we experience a tender field of feeling. Deep within the tenderness of feeling we experience the 'Myness' of feeling. We say, 'I feel like this.' 'I feel.' 'I feel *my* feelings.' So the I in the seat of all my myness is more tenderly located within the feeling. Deep within the I is a more tender level of creative intelligence which is 'I-ness'. The 'I-ness' is almost the abstract value of individual existence, intelligence. And deep within, that individual 'I-ness' is boundless – the unmanifest, non-changing, immortal, eternal reality.[346]

For most of the lecture the video camera would remain locked on to Maharishi's features, wandering only to home in on the portrait of his master or the freshly cut flowers surrounding the dais. Maharishi clearly enjoyed presenting these video lectures, and it appeared that he followed no prearranged script but would speak off-the-cuff, effortlessly and spontaneously.

At the conclusion of each lecture, the meditation teacher convening the

SCI course would then offer his or her interpretation of the lecture.

For the most part, the initial lectures were of Maharishi dealing with the basics of his philosophy.

> What is the nature of life? When we look around, we find that everything is growing, evolving, progressing. Progress, evolution, and growth are the nature of life.... This same tendency can be found in man's life. It is our experience that the natural tendency of the mind is to go to a field of greater happiness. Everyone wants more power, more happiness, and this desire expresses the tendency of life.[347]

Though the lectures afforded students an opportunity to hear Maharishi explaining his teachings very thoroughly, on problem with the SCI course was that participants had no proper chance to thrash out any of the points the lectures raised. There was no one to handle any objections to the sweeping generalizations Maharishi was prone to indulge in. Theoretically one could take such matters up with the attendant teacher, but in reality they were there to function of host to the event, leaving those attending merely to bear witness.

> Because the play of creative intelligence is in the direction of greater happiness, greater knowledge and greater achievement, it becomes obvious that life desires to be lived in the state of fulfillment, where everything would be of maximum value: maximum knowledge ... achievement.., strength ... power.., fulfillment. Life aspires to be lived on the level of abundance, on the level of affluence. To live infinity of life – that is life's natural tendency, and if the infinite value of life would become a living reality, that natural tendency would be satisfied.[348]

Of the higher states of consciousness that had been postulated by Maharishi, the sixth, known as 'God consciousness' was now referred to 'refined cosmic consciousness':

> In this further development, the liveliness of the infinite is cognized on the bed of the finite. This is only possible when the conscious mind has become vibrant with the infinite value and the perception has become so refined as to spontaneously cognize the finest relative values. In this situation, the finest relative perception rises to the level of the infinite value of perception.[349]

And what of the proposed 'seventh state of consciousness', the state of 'Unity', which Maharishi had also referred to as the state of 'Supreme Knowledge'?

> In this unified state of consciousness, the experiencer and the object of experience have both been brought to the same level of infinite value, and this encompasses the entire phenomenon of perception and action as well. The gulf between the knower and the object of his knowing has been bridged.[350]

The SCI course was, in terms of numbers, hugely successful. Not only did it appeal to existing meditators, but also with its new terms and packaging, Maharishi's meditation movement enjoyed a perceptible rise in clientele. In addition to gaining familiarity with the Science of Creative Intelligence, those who completed the course of videotaped lectures received a diploma.

There was also a certain amount of anxiety within the Maharishi's movement that others might cash in on the teaching of TM. So, to the horror of many, there was a bid to register Transcendental Meditation and TM as trademarks, raising questions as to whether or not a simple meditation technique could be the property of any one person or organisation.

When Maharishi Mahesh Yogi, appeared on the Speaking Freely show (on WNBC, hosted by Ed Newman), on Sunday, 8th July 1973, he was asked about the origins of TM:

> Ed Newman: Is it possible, Maharishi, that what you call Transcendental Meditation existed and was practiced before you began teaching fifteen years ago?
>
> Maharishi: Yes, yes, yes, because this is, what is it after all? This is knowledge of full value of life. Knowledge of full value of life. This value of full knowledge of life came along with life on earth. So ever since creation the Transcendental Meditation, this knowledge of full life, has always been there. For me it started to talk in English now, (laughs) Now because this is a scientific age we talk in terms of a science, because everything is systematic in this, and open to experience and verification by understanding. So we start to talk in terms of science of creative intelligence, but this knowledge of full value of life is as old as mankind.
>
> Ed Newman: Maharishi, you yourself, I believe, studied physics... errr?
>
> Maharishi: Back in my school days. (laughs)
>
> Ed Newman: Yes, you went to Allahabad University, if I am pronouncing that correctly...
>
> Maharishi: Yes, it's very good... [both laughing] Allahabad University.
>
> Ed Newman: What lead you into this? What was the, what were the steps by which you became a yogi?
>
> Maharishi: I think, just the mind of a scientist. To investigate more systematically the ultimate reality. What is deep within the mind? What is the ultimate reality? And if it can be experienced? Just this thing. Yogi is only, someone who has this inner awareness awakened in his consciousness. It's a simple word. But this, errr just this mind of a scientist... that if there is some

deeper reality, I must experience it. If there is that a full potential of life, I must have it. It's a very natural desire that rises in everyone. And fortunately I got a master who could just indicate to me an effortless natural way to it. And then I found it so beautiful, so wonderful, I thought I would like to share it with every man in the world.

Ed Newman: What, your Master, what did he call it? Did he have a particular name for, for the what you call Transcendental Meditation?

Maharishi: In, in Sanskrit, in Bhagavad Gita, we get this word *'bhavatit'*. *'bhavatit'*... 'beyond the thought', 'transcendental'... just that. *'bhavatit dhyan'*... *'dhyan'* is 'meditation'. *'bhavatit'* is 'transcendental'. This is common. But what was rare was the practice, the technique whereby one uses only the nature of the mind. And using the nature of the mind, the mental activity subsides and settles down to that inner calmness.

Ed Newman: Can you tell us anything about the technique, Maharishi? Can you explain what it consists of? I really you say it must be taught, people cannot learn it by themselves, but can you say anything about what it actually is?

Maharishi: There are two, two things to learn in Transcendental Meditation. One is, how the thought could be experienced in its finer state. We start thinking a thought and experience the finer state til the finest state is transcended and the active mind, experiencing mind, gains that steadiness, unbounded awareness. This one thing, how do we use the thought below mental thinking level so that the mental activity settles down? The other thing is, what thought to start with? These two things. So that we get else what thought to start, now even if.. There is one thing, thought is the word of being, in a thought. If I say, can, a rose, there is the sound 'rose' and then the meaning is lying in it. Someone who doesn't know English he just hears this sound 'rose', 'rose', he doesn't know the meaning. Now, meaning uninvolved in the practice of meditation takes the mind to experience the finer state of the sound, and the mind transcends the sound. If meaning is involved, then the mind remains on the thinking level. And mind on the thinking level is like swimming on the surface of the pond, on the horizontal level of activity. In Transcendental Meditation activity takes a vertical shift, and one transcends and gets to that unbounded awareness. So these two things; a specific thought, suitable to every individual, which the teacher selects. And, how the thought to be reduced, will be reduced below mental thinking levels. These two things, they are told within five minutes. [351]

1974 was optimistically dubbed the 'Year of Achievement for the World Plan', and Maharishi seemed intent on raising his public profile. He had not been seen in Britain since his ill-fated dalliance with The Beatles and it was a great relief to his followers when he was scheduled to appear at the Royal Albert Hall.
In the event, with Maharishi seated amidst a vast array of flowers sitting

impassively, listening to their flow, his entourage did most of the speaking. Perhaps Maharishi believed that they would present his message better than he, but the occasion lacked the warmth and spontaneity that characterized his former appearances. Before making his exit he paused a while to meet with well-wishers, a diminutive, fragile-looking man, beloved of so many, searching the eyes of his followers with an apparent sense of caution and restraint. There was no sign of the bubbling, mirthful man the press had dubbed 'the giggling *guru*'.

A rare appearance on British television showed Maharishi again smiling and laughing as of old, but the mood did not last. The interviewer asked him what became of the money derived from initiations and was rewarded with a particularly woeful look from Maharishi, and instead of answering the question directly he became strangely distant as he hesitantly pointed at his robe and murmured, 'I have no pockets!'

Some years earlier, Australian Bevan Morris had been recalled from *ashram* life in India, where he appeared to live the life of a *brahmachari*, wearing his hair and beard long, and draped in a *dhoti*. Bevan was required to complete his education, and so, conventionally attired and with his locks severely shorn, to Britain, having secured himself a place at Gonville and Caius College, Cambridge, to study comparative religion. Privately he had mentioned that Maharishi had got plans for him in relation to plans for a university.

Attention to the role of education was becoming a very big issue within the Transcendental Meditation movement, and by September 1974 Maharishi International University had found itself a new home at the former site of Parsons College, Fairfield, Iowa, and installed as its president Dr Bevan Morris.

In his bid to re-educate the world, Maharishi wanted to make an impact not only on the West but elsewhere too. It seems that the government of Nepal had expressed an interest in Transcendental Meditation, and Maharishi quickly responded by supplying video transmissions of his teachings. He addressed his audience in Nepal:

> The solutions to the pressing problems that concern our world can be found quickly and easily when every man is living the full potential of life. The knowledge is available to unfold the complete glory of humanity. The validation of the effectiveness of that knowledge has been sufficiently established for everyone to see its truly unlimited capacity to universally raise the quality of life on this planet. All that remains is for every responsible and interested citizen to lead or follow in this challenge – to bring lasting fulfillment to the highest aspirations of civilisation in our generation.[352]

On a comeback tour to promote his Science of Creative Intelligence, Maharishi is here pictured in London, 1975

21

───★───

DAWNING OF A NEW AGE

The suggestion had been made that by practising Transcendental Meditation meditators are contributing to world peace, but to substantiate this claim, it was necessary to gain the support of the scientific community. Essentially the premise of the 'Maharishi Effect' lay in the belief that each and every individual meditator spontaneously radiates waves of peace to his or her environment. Unfortunately, there was no known device which could measure such radiations. In the absence of positive proof Maharishi decided to bring the third law of thermodynamics into service:

> This law, the third law of thermodynamics, states that entropy (disorder) decreases when temperature (activity) decreases and that the condition of zero entropy, perfect orderliness, coincides with a temperature of absolute zero (absolutely no activity). In fact, the region near absolute zero temperature in physical systems is closely connected with a strong tendency towards wave coherence and synchrony and is exemplified in the onset of superfluidity and superconductivity near absolute zero temperature when activity is minimum.

> This suggests a striking analogy to the synchrony of brain waves induced by the very deep rest of TM. If we define for the purpose of comparison a 'mental temperature', corresponding to the level of mental and neurophysiological activity, and systematically reduce this through the technique of TM, we perceive a class of tendencies in the human mind that reminds us of the third law as seen in the realm of basic physics. This quantum mechanical analogy suggests that orderliness in the brain and in thinking is natural to man. TM accomplishes this orderliness by providing an opportunity for the mind to follow the natural tendency of the most general patterns of nature.[353]

The sheer weight of his vocabulary demanded attention, though when all was said and done, most would have been satisfied with a simpler explanation. Nevertheless, it is interesting to reflect on Maharishi's linkage of these two concepts of inactivity and orderliness. Not everyone would agree that science's relentless search for order will necessarily result in an improved or more peaceful world. The fear that science might eventually place undue constraint on freedom of perception once prompted Pre-Raphaelite painter Sir Edward Burne-Jones to protest, 'The more materialistic Science becomes, the more angels I shall paint.'[354]

A contemporary rumour told of a visit Maharishi made to a laboratory investigating genetics, throughout which he maintained an expressionless stoic silence, and when asked for an opinion of their work, he is said to have suggested, 'Why don't you investigate re-incarnation?'

On Sunday, 12th January 1975, Maharishi's birthday celebrations were in full swing aboard the Flagship *Gotthard* upon the still waters of Lake Lucerne, and Maharishi was to name the year and make his customary speech, but this year a special surprise was in store as, after 'coming out of silence', he announced the 'Dawn of the Age of Enlightenment'. He also announced that 1975 was to be the 'Year of Fulfilment of the World Plan'.

On hearing his speech, there could have been few present who did not believe that they would soon see an end to world strife and disorder. Although Maharishi had made many grand pronouncements before, the advent of an enlightened age was, even for him, an exceptional prediction. He explained his reasons for such optimism during his inaugural address:

> Jai Guru Dev. It is a very great and joyful time for us all today to be recognizing the dawn of the full potential of the human race on earth. We are recognizing, we are realizing today the full potential of the human race on earth, and that is in terms of unbounded happiness, harmony, peace, fulfilment.
>
> This we are recognizing on the basis of scientific verification, scientific validation of our teaching in the world for the last seventeen years. We have been teaching the knowledge that we received from Guru Dev, our Master, His Divinity – we like to adore him as His Divinity.[355]

It is worth noting that few of Maharishi's disciples were particularly well informed about the life or thoughts of the famed 'Guru Dev'. Most knew only what they had heard through Maharishi, so they must therefore have conceived a vision of this celebrated figure as being but a superior version of him. Since the former Shankaracharya was never directly quoted he remained a mystery with some wondering whether Maharishi was perhaps a greater teacher even than his master. Lesser or greater, it was Maharishi who was their teacher, telling them that the beginning of an enlightened age was at hand; a message they wanted to believe in.

A prayer was given, to bring forth support from the beyond for their activities for the coming year and more. This was a rare opportunity to see the devotional side of Maharishi; the following is an extract of the prayer he offered up:

I bow down to him who breathes out the Veda and creates the universe from it, remaining uninvolved, and who is the cherished shrine of pilgrimage for all the streams of knowledge.

Mother divine! Now on thine own, think of bringing the dawn of enlightenment to the whole world and destroying the fear of all that is not good. Do not wait for our prayers to reach thine altar, Ma! Thine immeasurable influence and strength is beyond the reach of prayers even from the Lord Almighty, the Lord of Creation, and the Lord of Dissolution.

I bow down to Shri Guru Dev, at whose door the impulses of creative intelligence assemble to pray for perfection day and night.[356]

In his announcement proclaiming the Dawn of Enlightenment, he was, in fact, only placing new clothes on his old ideas. Beneath the new declarations there still lay the notion that by the practice of TM (and the study of SCI), bliss would become an experience common to everyone. The novel twist came in the news that everyone would benefit, even those who did not meditate, a result of The Maharishi Effect.

It was a surprise to the people all over the world how we could dare to say, 'Life is bliss' when everywhere life was a struggle. Everywhere it is said, 'To err is human', as if man is born to make mistakes. When this has been the experience of life on earth, how could we dare to say 'Life is bliss'?

About two weeks ago I heard that there was large number of cities in the world where the crime rate had gone down. When the statistics were researched, we found that when the number in the city practising Transcendental Meditation reached one per cent then the crime rate went down. So if one per cent of the people with a little more orderly minds than others moving around on the streets could change the tendencies of the people, then we have just to give an expression that it's possible now to create a new world; its possible now to create a society free from problems; it's possible now to eliminate suffering from society, it's possible. Inauguration of the dawn of a new age is just declaring the possibility on the basis of scientific validation.[357]

The claim was that, courtesy of Maharishi, a situation had been arrived at where meditation could be scientifically assessed. But various objections were being raised regarding the lack of a blind control group (the inclusion of participants unaware of the nature of the experiments), and even more fundamental than this was the omission of any specific information on the basis of the technique of meditation, namely the *mantras*. And how could it be proved that those involved in the experiments were actually practising TM? Notwithstanding these issues, who could doubt Maharishi's sincerity when he stated:

We are in a scientific age. We have developed an age of science for us. Anything we want to do, anything we want to work on, we want to feel confident that we are not on false grounds. So on the basis of scientific experiments, on the basis of the scientific research carried out in different parts of the world during the last five years – we have confidence on the basis of what has been demonstrated in the lives of the individuals and in the lives of the cities as a whole.

When we designed the seven goals of the World Plan in 1972 we made one of the goals 'to enrich governmental achievements' based on our thought that the knowledge was so beautiful, the practice was so simple and natural, that once we called the attention of any government to it they would pick it up, We approached some governments. Through our feelers there we found that either the letter didn't reach the head of state or he knew of the letter, knew that such a letter was there, but he didn't have time to know it. He was so sunk in problems, so preoccupied, that he didn't have time to look to a call of solution. Now, when we are inaugurating the dawn of the Age of Enlightenment, we have a strength in ourselves. No matter what the governments want to do, or do, or don't do, irrespective of the attitudes of the governments towards themselves or towards us, the world is going to be a better world. Because to make the world better, now, does not depend on anything.[358]

There has not been and there will not be a place for the unfit. The fit will lead, and if the unfit are not coming along there is no place for them. In the place where light dominates there is no place for darkness. In the Age of Enlightenment there is no place for ignorant people. The ignorant will be made enlightened by a few orderly, enlightened people moving around. Nature will not allow ignorance to prevail. It just can't. Non-existence of the unfit has been the law of nature.[359]

When Maharishi appeared on the prestigious Merv Griffin Show, actor Clint Eastwood and actress Mary Tyler Moore joined him, and the broadcast stimulated a massive wave of interest in Transcendental Meditation (known in TM circles as the 'Merv Curve').

During March and April 1975 the message of the Dawn of the Age of Enlightenment was taken on tour, with inaugurations held in Britain, India, Canada, Argentina and on the Ivory Coast, and when Maharishi returned to Switzerland, to Lake Lucerne, he was just in time to join up with a celebration in nearby Seelisberg. Two lakeside hotels had been purchased and renovated for use of a newly founded organization, Maharishi European Research University, or MERU for short. Those familiar with Indian mythology might feel a twinge of recollection at the name, for it is on the fabled Mount Meru that the god Brahma is believed to reside and from its summit the river Ganges is said to flow to earth. Mount Meru is even conceived of as the heart of the cosmos. Maharishi defined the aims of MERU thus:

The first goal of Maharishi European Research University is to realize the ultimate goal of all scientific research by developing complete knowledge of the growth of human consciousness on the theoretical, experimental and experiential levels, and by then applying this knowledge so as to eliminate the causes of pain and suffering in all areas of human life, to render society free from problems, and to contribute maximum to progress and fulfilment – thereby creating an ideal society and ushering in the Age of Enlightenment.[360]

The basic role of MERU was to research the effects of TM and determine the existence of higher states of consciousness. In addition to its laboratory work, it was envisaged that it would also be responsible for promoting its findings, and to that end it would organize occasional conferences. Two such events took place in the latter part of the year, both in Switzerland and both attended by Maharishi. The first was promoted as the International Symposium on the Absolute Theory of Management and the other more simply as 'Evolutionary Models in Nature'.

According to reports, Maharishi found time to visit his other university, the MIU, in Fairfield, Iowa, and host a press conference there. The logo of the MIU utilised the image of a tree, and surrounding it the legend 'Knowledge is Structured in Consciousness'. The ancient symbol of the tree not only served to emphasize his message, but also conveyed the need to attend to both outer and inner needs; it was also an echo of Maharishi's maxim of 'watering the root'.

With the advent of video technology, the work of training new teachers could henceforth be undertaken without Maharishi's direct participation, but he seems to have had no desire to hand over the reins of his organizations. Though he made cameo public appearances and the annual pronouncements, he spent most of his time with his devotees.

Sometimes Maharishi would emerge to confer with some prominent dignitary or other, but generally he confined himself to the company of those he knew to be committed to his dreams. Tales abounded of his ability to function on a minimal intake of food and drink (subsisting on *urud dal*, *basmati* rice, vegetables, and *barfi* (an Indian sweetmeat not unlike milk fudge)., and just a few hours of sleep. From India *gangajal* (water from the River Ganges) was transported for him to Europe.

Disloyalty was not a characteristic common to Maharishi's devotees; adoration, adulation and awe were the norm, and he seldom encountered opposition or open confrontation. But of course there were those who quietly nursed feelings of disaffection until they either resolved their issues or gave up and jumped ship. Inevitably, there were departures, and occasionally even defections to other movements, but it appeared that no one was found disclosing the secrets of the *mantras*, at least not publicly. After a year spent searching for signs of a new enlightened age, in January

1976 the time came again for Maharishi to take stock and deliver his annual report. He had also to give the unborn year a name by which it could be distinguished, and 1976 was to be the 'Year of Government'. Again he chose the waters of Lake Lucerne and the trusty Flagship *Gotthard* from which to deliver his new-year greetings. In the previous year's speech, he had let slip that he had been less than overwhelmed by the response from heads of government to his letters of hope. This year he had something more impressive lined up; he was planning to form his *own* government, a World Government!

> It is a very great joy to inaugurate the World Government for the Age of Enlightenment. Last year we inaugurated the dawn of the Age of Enlightenment. Now the continued evidence of a better time dawning for the world has awakened our interest in establishing an organization suitable for administering the sunshine of the Age of Enlightenment. The World Government will be a global organization for administering the wellbeing and progress of society throughout the world. Already national, provincial, state, country, and city governments exist for maintaining well-being and progress on their respective levels, but despite all the power and resources at their disposal and despite all the intelligent people serving their cause, all governments throughout the ages have been submerged in problems. No government has succeeded in creating an ideal society. Something has been universally lacking and this has paralysed the capabilities of all governments throughout time.[361]

He was not speaking figuratively; ministers were soon chosen to oversee the new operation. Maharishi had surrounded himself with an inner circle comprising at least 100, some say 108, devotees (108 being a number cherished by Indian numerologists). Since all of them had private incomes, he found no shortage of willing candidates. When it came to sharing out the ministerial posts, Sanskrit scholar Vernon Katz, Brahmachari Nandikishore and Vesey Crichton were amongst those entitled to be addressed as 'Right Honorable'. The functions of the various ministries were to be as follows:

1. Development of Consciousness
2. Natural Law and Order
3. Cultural Integrity, Invincibility and World Harmony
4. Education and Enlightenment
5. Celebrations and Fulfilment
6. Prosperity and Progress
7. Information and Inspiration
8. All Possibilities: Research and Development
9. Capitals of the Age of Enlightenment
10. Health and Immortality

In addition to these posts, Maharishi envisaged his government as being supported by governors, whose role he defined in the following statement:

> To administer the Age of Enlightenment, Teachers and Governors of the Age of Enlightenment will be trained. A Governor of the Age of Enlightenment will be one who is spontaneously able to fulfil his desires.[362]

The pyramid of power was growing fast, with simple meditators relegated to the ranks. Over and above them lay a whole network of bureaucracy - checkers, teachers, course coordinators, national leaders, trustees, governors and ministers of the World Government. As a result of this structure, Maharishi became increasingly inaccessible to 'ordinary' people. Anyone wishing to meet him would first have to dig deep, very deep, in his or her pockets. Even after having attended all the videotaped SCI lectures they might still be thwarted in their desires, that is unless they happened to be extremely wealthy or politically powerful, hold a masters degree in science or be a Nobel prize-winner.

Of the spiritual missions targeting the West in the wake of Maharishi's lead, those that promoted devotional practices seemed to dominate. More often than not such missions were led by charismatic *guru* figures, worshipped by their followers. One might say that Maharishi discouraged his disciples from becoming consumed with adoration for him, by constantly redirecting their attention to his teaching and to the meditation. It was therefore something of a surprise when he agreed to meet with Swami Muktananda, the middle-aged and eccentric leader of a mission expounding the practice of *Siddha Yoga*.

Unlike Maharishi's movement, Swami Muktananda's organization was close-knit and small, and devotees had direct access to their teacher, and Muktananda's system of *yoga* centred on his ability to awaken the spiritual energy of his disciples. Taking his *darshan* frequently seemed to trigger off reactions resembling alternative practices of *yoga*: those being breathing exercises, meditation, devotion etc.

According to *Yoga Journal*, Maharishi announced:

> I am always thirsty to have the darshan of saints. It is really a blessing that one of the great saints of India is visiting us today. We hope to get something at his feet. I can describe at length the glory of Muktananda and Nityananda (Baba's guru). Swamiji's field is consciousness which is transcendental and in which everything grows. Swamiji's work is a blessing for us because we are trying to raise world consciousness. The work which Swamiji does in this direction is very necessary and a matter of great joy. The Vedas talk about consciousness which created this world. The same consciousness flows in the presence of Swamiji. Today you are getting the blessings of his presence.
>
> There is a difference between a brahmachari and a Swami. A brahmachari is one

who practices and goes on practicing TM. I am one such brahmachari. But a Swami is one who does not practice, but flows in his own nature. To flow in his own nature is the religion of a Swami. In him consciousness is in its own place. Not only does he flow within himself, but the world flows within him. Consciousness constantly flows with him. Muktananda is one such Swami. Today is the occasion to flow in that flowing consciousness. Therefore now we will go beyond words, and I request Swamiji to bless us either in silence with the flow of consciousness or in words. But I think he will bless us both ways.

Muktananda responded:

The meaning of the word Maharishi is great. Our scriptures say that his world was created by seven sages (rishis). Today one such Maharishi has created a new world here too. He is doing very good work. He has put many young people on the path of meditation by which they have benefited greatly. I have wanted to meet the Maharishi for a long time. Many people in America used to ask me if I knew TM and the Maharishi. I would tell them that I was gong to meet him. And today we have finally met. I knew his guru who was a great saint.

Today a guru is very necessary on the spiritual path. But what do we attain from the guru. Nothing new. We attain what we have already attained. The pure becomes pure. With the help of the guru we manifest God in us who is already manifest. It is very easy and natural to become pure in the presence of a pure being. I have not come here to give anything new. You already have it. You have within you that place, that state, attaining which a man regards pleasure or pain as ordinary things. This state is an easy chair in which yogis can sit comfortably. This is the place of attainment. [363]

Maharishi seemed to feel a kinship with the woolly-hatted *swami* with the sunglasses, and the feeling appeared mutual. Following the conference between the two leaders in Switzerland, students of *Siddha Yoga* claimed that not only had their teacher been accorded the title of 'Advisor to the Dawn of the Age of Enlightenment', but Muktananda had gained Maharishi's endorsement that he enjoyed the highest state of consciousness possible. It certainly appeared that Maharishi was becoming broader in his vision and he was now open to the suggestion that some contemporary teachers might have something to offer. But it was not to last, and it is alleged that soon after the meeting, Maharishi requested that all recordings made of conversations between the *swami* and himself be erased.

The 'Year of Government' saw more scientific conferences, held under the umbrella of MERU, and Maharishi attended some of them, in particular those convened in Switzerland. In March the theme was 'A New Awakening of Knowledge: All Possibilities in the Field of Consciousness'. But this did mean that everything is possible; Maharishi himself had declared as impossible the idea of altering the past. However, from as early as May 1959, he had upheld the possibility of acquiring *yogic* powers, the *siddhis* mentioned in Patanjali's *Yoga Sutras:*

> All the great powers, all the mystic powers, all the powers that you read in the *Yoga* of Patanjali and all that thing the *yogis* do could be done through this meditation.[364]

And he gave a clue as to how this might be achieved:

> If the mind is always on the surface level of the ocean of mind then the thought force is weak. And if the mind fathoms the deeper levels of consciousness, deeper levels of the ocean of mind and stirs all levels there, coming out it brings all the latent faculties up on the surface of the ocean of mind and then – one thought, and it is realised.[365]

In the third chapter of the *Yoga Sutras* are listed the many powers that can be attained through *yogic* discipline. Of the more astonishing are the abilities to remember past lives, know another's mind, become invisible, become strong as an elephant, hear the divine message, enter another's body (astral travel), and the power of aerial travel. According to Patanjali:

> By concentrating on the relation between air and body, and identifying himself with light things like cotton wool, the *yogi* moves in the sky.[366]

Levitation, as this latter power is generally called, has stirred the imagination of visitors to India since time immemorial, even though the consensus of opinion can be summed up as: 'If man were meant to fly he would have been given wings.' But when Maharishi set out to break the code of these *Yoga Sutras*, there was no lack of volunteers hoping to fly. Starting with a small group of long-term meditators Maharishi put Patanjali's formulae to the test.

Then the pioneers of the Maharishi Patanjali experiments began to train others and by December almost 1000 had signed up for instruction in what might be described as the art of the impossible. Astonishingly, the grapevine came alive with audacious claims of meditators disappearing and reappearing, materializing objects such as fruit out of nowhere, walking through walls and sailing through the air. The only catch was that no demonstrations of these '*siddhis*' (powers) were forthcoming in order to verify the claims.

The most evident power was that the claims, unproven as they were, still ensured an enormous interest in Maharishi's new 'technology'. If the promised ability to perform magic was not enough to draw the students in, there was always the lure of the conferred status, for graduation from the *siddhi* course conferred the exalted title of 'executive governor of consciousness'.

On hearing about the new developments, Charlie Lutes, Maharishi's friend from way back, allegedly confided in another former light of the movement, Nancy Cooke de Herrera (formerly Nancy Jackson). 'Just when he gets respectable, he comes out with something like this. The press will eat him up.'[367]

Maharishi Mahesh Yogi at London's Heathrow Airport, 1976
Alex Carpentier

With a 'world government' and meditators claiming *yogic* powers, Maharishi was in serious danger of losing some of the ground gained by previous efforts to reform his personal image. And when he saw the proof copies of the lavishly-produced bulletins and ostentatious commemorative publications his organizations were issuing, he must have realized that perhaps things were going too far, for in his next new-year pronouncements, instead of placing focus on the recent experiments, he chose the relatively safe domain of social ideals, announcing that 1977 would be the 'Year of Ideal Society':

> The time is right and the knowledge is available. It is my great joy to invite the responsible individuals, organisations, and governments of every country in the world to join in this global undertaking to create an ideal society.[368]

But opposition to Maharishi's ideas and the activities of his organizations was definitely in the air. Although the 1970's had witnessed a sustained flow of books advocating Transcendental Meditation, a few publications emerged with a very different point of view. These came mainly from fundamentalist Christian communities, and they forthrightly condemned Maharishi and his ideas, even going so far as to suggest that satanic forces were at play.

Back in the early 1960s Maharishi had believed that the lack of open opposition to his message was reasonable proof of his success. Now that the opposition forces were beginning to position themselves against him, was a change of fortune imminent? The anti-TM lobby in the USA claimed to be alarmed that the teaching of the techniques had spread to high schools, and in the state of New Jersey legal proceedings were instituted against the Maharishi's Movement. However, following Maharishi's mood of confident optimism, the Movement showed no signs of concern about this setback, with meditators getting on with their business, blissfully ignoring the critics.

Nadine Lewy, the wife of successful record producer, Henry Lewy, had been on the same course that The Beatles had attended back in 1968, and according to Jeffrey Ainis, Nadine confided that a decade or so later when she had been leaving to attend another course, George Harrison asked her to relay a message for him:

> At the course, Maharishi was on the stage before the session started. Nadine was arranging some flowers around him, and she gave him the message from George: "Give Maharishi my love".

> She said Maharishi lowered his eyes and said softly, "What do you want me to say? I gave them everything".

22

—★—

SUPERPOWERS

The advent of video technology was a godsend to Maharishi; for he could give lectures wherever and whenever he wanted. He was by no means camera shy, and he entered into the spirit of the new age with dedicated enthusiasm, giving performance after performance on any topic that took his fancy. Was it the worry that his teachings might one day be lost to the world that drove him on? Whatever his motives, countless miles of tape were being amassed. To the watching, waiting world Maharishi was no longer a man of flesh and blood, but a two-dimensional image, 625 lines high and compacted to fit inside a television screen. For many, this pre-packaged Master was as close as they would ever get to the real Maharishi who spent the major part of his time in the secure stronghold of the Capital of the Dawn of the Age of Enlightenment in Seelisberg, Switzerland, a virtual recluse.

Latecomers to the world of Maharishi had an unenviable task before them if all they wished for was just to learn the practise of Transcendental Meditation. The promise of an easy path to happiness was certainly alluring, but what were people to make of all the talk of an Age of Enlightenment, and the recent formation of a World Government? Although the attempts to nail down the verifiable aspects of the meditation were bold and imaginative, it was easy to become overwhelmed by the plethora of charts and statistics. Whilst it was apparent that the TM Movement was intent on promoting Maharishi and his views, new converts found themselves unable to gain access to any information about the man; there were no biographies and no commercial tapes of his lectures available. Personal and historical data on Maharishi being all but impossible to acquire, the only way to find out more about Maharishi was to go on a TM course and see the SCI videos.

However, those who were eager to become cosmically conscious, and unable to resist the temptation to become a latter day Peter Pan, were being encouraged to enrol for lessons in what might be seen as miracle working.

Meanwhile, many who helped Maharishi's meteoric rise to fame were being sidelined as new policies ousted the old order, and some grassroots meditators were becoming disenchanted with the Movement. Charlie Lutes, the former head of the SRM in the USA took a dim view of the changes, especially when he found himself debarred from gaining access to Maharishi. Returning home he fumed: 'Those idiots who surround him wouldn't let me in. They had me wait in the hallway.'[369] Apparently Maharishi telephoned him to apologize, but Charlie was not easily pacified:

> God damn it, Maharishi, I wouldn't wait more than an hour for Jesus Christ! I'd like to talk to you in private, so don't have any of those jerks along.

However, not all the changes were unwelcome to the old guard. The news that an 'ideal village' was to be created attracted a great deal of interest, especially from those without dependent relatives. Many had already speculated on what life might be like in a society of meditators, and here, in Skelmersdale, Lancashire, England was their chance to find out.

Apparently, on the new advanced courses, meditators were being encouraged to undergo experiments relating to Patanjali's *yoga sutras*, which involved bringing the *sutras* to mind whilst in a deep state of rest. Specifically, the *sutras* being used were those relating to the cultivation of qualities, such as *'maitri'* 'friendliness', *'karuna'* 'compassion' and *'mudita'* 'delight'. There were also experiments with *sutras* relating to *'siddhi'* 'powers', such as gaining *'hasti bala'* 'the strength of an elephant' and acquiring invisibility.

Not wishing to miss out on anything, many developed an insatiable curiosity to know what was happening in Switzerland. Nancy Cooke de Herrera was one of those who flew there to investigate, and whilst she was on the course she became disturbed at the activities of some of her fellow meditators:

> On one occasion, summoned downstairs to the phone, I heard ghastly sounds coming from the large conference room. It was as though cats, dogs, pigs, chickens, and a cow or two were fighting.
> '*Díos mio, qué es este ruído horrible?*' (My God, what is that horrible sound?) I asked the Spanish cleaning woman standing nearby.
> In Spanish, she explained, 'This goes on all the time. Sometimes we see heads go up and down – this is what they call their "flying room".'[370]

There were other things to worry newcomers to the Capital of the Age of Enlightenment, not least the news that Maharishi was now surrounded by a group of young Germans dubbed by meditators the 'Maharishi's gestapo'[371]

Whilst in Switzerland Nancy Cooke was fortunate in running into old friend Jerry Jarvis, who, like Charlie Lutes before him, was astonished at the conduct of some of the new wave of devotees. He exclaimed:

> Why do they behave this way? They have driven all the intelligent older people away from the organisation.[372]

Jarvis warned Nancy of some of the problems so far encountered in the experiments with the *siddhi* techniques:

> Using the *sutras* is a strain on the nervous system and some people flip out.

> In the last course, we worked on invisibility. Several of us accomplished it on occasion, but Maharishi decided it took too much concentration.[373]

> And there was more. It seems the local chiropractor was doing brisk business in dealing with back disorders allegedly brought on during the TM-Sidhi course.

Throughout May, June and July 1977, advertisements for public meetings made some extraordinary and extravagant claims:

SUPERNORMAL POWERS: REGULAR PRACTICE OF THE TM TECHNIQUE DEVELOPS SUPERNORMAL POWERS SUCH AS: Levitating the body at Will - Invisibility - Supernormal sight and hearing

DAWN of the AGE OF ENLIGHTENMENT NEW BREAKTHROUGHS IN HUMAN POTENTIAL - DEVELOP ENLIGHTENMENT THROUGH THE TRANSCENDENTAL MEDITATION PROGRAM Consciousness discovered as the field of all possibilities

LEVITATION, INVISIBILITY, MASTERY OVER NATURE, FULFILLMENT OF ALL DESIRES AND ASPIRATIONS, CREATION OF AN IDEAL SOCIETY IN THE AGE OF ENLIGHTENMENT

Regular Practice of the TM Technique Develops Supernormal Powers such as: Levitating the body at will, Invisibility, Supernormal sight and hearing

SCIENTIFIC SYMPOSIUM ON LEVITATION and the TRANSCENDENTAL MEDITATION PROGRAM

Lavish colour posters featured the image of a TM superhero - 'Siddha Man' - blonde haired, attired in an orange and yellow costume and light blue calf length boots, with the word 'SIDDHA' emblazoned across his chest!

STUDENTS INVITED TO DEVELOP POWERS OF A SUPERMAN

THROUGH THE TRANSCENDENTAL MEDITATION PROGRAM developed by **Maharishi European Research University**

Highly developed mind-body coordination enables the mind to successfully command the body to behave according to intention — even to the extent of making possible levitation, flying, invisibility, etc.

"The time has come for everyone now to realize the aspirations of their childhood—to become a superman, Infinite in the creative potential of man."
— Maharishi

Experience it yourself — learn the Transcendental Meditation technique first, then join the Age of Enlightenment courses conducted by Governors of the Age of Enlightenment to train you to develop the full potential of your consciousness and become a superman — a true Citizen of the Age of Enlightenment with the ability to fulfill your desires — command the laws of nature for the good of yourself and society.

FOR MORE INFORMATION CONTACT THE CAPITAL OF THE AGE OF ENLIGHTENMENT

The roller-coaster ride of declarations, conferences, inaugurations and assemblies that filled Maharishi's diary carried on unabated. The Transcendental Meditation business was booming, yet, a wave of envy, resentment and distrust was mounting. Disillusioned with the results of their meditations and disgruntled at the material trappings of the Movement, more and more voices were raised against it and, by implication, Maharishi.

When in late 1977 a rumour spread amongst meditators suggesting that the Movement had lost a case brought against it in New Jersey, they did not know what to think. Up until then Maharishi's sure touch had been taken for granted. Now it was a time for reflection.

On 19th October the federal court which had heard the case against TM decided to bar the teaching of Transcendental Meditation in schools in the state of New Jersey, believing that such teaching was in violation of the First Amendment to the Constitution, which requires separation of Church and State. The presiding judge, Judge Meanor concluded:

> The teaching of SCI/TM and the Puja are religious in nature, no other inference is permissible or reasonable ... although defendants have submitted well over 1500 pages of briefs, affidavits and deposition testimony in opposing plaintiffs' motion for summary judgement, defendants have failed to raise the slightest doubt as to the facts or as to the religious nature of the teaching of the Science of Creative Intelligence and the Puja. The teachings of SCI/TM courses in New Jersey violates the establishment clause of the First Amendment, and its teaching must be enjoined.[374]

Back on 13rd October 1977, at the International Capital of the Age of Enlightenment in Seelisberg, Maharishi launched the Inauguration of a Global Initiative for Invincibility to Every Nation, and on 21st October there was a celebration of this initiative. Addressing his World Government he skirted round the New Jersey judgement in his optimistic pronouncement about a new initiative called the 'TM-Sidhi programme':

> The celebration of Invincibility to Every Nation is a proof of rising purity in world consciousness, brought about by the Transcendental Meditation and TM-Sidhi programme. The world has changed. The conches and bells and trumpets which, in the past, were sounded to announce preparedness for war, are now being blown and rung to announce Invincibility to Every Nation – to announce the end of wars, the end of conflicts, the end of fears, and the end of hostility in life.[375]

It can be seen that Maharishi was coming from a highly religious culture where devotion, humility and resigned acceptance are seen as the indications of spiritual greatness, but those around Maharishi witnessed his search for perfection and his quest for absolutes as he weighed up ideas like age-reversal, invincibility and immortality. In truth, though he appeared to see everything as rosy and bright, he must privately have understood that life is not all a bowl of cherries. As would be expected, Maharishi's cohorts kept him informed about everyday news and global affairs, so some of the bleakness and suffering must therefore have seeped into his dreams of an ideal world. Whilst to some he might have looked like an ageing Indian monk enjoying the seclusion and beauty of his lakeside retreat, to others he was their *guru*. But at some time or another, those who looked up to Maharishi for guidance, had to ask themselves, as John Lennon had done, just how 'cosmic' he was. Yet to question his thinking was viewed by some as tantamount to disloyalty or worse.

A clue to Maharishi's continued, if not compulsive, flow of optimism lay in his seeing signals of progress.

> When we inaugurated the dawn of the Age of Enlightenment three years ago, it was still dark and there was great intensity of economic depression and inflation, and there were cries from everywhere. But we saw the forthcoming sunshine of the Age of Enlightenment, and we declared it -someone has to say what is going to come tomorrow. We have that golden vision to see only the right things, because we know the power of good is greater than any other power, and we see the power of good rising in the world.[376]

One cannot deny the simple sincerity of his sentiments, but it is an unfortunate fact that many who have held such views have not been spared great personal tragedy. The crucial issue really lay in whether or not he could vouchsafe his followers' welfare. Were the magic *mantras* really powerful enough to ensure their invincibility, their immortality even? Maharishi remained unequivocal, declaring: 'Life is immortal and invincible. It is bliss.'[377]

News of the forthcoming release of *Superman: the Movie* produced an extra lift to meditators' interest in special powers, especially when they noticed the inclusion of the magic letters 'TM' (which of course refers to Trade Mark, not Transcendental Meditation) on the billboards.

Maharishi continued his pastime of naming the years: 1978 became the 'Year of Invincibility to Every Nation'; 1979 became the 'Year of All Possibilities', and 1980, the 'Year of Pure Knowledge',

For those keen on the underlying concepts of Transcendental Meditation, and interested in exploring the spiritual heritage of the tradition that Maharishi identified with, there was always the possibility of getting an interview with Maharishi's fellow disciple, Shankaracharya Swami

Shantanand Saraswati, who could always be relied on to redirect one's attention from the material to the spiritual, from the contemplation of the gross towards the subtler regions of existence:

> Everyone is free but thinks that they are bound. In fact all those things that bind them are the expression of their own ignorance. This is what everyone has to understand. Here is an example. A special trick is used to catch monkeys. A round earthen pot with a small mouth is buried in the ground. Pieces of tasty food are put inside. When the monkeys smell them, they come close and put their hands inside and clutch the food, and then they cannot pull them out. The monkey doesn't know that he can be free. He doesn't want to release the piece of food, and yet wants to be free, so he cries, and can't run away. At that moment the man appears from his hiding place and catches the monkey. Most people who think that they are not free are acting like the monkey. They are holding on to something, maybe things of beauty, of fragrance. If only they could release their hold, they would be free, because in truth they are free.[378]

But it has to be said that even to the Shankaracharya, for all his humility and wisdom, fate played its games of trick or treat. Just below the monastery in Joshimath is the cave of Trotakacharya, and this had been acquired for the use of Swami Swaroopanand, an outspoken critic of Maharishi a claimant to the title of Shankaracharya. A local shopkeeper summarised the situation succinctly saying 'He (Swami Swaroopanand) has much money backing in Kashi (Benares), they have bought this *gupha* (cave) for him'.

It was now some thirty-two years since Swami Shantanand Saraswati had succeeded to the title of Shankaracharya of Jyotir Math. Even so, it came as a surprise when he announced his intention of retiring in favour of his foremost disciple, Swami Vishnudevanand Saraswati, a *'gurubhaiee'*, a 'brother disciple', of Swami Brahmananda. Criticism of Swami Shantanand's association with Maharishi might well have contributed to his decision to take to a quieter existence.

Swami Vishnudevanand, although not exactly young himself – his beard was already bleach white – would have greater stamina to endure the responsibilities of the post. Interestingly, one of Vishnudevanand's first decisions as Shankaracharya was to become better acquainted with Maharishi's thinking In order to take full advantage of Maharishi's presence in India, he made haste in arranging an extended stay with him at Maharishi Nagar.

After Shantanand's retirement, Maharishi approached him with a proposition.

> "Swamiji, now you do not have the bondage of the math. You will not be food for controversies if you visit other countries. I wish you bless the devotees

staying outside India". The reply was "I have spent my whole life on the holy feet of the lord. I have travelled only the holy places of this great motherland. Why should I travel abroad in this old age?"

Some people see more than their fair share of suffering. One such person is Dr Deepak Chopra a fellow countryman of Maharishi who lived in the USA. In 1980 he happened to purchase a book on TM and then became profoundly interested in its message. Coming as he did from a similar cultural background to Maharishi it is interesting to note the preconceptions he brought to the subject of mystic practices:

> It is impossible to come from India and not have a set of strong impressions about meditation. To me, meditation meant controlling the mind. The saying we all heard growing up was that the mind is like a drunken monkey, leaping this way and that in its maddened desires. Or it is like a flame that wavers in the wind and cannot be still. Or it is a wild elephant that can only be tamed by tying it to a post and waiting until exhaustion wore out the wildness.[379]

Not long after purchasing the book, Dr Chopra decided to get initiated into TM, and he found the technique to his liking:

> In this meditation the first experience was remarkable. As the teacher had suggested, it was quiet and serene and without strain. You didn't seem to be doing anything. But something more personal was occurring, like a curtain being drawn aside at midnight.[380]

1981 became the 'Year of Vedic Science'.

It is commonly assumed that Maharishi neither indulged in sensual pursuits nor had any interest in such matters, and it was said 'He is above these things'. Certainly, there is no evidence that he involved himself in licentious or lascivious behaviour, nor is there any record of his telling ribald jokes. In fact Maharishi's disinclination to speak of matters sexual might make one suspect that he was of a Puritanical bent. However, it is said that in response to a question concerning sex in marriage, he offered a veritable gem of an answer, directing the questioner to 'water the fruit and enjoy the fruit'. One is tempted to say that if he did not really utter these words then he definitely should have!

According to a British initiator, one of Maharishi's *brahmacharin* lapsed in his celibacy and had sexual intercourse.

'But, did you enjoy?' asked his master.
'Oh yes,' the *brahmachari* answered unreservedly.

Apparently, instead of admonishing the monk, Maharishi suggested that a *puja* should be performed.

And had Maharishi himself actually undertaken vows of celibacy? Leslie Smith of the BBC asked him about this back in October 1969.

> Leslie Smith: What is the vow you have taken?
> Maharishi: To refrain from the worldly joys of life – that is a monkish way of life.
> Leslie Smith: Have you renounced the world?
> Maharishi: I did renounce the world
> I had the idea that I must renounce the world in order to be really a spiritual man, a *yogi*. But what I found out is that this spiritual life is not dependent on the renunciation of the world. [381]:

Largely as a result of the undisputed allegations of Beatle John Lennon to rock magazine *Rolling Stone*, Maharishi had acquired a reputation for being something of a ladies' man. It is true that many young women easily became besotted with the man and his teaching, but so did a great many young men too.

Rumours have a limited life span, however, and this was no exception. It was almost dead until someone kicked over the dying embers and rekindled speculation about his interest in matters carnal. On Sunday, 23rd August 1981, *The News of the World* newspaper ran a story with the headline: 'Sexy Romps of the Beatles' Giggling Guru', with a quote from a Mrs Linda Pearce, saying 'I gave my mind to the Maharishi and he took my body'.

> After travelling to India to join the Transcendental Meditation movement, Mrs Linda Pearce says she fell completely under the Maharishi's spell. And then into his bed.
>
> "I was a virgin and knew nothing about sex," said 34-year-old Mrs Pearce. "He said he loved me and that I was the only one. 'You make my life so good" he told me.
> "When I asked about his celibacy he said; 'There are exceptions to every rule.'
> "He was a brilliant manipulator. I just couldn't see that he was dirty old man.
> "We made love regularly. And I don't think I was the only girl. At one stage I even thought I was pregnant by him."

Apparently, Linda Pearce had later married someone who was also involved in the Transcendental Meditation movement.

> 'Linda's 42-year-old husband, Peter, said; "When I confronted the Maharishi about sleeping with my wife he just laughed.
> "She was having terrible psychological problems because of it but he said that I should take her to the psychiatrist. He never denied it."'

Maharishi's aides decided to speak up for him:

'The Guru's man in Britain, Jonathan Hynde, who holds the grand title of Minister for the Development of Consciousness, defended his leader at their sumptuous £250,000 Mentmore Towers stately home H.Q.

Ex-public school boy Hynde, 26, said; "The Maharishi is celibate. He's a monk. He just couldn't lower himself to talk of this sort of thing.

"Mrs Pearce can say what she likes. I'll deny it on the Maharishi's behalf."'

When we start to weigh the allegations we soon recognise that, if such behaviour did occur, and if anyone held any evidence of it, there would be a possibility someone might think to blackmail Maharishi, as a sex scandal would have the potential to seriously impact upon his reputation as a trustworhty and respected teacher.

But were the women offering the truth, the scorn of disaffected devotees, or simply make-believe tales told in order to attract attention? Whatever it was, Ms Pearce's allegations caused quite a stir and meditation teachers, attempting to uphold Maharishi's reputation as a saint, must have puzzled at his continued silence and wondered how one young woman could, with so few words, cause so much discomfort for them, with the Age of Enlightenment apparently so close at hand.

Within weeks, Maharishi set up the 'Mother Divine' program (for women), and in October set up the 'Purusha' group (for men). These groups being intended for those with the time and inclination to participate in a full-time program of self-improvement; and celibacy is expected. So those who join the Mother Divine and Purusha groups are seen as being somewhat akin to nuns and monks.

Maharishi seemed very keen to instil in his followers an understanding of his vision of the ideal, virtuous woman.

The destiny of the world lies in the hands of women. Woman is the creator. She has beauty, charm, grace and wisdom. She has her hand in the hand of God. --- Woman is at the top of creation. This is her place and her *dharma*, and this she must never lose, for it she does, there will be wars, suffering and cruelty, because she is the opposite of all these things. The nervous system of a woman is by nature more refined and much more delicate. She is the first to sense the good, the pure, the beautiful, the divine. By nature, man is more gross. His position is to deal with the world, so he must be able to deal with stress. Woman is balance, a balance of all nature. She takes in all the stress of her husband and children and does not pass it on. Must not pass it on. Healing is in the lap of the mother; she heals the child's soul. Her place is to see that man goes for higher consciousness. The love of mother that comes through the hands of every woman is Mother Divine. A woman should not get so tired. Her structure is for finer things.[382]

~ *Brabmacbarya* ~

Brabmacbari is one who behaves as Brabman. Brabmacbari is Siddba.
Brabmacbari is completely self-sufficient. He breatbes bliss
consciousness. Supreme level of awakening on the pinnacle of Self.
On the practical level be is self-sufficient, fulfilled.
He is the source of all rules and duties. There is nothing to abstain from
and nothing to do. Do natural performance.
His action is on the level of unbounded awareness. Practice of
Brabmacbarya is gaining efficiency to work within bimself. Siddbi is one
technique. Added to that is bis attitude. He is working for bis Master.
He is working for bis Master in such a simple way that bis intellect is not
functioning. The Master is the beart of Brabmacbari. He completely and
innocently follows bis Master. Just obedience to Master – that's all.
That comes from within. Obedience is basic priority for rising to that
level of awareness.
I bave been through this, so I know this.
~ Prasbna Unanisbad: "Unless the disciple
becomes babituated to understand the spirit behind the words,
it is difficult to understand bis Master. ~
The attitude of service and respect is needed. When one understands the
babit of the teacher, there will not be that gap which obstructs the flow
of knowledge. Brabmacbari always says yes. Not even saying yes and
doubting. Whatever the Master says, be says out of love and in the
interest of the disciple. Individual is bis first concern. In case of
Brabmacbari first be is to be in unity consciousness. The relationship
with Master is laudable as it is one-sided. Relationship with others is as
good as others. Dbarana almost is a must in the life of a Siddba. Initiation
into Brabmacbarya serves as dbarana. Resolution should be on a very
reliable kind of method. A gentleman is a gentleman.
Brabmacbari does not seek a companion to cross the ocean of maya.
Brabnmacbari just sees bis way through. Technique of Brabmacbarya is
the growth of Brabman Consciousness.
Morning and evening TM-Siddbis; focus on the Master.
Brabmacbari is celibate. Awakening of enlightenment in the intellect bas
its basis in the physiology. Unity consciousness also bas its physiological
parallel. Whatever product we get from food is not to be wasted. Ojas is
that supreme valuable substance which gets built from all processes of
digestion. When the whole physiology is functioning with great order, then
ojas is produced in samadbi. So Brabmacbari is always punctual in bis
babits – sleeping, eating, etc. Therefore celibacy comes as a requirement.
For married people, the chance of enlightenment gets lessened.
Brabmacbarya is long known in terms of celibacy.

383

Apparently, to some students Maharishi advocated a lifestyle of *brahmacharya*, but the views outlined in this document seem to suggest that he was only recommending this *brahmachari* lifestyle to those who were unmarried.

In 1982, the 'Year of Natural Law' Maharishi managed to persuade Swami Shantanand to join with him and travel abroad to China; to help spread the word about Transcendental Meditation, as his assistant recalls.

> After staying for four to five days in Hong Kong we had to leave for China for the schedule made by Maharishi Mahesh Yogi. More than 250 yoga teachers in the Shanghai Airport with Vedic chanting gave us a hearty welcome. On the first day we took rest. On the second day we went to visit the Yangtze River which is the longest river of China. It flows in the midst of industrial area and ends in the ocean.

> Swamiji went in the steamer with all others. It flows almost 30 km to the ocean and loses itself in the might of the ocean. This huge river has its own strangeness that takes us into the different plane of life.

> We then went to Nanking, the capital city of China centuries back. We had an opportunity to meet the Buddhist religious scholars, progenies of former Buddhist Kings and to visit the old Buddhist temples there. The flow of Yangtze River in the Nanking city carries a beauty and a pride. One will cherish the experience for a long time. Later we were invited to by the vice-chancellor and head of the Department of Traditional Languages of Nanking University to deliver lectures on philosophy. We discussed many dimensions of philosophy and spirituality with them for hours. They were highly inspired by the thoughts of Swamiji. Later we came back to Shanghai.

> On the very next day we were invited to Shanghai University. They wanted Swamiji to enlighten them in the field of philosophy and spirituality. Some artists had exhibited their art works at the holy feet of Swamiji. There was a Bouddha Mahasabha [Buddhist Society] organized in the Jade Buddhist temple. It was supposed to be concluded. The chief of the Buddhist community insisted that Swamiji bless them by his presence in the concluding program. Swamiji accompanied by Mahesh Yogi and others attended the function.

> Swamiji accompanied by all the Vedic scholars had come to Beijing the present capital of China. The Yoga teachers of Beijing at the airport who also had made arrangements for the accommodation of Swamiji invited him. Beijing has a charismatic hoary tradition of forts and temples built for centuries ago. We had a very good time in visiting them. We were also invited by the officials of Indian embassy to their township.[384]

In 1983, the 'Year of Unified Field', Swami Shantanand again travelled with Maharishi to promote Transcendental Meditation, this time going to Africa; to visit Kenya (Nairobi Mombasa, Kisumu, Nakuru and Eldoret) and Zambia (Lusaka and Livingstone).

In October 1983 Maharishi took a trip to Ireland, telling RTÉ television viewers that 'TM and Sidhi Program is never a failure … ':

The conscious mind comes in tune with what physics has called 'Unified Field of all the laws of Nature'. And then, the thoughts and actions are according to Natural Law, they are supported by nature, and therefore one doesn't make a mistake. Problems in a country are created by the people who are not educated to think according to Natural law. But now through TM and Sidhi program, that worry is over.

It appeared that Maharishi was advancing TM and the TM-Sidhi program as a means of automatically resolving the political problems of Ireland. RTÉ commentator Emer O'Kelly questioned this:

23,000 people practise TM here yet we have unprecedented problems of violence and procession. Has the solution failed us?

Maharishi continued:

I think that we should think the other way because, when in all parts of the world the scientific research shows that the TM programme only produces positive results, we should be contented with the present level of crime or whatever. Otherwise who would know what would have happened to the south Ireland? Mmm? Things that are happening in the north?

TM and Sidhi program is never a failure...[385]

The 'TM-Sidhi' programme referred to by Maharishi - actually, the Sanskrit word is *siddhi* not *sidhi*, and means 'one who has acquired supernatural powers' - was not publicly demonstrated. Those who kept company with 'executive governors of consciousness', however, discovered to their surprise that the practice of the TM-Sidhi program required a launch pad of aerated foam.

The next year, 1984, Maharishi named the 'Year of Unified Field Based Civilization', though, if one were closely tracking developments, these years might rightly have been called by Maharishi the 'Years of the Real Estate', for the Movement had by now adopted a policy of acquiring run-down stately homes, vacant plots, in fact anything that looked good in terms of utility and long-term investment. To Maharishi goes the credit for negotiating down the asking price on the Fairfield, Iowa, site, and devotees followed his example by securing similarly good deals elsewhere.

One might have thought that the long-desired inner-city centres which were to be set aside for the exclusive use of meditation, might now become a reality, but this was not the case. The majority of properties purchased were situated out of town, some deep in the country, and were destined to house only the most dedicated followers and provide accommodation for those on residential courses.

23

— ★ —

QUEST FOR UTOPIA

During the early years of the Movement the funding and planning for the building of Shankaracharya Nagar had been raised from Western devotees, and since it had been envisaged that the *ashram* would forever be the international centre of the meditation movement, many looked forward to the time, when they might enjoy a visit there. However, within a decade or so, the site became more and more for the exclusive use of Indians, with Maharishi only making the occasional appearance.

The Academy of Meditation continued to draw visitors, Eastern and Western, meditators and non-meditators, all intent on soaking up the atmosphere and feeling the 'good vibrations' there. Indians were allowed ready access, but Westerners were shocked to find themselves barred entry. Even those who had earned themselves a place in the Movement's hierarchy were summarily refused admission. It would be hard to avoid the suspicion of racism at work, but this would not be a complete reflection of the situation. A statement from Maharishi on 'Cultural Integrity – the Unshakeable Foundation for Invincibility' goes some way to explain the underlying motives for vetting visitors at Shankaracharya Nagar:

> In the past, the mixing of cultures has been a drag on progress. People from one land, when they live in another's always miss their old habits and surroundings. This is not just a psychological weakness. The fact is that each land has a different culture according to its geographic and climatic conditions. So in each land the human nervous system is cultured differently, starting from birth. When a person moves to another land, his nervous system tries to adapt and often does succeed to a large extent. But even if the person fails to adapt to just one small factor, that will become a drag for him and for the host culture, because he will not be able to cohere fully with his environment. This mixing destroys cultures and hampers cultural integrity.[386]

One would have thought that he was referring to unwelcome foreign bodies rather than brethren. But he spoke from experience, for few had enjoyed the hospitality of a greater variety of 'host cultures' than he had. In view of the time he spent outside India, it was surprising he had not yet lost his Indian citizenship.

Within the perimeters of the *ashram*, Maharishi's deputy, Satyanand ruled supreme. He complained of a hectic work schedule and was heard to admit that he hardly found time to meditate. The *ashram* swarmed with *sadhus* (religious mendicants) who by their upbringing had been taught to revere the *guru* as God. It was not unknown at the *ashram* for a meditator to prostrate himself in front of 'Guru Dev' and to touch the image of his feet.

Indian journalist Dinesh Khare offered clarification about the position of 'Guru Dev' in regard to the teaching of TM:

> The initiation took place in front of a picture of Guru Dev and I was told that I should consider neither my initiator nor Maharishi Mahesh Yogi as my spiritual teacher but the Guru Dev himself. It was a thrilling experience and the very first day my turbulent mind experienced such a serene calm that when I got up after practising TM for the first time, I bowed my head to the lotus feet of Guru Dev and since that day have regarded him as my spiritual teacher and guide.[387]

Since religion is a way of life in the Indian subcontinent, it was not unnatural that religious customs surfaced at the academy too. *Shivalingas* (symbolic representations of the forces of cosmic energy) sprouted up on the *ashram* grounds, and the *sadhus* gathered together for *kirtan*, the singing of devotional songs to God. According to Satyanand, one of the *sadhus* who had been given the TM-Sidhi *sutras* 'leaned back and raised up several feet from the ground'[388]. In an amusing contrast to the somewhat sycophantic attitudes often adopted by followers towards Maharishi, an independent-minded resident Indian teacher of meditation at the academy openly admitted that he did not wish to attend one of Satyanand's afternoon lectures, saying: 'It is Test Match cricket, I listen to wireless.'

From time to time Maharishi returned to India, where he tried to find time for all those wishing to speak with him. On one such visit the writer Gita Mehta sought him out, finding him at New Delhi's most expensive hotel where he was holding court for a few days. Shown to his suite she joined the several hundred other people who were waiting to take audience with him in his bedroom. When Gita was shown in, others - a pair of Italian countesses and two scientists, one from Britain, the other an Indian nuclear physicist, joined her. The younger of the two *contessas* had a problem with her meditation.

'But, Swami,' ended the Countess, 'my *mantra* is not working anymore.'
'Oh dear,' said the Maharishi, and continued to smile. 'Then we must give you

another. Use the new *mantra* for four days, then let him know,' and he pointed to a man kneeling piously in the dark corner, 'whether it is working. I won't be here. I must fly back to Switzerland tomorrow. My work requires me there.'[389]

After the countesses had been dealt with, Maharishi addressed the two scientists:

'You see, my friends,' said the *guru*, 'science is only beginning to catch up with the knowledge that we Indian mystics have had through the ages. Once you have scientific words for what we know and teach, then you will accept the truth of what we say. Until then you will consider us fools. What it amounts to is that you wish to make up your own *mantras*.'
    The Maharishi giggled wickedly at the scientists.
    'For instance, anyone who is seriously interested and will not disturb, is welcome to come to Switzerland and see for themselves whether my students can levitate. But so many who come, go away and say they were hypnotized.'
    The Maharishi keeled over sideways in a fit of high-pitched laughter.[390]

The scientists did not know it, but they were privileged in not only being told about the floating populace of his centre in Switzerland, but also being offered an explanation as to the mechanics of levitation:

We teach our students that by concentration through meditation they can create an impenetrable field of energy between the ground and their bodies. The greater the field of energy, the higher the meditating man can rise. It is simple QED.[391]

Maharishi challenged the scientists to gain greater understanding of their disciplines by joining forces with him, and when he paused to present them with some flowers, Gita, who had been carefully monitoring the proceedings, thought she detected a noticeable reluctance in the Indian Physicist:

It was clear from the expression on his face that he suspected that the gift might drain some of the power he had acquired from a lifetime of pursuing the rational.[392]

Before inviting the scientists to attend a conference, to be held some months later, Maharishi decided to strengthen his links with them, and in an impassioned plea he invited them to rid themselves of their reservations:

'Come gentlemen. Let us join hands. It is Kaliyug. The Age of Darkness. We have no time to wait thirty or forty years for scientists to find the right words. The moral issues are already clear.
    Look around you. See what it is possible to achieve. Look how the world is thirsty. People everywhere are crying "Show us the Way!" Is it not funny that they are asking this during Kaliyug, the most immoral of eras?' The Maharishi giggled in delight.
    'But we can do it together, that is what is really funny. And only in these times

when your knowledge is so close to our wisdom.'[393]

Those meditators who could not afford to travel to India in search of illumination and a new *mantra,* or bring themselves to enrol on an SCI video course, were pretty much left to their own devices.

Those who browsed the shelves of bookshops in search of an inspirational book would find the odd TM title, sometimes useful, sometimes critical. In 1978 the brief appearance in the USA of *The Story of the Maharishi* by William Jefferson, filled the gap for those who could find it. Another profile, *Maharishi, the Guru,* edited by Martin Ebon also came and went without leaving much trace. *The TM Cookbook,* which included an account and photographs of one of the last international teacher-training courses in Rishikesh India, was destined to a similar fate.

In covering the teaching of Transcendental Meditation, the odd author, in an attempt to add weight to his writings, would let slip a TM *mantra* or two. Not all such books were anti-TM or even anti-Maharishi, but some most certainly were. Of these, few were informative or well researched, but there were occasional exceptions. From a number of directions their authors attacked what they saw as misconceptions about Maharishi's teachings, challenged the findings of his scientific experiments, questioned his ethics, attempted to expose the religious connotations of his teachings and even went so far as to brand his teaching a mirage and a confidence trick. All in all they presented a picture of the new Dawn of Enlightenment which greatly contrasted to that given out by the Movement.

Not all the authors who were critical of TM dismissed the benefits to be derived from its practice. The central question, for most of them, was not whether TM was a practical method of relaxation but whether it was in fact a religion by any other name. Armed with a transcript of the Sanskrit *puja* and a list of over a dozen *mantras,* they sought to dissuade upright Christian people from associating with Maharishi or his messengers. Disaffected initiators had they claimed, divulged the lists of *mantras,* and in disclosing them they also gave attention to the manner of selection, which was believed to be based on one criteria alone, the age of the initiate. Having convinced themselves that the *mantras* were the names of the principal gods and goddesses of the Hindu faith, they contended that their repetition was proof that TM constituted a form of Hindu worship. It was a reasonably powerful argument.

Maharishi's representatives were unhappy at this interpretation of their practice, and strenuously denied all charges, in particular that of being branded a religion. In order to evaluate this situation an unbiased definition of 'religion' is useful. *The Concise Oxford English Dictionary* offers an example of current thinking by defining religion as:

> Human recognition of superhuman controlling power and esp. of a personal God
> entitled to obedience; effect of such recognition on conduct and mental attitude.

From this it can safely be assumed that involvement in religion is a conscious act and not something that can be undertaken unwittingly, as a result of, say, chanting, making a gesture, or hearing of someone else's religious convictions. However, the moment one ascribes religious attributes to any such actions, it might reasonably be said that one was involving oneself in religion.

On the basis of this definition, therefore, it would be unreasonable to suggest that meditators, many of whom profess no religion, are involved in religion. The suggestion that by attending a ceremony conducted in a foreign tongue followed by instruction in the use a sound 'meaningless to us' one might become embroiled in a fledging offshoot of the Hindu religion is a little hard to accept. Few meditators would agree with this assertion since for the most part, they view TM as nothing more than a useful self-help technique, a way to relax after the upheavals that beset their everyday life. Having learned to meditate, only a small proportion then trouble themselves to make further contact with the Movement. It is unlikely that many practitioners of TM have more than a scant awareness of Maharishi's philosophy and fewer still knowledge about his religious convictions.

Although TM does not easily fall into the category of religion, it would be mistaken to infer that TM and its attendant philosophy is not a religion for any of its followers. If by the practice of TM, 'recognition' of a 'superhuman controlling power' came to the meditator, or if a meditator perceived Maharishi to be such a being, then TM could be considered a religion. Somebody who has given the subject considerable thought is Peter Russell. In one of his books, *The Awakening Earth,* he explains the function of the *mantra* in meditation:

> In transcendental meditation (TM), one of the most widespread practices in the West at present, the person sits down quietly and silently repeats a 'mantra', which as far as TM is concerned is just a meaningless sound, although in some other practices the mantra may have a specific meaning. In this meditation one attends to the mantra in a passive manner, not forcing it into any particular form or rhythm. This passive mode of attention is greatly helped by the fact that the mantra has no meaning; it does not, in itself, set you thinking on long trains of associative thought.[394]

Certainly this view of the TM technique is in perfect accord with the standpoint of TM teachers, and echoes Maharishi's comments on the subject. But things were not always thus.

Before surveying some of Maharishi's earlier allusions to the religious nature of his teachings, which meditators are largely ignorant of, it would be appropriate to look at his views on the right to freedom of information. Although Maharishi sometimes appeared cautious and highly selective about what information he chose to impart, it is unlikely that he would ever have agreed with the old maxim that 'ignorance is bliss'. At the Inauguration of the Dawn of the Age of Enlightenment on 12th January 1974 he put across his viewpoint very forcefully: 'Individuals don't have to remain in ignorance. Ignorance is the worst sin that a man can ever commit.'[395]

And to ignore the lessons of history would be to live a life in ignorance.

Maharishi's earliest recorded lectures were made in October 1955 and published under the title *Beacon Light of the Himalayas*. In the course of his expositions on 'the dawn of a happy era in the field of spiritual practices, mind control, peace and *atmananda*' he explained to his audience a little about the techniques he was imparting:

> We do not select any sound like mike, flower, table, pen, wall etc. because such ordinary sounds can do nothing more than merely sharpening the mind; whereas there are some special sounds which have the additional efficacy of producing vibrations whose effects are found to be congenial to our way of life. This is the scientific reason why we do not select any word at random. For our practice we select only the suitable *mantras* of personal Gods. Such *mantras* fetch to us the grace of personal Gods and make us happier in every walk of life.[396]

The following day he elaborated on this theme, explaining that a householder, in addition to his concerns for 'wife, children, friends, relatives, money, name and fame' might do well also to undertake devotion to 'his "ISHTAM" – his personal God – his beloved Deity -Almighty. "SAT-CHIT-ANANDAM".'[397]

This suggests that by repeating the *mantras* given by Maharishi a householder might readily cultivate devotion for supposed personal gods. He explained:

> When he devotes himself and meditates on the name and form (NAMA AND RUPA) of the LORD, he begins to experience some ANANDAM and also the Grace of the Lord in every walk of life.[398]

But isn't this 'Grace of the Lord' a 'recognition' of a 'superhuman controlling power'? Further, he appeared to be suggesting that the vital ingredient in securing this link is the power of love, the love of the deity:

> Love for the ISHTAM enables the Grihastha [householder] to feel the presence of his 'ISHTAM' always with him, in all his ways of life, in all his thought, speech and action.[399]

In a publication printed in Hawaii three years later entitled 'Meditation: easy system propounded by Maharishi Mahesh Yogi' there is to be found a series of questions which includes the following:

Q. How does meditation improve the fortune of a man?

A. Our system of meditation involves the All Mighty Power. We take the 'MANTRA' of some God according to our faith and meditate on that. The power of the 'MANTRA' brings to us the Almighty

Closer inspection of the published booklet of *'Beacon Light of the Himalayas'* reveals, on page fifty-nine, four Sanskrit verses forming a variant of a well-known prayer in veneration of the *guru,* or more particularly the *guru's* sandals. These verses are popularly known as the *Guru Paduka-Panchakam* and attributed to Adi Shankara, the founder of the Shankaracharya tradition of monks. Interestingly, one of these verses contains no fewer than three TM-style *bij mantras*. Transliteration of the particular Sanskrit verse is as follows:

ऐंकार ह्रींकार रहस्ययुक्त

श्रींकार गूदार्थ महाविभूत्या ।

ॐकार मर्म प्रतिपादिनीभ्याम्

नमो नमः श्री गुरुपादुकाभ्याम् ॥

ainkaara hreenkaara rahasyayukta
shreenkaara guudaartha mahaavibhuutyaa .
AUMkaara marma pratipaadineebhyaam
namo namah shri gurupaadukaabhyaam ..

'*ain*-practice & *hreen*-practice alongwith *shreen*-practice has hidden
meaning, mystery & great power,
Communicating the vital point of *OM*-practice,
I bow down again and again to the sandals of the blessed *guru*.'

Seemingly, this is compelling evidence of a connection between an older tradition of *bij mantra* meditation and the Transcendental Meditation taught by Maharishi.

In case anyone assumes that Maharishi went on to change the views he had expressed in 1955 they should be aware that many years later, when reflecting on that historic set of lectures, he was heard to comment:

As time goes on it looks as if it's just the more expanded commentary of what that book contains. The same message, the same thing.[400]

Back in 1959 Maharishi was asked how a *mantra* is selected.

Questioner: 'Maharishi, how may a person find, you know, which of the five materials are predominant in them?'

Maharishi: 'They, they have their method of, uh, oh, from the tendencies they know, from the, from the cut of the face they know. From the tendency. From the tendency.

Q. 'Do you take that into consideration when you give the person a *mantra*?

'I don't go into all these vibrations, botherations. I ask him "Which god you like?" He says "Shiva" - Okay, Shiva!

[Maharishi laughs, very loudly]

Where is the time to go into complications and all that? Ask him directly "What he likes?" and that is it.

[more laughter].

And somebody comes, "Oh my, I don't have any liking for anybody", then I trace behind, And then, "When you were young?" and "Which temple you were going more?" and "What your father was worshipping?" and then he comes round.

[Maharishi resumes the laughter]

Questioner: How would you apply this to the Westerners?

Maharishi: Oh here we don't go into these minute details.

[more laughter]

We get the *mantra* direct and that does all good for him.

[yet more laughter]

Into, not into so much details.'[401]

Although all the foregoing might appear to be conclusive evidence that TM is a religion, it is not necessarily the case, for at the 'Beacon Light' lectures, and to some extent thereafter, Maharishi was addressing an audience that in all probability consisted mainly of habituated to Indian thinking. By offering them a method by which they might deepen their faith, he was not offering them a religion, but an adjunct to their existing convictions. When years later he offered his techniques to those without religious beliefs, could it reasonably be suggested that he was therefore offering them a religion, that he was pulling the wool over their eyes? Perhaps not, but the presence of a passage in his commentary on the *Bhagavad-Gita*, published some twelve years after the 'Beacon Light' lectures, it does appear to confirm that meditation can be seen as having an essentially religious basis:

> By taking the name or form of the god and experiencing it in its subtler states until the mind transcends the subtlest state and attains transcendental consciousness. Those who are highly emotional, however, may even transcend through an increased feeling of love for the god during the process of making offerings.[402]

The debate as to whether or not the Transcendental Meditation method is totally unconnected with the Hindu faith has persisted throughout the years. As long ago as 1964, when Maharishi participated in the celebrated 'Meeting Point' debate, the presenter Robert Kee asked:

> Maharishi, I'm very struck by the apparent similarity of approach between you and the Abbot, but of course the basis of your meditation technique is the Hindu religion isn't it?[403]

It took more than this exceedingly direct question to goad Maharishi into impatience. Side-stepping the question he directed Kee's attention to the non-religious aspects of his teaching:

> The basis of my meditation is the desire of mind to go to a field of greater happiness the innate tendency of the mind to go to a field of greater happiness; and the Being is of blissful nature.

Although it is obvious that Maharishi disliked the meditation technique being linked with the Hindu religion, he was happy enough to admit its religious potential. The Abbot of Downside took him up on this topic:

> But there is one thing which I would really like to ask you about, Maharishi, if I may, because I think you would not entirely reject the statement that the condition which is reached in meditation is a condition in which we find God.

Maharishi was surprisingly and spectacularly forthcoming: 'Yes, yes. That is the only way to find God. The only way to find God.'

Someone once asked what interests, other than meditation, Maharishi pursued in his spare time, suggesting that perhaps he might be a collector or a connoisseur of antique furniture. Although most of us have leisure interests and hobbies, the prospect of the propounder of Transcendental Meditation, the Science of Creative Intelligence and the TM-Sidhi programme and the mastermind behind a host of other initiatives, finding satisfaction in the contemplation of a collection of Chippendale chairs or porcelain plates is somehow faintly ludicrous. However he was, in his own way, an avid collector of sorts. The themes of his collections were extremely diverse, and his appetite for acquiring new additions apparently insatiable, but the subject was always the same – people. At the start of his mission, the hunt was on to find willing and eager individuals ready to take up this meditation, then the emphasis moved to find volunteers with organizational skills and then to those who would be willing to teach. Those were simple, relatively carefree years when he was relatively unknown and giggled his way through interviews, apparently enjoying himself.

Maharishi's involvement with The Beatles and the uneven publicity it generated did not deter a great many celebrities from exploring his teachings. Over the years rumours have circulated in the media about who might be using Maharishi's *mantras,* which include Canadian Premier Pierre Trudeau, Emperor Haile Selassie of Ethiopia, and various musicians and singers such as Stevie Wonder, his ex-wife Syreeta, Cher, Paul Rodgers, singer-songwriter Justin Hayward and members of The Moody Blues, guitarist Billy Gibbons, actors Clint Eastwood, Burt Reynolds, Robert Powell, Efrem Zimbalist Jr, Patrick Stewart, Jim Carrey and Tom Hanks, actresses Jane Fonda, Shirley McLaine, Faye Dunaway, Goldie Hawn, Jennifer Aniston, Heather Graham and Anna Massey, comedians Jerry Seinfeld and Andy Kaufman, not to mention shock jock radio presenter Howard Stern, in addition to so many other entertainers, and various sportsmen and women.

But after his run-in with The Beatles, it was not the celebrities but the scientists that Maharishi had looked to 'collect'. And the scientists collected findings, and the findings collected new meditators and new helpers, who in time became recruited as new initiators, and so the process continued, forming circles within circles. Fresh inspirations led to new avenues, new themes to explore, creating newer ways of luring in candidates for initiation, leading to more donations. With an expanding source of revenue the organizations Maharishi had founded acquired printing presses, video technology, scientific technology and real estate, then even went so far as entering the arena of industry. What had started as an innocent, possibly naive attempt to spiritually regenerate the world was fast gaining the attention of the business community.

Actually, it seems a German cement manufacturer was amongst the first business to harness meditation for profit, allegedly quadrupling its production. John Lennon, in an interview for a teen magazine in 1967 had jokingly announced:

> Twenty minutes a day is prescribed for ze verkers. Twenty minutes in the morning and twenty minutes after verk. Makes you happy, intelligent and more energy.[404]

Boardroom interest in meditation was flourishing; instead of investing in new equipment, some companies calculated that better dividends might accrue from getting the workers meditating.

The main instruction which is given when one is learning the TM technique, and which is emphasized again and again, is 'Take it easy, take it as it comes, it is a simple natural innocent process, we do not expect anything.' But the suggestion that meditation is likely to bring wonderful improvements to one's life, and that such improvements are actually happening to thousands upon thousands of meditators, is surely enough to make people expect *something*! The TM-Sidhi courses took the situation beyond belief, with people expecting to fly, hoping to materialize objects at will, walk through walls and eventually to become immortals.

One of the many enticements offered to those adopting the practice of Transcendental Meditation was the promise of improved health. Maharishi's views on the relationship of mind and body immediately put one in mind of those of the Christian Science Church whose adherents assiduously avoid contact with doctors and drugs, preferring to neutralize disease by deliberately purging 'erroneous' thoughts. The contention that stresses and strains not only exacerbate existing symptoms of illness but also are sometimes the very cause of them, has received considerable backing from the medical profession over the years. And Maharishi asserted that not only would disorders originating from mental tension be eliminated but so too would those of an organic origin. In his book *Science of Being and Art of Living* he had thrown down the gauntlet, calling on the medical establishment to adopt the practice of Deep Meditation as a means of eradicating physical and mental problems. He painted a compelling picture of a life lived in bliss, a life where suffering had no place, where negativity could take no hold. Unlike other mortals his meditators would not have to endure the ups and downs of mundane reality; they would live a life free of headaches and heartaches, they would have no colds, no internal disorders, no problems at all!

But where was the evidence upon which he based these promises? At that time Maharishi had only been teaching Transcendental Meditation for a few years. So, how could he have been so certain of its benefits? The answer is twofold. First, he advocated that contact with Being could bring about a state of completeness and grace; this was his belief, his religious creed. If someone had been conscientiously following his guidance but had not been relieved from the anguish of disease or mental disorders, Maharishi would likely not have accepted this as disproving his claims. His faith concerning the preventative and curative powers of Being seems completely unshakeable, so that it is unlikely that anyone could have prevailed on him to change his beliefs, whatever the proof.

The other reason for his utter confidence in the healing power of meditation was more obvious. He himself enjoyed the rudest of health and saw no reason to doubt that this condition would continue. He *expected* it to be so.

In 1985, Maharishi's 'Year of Unified Field Based Education', Dr Chopra was offered his first opportunity to see the celebrated founder of TM, who as it happened was temporarily domiciled in Boston. Dr Chopra admits to having grown unexpectedly shy at the prospect of meeting Maharishi and acknowledges the likely source of his reluctance; that being a doctor he suspected he might find it particularly difficult to play the role of a patient follower. Dr Chopra also wished to retain the independence of thought and action that he valued so highly; he was concerned for his personal integrity. Perhaps unconsciously he understood the inherent dangers of becoming infatuated with a celebrity who had already turned so many people's heads. Dr Chopra describes his first impressions on seeing the 'Man of La Mantra', as one magazine dubbed Maharishi:

> I managed just barely to discern that the remote figure on the stage was indeed Maharishi, dressed in white silk and seated in lotus position on a divan. He rarely stirred, and even from a distance, one got the impression of immaculate stillness. As he talked, he gestured with a flower in his hand. His voice was unusually varied, rising and falling, often breaking out in a laugh.[405]

On this occasion, the topic of traditional Indian medicine was being presented by a variety of guest speakers including doctors and Indian *pandits*. For several hours, Dr Chopra and his wife listened, but since they had a plane to catch they slipped out early. Before going to the airport they stopped in the lobby for a glass of water.

> At just that moment, the doors to the hall opened and out came Maharishi. He walked very fast for such a small man. A group of people trailed behind him, but without warning he veered away from where they were going, towards the elevators, and walked to his left instead, right up to Rita and me.
> In his arms he carried a loose bundle of flowers, which had been given to him in the hail. He picked out a long-stemmed red rose and handed it to Rita, then another and handed it to me.
> 'Can you come up?' he asked us.[406]

With many volunteers to take care of the routine organizational tasks, Maharishi was free to retire into the background and survey his empire at leisure. After so many years committed to explaining his philosophy and practices, he might well have run out of steam had it not been for his ready audiences, who waited on his every word. With time to play with, he was able to devote his attention to drawing out the strands of ideas suggested in his earlier lectures and in particular those pertaining to the *Vedas*. When Maharishi attended functions, there would frequently be Vedic *pandits* with him, enveloped in intricately embroidered red woollen shawls, who would recite passages from these scriptures. Although their hymns were incomprehensible to most of those present, meditators were led to understand that the power of their chanting lay less in the meaning of the hymns than in the effects they produced (echoes of the *mantra* theory). Vedic *mantras* were also in vogue amongst those who practised the TM-Sidhi techniques, who were being advised to listen to tape-recorded selections from the *Sama Veda* as part of their meditation programme.

In announcing the formation of his World Government Maharishi cited the *Vedas* as the basis of its constitution. Those who took the trouble to investigate these texts were confronted with countless pages of largely unintelligible writings. Maharishi is alleged to have suggested that before any study of such works, students would do well to gain a thorough grounding in mathematics, presumably to sharpen their facility for analytical thinking. Reading from the *Vedas* had soon become obligatory for those practising the TM-Sidhi techniques, and they were supplied with translations of sections of the ninth, and tenth *mandalas* of the *Rig Veda*.

In July 1985 a World Assembly on Vedic Science was held in Washington DC, and attended by a collection of Maharishi's aides. Such assemblies had already been conducted elsewhere during the previous year. The Taste of Utopia Assembly had been staged at MIU in Iowa, followed by others in Holland, the Lebanon and Yugoslavia. All of them proposed that a Utopian age would soon occur, a direct result of the fusing of Vedic wisdom with the practise of the TM-Sidhi programme.

In his inaugural address to the Washington assembly on 9th July 1985 Maharishi declared:

> For centuries Vedic Science has been misinterpreted and misunderstood. But now modern science has dipped into the reality of the unity state of life at the basis of the infinite diversity in creation. If human intelligence is to proceed on the more fulfilling levels of knowledge and existence on earth, now is the time for the complete knowledge of life to be brought to human awareness. Vedic Science is that most fundamental, complete value of science, which has in store all the future progress of the world.[407]

Clearly, the TM-Sidhi programme, with its mixture of meditation and the mental murmuring of Patanjali's *sutras* ('thinking from a subtle level') was clearly giving Maharishi cause for increased optimism.

> Inaugurating this World Assembly on Vedic Science, I am so hopeful for the
> world. These thousands of experts in the Technology of the Unified Field are
> practical exponents of Vedic Science. They are assembled to understand
> thoroughly all the implications of this technology for human society throughout
> the world. When I started the Transcendental Meditation movement, I was one
> man who knew this is something which people need, which the world needs. I
> am very happy that those inspirations of the past 30 years, which took me
> around the world many times, are lively as we inaugurate the World Assembly
> of Vedic Science. The whole human race is now being set on the platform of
> perpetual, complete progress for living all possibilities in daily life. This is my
> great, great satisfaction.[408]

By referring to those who practised the TM-Sidhi techniques as 'experts in
the Technology of the Unified Field' Maharishi was making both implicit
and explicit claims for them. But how much did these students know of the
Vedas, how much of this 'Unified Field'? Surely it was time for these
'experts' to speak up and demonstrate their supposed abilities.

In his bid to convince audiences that his Vedic 'science' was no illusion,
Maharishi frequently took recourse to a mass of charts, graphs and
statistics, but Maharishi was not actually at the assembly but in a building
at the Capital of the Age of Enlightenment, in the 'land of the Ved'.
Maharishi had gone back home to India, and it was from there that he spoke
to the assembly in Washington:

> I would have liked to have participated in the Assembly, but I am digging deeper
> and deeper into Vedic Science here in India with the Vedic Pandits. India is very
> fortunate to have preserved this total knowledge of natural law in the ancient
> traditions, and each day I am busy enjoying different values of Vedic Science.[409]

Maharishi answered questions from the media by telephone, and when
someone asked him as to what effect the presence of certain religious
leaders have on world consciousness. Maharishi tried to explain:

> As positivity grows in the world consciousness, the Pope will enjoy more
> success with his followers and the Ayatollah Khomeini also will enjoy more
> harmony in his country. I'm sure he must be worried about all that is going on
> with his own religious people, and he must not be very happy with the
> differences with Iraq. And the Pope, of course, will never be happy with the
> violence on earth.[410]

According to one newspaper Maharishi had predicted that 'the time is
closing fast when the media will not report anything negative in world
events'. This statement is consistent with Maharishi's policy of giving but
scant attention to negative issues, but truly, the *Christian Science Monitor*
had long ago beaten him to it, with its policy of good news reportage.

Nevertheless, alas, tragedies still continued.

Amongst the many besuited speakers who took part in the World Assembly on Vedic Science were the master of ceremonies, Dr Bevan Morris, who was also President and Chairman of the Board of Trustees of Maharishi International University, and the Chief Minister of the Ministry of Education and Enlightenment, World Government of the Age of Enlightenment, and a fresh new face, the President of the American Association of AyurVedic Medicine and President and Chief of Staff of New England Memorial Hospital, Dr Deepak Chopra.

In 1981, after meeting the respected *ayurvedic* practitioner, Dr Brihaspati Dev Triguna (who was also present at the Washington assembly), Dr Chopra had evinced a great interest in the possibilities offered by alternative medicine. At the news conference Dr Chopra elucidated his views of *ayurveda:*

> As Maharishi has beautifully brought out, the basic premise of Ayurveda is very simple: nature is intelligent. As scientists we are able to study nature because it is intelligent. If nature were not intelligent, we would not get consistent results. Looking around us we can see the infinite organizing power of nature as it performs its operations with elegant simplicity. An individual is healthy to the extent that he allows nature to function spontaneously and effortlessly through his physiology. When he violates the laws of nature he creates stress, which obstructs the spontaneous flow of nature's creative intelligence. Ayurveda is a profound knowledge which allows one to live life spontaneously in accord with natural law.[411]

Meanwhile, in 'the land of the Ved', at the new town of Maharishi Nagar, Noida, Ghaziabad, near Delhi, a new nerve-centre of Maharishi's organization was emerging.

In 1985, 'Maharishi's World Plan for Perfect Health' had come into being, along with a World Centre for Ayurveda. No longer was Maharishi solely associated with being the one to have introduced Transcendental Meditation into the Western world, for now he was spearheading a massive promotion of a variety of Indian belief systems, all under the umbrella of his movement.

It had been decided to release a limited set of publicity photographs showing practitioners of the TM-Sidhi programme apparently hovering above the ground. As yet, however, there had been no public demonstration of these apparently extraordinary powers. It was approximately seven years since the *siddhi sutras* had first been taught, and considering Maharishi and his movement were by no means averse to publicity, it was only a matter of time before the world would be able to witness the results.

Instead, what occurred was that the Sivananda Yoga Vedanta Centre released pictures of some of their young students levitating, presumably to prove that Maharishi had no monopoly on mystical practices.

There were also those who, having learned the TM-Sidhi techniques, had since dropped out of Maharishi's movement and were ready to reveal all. In fact a steady stream of disaffected meditators, and even teachers, had already left the meditation movement, some taking up with the increasingly popular and famous Sathya Sai Baba who was said to manifest gifts for devotees out of the air. Some went to work alongside the South African Guru Raj, whilst others to join groups such as Mata Ji's Sahaja Yoga group, or to go it alone, or even to give the whole thing up altogether.

Ever since the introduction of the TM-Sidhi courses there had been an increase in open criticism of Maharishi's movement, concerning the magnitude of its claims, and the apparent lack of personal progress being made. The lack of spiritual progress might have been tolerable if there had been more evidence of material gains. Maharishi's message was that meditators were successful people in every task they performed: successful in their careers, content in their family life and able to make lots of friends. Now some of the meditators were prepared to admit to themselves that things just wasn't working out as they'd been led to believe; that the oft-quoted claim, that in meditation lay the key to realizing all one's desires, was becoming harder and harder to believe in.

Most put this inability to realize their dreams down to personal failings, concluding either that their *karma* must be incredibly bad or simply that they weren't worthy of higher experiences. Either way, they were not about to bite the hand that appeared so giving, and so they kept their reservations to themselves.

In 1986, the 'Year of Unified Field Based Perfect Health for All Mankind', plans were laid for mobilizing groups of *sidhas* - practitioners of the TM-Sidhi techniques - to perform for the masses. As a prelude to the first TM-Sidhi demonstration, Maharishi, on Sunday, 25th May 1986, announced his latest plan, a programme designed to bring about world peace:

> Time demands the rise of the supreme power in the world which can have authority over the dangerous rivalry of the superpowers and can act like a dear mother to all nations. Ten thousand experts in the Technology of the Unified Field together in India can create coherence in world consciousness, which will positively dominate over the dangerous rivalry of the superpowers. Everyone in the world family will rise together under an indomitable strength of evolutionary power of natural law. Every nation coming to the level of fulfilment will be no damage to the fulfilment of any other nation. This is what will establish a permanent state of world peace.[412]

24

AT THE HOP

On Wednesday, 9th July 1986 over 120 journalists gathered at the Capital Convention Center in Washington DC to witness the first official display of the TM-Sidhi techniques. As with TM, the TM-Sidhi techniques were aimed at bringing the meditator to a state of 'restful alertness'. Dr Chopra, who was by then a leading light of Maharishi's worldwide movement, clarified the connection between the practices of the TM-Sidhi program and levitation:

> When he has meditated and reached this silent, even state, the person must next apply the mental technique that will allow him to lift up from the ground. The phrase 'mental technique' simply means a correct thought. At first his body will not co-operate with the thought. If one sits in an armchair and thinks, 'I want to fly', the body will not co-operate, but if the mind is in *samadhi*, there will be a result.[413]

Maharishi's own explanation of the deeper value of experiencing this phenomenon is also worth noting:

> 'Yogic flying' demonstrates the ability of the individual to act from the unified field and enliven the total potential of natural law in all its expressions – mind, body, behaviour, and environment. 'Yogic flying' presents in miniature the flight of galaxies in space, all unified in perfect order by natural law.[414]

On Tuesday, 8th July 1986, the day before the 'yogic flying competition', 3,000 *sidhas* gathered for the World Assembly on Perfect Health in Washington to listen to an inaugural pep-talk from Maharishi, courtesy of the latest time-lapse technology, with him explaining his latest initiative, a Programme to Create World Peace.

> The political history in the world has not been very worthwhile, with all the wars and now with something worse than war – the present state of terrorism. Terrorism can burst out at any place at any time, and terrorism involving the superpowers has created a terrible time for the whole human race.[415]

This seemed to be a very different Maharishi from the old days, what had happened to his theories concerning the infallible laws of *karma*? Surely one reaps only that which one has sown. Were not the recipients of violence only receiving their just desserts? Apparently not, for he declared:

> Whatever wars are seen here and there – the Iran-Iraq war, so much misfortune in South Africa and in Lebanon – all these negative things which should not be there will simply disappear.[416]

Was he seriously suggesting that he could undertake to deliver world peace on the strength of research into the TM-Sidhi programme?

> Already, trends are seen in this direction. This has resulted from the purifying influence in world consciousness generated by such world assemblies as we have here today.[417]

These words were as music to his devotees' ears, for they believed that out of a world population of many, many millions, only they and their kind held the secret of improving life on earth for others.

The day of the 'yogic flying' demonstrations arrived and the press gathered to witness the spectacle. They were primed for the big moment by a panel of sharp-suited men, thoroughly conversant with Maharishi-speak, who indulged in lengthy explanations about the theories connecting the practice of the TM-Sidhi programme with the goal of world peace. But the media had only come to watch the 'flying', and the cameramen waited impatiently. The press was only there in order to determine the truth of the Movement's claims.

Giving themselves a preliminary booster, the 'experts in the Technology of the Unified Field', dressed in athletic costumes and seated on foam mattresses arranged across the auditorium, took part in a brief meditation. The cameramen steadied their cameras and waited, fingers itching, waiting for the first signs of flight. And then it happened…

It took a while for the reality of the event to sink in, for the sight of 22 young people hopping, hopping about like frogs, and trying to project themselves across the vast expanse of the hall, was a long, long way from the long-awaited, long-anticipated, act of 'flying'.

> The Washington Post reported, 'When the final race, the 50-metre dash was completed, the contestants were utterly animated. While the audience rose to their feet in applause, the hoppers remained seated, hopping vigorously amongst themselves …'[418]

It is thought that the audience referred to was about 1,000 strong, and was composed exclusively of meditators.

The name of His Divinity Swami Brahmananda Saraswati Maharaj, Jagadguru Shankaracharya of Jyotir Math, Himalayas was still murmured with reverence by the faithful, and he was worshipped as 'the supreme teacher'. Each July, on the day of full moon (known to Hindus as *Guru Purnima*), Maharishi's closest disciples offered their devotions to a man, the life story and philosophy of which they were largely ignorant. In 1986 *Guru Purnima* fell on Monday, 21st July, and this auspicious day was chosen for the First International 'Yogic Flying' Competition at the Indira Gandhi Indoor Stadium in New Delhi, India. Surrounding the foam-mattressed arena were advertisements proclaiming 'Maharishi's Programme to Create World Peace' and 'Maharishi Ayurveda Perfect Health for All Mankind'. To a capacity audience of 10,000 seventy-odd *sidhas* from across the world, came to exhibit their ability to defy gravity. The new Shankaracharya, Swami Vishnudevanand opened the proceedings, with his arrival prompting a group of Vedic *pandits* to begin their recitations. Following on from the Shankaracharya's appearance came Dr Bevan Morris and a succession of other speakers, mainly Indian.

Then it was time for the show to commence. After a few minutes of *mantra* meditation, the 'levitating' athletes sprang about, rather like Chinese crackers. Earnestly they hop-jumped, hop-raced and hurdle-hopped in their bid to demonstrate the 'Mechanics to Create Coherence in World Consciousness, the Basis of World Peace'.

Whilst waiting for the results, members of the audience were treated to a series of 'inaugurations' given by senior people from institutions connected with Maharishi. Dr Brihaspati Triguna spoke on behalf of Maharishi World Centre for Ayurveda and World Hospital of Ayurveda, and Dr B V Raman appeared for the World Centre for Jyotish (Indian Astrology), whilst its performers, who gave a recital of some selections of Indian classical music, represented Maharishi World Centre for Gandharva Veda.

It is said that a *sidha's* capacity to produce 'increased coherence' and assist world peace is calculated at 100 times that of one who practises the regular TM technique. With approximately 50,000 supermeditators available worldwide, a plan was devised which would draw greater attention to the phenomenon of 'yogic flying' and also generate cash contributions for the peace initiative. And on Friday, 15th August 1986, right around the world, *sidhas* twitched, convulsed and hopped their way to short-term fame, but the ambitious goal of raising $100 million for the World Peace Fund was not achieved. However, the still photographs portraying the lotus positioned peaceniks did make it look as if they had floated above *terra firma* and that magic had been done that day.

For Dr Morris, Maharishi's right-hand man, August was a very busy month. He appeared at numerous gatherings and press conferences; in fact, so ubiquitous was he becoming, that one might have thought he possessed some of the extraordinary powers that had been promised, but so far not been seen. As he faced the press in London's Royal Garden Hotel, he told BBC Radio 4's Trevor Barnes:

> When the person practises Transcendental Meditation their mind settles down to a completely silent state, a state of pure consciousness. Then they begin to practise a technique from the ancient *Yoga Sutras* of Patanjali which is supposed to produce flying. The brain becomes intensely coherent, and inside what you feel is an incredible surge of energy and great waves and thrills of bliss from head to toe and then the mind.

At this point he was interrupted by Barnes who, spotting the first signs of activity, wanted to keep his radio listeners informed:

> The first one has started to hop towards us. It looks like a physical thing. He could just be propelling himself along with his hands.[419]

It fell to Dr Morris to answer the central question of whether or not the 'yogic flying' had yet progressed past the phase of hopping. With visible reluctance he said that, of the three postulated stages of levitation -hopping, hovering and floating – only examples of the first stage had been witnessed amongst practitioners of the TM-Sidhi programme. He did, however, emphasize his conviction that it would one day be possible to go beyond this stage, and pointed to the historical wealth of accounts of such phenomena.

The flyers themselves were apparently seeing an altogether show. For them the real excitement was in the idea that increased brain coherence might be generated by these exercises, and the feelings of bliss that were said to course through participants' bodies, impelling them to take their next jump.

One might wonder why people expected so much from the 'flyers'? But there was of course Maharishi's forecast that his disciples would soon be flying over Lake Lucerne. According to Dr Chopra, a young man had suggested that 'yogic flying' would never be used as a method of transport, but on hearing this, Maharishi had contradicted him: ' "Oh, no," he said, "we will fly outside the buses, even if just for fun." '[420]

Not all the disciples of Swami Brahmananda were enthusiastic about Maharishi's teachings. Swami Swaroopanand Saraswati, born in the same area of India as Maharishi, and initiated into *sannyas* by Swami Brahmananda, had inherited the seat of The Shankaracharya of Dwarka. He was approached by a meditator (and practitioner of the TM-Sidhi program) who queried him about Maharishi's qualifications.

> Questioner: Mahesh Yogi claims that he preaches *yoga* according to the instruction of his *guru*. The truth of the matter, however, is that Guru Dev never asked anyone who is not a *Brahmin* by birth to go and spread his teachings. What is your opinion?

> Shankaracharya: This is true. In reality, preaching, initiating, guiding people engaged in spiritual pursuits, is the duty of those who are born in a *Brahmin* family. If he is a follower of *Sanatan Dharma* (the Hindu religion), he should not do what he is doing. This is against the orders of his *guru*. Moreover, making others write *puujya* (revered), calling himself Maharishi (a great seer) is totally inappropriate. No assembly of saints has either conferred upon him a title of Maharishi nor has announced him *puujya*. In the ashram he was doing the work of typing and writing and translation. Then he became a *sadhu*. However, he has never practiced *yoga*. It is said that Guru Dev was given poison. Who gave that poison we don't know but we know that there was poison in his body. When Guru Dev's body became unwell, then we wanted him to go to Kashi [Varanasi] to rest. But he (Mahesh) removed him from that trip forcibly and took him to speak in Calcutta. There he died. [421]

Each year at the beginning of January, Maharishi would 'go into silence' for about ten days, and then again in July, and it thought this is in order to recharge his energies. However, Nancy Cooke de Herrera recounts that Charlie Lutes suggested an alternate reason for these periods of seclusion:

> It's also a time when he gets to talk with the Hierarchy. It [the Hierarchy] is the government of the cosmic force which controls the universe. Maharishi consults it in his silences when he needs guidance for his world mission. He obeys Mother Divine and honors this force, although the name is not mentioned in public. [422]

Benjamin Creme, the representative of an Eastern missionary known as Maitreya, was asked:

> Questioner: Which position does Maharishi Mahesh Yogi hold in the hierarchy of the Masters?
> Benjamin Crème: He is a disciple of a 6th ray Master of the 6th degree known as Guru Dev, Who is not in incarnation. [423]

> Questioner: Is Swami Brahmananda Saraswati [Guru Dev] now on Sirius and connected through Maharishi Mahesh Yogi to planet Earth?
> Benjamin Crème: No. Guru Dev still works on the inner [higher] planes of this Earth. [424]

When the 12th January1987 celebrations came around the year was declared as the 'Year of World Peace'.

Although Maharishi still contended that everyone should become blissful, nowadays he seemed less concerned about the means:

> Enjoy your life and be happy. Being happy is of the utmost importance. Success in anything is through happiness. More support of Nature comes from being happy. Under all circumstances be happy, even if you have to force it a bit to change long standing habits.

> Just think of any negativity that comes at you as a raindrop falling into the ocean of your bliss. You may not always have an ocean of bliss, but think that way anyway and it will help it come. Doubting is not blissful and does not create happiness. Be happy, healthy and let that love flow through your heart.[425]

He told of his hopes, that by amassing large groups of *sidhas*, world peace would occur. On hearing this announcement at least some people must have had a strange feeling of *déjà vu*. Almost a decade before, one of the Movement's magazines had announced the triumph of Maharishi's peace forces in having created world peace.

The *World Government News* was a lavish production, a expensive looking publication which left the hands of readers smeared with specks of gold ink.. In the January 1979 issue of the magazine, under a gilt-framed photograph of Maharishi, the text ran:

> During October, in a historically unprecedented global initiative, the World Government of the Age of Enlightenment sent Governors of the Age of Enlightenment to restore peace in the five most troubled areas of the world. Through this initiative, inspired by His Holiness Maharishi Mahesh Yogi, founder of the World Government of the Age of Enlightenment, world peace has been achieved and large-scale violence and conflict, and consequent mass pain and suffering of humanity, have been vanquished from the face of the earth.[426]

Maharishi really did seem to believe that he could create a situation where world peace might become an all-time reality, but only if it were expanded to 10,000 *sidhas* and maintained by a $100 million World Peace Fund,:

> 10,000 Vedic Scientists in one place on earth, Maharishi Nagar, India, will enliven the supreme power of natural law in world consciousness, which will nourish all nations and disallow the rise of any negative or destructive influence in any part of the world.[427]

Whether Maharishi liked it or not, whether he acknowledged it or not, the world beyond his movement could not easily be brought under the control of 'orderly thinking'. However he must have been warmed to hear from his teachers that approximately 3½ million people had by now received instruction in TM and to know that he could rely on others to spread the word. In one of the Movement's books, *Feel Great With TM*, an eminent doctor, Desmond Kelly, MD, FRCP, FRCPsych, endorsed the technique, saying amongst other things:

> Setting aside 20 minutes twice a day for Transcendental Meditation enables the brain to be quiet and tranquil. It helps people think more clearly and positively, to have creative ideas, and to cope with the stress of a busy life. People sleep more soundly. TM also elevates the good-mood neurotransmitters in the brain, and because it acts on the brain directly it is much more than just another relaxation technique ...[428]

Notwithstanding, the fact that Maharishi was mute about his origins and his personal history, rumour had it that members of his family held posts in his various organisations.

In January 1988 the *Illustrated Weekly of India* published a long in-depth article about Maharishi, entitled *The Troubled Guru.*

> Among the yogi's relatives, his brother J P Srivastava's sons, Anand and Ajay Prakash, seem to be in charge of accounts and administration. The brother, reportedly, is not given much importance in the family hierarchy, for reasons that date back to the illustrious younger sibling's youth. Mahesh Yogi, apparently, had early in life forsaken hearth and home after being allegedly ill-treated by his brother and the memory seems to still rankle. So J.P. Srivastava has been relegated to an insignificant position...

> The yogi, is reportedly, fondest of his niece, Kirti, his sister Indira's daughter. She is in charge of the women's wing. Apart from Brahmachari Nandikishore, she is the person reported to be closet to him. She has two brothers, Praful and Pramod. While Pramod has settled in West Germany through the benevolence of his uncle, Praful operates from India, say sources. The Maharishi's munificence extends to more distant relatives as well. Girish Varma, the son of one of the yogi's paternal uncles, has comfortably settled at NOIDA.[429]

Though 1989 was dubbed 'Year of Heaven on Earth', there were no obvious signs of world peace, but this did not stop Maharishi from continuing to talk about the better times to come:

> Heaven on Earth has been the most laudable aspiration of the wise throughout the ages. Creation of Heaven on Earth is the most desirable project in entire history of the human race.
>
> Everyone can now enjoy Heaven on Earth through perfect alliance with natural law, through the enlivenment of the total potential of natural law in one's own consciousness. Perfect alliance with natural law is now available to every individual and every nation through my Vedic Science and Technology – the perfect science and technology of life which offers to enrich and raise to perfection all fields of daily life and create Heaven on Earth.[430]

In his earlier lectures and writings Maharishi had assiduously avoided the use of the words 'I' and 'my' in favour of 'we' and 'our'. The names of his movements were similarly impersonal until his university in Iowa was named Maharishi International University. Then, virtually everything associated with him took on his name. In 1989 he inaugurated Maharishi's Global Green Revolution, Maharishi's Global Rural Development, Maharishi's Global Urban Renewal and Maharishi's Global Industrial Revolution, programmes aimed at eradicating poverty. There was even attempts to re-brand Transcendental Meditation as Maharishi's Transcendental Meditation and Science of Creative Intelligence as Maharishi's Science of Creative Intelligence. The market diversification had also led to the introduction of Maharishi AyurVedic preparations and Maharishi Gandharva music cassettes, products to ring in the new Age of Enlightenment or Heaven on Earth:

> The inspiration to create Heaven on Earth comes from the great achievements of my Movement around the world during the last thirty years and above all from the discovery of the Ved, the infinite creative intelligence of natural law, in the self-referral consciousness, transcendental consciousness of everyone.[431]

In November 1989, Dandi Swami Vishnudevanand Saraswati died, and it is suggested the post of Shankaracharya of Jyotir Math was then offered to Dandi Swami Narayananand Saraswati (a devotee of Swami Brahmananda and close *gurubhaiee* of Swami Shantanand) but that he refused it, choosing instead a life of seclusion and solitude. Anyway, in the event, the new Shankaracharya was named as Swami Vasudevanand Saraswati, who until then had worked as a teacher at the Sanskrit Mahavidyalaya, Alopibagh, Allahabad, where he is said to have been the head of the Vedanta Department. Before taking the title of Swami Vasudevanand he was called Brahmachari Somnath, prior to which he was variously known as Somnath Dwivedi, and Shobhnath Dwivedi.

On 12th January 1990, Maharishi Mahesh Yogi, from the World Capital of the Age of Enlightenment, Maharishi Nagar, Delhi, India, In the company of some half dozen of his *brahmacharin*, amongst them Satyanand, and to the sound of Vedic chanting, Maharishi made his way across the hall. His face (remarkably aged) beamed with a particularly joyous expression as with palms placed together he acknowledged the crowds of disciples. Amongst the assembled throng sat row upon row of young Brahmin boys in Nehru hats, known as the 1000 Headed Purusha; perhaps out there too were the 1000 young girls collectively known as Divine Mother. Also there to witness the celebrations were the VIPs, who had been allotted comfortable orange armchairs, and others, presumably lesser beings, the rank and file, who stood beside their white tubular chairs. Marked with the Hindu ritual red *tilak* upon his forehead with garlands of seasonal flowers around his neck, Maharishi stood before a painting of his 'Guru Dev' placed upon a long altar replete with fruit, flowers and other symbolic offerings such as candles and incense. All present joined together in singing the *puja*, the prayer to the Masters of the Holy Tradition.

Maharishi proclaimed to his audience, and to all the devotees who were viewing him across the world on satellite link-up, that the Sixteenth Year of the Age of Enlightenment would be the 'Year of Alliance with Nature's Government'.

Vedic *pandits* had recited some more ancient chants, the speeches commenced, and a succession of Indian speakers came and went, Dr Triguna and Dr Chopra amongst them.

Apparently, Dr Chopra had brought some news, on hearing which Maharishi became unusually animated:

> I was just waiting for this news today. Just this morning thought came to me 'How cruel is the health law of USA which prohibits things for health which have worked for thousands of years?' but that idea has now got this beautiful news and I am going to congratulate America for this. I congratulate the Medical Association of America, you have taken a timely stand for perfect health of human race. America has proved to be the most creative country in the world and now I see my feeling for years that USA is the most creative country in the world is materialized now in this news, if the news is true. If the news is true.[432]

Dr Chopra assured Maharishi the news was true that the American Medical Association was giving credit for a course on Maharishi Ayurveda. This pleased its founder no end:

> Then from today I'll cease to think that American Medical Association have been and is continuing to be a puppet of the multinationals. I'll change my views.[433]

Then Maharishi launched into praise for those leading his *ayurveda* initiative and the promotion of its value, making the point that the fundamental strength of *ayurveda* lay in its ability to prevent illness.

He was in particularly good form, his delivery bubbly and enthusiastic. As he glanced around him his eyes danced and sparkled. This was not to say he never hesitated or found himself grasping for words, as when the name he had applied to the year of 1990 for some moments eluded him, but after quickly referring to his notes he continued undaunted, stating that he perceived 'an upsurge in friendliness in the world today' which he attributed to the practice of accessing transcendental consciousness:

Freshness is blossoming in world consciousness, negativity is subsiding in the world behaviour. It is a very good time for the human race, that this knowledge is fully enlivened. Today we have the total knowledge of natural law in our fingertips. This is the time that we feel, we are the custodians of heaven and earth so we want to bring them together. We want to create heaven on earth because we have that knowledge, that pure knowledge, that total knowledge of natural law. That reigns life in heaven just as much as it reigns life on earth.

A common intelligence which reigns the whole universe is available now through my Vedic science to every individual in his own self-awareness, in his transcendental consciousness.[434]

Maharishi continued on with a marathon speech. He was clearly in high spirits and in an especially confident mood. Although his outer appearance was showing his age, his strength of purpose and his capacity to express himself told another story. With head and body bobbing up and down, his toothsome, smiling face emitted hope and generosity. His words tumbled amidst bubbles of humour. The man seemed to be on a perpetual 'high'. Was it any wonder that, on the strength of his personality, so many had taken to his teachings? His passion and optimism flowed out in seemingly endless torrents of speech. He had the power, he had the charisma, and he had that certain something, a magnetism that drew people near.

In a passing reference to world peace, he stated it had already been gained, confiding:

I am very happy today that those days should now be over for those powerful governments. That they hush up the great discoveries in order that 'no other government can have it and I will have a more powerful weapon'. The days of weapons are over.

We have achieved the first year of the heaven on earth and now what will prevail in the world? Friendliness, sincerity, protection, nourishment, motherly and fatherly affection towards human race.[435]

Had his followers had been forbidden to pass on any bad news to him? But one might be forgiven for believing his assurances, for he sounded so knowledgeable, so convincing, so right, and with so much more to say. Many more speakers were to have their say, but the star of the show, as always, was still Maharishi.

A novel twist to the proceedings came with a guest appearance of sorts, a pre-recorded video statement from the Delhi Police Commissioner, Raja Vijay Karan. He looked an intelligent man, conscientious but beleaguered with the problems of running an overworked police force of some 52,000 (Delhi was believed to be the largest metropolitan force in the world at that time). His concern was that his officers had to work very long hours, seven days a week, and were therefore subjected to unbearably high levels of stress, and he was looking for a way to assist them. Presumably he was unable to offer his staff shorter working hours, so had to find an alternative way of keeping them fresh. It is unlikely that such a down-to-earth sort of person would have otherwise given much credence to the Movement's claims, about being able to create an ideal society, but he was happy enough for his staff to give the meditation a try:

> So we hope with the introduction of Transcendental Meditation in the Delhi Police, the Delhi policeman will be less stressful, will suffer from less anxiety. He will be more fresh in his duty and will be able to perform the 12-14 hours of duty every day with greater cheer, with greater energy and with greater happiness and service to the people. Thank you.[436]

Following the Police Commissioner came another surprise speaker, one Anil Anatha Krishna, President of a division of a major Maharishi endeavour, the Maharishi Heaven on Earth Development Corporation, and the subject of his presentation was the provocatively named Electric Chariots Project:

> Maharishi has given me this opportunity to exercise my technological capabilities to initiate and implement an electric vehicle project, to bring about a pollution-free world. With the blessings and guidance of Maharishi, we are gearing up for massive commercial production and marketing of pollution-free electric vehicles scheduled for commercial release by March 1990.
>
> In March we march to bring about heaven on earth with the introduction of pollution-free personal and public transportation system electric vehicles in the classes of two-, three- and four-wheelers.[437]

Statue of Guru Dev at Shankaracharya Nagar

25

★

CORPORATE STRUCTURE

During the 12th January 1990 celebrations, Maharishi accorded one of his associates some generous praise; Dr Chopra, he said, had given up a highly lucrative career in medicine to involve himself in the study and promotion of Maharishi Ayur-ved. However he made no mention that Dr Chopra was now so highly placed within the Movement that he was tipped as the most likely contender for succession to the leadership of Maharishi's organizations. The New Year saw the publication of a new book from Dr Chopra's books, the fourth in as many years, and the release of a package of six tape recordings under the title *Magical Mind, Magical Body*. Both his written and his recorded material were being heavily promoted within the Movement, with Dr Chopra himself in ever-greater demand. Reading between the lines, it seems as though Maharishi wished Dr Chopra to have greater exposure, and was gently divesting himself of his own responsibilities in order to retire at last.

It appeared somewhat ironic that after several decades in which Maharishi and his spokespeople had strenuously upheld the all-embracing nature of meditation's benefits, the Movement suddenly evince interest in 'alternative' medicine. Maharishi Ayur-Ved and its principal product *Amrita Kalash,* said to be 'known in the ancient Vedic civilisation as the nectar of immortality'[438] had first surfaced in 1986. In just five years the promotion of Maharishi Ayur-Ved had burgeoned to the point where a 500-room Maharishi Ayur-Ved Prevention Centre was to be set up in every continent, with 1,000 Maharishi Ayur-Ved Health and Rejuvenation Centres in North America alone. In pursuance of Maharishi's commitment to his belief in the merits of 'yogic flying' a permanent group of 7,000 'Vedic scientists' was to be established at Maharishi Ved Vigyan Peeth, Maharishi Nagar, Delhi.

Maharishi's simple teaching had, for the first decade and a half of his mission, focussed solely on the merits of regular practice of Transcendental

Meditation.

> Heaven on Earth will have lots of people as successors of this knowledge. By now there are about 40,000 teachers of Transcendental Meditation and they're all the successors of this beautiful Vedic wisdom.[439]

The new upsurge of interest in *ayurveda* centred around the names of Dr V. M. Dwivedi, Dr Brihaspati-Dev Triguna and Dr Balraj Maharshi, Dr Hari Sharma and Dr Deepak Chopra.

Maharishi offered his unreserved and unconditional support for *ayurvedic* medicine:

> Ayur-Ved is that simple, natural program for perfect health that eliminates all imbalances – in the physiology, psychology, behaviour, and environment. All the different health systems of the world are going to be fulfilled with support and enrichment from Ayur-Ved.[440]

Maharishi's style of *ayurvedic* medicine offered more than just a range of herbal preparations, it offered 'pulse diagnosis' and the intriguingly named 'primordial sound techniques'.

According to Dr Chopra, whilst he was staying at Maharishi Nagar once, Maharishi had summoned him to his quarters and told him:

> I have been waiting a long time to bring out some special techniques. I believe they will become the medicine of the future. They were known in the distant past but were lost in the confusion of time; now I want you to learn them, and at the same time I want you to explain, clearly and scientifically, how they work.[441]

Maharishi then revealed certain simple sounds to him and explained how they should be used. He ended their meeting on a note of caution:

> 'This knowledge is extremely powerful,' he repeated. 'By comparison, the drugs and surgery you are used to using are very crude. It will take time, but people will grow to realize this.'[442]

Apparently Dr Chopra was convinced of the healing potential of these sounds, for they soon came to be offered as part of Maharishi's package of measures designed to usher in his dream of a perfect society:

> Through the application of the prevention value of Maharishi Ayur-Ved, we envision a time in which life is lived in perfect health, free from sickness and suffering, and every nation, on the basis of perfect health, enjoys self-sufficiency, cultural integrity, and invincibility in the perpetual sunshine of the Age of Enlightenment.[443]

Having entered the field of alternative medicine, it was perhaps only natural that Maharishi would not stop at *ayurveda*. Meditators had become involved in a whole series of commercial endeavours, ranging from selling air-freshening ionizing units to putting in a bid for the construction toy giant Meccano, playing with stocks and shares and selling precious gems. With the introduction of Maharishi Ayur-Ved, the scope for new businesses appeared to be unlimited. There seemed to be no good reason why they should not go the whole hog and explain all the other magical possibilities offered by ancient thought (making sure of course, that they were offered in a scientific way).

Serious consideration was being given to the environment, therefore it was good time to research, revive and re-establish traditional Indian ideas relating to architecture and planning. This new initiative was dubbed Maharishi Sthapatya-Ved:

> 'Our homes should be celestial, highly artistic homes worthy of Heaven on Earth,' says a spokesman for the World centre for Sthapatya-Ved. 'Using good materials is not enough. All the surfaces should be richly carved inside and out. The artists and the architect should work together to create a formidable, magical piece of art, stunning to the senses and fulfilling to the heart.'[444]

Armenia, recently the victim of severe earthquakes, was to serve as a model for this new architecture, and the town of Leninakan was chosen to be a City of Immortals.

Indian perspectives on astrology were also reviewed, and also brought into service, suitably approved and branded:

> Maharishi Jyotish is that precious and intimate aspect of Vedic Science representing the inner light of consciousness which brings the full knowledge of past, present and future.[445]

Another intriguing subject which was awaiting the attention of Maharishi's team, was the ancient practice of ritual performances known as *yagya*:

> Maharishi Yagyas are ancient precise performances by specially trained Vedic *pandits* at Maharishi Ved Vigyan Vidya Peeth in India which create specific life-supporting influences from the field of pure consciousness, the source of natural law, to counteract any negative effects which are going to come from our past actions.[446]

In effect, what was being offered was a sort of dial-a-prayer service for those with problems with their past *karma*.

After years of concern about his movement's image, this swing towards wholesale Hindu revivalism might suggest that Maharishi had given up his dreams of trying to win the support of scientists. Certainly, sceptics such as American author James Randi were challenging him:

> Ever since I heard that the Maharishi Mahesh Yogi of Transcendental

Meditation fame has a doctorate in physics, I've been wary of scientists who have lots of education but aren't very scientific. This yogic person, in common with most amateur philosophers, gropes about for a simple analogy to demonstrate a novel notion, failing to recognize that analogies are only for purposes of illustration and simplification, and do not often represent parallels. The Maharishi actually equates the solar system, with its planets orbiting about central Sun, with the atom and its accompanying electrons orbiting a central nucleus. It doesn't take much science to recognize that not only is His Holiness thereby ignorant of the actual state of the atom, but that his parallel is ludicrous.

The Maharishi's solar system-atom analogy is not only crackpot, it is very bad crackpot.[447]

Another detractor was a fellow-countryman, who coincidentally hailed from the same region of India, Jabalpur. Acharya Rajneesh, now known as Bhagwan Rajneesh, openly disparaged Maharishi.

Cheechli was the birthplace of Maharishi Mahesh Yogi. He never mentions it. There are reasons why he does not mention where he was born, because he belongs to the *sudra* class in India. Just to mention that you come from a certain village, certain caste, or profession - and Indians are very uncultured about that. They may just stop you on the road and ask you, "What is your caste?" Nobody thinks that this is an interference.

Maharishi Mahesh Yogi was born on the other side of the station, but because he is a *sudra*, he can neither mention the village - because it is a village of only *sudras*, the lowest caste in the Indian hierarchy - nor can he use his surname. That too will immediately reveal who he is.

His full name is Mahesh Kumar Shrivastava, but "Shrivastava" would put a stop to all his pretensions, at least in India, and that would affect others too. He is not an initiated *sannyasin* in any of the old orders, because again, there are only ten *sannyasin* orders in India. I have been trying to destroy them, that is why they are all angry with me.

These orders are again castes, but of *sannyasins*. Maharishi Mahesh Yogi cannot be a *sannyasin* because no *sudra* can become an initiate. That's why he does not write "Swami" before his name. He cannot, nobody has given him that name. He does not write behind his name, as Hindu *sannyasins* do, Bharti, Saraswati, Giri et cetera; they have their ten names.

He has created his own name - "Yogi." It does not mean anything. Anybody trying to stand on his head, and of course falling again and again, can call himself a *yogi*, there is no restriction on it.

A *sudra* can be a *yogi*, and the name Maharishi is something to replace "Swami," because in India things are such that if the name "Swami" is missing, then people would suspect something is wrong.

You have to put something else there just to cover up the gap.

He invented "Maharishi." He is not even a *rishi*; *rishi* means "seer," and *maharishi* means "great seer."

He can't even see beyond his nose. All he can do when you ask him relevant questions is giggle.

In fact, I will call him "Swami Gigglananda," that will fit him perfectly. That giggling is not something respectable, it is really a strategy to avoid questions. He cannot answer any question.[448]

***

Apparently, Deepak Chopra first became aware there was something amiss when Maharishi failed to make a call to a meditation course in Iowa.

Maharishi was supposed to address the assembly on speaker phone from India, but the phone call didn't come through at the appointed time. We all dispersed.

A couple of hours later when I was in meditation I had a vision of Maharishi lying in a hospital bed with intravenous tubes in his body breathing on a respirator. I quickly got out of the meditation and phoned my parents in New Delhi. My mother picked up the phone and told me that Maharishi was very sick. "They think he's been poisoned. Come quickly," she said. I asked to speak to my father, who was a cardiologist. She said, "Your father isn't here. He's taking care of Maharishi." This began a journey that took me to the very heart of who the guru is and who he is expected to be. The two can be in jarring opposition.

I immediately left Fairfield for Chicago, where a wealthy TM donor had been kind enough to charter a plane for me. When I arrived in Delhi, it was past midnight. I first went home. My father was not there, and my mother told me he was still with Maharishi in a house in Golflinks, a private reserve in the city. One room had been converted into an intensive care unit presided over by my father and other doctors. I arrived at the house at 2:00 am, and when I entered the makeshift ICU I saw Maharishi lying unconscious in a bed with IV tubes and a respirator just as I had foreseen. My father informed me darkly that after drinking a glass of orange juice given to him by "a foreign disciple," Maharishi had suffered severe abdominal pain and inflammation of the pancreas, along with kidney failure followed by a heart attack. Poisoning was suspected. Over the next few days Maharishi's condition worsened. The pancreas and kidney functions continued to deteriorate, and his heart didn't improve. My father was of the opinion that Maharishi should be taken to England for a course of kidney dialysis. The Indian TM organization, centered around Maharishi's nephews, Prakash and Anand Shrivastava, were adamant that no one in the movement should find out that Maharishi was grievously ill. The rationale was that his followers would panic and lose faith.

Maharishi's complete recovery happened slowly. There was a point where the doctor informed us that he had sevre anemia and needed a blood transfusion.

When they typed and cross-matched Maharishi's blood, I turned out to be the only match - this, of course, only increased my sense of being a participant in a drama shaped by forces outside myself. When he was informed about the situation, however, Maharishi refused to accept my blood but would give no reason. Considering that much had been made of how he had studied physics in college and had insisted on the scientific validity of TM, this was a baffling decision. Then I had a sudden insight. He didn't want my blood because he didn't want my karma. After all, I had been a smoker, had indulged in alcohol and sex and had even experimented with LSD years before. I went to Maharishi and confronted him with my realization. I asked if he believed that karma could be transmitted in the blood. He responded reluctantly, "That's true." I told him that red blood cells do not have a nucleus and therefore contain no DNA. Without genetic information my blood would only be giving him the hemoglobin he needed without karmic infection. At first he was suspicious, but I had the hematologist explain to him that memory and information is not transferred through a red blood transfusion. Eventually he accepted my blood. As he regained strength, we removed him from the hospital, and he was brought to a London hotel to continue recuperating.

This began a period of increased intimacy between us. We would go for long walks in Hyde Park, which felt strange given the complete blackout of news to the TM movement, which was told that Maharishi had decided to go into silence for the time being. On one occasion, a stranger ran up to us in the park and asked, "Aren't you the guru of the Beatles?" My wife Rita, who had joined us that day, quickly interjected, "He's my father-in-law. Please leave him alone." In the end we felt that staying in London risked unnecessary publicity. So Maharishi was moved to a country home in the southwest of England where I spent hours personally nursing him.

In all, Maharishi was out of circulation for almost a year; few in the TM movement knew where he was, and almost no one was willing to concede that he had been sick. After he was fully recovered we flew him via helicopter back to his chosen residence, which wasn't in either India or the U.S. but the obscure village of Vlodrop in Holland.[449]

Allegedly, it was only intended for Maharishi to stay in Holland a few days, but the stopover was extended, first by days, and then by weeks. Then everything was packed in order to move him back to India, and a chartered flight flew him out from Maastricht, but before very long Maharishi requested the pilot turn the plane around and land again, whereupon Maharishi returned to Vlodrop.

In January 1992, from his new top-security base in a converted monastery in Vlodrop, Holland, the Maharishi Continental Capital of the Age of Enlightenment for Europe, Maharishi broadcast his new year's message, and with the help of satellite technology the scrambled signals made their way through the ethers. He announced to his faithful supporters, clustered around television monitors around the world, that the Eighteenth Year of the Age of Enlightenment was to be 'Maharishi's Year of the Constitution of the Universe'.

On 1st April 1992 (April Fool's Day) former Beatle George Harrison announced his intention to perform at a concert to benefit a new political party. But was he joking?

The Natural Law Party was the inspiration of Maharishi Mahesh Yogi, and when it was launched it was decided to field over 300 candidates in the British General Election. Few in Britain would then be able to remain ignorant of this new political force, since the Natural Law Party's manifesto had been dropped through letterboxes across the land. George Harrison's involvement seems to have been spurred by his attendance at a lecture on Ayur-Ved by Dr Chopra some weeks earlier in London. Then he was approached to lend his support to the campaign, and he unhesitatingly agreed and set about rehearsing with musicians he had been touring with in Japan.

Though George Harrison was prepared to stand up and be counted as one of Maharishi's meditators, did he seriously believe that the practice of meditation automatically endowed it's practitioners with the ability to govern others?

> I believe this Party offers the only option to get out of our problems and create the beautiful nation we would all like to have. The General Election should be a celebration of democracy and our right to vote. The Natural Law Party is turning this election into a wonderful, national celebration and I am with them all the way.[450]

George Harrison's appearance at the Royal Albert Hall, London, billed as his first UK show since leaving The Beatles, proved hugely successful for his reputation and for the spread of Transcendental Meditation. Before the concert he announced:

> I still practice Transcendental Meditation and I think it's great. Maharishi only ever did good for us, and although I have not been with him physically, I never left him.[451]

But it was going to take more than the return of this quiet former superstar to win over the voters. The fledgling offshoot of the World Government of the Age of Enlightenment had its headquarters in rural Buckinghamshire, at the splendid country mansion of Mentmore Towers, and Geoffrey Clements, the leader of the party, was asked what would happen if the

Natural Law Party won no seats. 'That's a scenario that isn't going to unfold,' he replied confidently.[452]

Not everyone was with them all the way, and Simon Garfield of the *Independent* newspaper wrote:

> There appears to be nothing illegal about the activities of the Natural Law Party, but there is a vaguely sinister air to its HQ; amid dripping candles and incense, secret doors and dank passageways, cracked masonry and tarnished gilt, it is as though New Agers were making gothic horror movies. Visitors to Mentmore may arrive with an open mind, but they will almost certainly come away converted. The problem is, they will be converted to Conservatism.[453]

When the NLP Party had approached George Harrison to become a candidate, he in turn contacted Paul McCartney.

> Paul McCartney- 'A week before the British elections of 1992, the ones where the Maharishi's Natural Law Party took double-page ads in all the papers, George asked me to stand as the Natural Law Party Member of Parliament for Liverpool. Just one week before the last general election. George rang me giggling from LA. He said, "I've been up all night and you may think this is a bit silly, but Maharishi would like you, me and Ringo to stand as Members of Parliament for Liverpool." He said, "We'll win." I said "Yeeeessss!" He said, "It'll be great." I said, "Why, what'll we do?" He said, "Well, we'll introduce meditation for everyone." I said, "Wait a minute, this is a quite far-out idea this, you know." I think, as George's wife pointed out to him, he just wouldn't want the work. If you send George a bunch of papers, he says, "I'm not looking at that!", but if you're an MP, you've got to look at those papers, there's no getting round it. But it was quite funny. I said, "George, let's get one thing straight. No way am I gonna do it. I don't want to put a damper on, I don't want to rain on your parade or anything. You do it if you want. I'll support you. I'll back you up. But there's no way in heaven I am going to stand as a Member of Parliament a week before the election! You've gotta be kidding!" Well, they put 230 candidates out and I think every one of them lost their deposit. That may be a slight exaggeration but I don't recall any of them getting in. It showed they had a bit of dough, though. But they were talking mad things. George was saying, "You know places like Bradford and Blackburn or Southall where they have a big Indian community? They're going to bring in Indian guys, holy men, people like that to be candidates." He said, "Well, they'll definitely win in all those Indian communities." There was lots of talk, it was talk.'[454]

Even Canadian magician, Doug Henning, was targeted to become an MP. Henning was at that time involved in a $1.5 billion scheme to open up a 1,400 acre theme park at Niagara Falls to promote Maharishi's teachings. Although several other similar projects had been mooted in Florida, California, India and Holland, and substantial plots of land had been purchased, none had been developed. The theme park ideas seem to stem from Maharishi's visit to Disneyland some years before, and the park to be created at Niagara Falls, in addition to educational facilities, planned to offer such attractions as the 'Seven States of Consciousness', a 'Ride into the Molecular Structure of a Flower', and a 'levitating' building referred to as the 'Courtyard of Illusions'.

Henning was interviewed for Canadian radio and asked what involvement Maharishi had in these projects:

> Oh he isn't in the corporate structure. He's … you might say the knowledge aspect and the enlightenment aspect. He's a sage. He is a monk. He doesn't make money. He doesn't have any money. He just is there and he gives the knowledge.[455]

Doug Henning's bid to become a Member of Parliament for Blackpool South appeared somewhat flawed, for he had never even been there:

> But I've read all about it, I'll be going in a few days. My platform in Blackpool is to beautify it with beautiful fountains and flowers and trees and waterfalls, and create more high-quality attractions and improve life for everybody and phase out VAT [Value Added Tax].[456]

He was not the only 'out-of-town' candidate; for amongst the others were Australians Byron Rigby and President of Maharishi International University Dr Bevan Morris, who had been flown in especially for the election. Most of the candidates, however, were British residents and teachers of meditation, and not all of them unknown.

> Dr Henning has recently been seen on BBC television, presenting his magic shows, as have Leslie Davis and Roger Chalmers, two members of the party's executive council. But their appearance was rather less glamorous, coming as it did on the BBC news last October after being struck off the medical register for offering herbal treatments for AIDS. The treatment was part of the Ayur-Ved health programme, practised and promoted by the Natural Law Party.[457]

Heaven on earth sounded attractive enough, but some of the voters were left unconvinced of the NLP's ability to provide 'perpetual sunshine of the Age of Enlightenment; always and everywhere a rainbow in the sky – coherent light of good luck for everyone'. Even meditators were divided about it, wondering whether the Movement's involvement in politics was ill-advised. The Party's main appeal was to the floating voter, but it won no seats; indeed, none of it's candidates came anywhere close to being elected.

In Southport, where NLP's leader, Geoffrey Clements, stood for election, of the 55,440 people who turned out to vote only 159 supported him. Doug Henning fared a little better, gaining 173 votes out of 43,941 cast, but all candidates lost their deposits. Many of Maharishi's followers must have wished that he had not suggested their getting embroiled in the mundane and pressurized world of politics.

One would have thought that this debacle would mark the end of Maharishi's involvement with politics, but he tried again in May 1992 in Israel and again in August 1992 in the USA, with no better results.

When 1993 came, Maharishi had still not returned to his native India, and was still in Vlodrop, Holland. Many thought his reasons for staying in Europe was on account of tax problems back in India, but Maharishi himself offered a rather different reason:

> The leaders in Europe have been trying to integrate, so I thought to establish a Vedic Science university here to help integrate the collective consciousness of all the countries in Europe.[458]

His continued presence in Holland did not, however, prevent him from attending numerous assemblies, or from speaking with his followers all over the world by conference telephone and satellite broadcasts.

The image of the laughing, bouncing, giggling *guru* with the long, flowing hair and a twinkle in his eye had, by repeated exposure, become etched in the minds of his followers. His oft-repeated claim that Transcendental Meditation contributes to perfect health and a reversal of the ageing process, justified expectation that he at least, would demonstrate these benefits. But the 12th January 1993 broadcast belied these promises.

Maharishi was almost totally bald, his forehead furrowed with deep lines, and his eyes no longer darted about as he spoke. They now appeared unseeing, the pupils all but permanently veiled by his heavily hooded eyelids. In the three-quarters of an hour that he spoke, he gave the impression of one who had great difficulty rising to the occasion. Subdued beyond belief, his words no longer bubbled up spontaneously from a well of inspiration. He delivered his annual speech hesitantly and almost without humour. Naming 1993 the 'Year of Administration Through Natural Law', Maharishi spoke at length of the greatness of Nature's government, saying that it:

> ... maintains perfect order in the infinite diversity of the universe, whole galactic life, infinite dynamism in all directions, all the time. With such speed everything is moving in the empty space, but no collisions, no problems for anyone.[459]

His latest message to the world was that it was possible for life on earth to exemplify the qualities of order and perfection:

> It's a very great joy for us today with this ability that it's completely within our reach, to create a perfect government, as competent as the government of the universe, absolute government. And on that basis have the life of every individual in the nation and the collective life of the nation as a whole to be fully

alert, and this will be the society that we envision now. Because of the ability of this pure knowledge.[460]

Maharishi went on to claim that some time in the distant past, earth had witnessed ideal or perfect civilizations:

> We have great records of such times when such societies existed. Our ancient record of knowledge, not speaking of the modern historians, but our ancient record of civilizations has given us beautiful records and the golden records of ideal civilizations that existed. Golden records of ideal governments that have existed. So we know from the ability of knowledge that we have to make life great, fully according to natural law.[461]

The belief was that, if sufficient numbers achieved transcendental consciousness, an administration governed by natural law would result, in which all good to everybody would prevail. He went on to describe his vision of the panorama of cosmic life:

> The whole universe, infinite number of galaxies moving in empty space with infinite speed, all the time, but well ordered.
>
> Empty space permeates the universe and there is the performance of that infinite creative intelligence which maintains order at every moment in the huge, expanding universe.[462]

The thrust of his present initiative was that each nation should be encouraged to maintain a group of individuals (supported by donations rather than by taxes) dedicated to making contact with 'Nature's government'. Governments in the countries that housed these groups would then, he assured his audience, be able to function with a 'cool head' and 'warm heart':

> It is a very great joy to inaugurate that administration, that global administration through natural law today that is going to transform the history of mankind. The history of so many thousands of years is now going to be transformed into a golden age.[463]

During 1993 the Natural Law Party continued to try to gain influence, contesting elections in Canada, New Zealand and Australia, but without any success.

Apparently Maharishi was still keen to see some results from his initiative to join the political scene; according to *Maharishi European Sidhaland News*, on 24th October 1993 (dubbed Invincibility Day), he proclaimed:

> The Natural Law Party is purifying the last and deepest layer of ignorance in the world – the field of politics.[464]

The publicity generated by the various innovative campaigns must have gained the Movement at least a few new converts, but not enough to leave initiators feeling satisfied. A suggested remedy, which would do away with the need for people to pay substantial fees for initiation, was the suggestion that the teaching of Transcendental Meditation might be offered in Great Britain as part of the National Health Service.

The Twentieth Year of the Age of Enlightenment, 1994, started with the announcement that 'donations' for learning to meditate were to be increased to £470. On 12th January, Maharishi again came onto the television screens in meditation centres equipped with decoding devices and satellite dishes, and once again his appearance was prefaced by a preamble from Dr Bevan Morris, from whom viewers learned that this was to be Maharishi's 'Year of Discovery of Veda in Human Physiology'. The man himself, now seventy-six years of age looked in better shape than in the previous year. As he sat, surrounded by a veritable garden of flowers, plants, birthday cakes, and the Vedic *pandits* and his devotees, he spoke at length on the topic of the 'Veda in Human Physiology'. Interspersed with his explanations of a new 'discovery', he spoke of the 'dawn of perfection for every individual', of the 'vision or the reality of the fabric of immortality' and of the 'fruit of knowledge', that 'knowledgeable life will be mistake-free life'. He offered an answer to the eternal question of why humans suffer: 'It is the basic violation of natural law that is the cause of all kinds of disorders and suffering ...'[465]

It was calculated that several million people having been taught Transcendental Meditation, so there could be little doubt that the practice of meditation would continue to occupy the attention of many people for years to come, although not necessarily under the monopoly of Maharishi's movement. It is unlikely that the *mantras* would remain secret, and there were already divisions over the true nature of his teaching – whether it was secular or religious – there were already splits in the ranks of followers. Clearly, at some time, Maharishi would pass on the mantle of power, probably to someone younger.

Born on Sunday, 13rd May 1956 in Papanasam, Tamil Nadu, South India, and named Ravi Ratnam, Ravi Shankar joined Maharishi in 1975 and was for several years his personal secretary. But, for whatever reason, Ravi became distanced from Maharishi and the TM movement, and was obliged to modify his name to Sri Sri Ravi Shankar (aka Ravishankar) after the world-famous musician Ravi Shankar objected to his adopting the name.

Ravi now heads his own organisation - the Art of Living Foundation -

which he started in 1983 - and though he identifies as being part of the same Holy Tradition as Maharishi, he teaches a different practice, the Sudarshan Kriya Yoga (SKY), a breathing technique.

Dr Chopra had also seen as a likely future head the head of the movement, but also parted company with Maharishi after The *Journal of the American Medical Association* first published an extremely positive profile of Maharishi Ayur-Ved, then changed its stance and followed it with an article seeking to expose alleged malpractice.

The year of 1998 was announced as Maharishi's Second Year of Global Administration through Natural Law; with 1999 becoming Maharishi's Third Year of Global Administration through Natural Law; and 2000 being Maharishi's Fourth Year of Global Administration through Natural Law.

In 1931 an Indian called Dr V.G. Rele had authored *The Vedic Gods as Figures of Biology,* an exploratory work connecting human anatomy and Vedic Scriptures. In 2000, Dr Tony Nader revived this idea in a work titled *Human Physiology: Expression of Veda and the Vedic Literature,* for which Dr Nader was rewarded by being given his weight in gold, and was, during a four-day Vedic ceremony, bestowed the title of 'Maharaja Adhiraj Rajaraam' and responsibility for the 'Global Country of World Peace'.

Meanwhile, at Shankaracharya Nagar in Rishikesh, the elderly but good-natured and blissful Dandi Swami Narayananand Saraswati, *gurubhaiee* of Maharishi and Swami Shantanand, and devotee of Shankaracharya Swami Brahmananda Saraswati, stayed amidst the crumbling ruins of the former *ashram*, amidst the jungle, living out his self-disciplined simple existence, observing a vow of *maun* (talking to no one).

An Indian TM teacher, Mr. Thakur, had this to say of Dandi Swami Narayananand:

'Dandi Swami is very *guru*, he has enlightenment.'

Dandi Swami Narayananand Saraswati
seated outside his *kutir* at Shankaracharya Nagar, 2000

26

MAHASAMADHI

The naming of the years continued, with 2001 becoming 'Maharishi's Year of Global Country of World Peace', and later that year there was the surprise announcement, from Maharishi's camp, of the creation of a new currency;

> The Raam, or the World Peace Bond as it is also known, was launched on October 26th, 2001 by Maharishi Global Financing, one of the financial arms of the Maharishi Mahesh Yogi of Transcendental Meditation (TM) to become "the global development currency of the global country of world peace."[466]

Accordingly, a few months later, the new year of 2002 became 'Maharishi's Year of Raam Mudra' ('*mudra*' being Sanskrit for 'seal', 'mark', 'gesture', 'money', from the root words '*mud*' = 'joy', and '*ra*' = 'to give' ie 'to give joy').

To all intents and purposes, Maharishi was no longer visible to the world at large, so it was a big surprise when, on Sunday, 12th May 2002, at 21:00 (EST), CNN America screened a live interview between veteran interviewer Larry King (wearing his trademark braces) in New York, and Maharishi Mahesh Yogi in Vlodrop, Holland.

Answering a long string of questions from the show's host, Maharishi seemed in good shape, smiling and laughing through much of the exchange. It must be acknowledged that Maharishi showed all the usual physical signs of ageing that might be expected of a man of his years (he was now 84), and was by now almost completely bald, his remaining hair and beard a snowy white.

Larry King asked some good questions:

> Larry King: It's a great pleasure to welcome to Larry King Live, from Vlodrop, Holland, Maharishi Mahesh Yogi. He is the author of the famous book, *Science of Being and Art of Living: Transcendental Meditation.* He has not done an

interview in 25 years. The book has been newly revised and updated. And it's an honour to welcome him to this program. Is Maharishi a title or a name?

Maharishi: Title, I think. People begin to call significance of the characteristic of the word "*maharishi*." "*maha*" means "great" and "*rishi*" is a "seer". "The Seer of Reality". The Seer, that's what people called, and it became a sort of name.

. . . .

Larry King: Why have you been quiet for some time now? Why have you not, have we not seen you much?

Maharishi: No, I was not quiet. Only, I got into creating the effect. I was teaching transcendental meditation for 30, 40 years, but I found that the world is not yet to the extent of possibility in the field of good.

So I realized that talking about like this, and on and on -- I realized that talking is not too much important. Creating the effect in the world.. and now I am engaging in creating the effect in the world.

. . . .

Larry King: We know that your good friends George Harrison and John Lennon are gone. What do you believe happens upon death?

Maharishi: Death is just a .. it gives a new start for a new journey. In the process of evolution, the body lasts for some time and then will take other body and take other body and take other body until the final redemption from diversity is transcended.

. . . .

How do you deal personally with sadness? George Harrison just died. I know he was a friend of yours. How do you deal when someone you love or like is gone?

Maharishi: It's human nature to like those whom you like, and when they go it's natural to be sad about them. But it is inevitable. It's inevitable.

. . . .

Larry King: Do you weep? Do you cry when someone you love dies?

Maharishi: There is no reason to cry, because I know that everyone has to go on and on, on the path of progress, path of progress, path of progress. There is nothing to cry about something.

When the sun sets at the end of the day, one doesn't cry for the sun. It's happening, it's happening. The same sun that is setting is going to rise again and again set, and again rise, and again set.

. . . .

Larry King: There have been stories that you're the... you're.. that you have started what is a multi-billion dollar business.

Maharishi: I lack only $1 billion to make the world a better world.

So many months ago, I had publicized in the American papers that $1 billion endowment fund will raise enough this Vedic *pandits* to fly about. We want to engage 40,000 people on a permanent basis, and they will have enough intense influence of coherency in the world consciousness. And anybody who wants to have peace -- and everyone wants peace -- they were invited to donate.

But I realized later that I was talking to the.. this capitalist country. And capitalist country in their own fog. Unless they get something privately themselves, they'll not indulge into it.

So money has become prominent in a world of capitalism. That I realized when nobody sponsored for world peace, and everybody wants world peace. But they will not...

Larry King: Take part.

Maharishi: ... part with some of their huge billions and millions in the bank. So I said, "All right".

. . . .

Larry King: Do you have a family?

Maharishi: The world is my family. I count them...

Larry King: You have no children of your own?

Maharishi: That is what a family means -- all the children of the world.

Larry King: I know, but I'm just asking if you have children from your loins?

Maharishi: I am a single person. I'm a *purusha*. I'm a... what do you call it.. *sannyasi*, if you understand the word. I'm a monk, if you understand it...

Larry King: You're a bachelor?

Maharishi: Monk.

Larry King: Do you have special diets that you eat?

Maharishi: I think that diet that I eat, everyone eats the same thing -- some rice, some *dal,* some *chapatis*, something vegetables. But I like this organic, organic. I recommend to people organic agriculture -- Vedic organic agriculture. Huge amount of scientific research has shown that with the Vedic hymns, with the Vedic melodies, the nutrients grow in the trees very much in the fruits, in the crops, in the vegetables.

So that is why.. what I am promoting in the world.

Larry King: How old are you?

Maharishi: I have almost forgotten when I was born. I was told before.

(laughter) I never look back. In my habit, I never looked back. I never looked back.

Larry King: Are you in good health?

Maharishi: I am in fairly good health. Yes, yes, fairly good health.

Larry King: Do you go to doctors?

Maharishi: Doctors come to me even before calling them. They like to see me year after year the same way, like that, like that.

But the main thing is not so important what I am. What is important is my program for the world, that the world will be a better world. It will be free from sins. Governments will be preventive administrations in the world. That is important.

I'm not important for the world. I'm here for some time, gone. And everyone will finish the whole story.

But I have promoted a program which is practical, positive and simple for every individual...

Larry King: Where...?

Maharishi: ... and for every nation.

Larry King: Where did you learn it?

Maharishi: I learned it from my master. I address him as His Divinity, Swami Brahmananda Saraswati, in the Himalayas in India. And that I hold to be the tradition of Vedic masters.

. . . .

Larry King: Do you believe in a god?

Maharishi: I believe in God. And I believe in the custody of God vested in kings. And I'm very happy to have your name as "King." It's the King!

Larry King: I'm a King.

Maharishi: I want to establish a government in every country that will support life in the country. This drama of four years, five years, change the government, change the government, is only useful to the foreign powers.

They think democracy... I used to say "Damn The Democracy," because it's not a stable government, it's only useful for foreign powers. It's a bad thing for any nation to change the... a man comes for four years, now he is the President. And then he goes to jail tomorrow -- here, there. Such inadequacy in the field of administration must create a very chaotic population in every country. And that is the situation in the world.

It's clear that, to a large degree, the future of the teaching of Transcendental Meditation lies in its teachers, but since so many had already gone their own way, what was Maharishi's view of these 'independent' teachers of meditation? At a press conference on 14th May 2003, in the year of 'Maharishi's Year of Ideal Government—Raam Raj' Maharishi spoke on this very issue:

> What I have taught, because it has it's eternal authenticity in the Vedic literature and you should know that, how many? 30 – 40 thousand teachers of TM I have trained and many of them have gone on there own and they may not call it Maharishi's TM but they are teaching it in some different name here and there. So there's a lot of these, artificial things are going on, doesn't matter, as long as the man is getting something useful to make his life better, we are satisfied.[467]

Transcendental Meditation had become extremely expensive, so some breakaway teachers were offering meditation at a budget price whilst others taught it for free.

With the explosion of PC, tablet and mobile phone usage giving ever-wider access to the Internet, the Movement was now establishing a web presence in order to promote TM, and Maharishi's multifarious commercial and educational ventures.

In 2005, David Lynch, the world famous American Filmmaker, established the David Lynch Foundation (DLF), a non-profit educational organization for 'Consciousness-Based Education and World Peace' to ensure that every child anywhere in the world who wants to learn to learn Transcendental Meditation can do so.

> Lynch hopes through this organisation to make the teaching of transcendental meditation (TM) available to students in every school in America. He calculates that introducing students to the discipline will help to lower stress, anxiety and blood-pressure in the country's classrooms. Where there is bullying there will be bliss. Excellence will replace mediocrity. And so on.

> Students who meditate, Lynch assured the New York Post yesterday, will: "Start shining like a bright, shiny penny and their anxieties will go away. By diving within, they will attain a field of pure consciousness, pure bliss, creativity, intelligence, dynamic peace. You enliven the field, and every day it gets better. Negativity recedes."[468]

So it looked as though Transcendental Meditation would be gaining better acceptance and better press. But, on Monday, 15th August 2005, the BBC announced Maharishi's decision to suspend the teaching Transcendental Meditation in Great Britain, describing the country as a 'Scorpion Nation'. *The Guardian* newspaper announced:

> Disgusted at Tony Blair's support for the US in the Iraq war and the British

electorate's failure to unseat the prime minister at the general election, the 95-year-old guru says there is no point continuing to waste the "beautiful nectar" of TM on a "scorpion" nation.

"The good effects of transcendental meditation - increased creativity and long life - should not be given to a dangerous country that is constantly busy destroying the world," said the maharishi, speaking at one his regular press conferences in the Netherlands. "TM is a gift from me to those who want to create peace and harmony in the world."

Mike Owen, a psychotherapist with Sunabitur Healthcare, who has recommended TM to many of his patients, said that, for many, flying overseas was both impractical and prohibitively expensive.

"Whatever you think of the maharishi's wilder theories, TM is a proven tool for reducing stress and anxiety," he said. "It seems a shame to deprive ordinary people of that just because the maharishi considers our government bellicose and warlike."

The two best-known British advocates of TM are the former Tory party leader William Hague and the industrialist and broadcaster Sir John Harvey-Jones. Sir John says TM has made him a much easier person to live with: "I don't make a drama out of a crisis. If I gave it up now, my wife would leave me." [469]

The tirade against Blair is best understood in the context of Maharishi's apparent preference for monarchy, even dictatorship, over democracy. It was even rumoured that at that time he was offering the opportunity of special one-to-one enlightenment courses for anyone with enough wealth (a sum of a million dollars was mentioned), who afterwards would be awarded the title of '*Raja*' ('King'), Indeed, news spread of the crowning of one of his aides, Dr Tony Nader - Tanios Maurice Abou Nader, born 10th January 1955, Beirut, Lebanon, who Maharishi conferred the name or title of 'Raja Ram'.

Maharishi's announcements about Britain being a Scorpion Nation had no doubt raised some eyebrows in the outside world, but even insiders were shocked, and none more so than when they heard that TM teachers were now expected to become 're-certified'. Initiators were being asked to attend a specially arranged course, equipped with video conferencing direct to Maharishi, and to sign an updated legal agreement. The news was this met with a very mixed reception, after all, the *puja* was not to be changed, nor were the teaching methods, and nor were the checking points. Accordingly, the loyalties of many were being strained to the full.

The New Year of 2006 became 'Maharishi's Year of Global Reconstruction for the Whole World to be Heaven on Earth—First Year of Sat-Yuga'

On Wednesday, 8th March 2006, reporter David Jones visited Maharishi's residence in Vlodrop, Holland, and was granted a rare interview with the aged, frail and increasingly reclusive Maharishi, by televised link, with Maharishi remaining in his accommodation upstairs. Jones seems to have been briefed not to mention a particular subject, but...

David Jones: 'I hesitate to mention the "Beatles" word, I know you don't particularly like going back all those years, but British.. English people, of course associate you with The Beatles and with that period and they haven't themselves.. they haven't enjoyed always a particularly good fate since their encounter with Transcendental Meditation.'

Maharishi does not answer the question directly, and instead advises the reporter, that rather than trying to get a news story he instead investigate Transcendental Meditation for himself.

Maharishi: 'You know that phrase, English phrase, "Taste of pudding is in eating"? Taste of Transcendental Consciousness is in experiencing.'

The reporter is not put off and he soon steers the interview back to the topic of his choice by asking Maharishi about the importance of celebrity in the modern world. Then he is more forthright.

David Jones: 'One more question then on that subject, about, and it is about The Beatles. Do you regret now having ever becoming involved with them? Because then your movement became associated with celebrity, with, you know, popular music and so on? Do you regret that period?'

Maharishi: 'Forget about it. If at all, Beatles became substantial due to my contact. I did not become great by the association of The Beatles. These boys may be musicians, Beatles, [but] it's wrong for the English Press to make the business perverted wherever, even after these fifty years. *"Beatles make the Maharishi great"*, it's a waste of thought, you know. It waned.

What? These little singers boys, singer boys, conquered the Field of Divine Integrity?

It's not good enough that they followed; they had a good - what they call it - a teacher or a guide? [manager, Brian Epstein] But when he was no more, they all scattered here and there and there. So he was the guide who made these four boys pull together, and made Beatles. And British Press made, "wherever they'll be I'll be" after so many years. All *"Beatles, Maharishi, Beatles"*. (laughs) It's a waste of thought, you know.'[470]

A week later, *New York Times* journalist Lily Koppel was also granted an interview with Maharishi.

Maharishi, who is believed to be 89, now confines himself to two rooms in his golden-hued log house in the small Dutch village of Vlodrop. Although he has emerged only a few times in the past year — for fresh air on a chauffeured drive — he contends that his most important work lies ahead of him. His first 50 years, he says, were merely a "warm-up" for his goal of creating world peace by, among other things, rebuilding national capitals according to his harmony-producing precepts. Inner peace, it turns out, is not enough.

Maharishi agreed to a rare interview. I was permitted in his house but was not allowed into his upstairs quarters. His followers told me that seclusion preserves his energy and that he talks in person to only a small circle of attendants. I spoke to Maharishi by videoconference from a downstairs room where his red velvet gilded throne sat empty.

Framed in a flat-screen monitor, he appeared more than ever a mystical creature, his thin face sketched with a white beard. He was dressed in his customary white silk dhoti, a fresh necklace of yellow petals around his neck. His aim, he explained in English, is to create coherence in a world undone by our stressed brains, artificial national borders, terrorism and irrational violence. "My coherence-creating groups are going to put out all this mischief-mongership in the world," he said in a high-pitched voice, holding President Bush up as the greatest mischief-monger of all. "The world is going to come out to be a neat and clean world. All these countries will fade away."[471]

Maharishi continued to remain hidden in the fastnesses of his base in Vlodrop, where only his closest aides had access to him. And on Sunday, 21st October 2007, Maharishi reflected on when, back to 1955, he had begun his mission to spread the practice of meditation.

And now I remember when I begin to look into the past, what I, what happened, the first such thing happened somewhere in Kerala, where I went from Uttar Kashi to Kerala, *dakshina* [Hindi for 'south'].. South India, and people wanted to learn this practice of meditation.
I thought: "What to do, what to do, what to do?" then I thought, "I should teach them all in the name of Guru Dev. I should design a system, a system of *puja* to Guru Dev."
And in that *puja* the reality came out, the reality of Guru Dev, the totality of Guru Dev and what it was:
"Gurur Brahma", the Creator, *"Gurur Vishnur"*, the Maintainer, *"Gurur Brahma"*, the Creator, *"Gurur Vishnur"*, the Maintainer, the Administrator, *"Guruh Sakshat Param Brahma"*, totality of knowledge, totality of enlightenment. *"Gurur Brahma, Gurur Vishnur, Gurur Devo Maheshvarah"*, silence, *"Shiva, Gurur Brahma, Gurur Vishnur, Gurur Devo Maheshvarah, Shiva"*, silence, eternal Purusha. *"Guruh Sakshat, Param Brahma"*, transcendental *"Brahma"*
Totality of all, infinite diversity, that is the *guru* – *"na guror adhikam"*[104], *"na*

guror adhikam" – "there is no one greater than *guru*", *guru* is everything, Creator, Maintainer, Sustainer, everything is the *guru*, the *guru*, the *guru*.

I formulated the *puja* to Guru Dev; I started through that instrumentality to transfer Guru Dev's reality to the one who wanted to teach meditation [the *brahmachari* himself]. So what flowed was, totality of Guru Dev, flowed through the *puja*.[472]

On Friday, 11th January 2008 the founding of a fresh initiative was celebrated, a new charity called the Brahmananda Saraswati Trust. A measure of Maharishi's current health situation could be discerned from his faltering address to his audience; his voice sounded croaky and he spoke with difficulty between long pauses and outbursts of coughing, his words were sometimes quite difficult to discern.

When I am listening... all this.. my mind goes to "from where all this was happening?" I did not know from where all this was happening. It was happening, and all that I know. It was the destiny of the world. It was fortune of the world that was being shaped, being designed. By whom? I did not know. By some skill, some skill, by some skill beyond my fathomability! I was simply working. I was simply working. I was simply working. I did not know from where all the instruments are coming, to give shape to the world, here, there, and everywhere. I was only working. Because when I am hearing all these, beautiful sentiments, I was led on to find out, from where this was happening

The depth, of Vedic Wisdom for life is so enormous, that it is, completely self-sufficient, in its articulating, everything. One would never know, from where one is acting. When I hear all these sentiments, the only thing I could say, "I started to find out from where I was doing - I was not doing - it was happening." From place to place I was moving around. It was happening, but it was not I that was instrumental to it in any way. So I find no source of it. This is because unfathomable is the field of Natural Law; unfathomable is the field of Natural Law. And it happens, and it happens, and it works out the destiny of everyone. You go to find this logic, that logic, that logic, that logic. You are not able to pinpoint from where it is happening, and ultimately you are left to, left to something that you can only say, "Jai Guru Dev". It's from where there that it is happening.

I remember a Vedic saying:

न गुरोरधिकं न गुरोरधिकं न गुरोरधिकं न गुरोरधिकं

"*Na Guror adhikam, na Guror adhikam, na Guror adhikam, na Guror adhikam*" - "There is nothing greater than Guru Dev. Nothing greater than Guru Dev." "*Gurur Brahmaa*"; this is how Guru Dev is defined.

गुरुब्रह्मा गुरुविष्णुः गुरुदेवो महेश्वरः

Guru Brahmaa Guru Vishnuh Guru Devo Maheshvarah

And above all:

गुरुः साक्षात् परब्रह्म तस्मै श्रीगुरवे नमः

Guru Saakshaat parabrahma tasmai shri gurave namah [473]

I end up with something, beyond anything, and that is the reality of life. You can't find the source, because the course is all over. Where ends intellect? Where ends everything? In the Transcendental is the reality of all poss-ibil-ities. So, "Glory to Guru Dev. Glory to Guru Dev. Glory to Guru Dev". And we got to that, we got to that course of action; we got to that course of action from where everything is a possibility, automatically. [474]

On Saturday, 12th January 2008, Donovan made a visit to Vlodrop, Holland, in order join in celebrations on Maharishi's birthday, by playing a few songs.

Later that month, on Thursday, 31st January 2008, *The Indian Express* newspaper reported news of Maharishi's retirement:

Maharishi Mahesh Yogi, who soared to worldwide fame as the guru to the Beatles and creator of the Transcendental Meditation I technique, has retreated into near silence and turned over the day-to-day running of his global network to senior aides, a close adviser said on Tuesday.

"He had been involved very dynamically in his worldwide movement for over 50 years, so it's quite a significant change to see him dive back into knowledge and let others take care of the administration," adviser John Hagelin, an American physicist, said on telephone.

The silver-bearded Maharishi is thought to be 91 and is losing the strength to keep up his punishing administrative workload. "He is not as young as he once was," said Hagelin. "I think he probably has a more limited reserve of physical energy to draw upon. He was working 20-hour- a-day for years."

The Maharishi told senior aides at a January 8 meeting in the Netherlands of his plan to withdraw from administration duties and spend time absorbed in the ancient Indian texts that underpin his movement—catching many followers off guard. Many people have been trained for years to carry on the Maharishi's various tasks, he added.

The Maharishi now spends his days in silence contemplating and preparing a commentary on the Vedas from which he evolves solutions for today's troubled world. "I think everybody's quietly feeling some sense of celebration that he's finally going to complete his commentary on the Vedas, which probably will have a longer-term impact. It's a vitally important body of literature," Hagelin said.

Less than a week later Maharishi's aides announced that at about 19:00hrs (CET), Tuesday, 5th February 2008, Maharishi Mahesh Yogi had died in his sleep, at his compound in Vlodrop, in Holland. His death came in the wake of rumours about his rapidly declining health and need for hospitalisation.

On Friday, 8th February Maharishi's body was flown to India by chartered flight to Varanasi Airport, and after customs clearance the body was then taken by road to Allahabad (also known as Prayag). It was rumoured that the body was to be immersed in the river Ganga, (as had the body of Swami Brahmananda been back in 1953). But perhaps there was difficulty in arranging for an immersion, and word then came that his body was to be cremated instead. The body was laid for several hours at one of the former *ashrams* of his master, the building known as Brahma Nivas, in Alopi Bhag. Then from there it was taken 30km to the south to the 120-acre site of Maharishi Ved Vidyapeeth at Arail, Naini, where it was seated upright in the crossed-legged lotus position on a long couch, and draped in white silk. Over the weekend a stream of several thousand visitors filed past to see Maharishi's mortal remains - images of the scene were intermittently transmitted via the website of one of Maharishi's organisation's.

On Saturday, 9th February 2008, *The Times of India* reported.

'Call it cosmic coincidence. Close on the heels of NASA's announcement that the Beatles' song Across the Universe would be transmitted to the distant Polaris star system in the hope of making contact with intelligent, extraterrestrial life, came the news that the Indian mystic who inspired the Beatles to write the song had passed away. Ascended to a new plane of consciousness, perhaps, where he and those of the Fab Four no longer with us could produce more chart-busting music.

Maharishi Mahesh Yogi, also known for his introduction of transcendental meditation I to the world, leaves behind a global business empire. But it was his impact on music and counterculture that first brought his movement attention from the world. Most famously, of course, he got the Beatles to replace LSD with a different kind of high.'

'Though his association with George Harrison, in particular, made him famous, the Maharishi's contribution in popularising Indian spiritualism across the world cannot be overstated. His theory of transcendental meditation has proved to be a treasure-trove of tips for management courses. TM, which he trademarked, offers a means of achieving enlightenment without self-denial. Dismissed by critics as a hippie mystic earlier, the Maharishi's interpretation of ancient yogic techniques has led to a multibillion dollar self-help industry. He moved into what he called consciousness-based education and set up several colleges and universities. Since TM became popular, there has been no shortage of scientists to study its techniques. Many of them have found that meditation does promote mental and physical well-being, and especially aids in reducing stress. He was both a businessman and a guru, a spiritual man who sought a world stage from where to advance the joys of inner happiness. As the refrain from Across the Universe went, Jai Guru Deva, here and perhaps one day in Polaris.'

On Monday, 11th February 2008, the body of Maharishi was taken in a wooden coffin along the mile long route to the hilltop overlooking the Sangam (the meeting of the rivers) where around midday the body was laid on a raised platform and once there Maharishi's male relatives went on to perform the last rites, and eventually to set light to the pyre, observed by thousands of onlookers. Live transmission of the event was broadcast across the world on the Internet by 'Saadhana', a team of Indian broadcasters. As the flames slowly intensified the air vibrated to repeated chants of "Shri Ram, Jaya Ram, Jaya Jaya Ram." - 'Blessed Rama, Victory to Rama, Victory Victory to Rama'.

Hours later *The Times of India* newspaper reported:

'The remains would be picked on Tuesday and the ashes would be immersed in Sangam on Wednesday. The Shashtodhasi ceremony would take place on February 21st.' According to a report by Associated Press, a marble tomb is to be built over the ashes.'

Another report detailed the day's ceremonies

Tuesday, 12th February 2008, Allahabad - The ashes of Maharishi Mahesh Yogi, who introduced the world to Transcendental Meditation and was known as the guru of the Beatles, were immersed yesterday in the river in Sangam, a holy place for Hindus.

The ashes and funeral flowers, gathered in brass urns, and wrapped in white cloth and garlands of roses, were carried to the Sangam, where the Ganges, the Yamuna and mythical Saraswati meet, in an elaborate procession led by Vedic pundits from the Jyotirmath of the Shankaracharya, the spiritual order to which the seer belonged.

They were followed by the 35 "rajas" or kings who are national heads for the Maharishi's TM organisation, including his nominated heir Maharaja Tony Nader or Adi Ram, the name by which he is now known.

Thousands of devotees and local residents accompanied the procession that set off at 12pm from the Shanti Sthal, where the funeral pyre was lit on Monday. Girish Varma, the seer's kin and a functionary in the organisation in India, and members of the seers' family presided over the ceremony along with the priests. Around 1:30pm, the ashes were released into the waters of the Sangam.[475]

On the passing of Maharishi Mahesh Yogi

Deepak Chopra: Maharishi, the Guru from whom I learned everything took "Mahasamadhi" (the big meditation) on the evening of February 5, 2008.[476]

Sri Sri Ravishankar: Meditation is the gift he gave to the world. Fifty years ago, meditation was not the household name that it is today. He popularised meditation and the Vedas.[477]

David Lynch: In life, he revolutionized the lives of millions of people. In twenty, fifty, five hundred years there will be millions of people who will know and understand what the Maharishi has done.[478]

Paul McCartney: 'I was asked for my thoughts on the passing of Maharishi Mahesh Yogi and I can only say that whilst I am deeply saddened by his passing, my memories of him will only be joyful ones.'

'He was a great man who worked tirelessly for the people of the world and the cause of unity. I will never forget the dedication that he wrote inside a book he once gave me, which read "radiate bliss consciousness", and that to me says it all. I will miss him but will always think of him with a smile.'

Ringo Starr: 'One of the wise men I met in my life was the Maharishi. I always was impressed by his joy and I truly believe he knows where he is going.'

Cynthia Lennon: 'Maharishi had a laugh like a tinkling bell. He had an aura. I was as cynical as anyone to begin with, but I suppose I'm a perpetual student. I felt he was someone I could learn from. '

Donovan: 'Maharishi brought the pure transcendental meditation back to the world, reuniting us with our own true self. As a poet I can find no words to describe how grateful I am to Maharishi for his gift.'[479]

***

A journalist once put it to Maharishi that he was 'working on a very high state' and asked whether or not this was his last incarnation:

Last incarnation? I think I leave a better world than what I found it, and then I have done my duty to the world – don't have to come back. Sure I'm going to leave a better world than what I found it.[480]

Glossary

Adharma Vice, sin
Amrita Nectar
Ananda Joy, bliss
Arya Noble
Ashram Hermitage
Ashrama Stage of life
Atma, Atman Soul
Avataar Incarnation
Bal Brahmachari Life celibate student
Bhagavan Bhagwan God
Bhajan Hymn
Bhakti Devotion
Bharat India
Bhavateet Transcendental
Bij Seed
Brahma Hindu god of creation
Brahmanand, Brahmananda Absolute bliss
Brahmachari Celibate student
Brahman The Absolute
Brahmin Learned or priestly caste
Charan Ray of sun or moon
Chela Disciple
Chit Consciousness
Darshan Holy look
Deepak Light, lamp
Dharma Duty
Dhoop Sticky incense, fragrant lamp
Dhoti Sheet
Dhyan Meditation
Diksha Initiation
Ganapati Ganesha Hindu god with elephant trunk
Gandharva-Ved Indian classical music
Gandharvas Celestial musicians
Ganja Marijuana

Gita Song
Grihastha Householder
Guna Quality
Hare Lord
Gupha Cave
Guru Teacher, master
Gurudwara Sikh temple
Gyan, Gyaan, Gnan, Jyaan Knowledge
Hansa Swan
Hawaii Pertaining to the air
Ishtam gods
Jagadguru World-*guru*
Jai, Jay, Jaya Hail, glory
Japa Repetition of *mantra*
Ji Term of respect
Jyotir Light
Jyotishi Indian astrology
Kalpa Period of time
Kamandalu Wooden pot
Karma Law of action and reaction
Kashi Benares, Varanasi
Kaupeen Loincloth
Krishna Dark, name of principal character of *Mahabharata* poem
Kshatriya Caste of warriors, administrators
Lingam Phallus
Maharaj(ah) King
Maharishi (*Maharshi*) Great sage
Mahesh Name of Hindu god Shiva
Mala Rosary
Mandir Hindu temple
Mantra Word or words of spiritual power
Manu Smriti or *Manu Samhita* Law book
Math Monastery
Mudra sign, mark, seal, money
Mukti Liberation
Nagar Town
Pandit Learned man
Paramatma Supreme Spirit, God
Prana Breath
Pranava Name of *om mantra*
Prasad Blessing
Puja Ceremony, ritual

Purnima Full moon night

Purusha a person who is fully self-controlled

Raj Royal

Rajasic Energetic, passionate

Rama Name of hero of *Ramayana* poem

Rishi Wise man

Rudra Name of Hindu god Shiva

Sadhana Spiritual discipline

Sadhu Wandering holy man

Samadhi Stillness of the mind

Sannyas Vow of renunciation

Saraswati Name of Hindu goddess of learning, name of river

Satsang To take the company of the good or pious

Sattvic Pure

Satya Truth

Shankar Name of Hindu god Shiva

Shanti Peace

Shiva Name of Hindu god of destruction, lord of the *yogis*

Shivalinga Symbol of creative forces

Shivaratri Night(s) dedicated to worship of Hindu deities Shiva and his consort Shakti

Shloka Verse

Shri Blessed

Siddha Perfected being

Siddhi One who has acquired supernatural powers

Smriti Remembered texts

Sutra an aphorism, a formula

Swami Renunciate

Swaroop Divine form

Tilak Mark of sandalwood paste applied to forehead

Tri Three

Upadesh Lecture

Upanishad Texts on *yoga*, to sit near

Vanaprasthas Forest dwellers

Varna Caste

Vishnu Hindu god of preservation

Yagya, *Yajna* Ritual, sacrifice

Yantra, a mystical geometrical diagram or object

Yatra Tour, pilgrimage

Yuga Period of time

Notes

[1] *Intro*, issue 1, September 1967, p.7.

[2] Maharishi Mahesh Yogi, *Thirty Years Around the World*, vol. 1, p.244.

[3] Circulated transcript.

[4] Elsa Dragemark, *The Way to Maharishi's Himalayas*, p.257.

[5] It is written that on Thursday, 21st December 1871 (Vikram Samvat 1928th, Marg Shirsh Shukla Dasmi) in the village of Gana close to Ayodhya, Rajaram Mishra was born. In the Hindi biography of Guru Dev (*Shri Jyotishpeethaddharaka* by Shri Rameshwar Tiwari, published 1965) Guru Dev's birthdate is given as *'maargashiirshha shukla dashamii, vikrama samvat 1928th'* i.e. Margashirsha 10th 1928th, whilst the Western calendar date was then calculated to be 'December 21st, 1870'. Additionally, in 'Our Guiding Light', a profile of Guru Dev included in a book entitled 'The Beacon Light of the Himalayas', published 1955, it is stated by Bala Brahmachari Mahesh (later known as Maharishi Mahesh Yogi): 'He was born on Margashirsh Shukla 10 Samvat 1928th (equivalent to December 1871)'. In the re-published text edition of 'Our Guiding Light' a birth date of 20th December 1868 is offered. However, this date would convert to Sunday Pausha 6th 1925 in the Vikrami calendar - a day and date hitherto unmentioned in connection with Guru Dev's birth.

It is generally accepted that there is a difference of fifty-six / fifty-seven years between the Vikram and Gregorian calendars. Accordingly, the Vikrami date of Margashirsh Shukla 10 Samvat 1928th is shown to correspond to Thursday 21st December 1871 in the Gregorian calendar.

[6] Paul Mason, *Biography of Guru Dev*, p.18.

[7] Paul Mason, *Biography of Guru Dev*, p.44.

[8] Paul Mason, *Biography of Guru Dev*, p.66.

[9] Paul Mason, *Biography of Guru Dev*, pp.67-8.

[10] Paul Mason, *Biography of Guru Dev*, p.91.

[11] Swami Rama, *Living with the Himalayan Masters*, pp.257-8.

[12] Maharishi Mahesh Yogi, *Meditations of Maharishi Mahesh Yogi*, pp.39-40.

[13] Maharishi Mahesh Yogi, *Science of Being and Art of Living*, p.181.

[14] Maharishi Mahesh Yogi, *Meditations*, p.61.

[15] *MIU World*, vol. 1, no. 2, 1991.

[16] Jugal Kishore Shrivastava, *Vedanta Incarnate*, 2009, p.48.

[17] typewritten report, Maharishi speaking on 18th July 1965, at Lago di Braies.

[18] Circulated transcript.

[19] quoted in, Jugal Kishore Shrivastava, *Vedanta Incarnate*, 2009, p.48.

[20] typewritten report, Maharishi speaking on 18th July 1965, at Lago di Braies.

[21] quoted in, Jugal Kishore Shrivastava, *Vedanta Incarnate*,2009, p.48.

[22] Author's transcript of recording of Maharishi Mahesh Yogi.

[23] Circulated transcript.

[24] Author's transcript of recording of Maharishi Mahesh Yogi.

[25] Jugal Kishor Shrivastava, *Sansmarana*, p13.

[26] Author's transcript of recording entitled *India, Love and Marriage.*

[27] *International Times*, 15th December 1967.

[28] B.D. Tripathi, *Sadhus of India,* Pilgrims, 1978, revised 2004, p.221.

[29] Maharishi Mahesh Yogi, *Thirty Years*, p.185.

[30] Author's transcript from a recording.

[31] Maharishi Mahesh Yogi, *Thirty Years*, p.185.

[32] Elsa Dragemark, *The Way to Maharishi's Himalayas*, p.259.

[33] Transcript of Mahrishi answering questions at Hochgurgl 22nd July 1964

[34] Excerpt from *Shri Shankaracharya Vaaksudha* (translation by Paul Mason).

[35] Paul Mason, *Roots of TM* p.85.

[36] B.D. Tripathi, *Sadhus of India,* Pilgrims, 1978, revised 2004, p.222.

[37] Swami Rama, *Living with the Himalayan Masters*, p.260.

[38] Paul Mason, *Biography of Guru Dev* p.245.

[39] Elsa Dragemark, *The Way to Maharishi's Himalayas*, p.238.

[40] Herbert Tichy, *Himalaya*, p.50.

[41] Author's translation of Hindi speech from sound recording.

[42] Paul Mason, *Guru Dev as Presented by Maharishi* (excerpts) pp.3-8.

[43] Paul Mason, *Biography of Guru Dev* p.245.

[44] Maharishi Mahesh Yogi, *Love and God*, p.10.

[45] B.D. Tripathi, *Sadhus of India,* Pilgrims, 1978, revised 2004, p.223

[46] Paul Mason, *Biography of Guru Dev* pp.307-8.

[47] Paul Mason, *108 Discourses of Guru Dev* p.62.

[48] Author's transcript of recording, of talk given c1967, by one of Maharishi's *brahmachari's*, Swami Satyananand.

[49] Paul Mason, *Biography of Guru Dev* p.245.

[50] B.D. Tripathi, *Sadhus of India,* Pilgrims, 1978, revised 2004, p.264.

[51] Extracts from *'Hamare Gurudeva'*, compiled by Swami Vasudevanand, pp.60-2, translated from the Hindi into English.

[52] Helena Olson, *Hermit in the House*, p.67.

[53] Robert Hollings, *Transcendental Meditation*, p.83.

[54] Maharishi Mahesh Yogi, *History of the Movement* pp7-8.

[55] Swami Srikanta Bharathi, *Deva Doota Maharishi Mahesh Yogi*

[56] *History of the Movement* pp8-9.

[57] Author's transcript from a recording.

[58] Author's transcript from a recording.

[59] Quote from speech of Mrs Thankamma N Menon, October 1955, from *Beacon Light of the Himalayas*, published 1956, p,50.

[60] Quote from speech of Sri C R Vaidyanathan, October 1955, from *Beacon Light*

of the Himalayas, published 1956, pp.36-7.
[61] Quote from speech of Professor P S Atchuthan Pillai, October 1955, from *Beacon Light of the Himalayas,* published 1956, p.79.
[62] Excerpts of speech by Bala Brahmachari Mahesh, *Beacon Light of the Himalayas*, published 1956, pp.66-67.
[63] Maharishi Mahesh Yogi, *Beacon Light of the Himalayas*, p.26.
[64] Maharishi Mahesh Yogi, *Beacon Light of the Himalayas*, p.43.
[65] Maharishi Mahesh Yogi, *Beacon Light of the Himalayas*, p.46.
[66] Maharishi Mahesh Yogi, *Beacon Light of the Himalayas*, p.62.
[67] Maharishi Mahesh Yogi, *Beacon Light of the Himalayas*, p.62.
[68] Maharishi Mahesh Yogi, *Beacon Light*, p.66.
[69] Maharishi Mahesh Yogi, *Beacon Light*, p.66.
[70] Maharishi Mahesh Yogi, *Beacon Light*, p.76.
[71] Maharishi speaking at Poland Spring USA on12 July 1970.
[72] *Beacon Light of the Himalayas*, p.17.
[73] Maharishi Mahesh Yogi, *Beacon Light*, introduction.
[74] Maharishi Mahesh Yogi, *History of the Movement* p10.
[75] *Torch Divine* Vol 1 No. 1 July 1958, pp 8-9.
[76] Maharishi Mahesh Yogi, *Beacon Light*, p.77.
[77] Maharishi Mahesh Yogi, *Thirty Years*, p.208.
[78] Maharishi Mahesh Yogi, *Bhagavad-Gita*, p.9.
[79] *International Times*, 15th December 1967.
[80] Maharishi Mahesh Yogi, *History of the Movement* p14.
[81] Maharishi Mahesh Yogi, *History of the Movement* p28th.
[82] Maharishi Mahesh Yogi, *History of the Movement* pp14-15.
[83] Maharishi Mahesh Yogi, *Thirty Years*, p.213.
[84] *Straits Echo and Times* 22nd May 1958.
[85] Maharishi Mahesh Yogi, *Thirty Years*, pp.217ff.
[86] Maharishi Mahesh Yogi, *Thirty Years*, p.213.
[87] Maharishi Mahesh Yogi, *Thirty Years*, p.223.
[88] Vesey Crichton, Obituary of David Morgan, https://www.theguardian.com/lifeandstyle/2017/aug/29/david-morgan-obituary
[89] Maharishi Mahesh Yogi, *History of the Movement* pp.16-17.
[90] Maharishi Mahesh Yogi, *Thirty Years*, p.227.
[91] Maharishi Mahesh Yogi, *Thirty Years*, p.229.
[92] Maharishi Mahesh Yogi, *History of the Movement* pp.17-18
[93] *International Times*, 15th December 1967.
[94] Maharishi Mahesh Yogi, *History of the Movement* p.p20-21.
[95] *International Times*, 15th December 1967.
[96] Maharishi Mahesh Yogi, *Thirty Years*, p.242.
[97] Maharishi Mahesh Yogi, *Thirty Years*, p.243.
[98] Helena Olson, *Hermit in the House*, pp.21-2.
[99] Helena Olson, *Hermit in the House*, p.43.
[100] Helena Olson, *Hermit in the House*, p.44.

101 Helena Olson, *Hermit in the House*, p.44.
102 Helena Olson, *Hermit in the House*, p.50.
103 Helena Olson, *Hermit in the House*, p.51.
104 Helena Olson, *Hermit in the House*, p.53.
105 Helena Olson, *Hermit in the House*, p.79.
106 Helena Olson, *Hermit in the House*, p.160.
107 Charlie Lutes & Martin Zucker, *'Messenger of Bliss'* YogiVinceBooks, 2006.
108 Maharishi Mahesh Yogi, *Deep Meditation*.
109 Helena Olson, *Hermit in the House*, p.104.
110 Helena Olson, *Hermit in the House*, p.148.
111 Maharishi Mahesh Yogi, *Thirty Years*, p.252.
112 Helena Olson, *Hermit in the House*, pp.160-1.
113 Helena Olson, *Hermit in the House*, p.165.
114 Maharishi Mahesh Yogi, *Thirty Years*, p.264.
115 Maharishi Mahesh Yogi, *History of the Movement* pp.23-25.
116 Maharishi Mahesh Yogi, *Maharishi Mahesh Yogi*. LP.
117 Maharishi Mahesh Yogi, *Maharishi Mahesh Yogi*. LP.
118 Maharishi Mahesh Yogi, *Thirty Years*, p.301.
119 Maharishi Mahesh Yogi, *Deep Meditation*.
120 Maharishi Mahesh Yogi, *Thirty Years*, p.314.
121 Maharishi Mahesh Yogi, *History of the Movement* pp.25-26.
122 Elsa Dragemark, *The Way to Maharishi's Himalayas*, pp.43-4.
123 Maharishi Mahesh Yogi, *History of the Movement* p32.
124 Elsa Dragemark, *The Way to Maharishi's Himalayas*, p.44.
125 Elsa Dragemark, *The Way to Maharishi's Himalayas*, p.351.
126 https://studysociety.org/recordPDF/1961%20Revised%20Nov%202008.pdf
127 Elsa Dragemark, *The Way to Maharishi's Himalayas*, p.352.
128 Elsa Dragemark, *The Way to Maharishi's Himalayas*, p.354.
129 Maharishi Mahesh Yogi, *Love and God*, p.50.
130 *A Six Month Course in Yoga Asanas*, p.3.
131 circulated copy; Maharishi Mahesh Yogi, 27th Febuary 1962
132 Maharishi Mahesh Yogi, *Meditations*, p.143.
133 Maharishi Mahesh Yogi, *Meditations*, p.185.
134 Communicated by David Fiske to author.
135 David Fiske, *Stalking Personal Power & Peace*
    http://www.esotericarts.org/SPP&P.pdf
136 Maharishi Mahesh Yogi, *Meditations*, p.123.
137 Maharishi Mahesh Yogi, *Science of Being*, revised edition, p.xv.
138 *Science of Being*, first edition, p.xviii.
139 *Science of Being*, revised edition, p.97-8.
140 *Science of Being*, revised edition, p.271.
141 *Science of Being*, revised edition, p.272.
142 *Science of Being*, revised edition, p.238.
143 *Science of Being*, revised edition, p.238.

[144] *Science of Being*, revised edition, p.259.
[145] *Science of Being*, revised edition, p.240.
[146] *Science of Being*, revised edition, p.300.
[147] B.D. Tripathi, *Sadhus of India,* Pilgrims, 1978, revised 2004, p.222.
[148] Paul Mason, *Biography of Guru Dev,* p.28th.
[149] Maharishi Mahesh Yogi, *Maharishi Mahesh Yogi,* LP.
[150] Maharishi Mahesh Yogi, *Thirty Years*, p.542.
[151] Maharishi Mahesh Yogi et al, *The Maharishi and the Abbot.*
[152] Elsa Dragemark, *The Way to Maharishi's Himalayas*, p.45.
[153] Elsa Dragemark, *The Way to Maharishi's Himalayas*, p.46
[154] Communicated by David Fiske to author.
[155] David Fiske, *Stalking Personal Power & Peace*
http://www.esotericarts.org/SPP&P.pdf
[156] Maharishi Mahesh Yogi, *Thirty Years*, p.572.
[157] Maharishi Mahesh Yogi, *Meditations*, pp 13ff.
[158] Maharishi Mahesh Yogi, *Meditations*, p 15.
[159] Maharishi Mahesh Yogi, *Meditations*, pp 17-18.
[160] Maharishi Mahesh Yogi, *Meditations*, p32.
[161] Maharishi Mahesh Yogi, *Meditations*, p50.
[162] Maharishi Mahesh Yogi, *Science of Being*, pp.98-9.
[163] Elsa Dragemark, *The Way to Maharishi's Himalayas*, p.259.
[164] Maharishi Mahesh Yogi, *Meditations*, p.64.
[165] Maharishi Mahesh Yogi, *Meditations*, pp 110-11.
[166] Maharishi Mahesh Yogi, *Bhagavad-Gita*, p.8.
[167] Maharishi Mahesh Yogi, *Meditations*, pp.187-8.
[168] Maharishi Mahesh Yogi, *Meditations*, p.134.
[169] Maharishi Mahesh Yogi, *Love and God*, pp.7-8.
[170] Maharishi Mahesh Yogi, *Love and God*, p.6.
[171] Aldous Huxley, *The Doors of Perception*, pp.16-17.
[172] Aldous Huxley, *The Doors of Perception*, p.18.
[173] John Densmore, *Riders on the Storm*, p.33.
[174] John Densmore, *Riders on the Storm*, p.33.
[175] Circulated transcript from recording.
[176] Ved Mehta, *Portrait of India*, p.94.
[177] Ved Mehta, *Portrait of India*, p.95-6.
[178] Ved Mehta, *Portrait of India*, p.96.
[179] Ved Mehta, *Portrait of India*, p.97.
[180] Nancy Cooke de Herrara, *Beyond Gurus*, p.165.
[181] Nancy Cooke de Herrara, *Beyond Gurus*, p.175.
[182] Paul Horn, *A Special Edition.*
[183] Paul Horn, *Paul Horn in India.*
[184] Maharishi Mahesh Yogi, *Seven States of Consciousness.*
[185] Author's transcript from a recording.
[186] Maharishi Mahesh Yogi, *Bhagavad-Gita*, p.8.

[187] Maharishi Mahesh Yogi, *Bhagavad-Gita*, p.184.
[188] Maharishi Mahesh Yogi, *Bhagavad-Gita*, p.184.
[189] Maharishi Mahesh Yogi, *Bhagavad-Gita*, p.185.
[190] Maharishi Mahesh Yogi, *Bhagavad-Gita*, p.340.
[191] Maharishi Mahesh Yogi, *Bhagavad-Gita*, p.342.
[192] Maharishi Mahesh Yogi, *Bhagavad-Gita*, p.88.
[193] Maharishi Mahesh Yogi, *Bhagavad-Gita*, p.169.
[194] Maharishi Mahesh Yogi, *Bhagavad-Gita*, pp 139-40.
[195] Maharishi Mahesh Yogi, *Bhagavad-Gita*, p.93.
[196] Maharishi Mahesh Yogi, *Bhagavad-Gita*, p.144.
[197] Maharishi Mahesh Yogi, *Bhagavad-Gita*, p.144.
[198] Maharishi Mahesh Yogi, *Bhagavad-Gita*, p.94.
[199] *International Times*, 13rd May 1967.
[200] *Observer*, 26th November 1967.
[201] *Observer*, 26th November 1967.
[202] *Observer*, 26th November 1967.
[203] *Intro*, issue 1, September 1967.
[204] Albert Goldman, *The Lives of John Lennon*, pp.324-5.
[205] *The Beatles, Drugs, Mysticism & India*, p.38.
[206] *The Beatles, Drugs, Mysticism & India*, p.38.
[207] *The Beatles, Drugs, Mysticism & India*, p.38.
[208] *Daily Express*, 27th August 1967.
[209] *Daily Express*, 27th August 1967.
[210] *Associated Newspapers*, 26th August 1967.
[211] Author's transcript from radio broadcast.
[212] Derek Taylor, *Thirty Years Ago Today*, p.132.
[213] *Intro*, issue 1, September 1967.
[214] *Intro*, issue 1, September 1967.
[215] Author's transcript from a recording.
[216] Author's transcript from a recording.
[217] Author's transcript from a recording.
[218] Author's transcript of BBC Home Service radio broadcast on 17th September 1967, entitled *The Spirit and the Flesh*,[218]
[219] Peter Shotton and Nicholas Schaffer, *John Lennon – In My Life*, p.138.
[220] Peter Shotton and Nicholas Schaffer, *John Lennon – In My Life*, p.139.
[221] Pageant Magazine, April 1968.
[222] Author's transcript from a recording.
[223] *Gurudevastuti*, v. 5 / *Guru Gita*, v. 34.
[224] The quotations that follow are taken from the author's transcript from the broadcast.
[225] Richard Neville, *Playpower*, p.79.
[226] Peter Brown and Steven Gaines, *The Love You Make*, p.249.
[227] Steven Gaines, *Heroes and Villains*, pp.238-9.
[228] Steven Gaines, *Heroes and Villains*, pp.239.

229 Peter Shotton and Nicholas Schaffer, *John Lennon – In My Life*, p.161.
230 Peter Shotton and Nicholas Schaffer, *John Lennon – In My Life*, p.161.
231 Peter Shotton and Nicholas Schaffer, *John Lennon – In My Life*, p.161.
232 Peter Shotton and Nicholas Schaffer, *John Lennon – In My Life*, p.161.
233 Peter Shotton and Nicholas Schaffer, *John Lennon – In My Life*, p.161.
234 Peter Shotton and Nicholas Schaffer, *John Lennon – In My Life*, p.161.
235 *International Times*, 26th February 1968.
236 Maharishi Mahesh Yogi, *Meditations*, p.32.
237 Circulated transcript of recording.
238 Elsa Dragemark, *The Way to Maharishi's Himalayas*, pp.169ff.
239 Author's transcript from a recording.
240 Albert Goldman, *The Lives of John Lennon*, p.351.
241 Elsa Dragemark, *The Way to Maharishi's Himalayas*, p.170.
242 *The Beatles, Drugs, Mysticism & India* p.147.
243 Cynthia Lennon, *Twist of Lennon*, pp.154-5.
244 Author's transcript from a recording.
245 *Rave*, May 1968.
246 Denny and Kathleen Somach, *Ticket to Ride*, p.122.
247 *The Secret of the Mantras*, Richard Blakely, 2012, p.195.
248 Elsa Dragemark, *The Way to Maharishi's Himalayas*, p.178.
249 *The Beatles Book*, issue 58, May 1968.
250 Peter Brown and Steven Gaines, *The Love You Make*, p.253.
251 http://www.beatlesinterviews.org/db68.html quoted in 'The Beatles, Drugs, Mysticism & India' p213
252 Cynthia Lennon, *Twist of Lennon*, pp.156-7.
253 Cynthia Lennon, *Twist of Lennon*, pp.160.
254 Philip Norman, *Shout*, p.320.
255 Jonathon Greene, *Days in the Life*, pp.160-1.
256 Peter Brown and Steven Gaines, *The Love You Make*, p.253.
257 Peter Brown and Steven Gaines, *The Love You Make*, p.253.
258 Paul Mason, *'The Beatles, Drugs, Mysticism & India'* -/- http://graphics8.nytimes.com/packages/pdf/arts/Mardas.pdf
259 *The Beatles, Drugs, Mysticism & India* -/- http://graphics8.nytimes.com/packages/pdf/arts/Mardas.pdf
260 Jan Wenner, *Lennon Remembers*, p.56.
261 Jan Wenner, *Lennon Remembers*, p.56.
262 Cynthia Lennon, *Twist of Lennon*, p.161.
263 Cynthia Lennon, *Twist of Lennon*, pp.159-60.
264 Cynthia Lennon, *Twist of Lennon*, p.161.
265 Thakur Raghvendra Singh BSc, met and initiated into TM by Maharishi c1962
266 Paul Mason, *'The Beatles, Drugs, Mysticism & India'*, p.237-8.
267 Nancy Cooke de Herrara, Beyond Gurus, p264
268 Peter Shotton and Nicholas Schaffer, *John Lennon – In My Life*, p.162.

269 Paul Horn, *Special Edition*.
270 Nancy Cooke de Herrara, *Beyond Gurus*, p.28th1.
271 Nancy Cooke de Herrara, *Beyond Gurus*, p.28th2.
272 Peter McCabe and Robert D. Schonfield, *Apple to the Core*, p.95.
273 Steven Gaines, *Heroes and Villains*, p.243.
274 Steven Gaines, *Heroes and Villains*, p.244.
275 Paul Mason, *Biography of Guru Dev*, p.143.
276 Paul Mason, *Biography of Guru Dev*, p.141.
277 Paul Mason, *Biography of Guru Dev*, p.141.
278 Paul Mason, *Biography of Guru Dev*, p.142.
279 Author's transcript from a recording.
280 Author's transcript from a recording.
281 Nancy Cooke de Herrara, *Beyond Gurus*, p.298.
282 Message from Diane Rousseau, a close student of Charlie Lutes.
283 Charlie Lutes & Martin Zucker, *Messenger of Bliss,* YogiVinceBooks, 2006
284 Author's transcript from a recording.
285 Nancy Cooke de Herrara, *Beyond Gurus*, p.299.
286 *The Ottawa Journal* Saturday, 22nd June 1968.
287 Alistair Shearer and Peter Russell, *The Upanishads*, p.65.
288 Alistair Shearer and Peter Russell, *The Upanishads*, p.33.
289 Maharishi Mahesh Yogi, *Love and God*, p.10.
290 Author's transcript from a recording.
291 Author's transcript from a recording.
292 *Vedic Hymns and Prayers*, RV. I. 2. 15.
293 Jean Le Mee and Ingbert Gruttner, *Hymns from the Riq-Veda*, RV. IX. 112.1-4.
294 This and the quotations that follow are taken from the author's transcript from a recording.
295 David Fiske, *Stalking Personal Power & Peace*
http://www.esotericarts.org/SPP&P.pdf
296 *International Times*, 15th December 1967.
297 Lyall Watson, *Supernature*, pp.178-9.
298 This and the quotations that follow are taken from the author's transcript from a recording.
299 This and the quotations that follow are taken from the author's transcript from a recording.
300 Paul Mason, *Roots of TM*, pp.60-1.
301 Author's transcript from a recording.
302 Maharishi Mahesh Yogi, *Meditations*, p.95.
303 This and the quotations that follow are transcript from a recording.
304 *International Times*, 15th December 1967.
305 This and the quotations that follow are taken from the author's transcript from a recording.
306 This and the quotations that follow are taken from the author's transcript from a recording.

[307] Swami Sivananda, *Triple Yoga*, p.3.

[308] This and the quotations that follow are taken from the author's transcript from a recording.

[309] *International Times*, 15th December 1967.

[310] This and the quotations that follow are taken from the author's transcript from a recording.

[311] http://oshosearch.net/Convert/Articles_Osho/Glimpses_of_a_Golden_Childhood /Osho-Glimpses-of-a-Golden-Childhood-00000047.html

[312] http://oshoworld.com/onlinebooks/BookXMLMain.asp?BookName=miscellaneo us/early%20talks.txt chapter 7 pp 1-38.

[313] http://oshosearch.net/Convert/Articles_Osho/Glimpses_of_a_Golden_Childhood /Osho-Glimpses-of-a-Golden-Childhood-00000047.html

[314] http://oshoworld.com/onlinebooks/BookXMLMain.asp?BookName=miscellaneo us/early%20talks.txt chapter 7 pp 1-38.

[315] http://oshosearch.net/Convert/Articles_Osho/Glimpses_of_a_Golden_Childhood /Osho-Glimpses-of-a-Golden-Childhood-00000047.html

[316] *International Times*, 29th August 1969.

[317] *International Times*, 29th August 1969.

[318] Maharishi Mahesh Yogi, *Science of Being*, revised edition, p.155.

[319] Author's transcript from a recording.

[320] Author's transcript from a recording.

[321] Shankaracharya Shantanand, *Good Company*, p.128th.

[322] Shankaracharya Shantanand, *Good Company*, pp.129-30.

[323] Author's transcript from a recording.

[324] Author's transcript from a recording.

[325] Author's transcript from a recording.

[326] Shankaracharya Shantanand, *Good Company*, p.43.

[327] Swami Sivananda, *The Bhagavad Gita*, p.80.

[328] Author's transcript from a recording.

[329] Wendy Doniger and Brian K. Smith, *The Laws of Manu*, p.87.

[330] Wendy Doniger and Brian K. Smith, *The Laws of Manu*, p.xxiii.

[331] Author's transcript from a recording.

[332] Author's transcript from a recording - 'Irish' here interpreted as 'paradoxical'.

[333] Transcript of Maharishi speaking in Rishikesh, March 16th 1970

[334] Transcript of Maharishi speaking in Rishikesh, 1st April 1970

[335] Jan Wenner, *Lennon Remembers*, p.55.

[336] Jan Wenner, *Lennon Remembers*, p.55.

[337] Maharishi Mahesh Yogi, on 8th July 1971 in Amherst, U.S.A.

[338] Jack Forem, *Transcendental Meditation*, p.108.

[339] Jack Forem, *Transcendental Meditation*, p.108.

[340] Jack Forem, *Transcendental Meditation*, p.15.

[341] Harold Bloomfield et al., *TM**, p.224.

[342] Photocopied and circulated transcript.

[343] Robert Hollings, *Transcendental Meditation*, p.57.

[344] Paul Mason, *The Beatle, Drugs, Mysticism & Drugs* p.277.
[345] Paul Mason, *The Beatle, Drugs, Mysticism & Drugs* p.277.
[346] Harold Bloomfield et al., *TM**, p.162.
[347] Harold Bloomfield et al., *TM**, p.165.
[348] Harold Bloomfield et al., *TM**, p.166.
[349] Harold Bloomfield et al., *TM**, pp.183-4.
[350] Harold Bloomfield et al., *TM**, p.184.
[351] Author's transcript of recording of TV broadcast.
[352] Harold Bloomfield et al., *TM**, p.228th.
[353] Peter Russell, *The TM Technique*, p.85.
[354] Richard Tames, *William Morris – Lifelines 3*, p.11.
[355] *Inauguration of the Dawn of the Age of Enlightenment*, p.23.
[356] *Inauguration of the Dawn of the Age of Enlightenment*, p.23.
[357] *Inauguration of the Dawn of the Age of Enlightenment*, p.25.
[358] *Inauguration of the Dawn of the Age of Enlightenment*, p.27.
[359] *Inauguration of the Dawn of the Age of Enlightenment*, p.47.
[360] *Creating an Ideal Society: A Global Undertaking*, p.96.
[361] *Creating an Ideal Society: A Global Undertaking*, p.109.
[362] *Enlightenment and Invincibility to Every Individual and to Every Nation*, p.254.
[363] *Yoga Journal* March 1977 *East Meets in the West* by Raghu Butler, pp41-2
[364] Maharishi Mahesh Yogi, *Deep Meditation*. LP.
[365] Maharishi Mahesh Yogi, *Deep Meditation*. LP.
[366] Shree Purohit Swami and W.B. Yeats, *Aphorisms of Yoga* Bhagwan Shree Patanjali, p.48.
[367] Nancy Cooke de Herrara, *Beyond Gurus*, p.432.
[368] Creating an Ideal Society, p.5.
[369] Nancy Cooke de Herrara, *Beyond Gurus*, p.432.
[370] Nancy Cooke de Herrara, *Beyond Gurus*, p.438.
[371] Nancy Cooke de Herrara, *Beyond Gurus*, p.438
[372] Nancy Cooke de Herrara, *Beyond Gurus*, pp.452-3.
[373] Nancy Cooke de Herrara, *Beyond Gurus*, p.456.
[374] *United States District Court, District of New Jersey, Civil Action No. 76-341*, quoted in > Josh McDowell and Don Stewart, Understanding the Cults, p.108.
[375] *Enlightenment and Invincibility*, p.51.
[376] *Enlightenment and Invincibility*, p.59.
[377] *Enlightenment and Invincibility*, p.51.
[378] Shankaracharya Shantanand, *Good Company*, p.88.
[379] Deepak Chopra, *Return of the Rishi*, p.123.
[380] Deepak Chopra, *Return of the Rishi*, p.127.
[381] Author's transcript of recording.
[382] Circulated copy of Maharishi's talk.
[383] Circulated document, attributed to 'Maharishi in Rishikesh'
[384] Translations of excerpts of *Humaare Gurudeva*, the Hindi biography of Swami Shantanand Saraswati, by Swami Vasudevanand Saraswati, 1983.

385 https://www.rte.ie/archives/2018/1022/1005811-maharishi-mahesh-yogi/
386 *Enlightenment and Invincibility*, p.141.
387 Raj Varma, *Strange Facts About A Great Saint,* Introduction.
388 Told by Satyanand to the author.
389 Gita Mehta, *Karma Cola*, pp.110-11.
390 Gita Mehta, *Karma Cola*, p.112.
391 Gita Mehta, *Karma Cola*, p.113.
392 Gita Mehta, *Karma Cola*, p.113.
393 Gita Mehta, *Karma Cola*, pp.113-14
394 Peter Russell, *The Awakening Earth*, p.148.
395 *Enlightenment and Invincibility*, p.386.
396 Maharishi Mahesh Yogi, *Beacon Light of the Himalayas*, p.65.
397 Maharishi Mahesh Yogi, *Beacon Light of the Himalayas*, p.75.
398 Maharishi Mahesh Yogi, *Beacon Light of the Himalayas*, p.76.
399 Maharishi Mahesh Yogi, *Beacon Light of the Himalayas*, p.76.
400 Maharishi Mahesh Yogi, *Thirty Years*, p.194.
401 Author's transcript from a recording.
402 Maharishi Mahesh Yogi, *Bhagavad-Gita*, pp.213-14.
403 Maharishi Mahesh Yogi et al. *The Maharishi and the Abbot.*
404 *Intro*, issue 1, September 1967.
405 Deepak Chopra, *Return of the Rishi*, p.139.
406 Deepak Chopra, *Return of the Rishi*, pp.139-40.
407 *Life Supported by Natural Law*, p.35.
408 *Life Supported by Natural Law*, p.36.
409 *Life Supported by Natural Law*, p.36.
410 *Life Supported by Natural Law*, p.165.
411 *Life Supported by Natural Law*, p.182.
412 *Maharishi's Programme to Create World Peace*, p.2.
413 Deepak Chopra, *Return of the Rishi*, p.183.
414 *Maharishi's Programme to Create World Peace*, p.vii.
415 *Maharishi's Programme to Create World Peace*, p.4.
416 *Maharishi's Programme to Create World Peace*, p.8.
417 *Maharishi's Programme to Create World Peace*, p.8.
418 *Maharishi's Programme to Create World Peace*, p.33.
419 *Maharishi's Programme to Create World Peace*, p.301.
420 Deepak Chopra, *Return of the Rishi*, p.185.
421 Robert Kropinski, *A Visit to the Shankaracharya.*
422 Nancy Cooke de Herrara, *Beyond Gurus*, p.111.
423 Benjamin Creme, *Maitreya's Mission*, vol. 2, p.79.
424 Benjamin Creme, *Maitreya's Mission*, vol. 2, p.79.
425 Displayed at the London centre, 1993.
426 *World Government News*, issue 11, November/December 1978, January 1979.
427 *Maharishi's Programme to Create Heaven on Earth*, p.39.
428 Bill Stevens and Jim Anderson, *Feel Great with TM*, p.7.

[429] *Illustrated Weekly of India,* 17-23 January 1988, p.13.
[430] *Maharishi's Programme to Create Heaven on Earth*, p.5.
[431] *Maharishi's Programme to Create Heaven on Earth*, p.5.
[432] Author's transcript from a recording.
[433] Author's transcript from a recording.
[434] Author's transcript from a recording.
[435] Author's transcript from a recording.
[436] Author's transcript from a recording.
[437] Author's transcript from a recording.
[438] *Maharishi's Programme to Create Heaven on Earth*, p.126.
[439] *MIU World*, vol. 1, no. 2, 1991, p.18.
[440] *Maharishi's Programme to Create Heaven on Earth*, p.46.
[441] Deepak Chopra, *Quantum Healing*, p.3.
[442] Deepak Chopra, *Quantum Healing*, p.4.
[443] *Maharishi's Programme to Create Heaven on Earth*, p.52.
[444] Rachel Storm, *In Search of Heaven on Earth*, p.111.
[445] Maharishi's *Programme to Create Heaven on Earth*, p.54.
[446] Maharishi's *Programme to Create Heaven on Earth*, p.56.
[447] James Randi, *Psychic Investigator*, p.32.
[448] Osho World Online Magazine - June 2004.
[449] https://www.huffpost.com › entry › the-maharishi-years-the-u_b_86412
_3 Feb 2008
[450] Press release.
[451] Press release.
[452] Independent, 4th April 1992.
[453] Independent, 4th April 1992.
[454] Paul McCartney, *Many Years From Now*, Barry Miles, Vintage, 1998.
[455] Author's transcript from radio broadcast.
[456] *Independent*, 4th April 1992.
[457] *Independent*, 4th April 1992.
[458] *MIU World*, vol. 1, no. 2, 1991, p.19.
[459] Author's transcript from a recording.
[460] Author's transcript from a recording.
[461] Author's transcript from a recording.
[462] Author's transcript from a recording.
[463] Author's transcript from a recording.
[464] *Maharishi European Sidhaland News*, December 1993.
[465] Author's transcript from a recording.
[466] http://www.appropriate-economics.org/materials/raam.html
[467] Author's transcript from a recording.
[468] https://www.independent.co.uk/news/people/profiles/david-lynch-the-weird-world-of-david-lynch-300613.html
[469] https://www.theguardian.com/uk/2005/aug/15/health.healthandwellbeing
[470] Paul Mason, *The Beatle, Drugs, Mysticism & Drugs* p.294.

[471] https://www.nytimes.com/2006/10/08/magazine/08wwln_essay.html
[472] Author's transcript from a recording.
[473] *'Guru* is Brahma, *guru* is Vishnu, *guru* is the god Maheshwara (Shiva),
In the presence of the *guru*, the transcendental *brahman*, to him the blessed *guru*, I
bow down.' - from *Gurudevastuti* v. 6 /*Guru Mantra* / TM Puja.
[474] Author's transcript from a recording.
[475] *Gulf News* 13rd February 2008.
[476] https://www.bienfaits-meditation.com/en/the_beatles_and_tm/celebrities
/deepak_chopra_en
[477] https://www.rediff.com/news/2008/feb/11guest.htm
[478] *The Expansion of Happiness* by Mack Travis, Tadorna, 2014.
[479] *The Beatles, Drugs, Mysticism & India* pp.295-6.
[480] *International Times*, 15th December 1967.

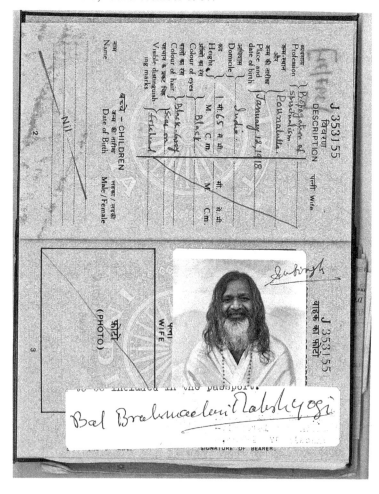

Bibliography

Bloomfield, Harold, Michael Cain and Dennis Jaffe. *TM* * Delcarte, 1976.
Brown, Peter and Steven Gaines. *The Love You Make.* Macmillan, 1983.
Chopra, Deepak. *Return of the Rishi.* Houghton Mifflin, 1991.
Collin-Smith, Joyce. *Call No Man Master.* Gateway, 1988.
Cooke de Herrara, Nancy. *Beyond Gurus.* Blue Dolphin, 1992.
Creating an Ideal Society: A Global Undertaking. International Association for the Advancement of the Science of Creative Intelligence, 1976.
Creme, Benjamin. *Maitreya's Mission, vol. 2.* Share International Foundation, 1993.
Das, A.C. *R.g Vedic India*, Motilal Banarsidass, 1920.
Densmore, John. *Riders on the Storm.* Bloomsbury, 1991.
Doniger, Wendy and Brian K. Smith. *The Laws of Manu.* Penguin, 1991.
Dragemark, Elsa. *The Way to Maharishi's Himalayas.* Stockholm, 1972.
Enlightenment and Invincibility to Every Individual and to Every Nation. International Association for the Advancement of the Science of Creative Intelligence, 1978.
Forem, Jack. *Transcendental Meditation.* Allen & Unwin, 1974.
Gaines, Steven. *Heroes and Villains.* Grafton, 1986.
Goldman, Albert. *The Lives of John Lennon.* Bantam, 1989.
Greene, Jonathon. *Days in the Life.* Minerva, 1988.
Hollings, Robert. *Transcendental Meditation.* Aquarian, 1982.
Horn, Paul. *Paul Horn in India*, record sleeve notes. Blue Note BN-LA529-H2, 1975.
Horn, Paul. *Special Edition*, record sleeve notes. Island Records ISLD6, 1974.
Huxley, Aldous. *The Doors of Perception.* Penguin, 1972. *Inauguration of the Dawn of the Age of Enlightenment.* Maharishi International University, 1975.
Le Mee, Jean and Ingbert Gruttner. *Hymns from the Rig- Veda.* Cape, 1975.
Lennon, Cynthia. *Twist of Lennon.* Star, 1978.
Life Supported by Natural Law. Age of Enlightenment Press, 1988.
McCabe, Peter and Robert D. Schonfield. *Apple to the Core.* Sphere, 1973.
McDowell, Josh and Don Stewart. *Understanding the Cults.* Here's Life, 1982.
Maharishi's Programmes to Create Heaven on Earth. Global Video

Productions, 1992.

Maharishi's Programme to Create World Peace. MERU and Age of Enlightenment Presses, 1987.

Mahesh Yogi, Maharshi Bala Brahmachari. *Beacon Light of the Himalayas – The Dawn of the Happy New Era.* Adhyatmic Vikas Mandal, Kerala, 1955.

Mahesh Yogi, Maharishi. *Bhagavad-Gita.* International SRM Publications, 1967.

Mahesh Yogi, Maharishi. *Deep Meditation.* IMS Records WP1420, 1962.

Maharishi Mahesh Yogi, *History of the Movement: A Portion of the talk given by Maharishi Mahesh Yogi,* published International Meditation Centre, Dal Lake, Kashmir, April 1969

Mahesh Yogi, Maharishi. *Love and God.* SRM Oslo, 1965.

Mahesh Yogi, Maharishi. *Maharishi Mahesh Yogi.* World Pacific Records WPS21446/Liberty Records LBS83075, 1967.

Mahesh Yogi, Maharishi. *Meditations of Maharishi Mahesh Yogi.* Bantam, 1968.

Mahesh Yogi, Maharishi. *Science of Being and Art of Living.* First edition, Allied Publishers (Private) India, 1963.

Mahesh Yogi, Maharishi. *Science of Being and Art of Living.* Revised edition, Signet, 1968.

Mahesh Yogi, Maharishi. *Seven States of Consciousness.* World Pacific Records WPS21446, 1968.

Mahesh Yogi, Maharishi. *Thirty Years Around the World – Dawn of the Age of Enlightenment, vol. 1 1957-64.* Maharishi Vedic University, 1986.

Mahesh Yogi, Maharishi, Abbot of Downside and Robert Kee. *The Maharishi and the Abbot.* International SRM Publications, 1964.

Mason, Paul, *108 Discourses of Guru Dev*, Premanand, 2009.

Mason, Paul, *Biography of Guru Dev*, Premanand, 2009.

Mason, Paul, *Dandi Swami: The Story of the Guru's Will, Maharishi Mahesh Yogi, the Shankaracharyas of Jyotir Math & Meetings with Dandi Swami Narayananand Saraswati*, Premanand, 2014.

Mason, Paul, *Guru Dev as Presented* by Maharishi Mahesh Yogi, Premanand, 2009.

Mason, Paul, *Roots of TM: The Transcendental Meditation of Guru Dev & Maharishi Mahesh Yogi,* Premanand, 2015.

Mason, Paul, *The Beatles, Drugs, Mysticism & India:* Maharishi Mahesh Yogi - Transcendental Meditation - Jai Guru Deva OM, Premanand, 2017. *Maharishi Mahesh Yogi - Transcendental Meditation- Jai Guru Deva OM*, Premanand, 2017.

Mehta, Gita. *Karma Cola.* Cape, 1980.

Mehta, Ved. *Portrait of India.* Weidenfeld & Nicolson, 1970.

Neville, Richard. *Playpower*. Paladin, 1971.

Norman, Philip. *Shout*. Penguin, 1993.

Olson, Helena. *Hermit in the House*. Los Angeles, 1967.

Purohit Swami, Shree and W.B. Yeats. *Aphorisms of Yoga Bhagwan Shree Patanjali*. Faber & Faber, 1987.

Rama, Swami. *Living with the Himalayan Masters*. Himalayan Institute of Yoga Science and Philosophy of the USA, 1978.

Randi, James. *Psychic Investigator*. Boxtree, 1991.

Russell, Peter. *The Awakening Earth*. Routledge & Kegan Paul, 1982.

Russell, Peter. *The TM Technique*. Routledge & Kegan Paul, 1976.

Shantanand, Shankaracharya. *Good Company*. Element, 1992.

Shearer, Alistair and Peter Russell. *The Upanishads*. Wildwood, 1978.

Shotton, Peter and Nicholas Schaffer. *John Lennon – In My Life*. Coronet, 1984.

Sivananda, Swami. *The Bhagavad Gita*. Divine Life Society, 1939.

Sivananda, Swami. *Triple Yoga*. Divine Life Society, 1986.

A Six Month Course in Yoga Asanas. International SRM Publications, 1962.

Somach, Denny and Kathleen. *Ticket to Ride*. Macdonald, 1989.

Stevens, Bill and Jim Anderson. *Feel Great with TM*. Golden Arrow Publications, 1988.

Storm, Rachel. *In Search of Heaven on Earth*. Bloomsbury, 1991.

Tames, Richard. *William Morris – Lifelines 3*. Shire, 1972.

Taylor, Derek. *Thirty Years Ago Today*. Bantam, 1987.

Tichy, Herbert. *Himalaya*. Vikas, 1970.

Tiwari, Rameshwar. *Shri Jyotishpeethaddharaka*, Biography of Swami Brahmananda Saraswati (in Hindi) 1965

Tiwari, Rameshwar. *Shri Shankaracharya Upadeshamrita*, (in Hindi), 1969

Varma, Raj. *Strange Facts About a Great Saint*, 1980.

Vedic Hymns and Prayers. All India Arya (Hindu) Dharma Sewa Sangha, 1978.

Watson, Lyall. *Supernature*. Coronet, 1971.

Wenner, Jan. *Lennon Remembers*. Penguin, 1975.

Index

Hand-written message
from Maharishi Mahesh Yogi

Sing the Song of life
and let it echo for
all to enjoy

'There is no reason to cry, because I know that everyone has to go on and on, on the path of progress, path of progress, path of progress. There is nothing to cry about something.

When the sun sets at the end of the day, one doesn't cry for the sun. It's happening, it's happening. The same sun that is setting is going to rise again and again set, and again rise, and again set.'

- Maharishi Mahesh Yogi
Sunday, 12th May 2002

CPSIA information can be obtained
at www.ICGtesting.com
Printed in the USA
LVHW080331040720
659661LV00002B/55